JE CROIS EN MOI

MORIARTY
THE PATRIOT

BASED ON THE WORKS OF Sir Arthur Conan Doyle
STORYBOARDS BY Ryosuke Takeuchi
ART BY Hikaru Miyoshi

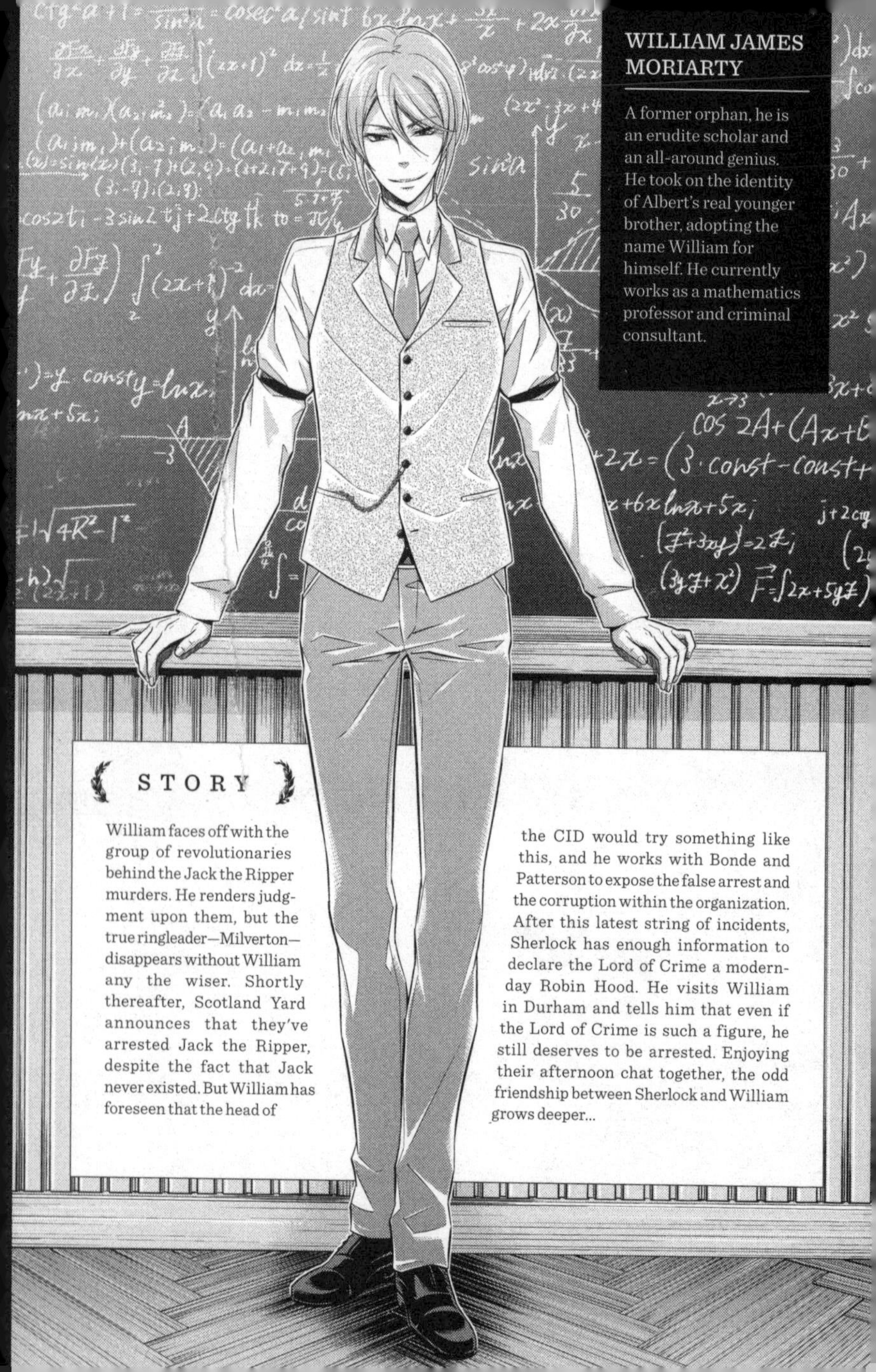

WILLIAM JAMES MORIARTY

A former orphan, he is an erudite scholar and an all-around genius. He took on the identity of Albert's real younger brother, adopting the name William for himself. He currently works as a mathematics professor and criminal consultant.

STORY

William faces off with the group of revolutionaries behind the Jack the Ripper murders. He renders judgment upon them, but the true ringleader—Milverton—disappears without William any the wiser. Shortly thereafter, Scotland Yard announces that they've arrested Jack the Ripper, despite the fact that Jack never existed. But William has foreseen that the head of the CID would try something like this, and he works with Bonde and Patterson to expose the false arrest and the corruption within the organization. After this latest string of incidents, Sherlock has enough information to declare the Lord of Crime a modern-day Robin Hood. He visits William in Durham and tells him that even if the Lord of Crime is such a figure, he still deserves to be arrested. Enjoying their afternoon chat together, the odd friendship between Sherlock and William grows deeper...

CHARACTERS

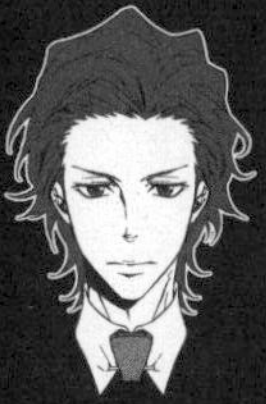

ALBERT JAMES MORIARTY

A count who inherited his family estate at a young age. Works as the director of Universal Exports, a shell company for MI6.

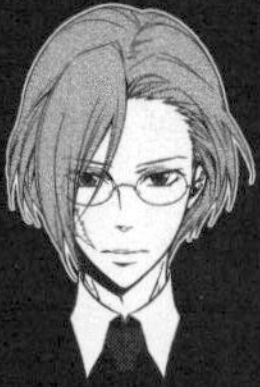

LOUIS JAMES MORIARTY

William's younger brother. He's in charge of maintaining the family estate and assets.

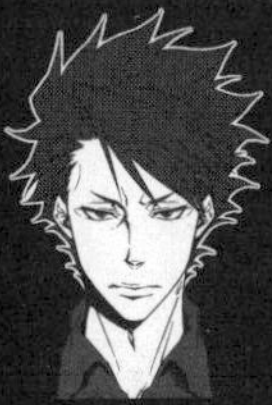

SEBASTIAN MORAN

A master gunman and former army soldier who is quick to throw punches. Supports William as one of his henchmen.

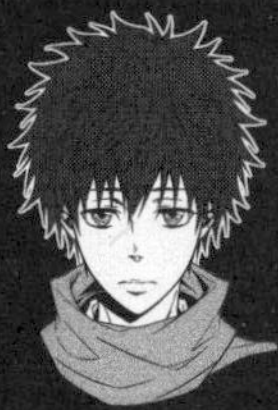

FRED PORLOCK

A young man with connections to a criminal network in England. He is proficient in covert operations and the art of disguise.

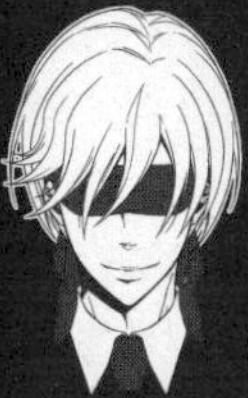

VON HERDER

A blind engineering genius from Germany. He works as the quartermaster for MI6. His code name is Que.

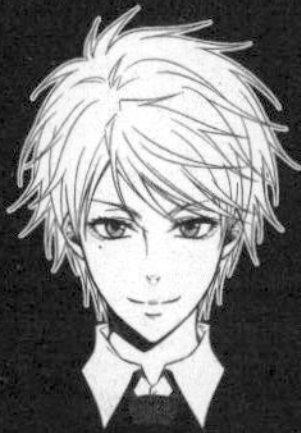

JAMES BONDE

A member of MI6, and the seventh agent granted a license to kill. Irene Adler took on this identity to save her life.

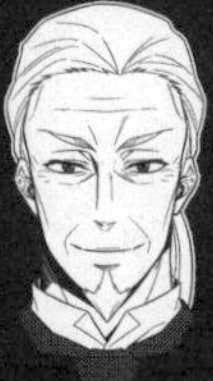

JACK RENFIELD

A proficient soldier during the Afghan Wars. Feared by both enemy and ally, he earned the nickname "Jack the Ripper."

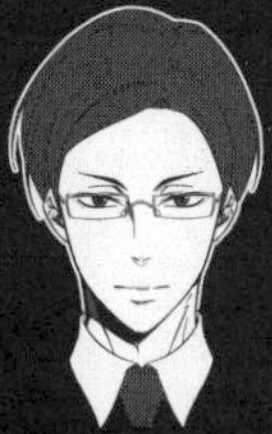

ZACH PATTERSON

An officer with Scotland Yard and a mole for MI6. He was promoted to chief inspector of the CID.

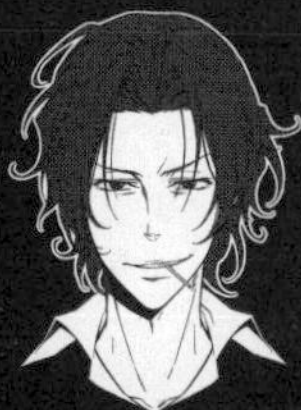

SHERLOCK HOLMES

The world's only consulting detective, he uses his extraordinary powers of observation and deduction to solve mysteries.

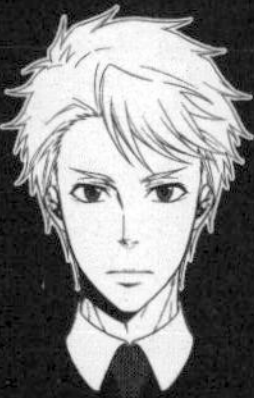

JOHN H. WATSON

A former army medic back from the Afghan War. Shares a flat with Sherlock at 221B Baker Street.

CONTENTS

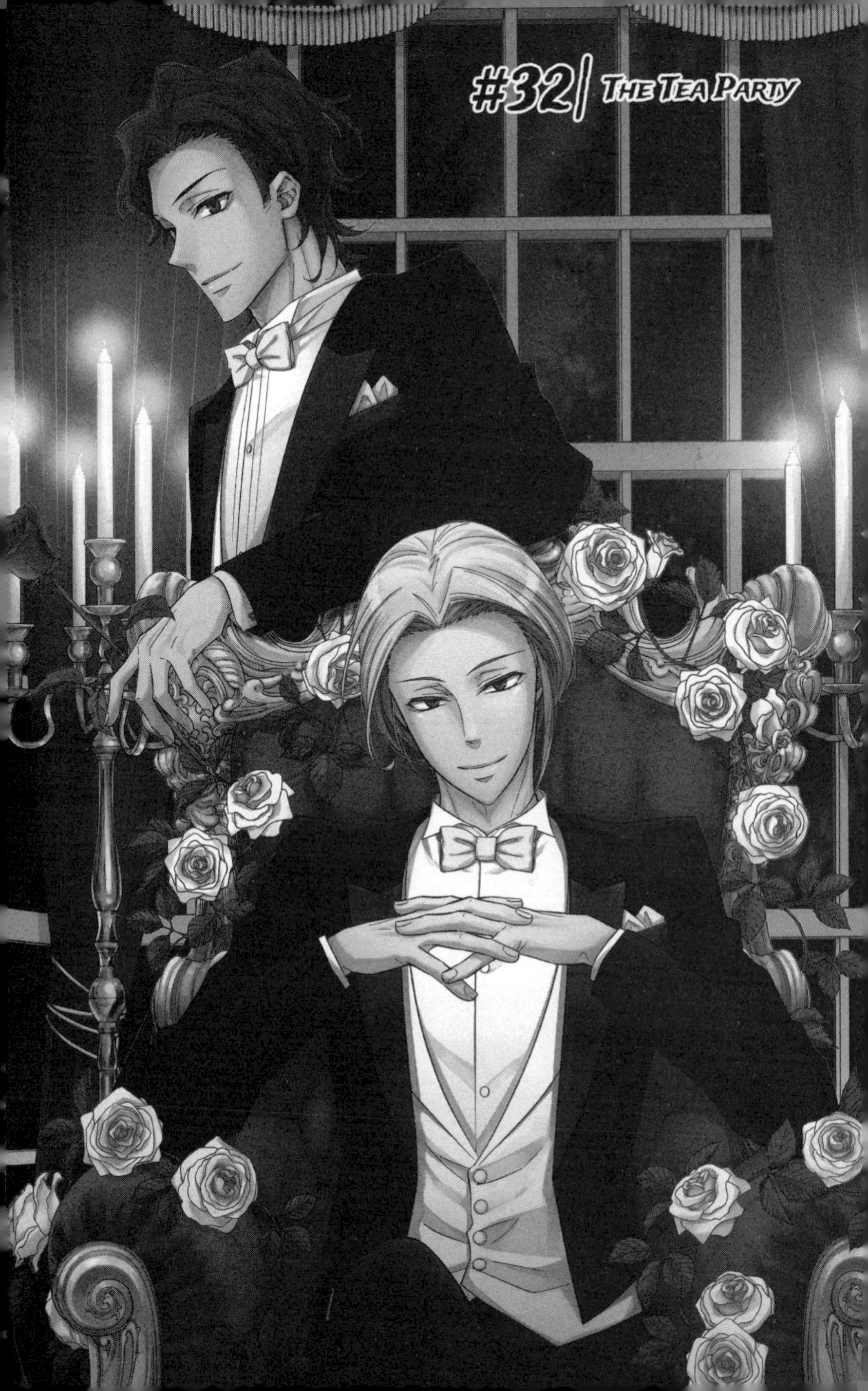
#32 | The Tea Party

MORIARTY
THE PATRIOT

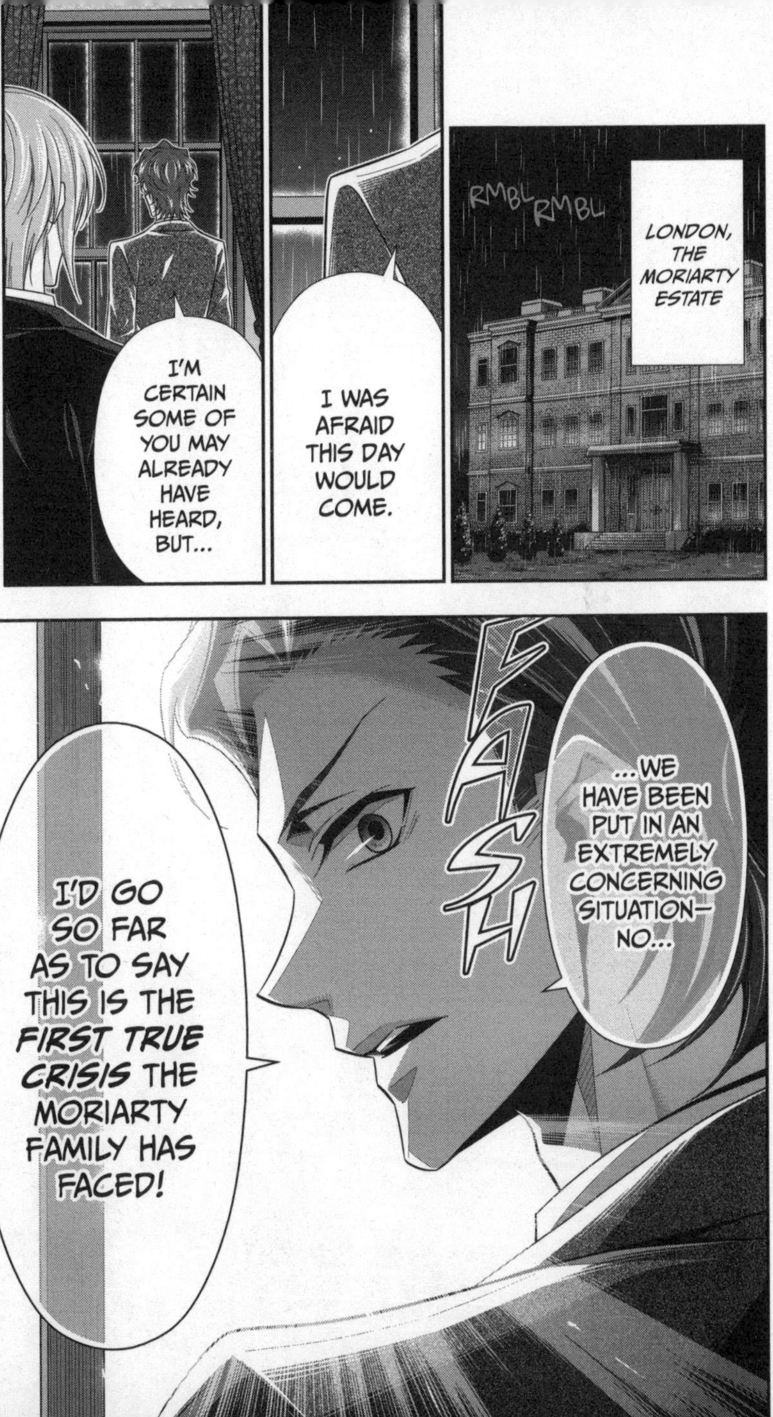
RMBL RMBL
LONDON, THE MORIARTY ESTATE
I WAS AFRAID THIS DAY WOULD COME.
I'M CERTAIN SOME OF YOU MAY ALREADY HAVE HEARD, BUT...
...WE HAVE BEEN PUT IN AN EXTREMELY CONCERNING SITUATION—NO...
FASH
I'D GO SO FAR AS TO SAY THIS IS THE *FIRST TRUE CRISIS* THE MORIARTY FAMILY HAS FACED!

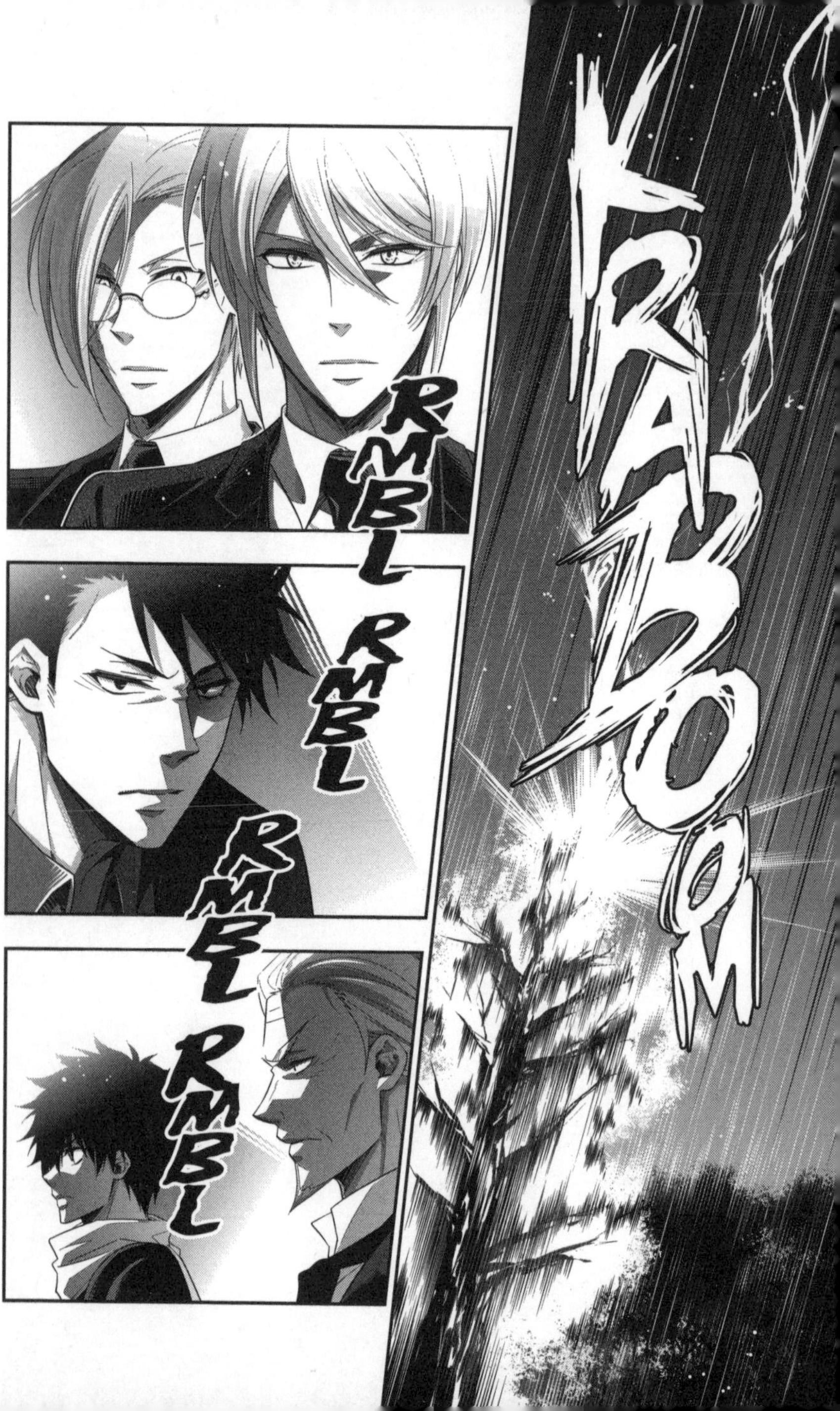
KRABOOM
RMBL
RMBL
RMBL
RMBL

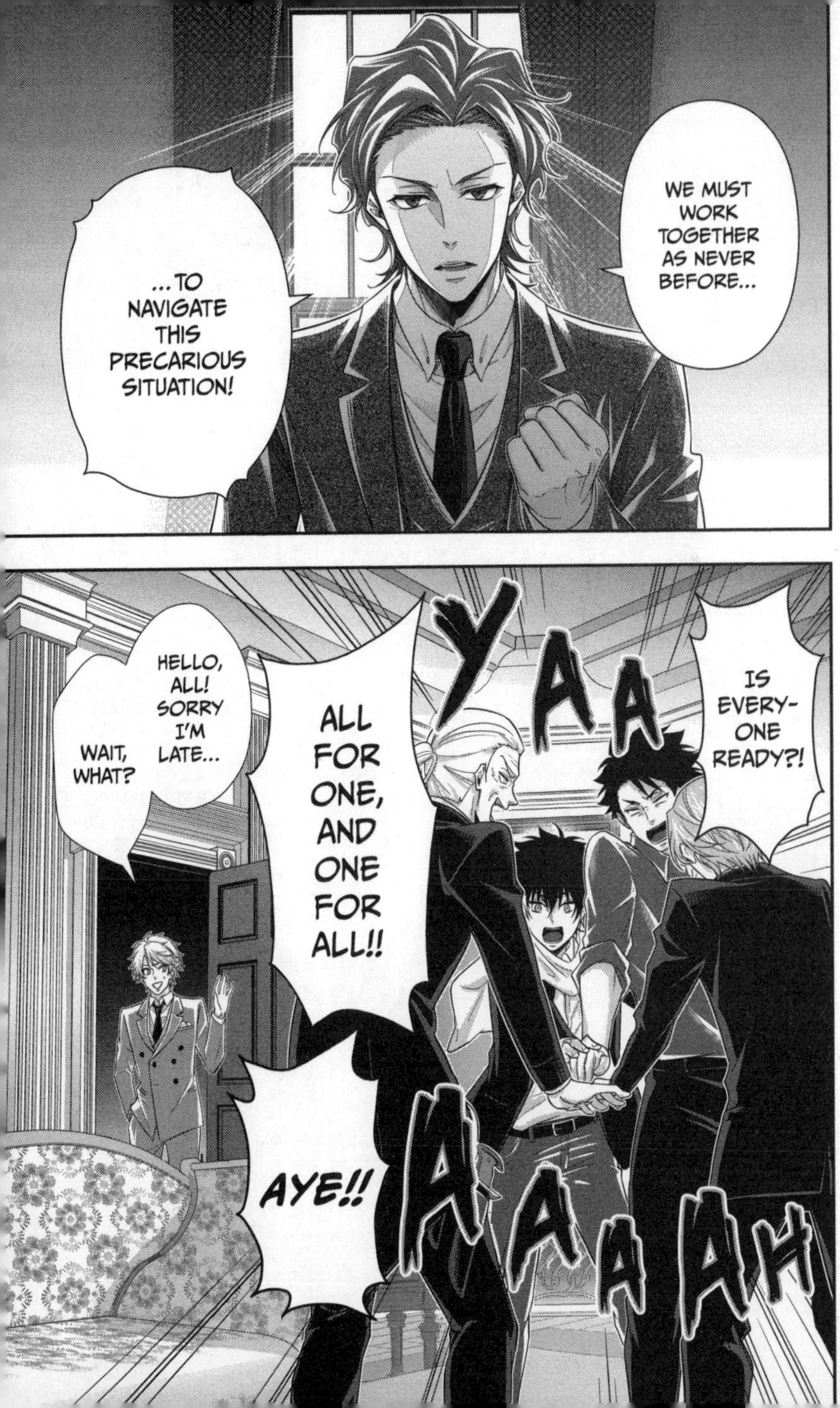
WE MUST WORK TOGETHER AS NEVER BEFORE...
...TO NAVIGATE THIS PRECARIOUS SITUATION!
IS EVERY-ONE READY?!
YAA
ALL FOR ONE, AND ONE FOR ALL!!
HELLO, ALL! SORRY I'M LATE...
WAIT, WHAT?
AAAAH
AYE!!

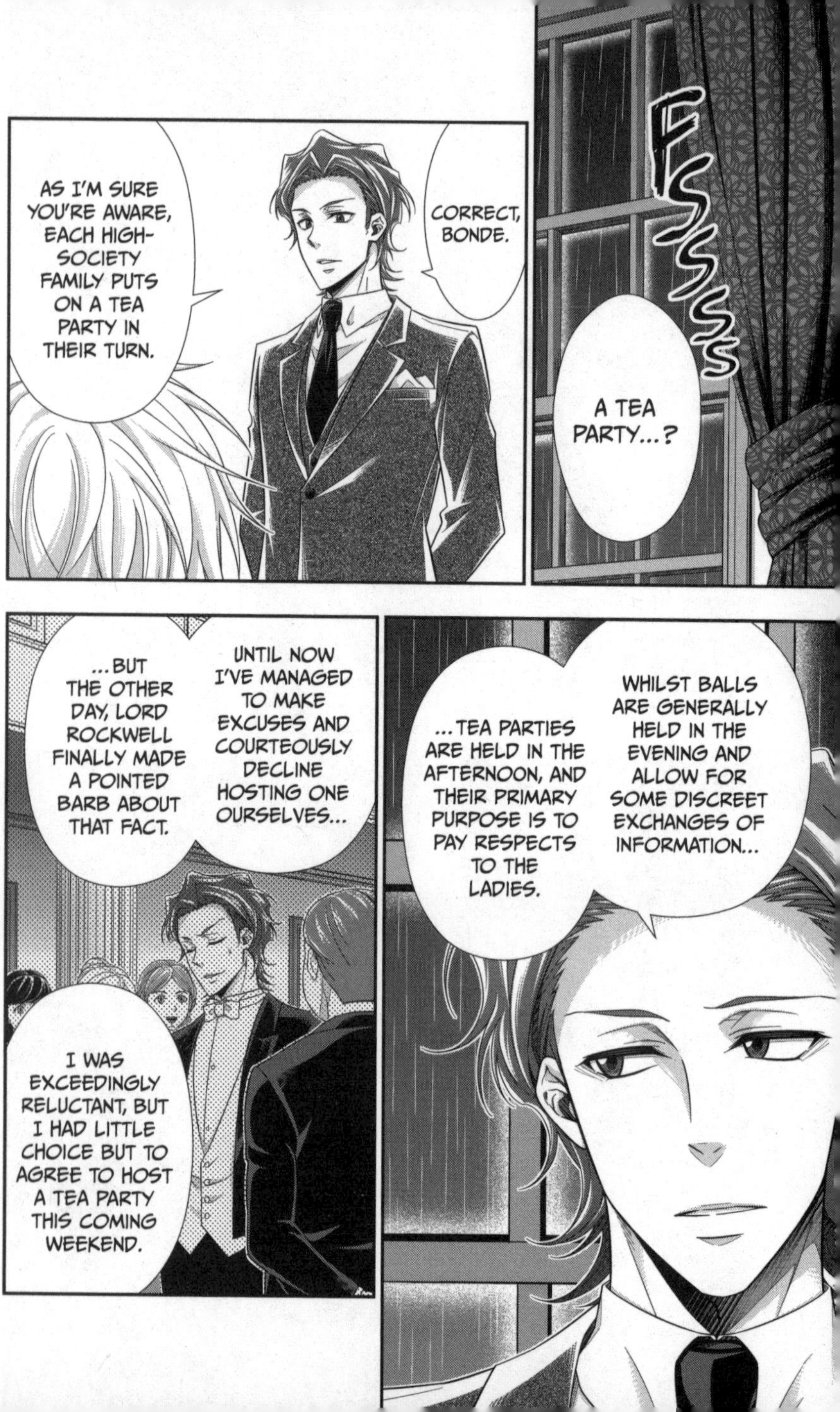
FSSSSS
A TEA PARTY...?
CORRECT, BONDE.
AS I'M SURE YOU'RE AWARE, EACH HIGH-SOCIETY FAMILY PUTS ON A TEA PARTY IN THEIR TURN.
WHILST BALLS ARE GENERALLY HELD IN THE EVENING AND ALLOW FOR SOME DISCREET EXCHANGES OF INFORMATION...
...TEA PARTIES ARE HELD IN THE AFTERNOON, AND THEIR PRIMARY PURPOSE IS TO PAY RESPECTS TO THE LADIES.
UNTIL NOW I'VE MANAGED TO MAKE EXCUSES AND COURTEOUSLY DECLINE HOSTING ONE OURSELVES...
...BUT THE OTHER DAY, LORD ROCKWELL FINALLY MADE A POINTED BARB ABOUT THAT FACT.
I WAS EXCEEDINGLY RELUCTANT, BUT I HAD LITTLE CHOICE BUT TO AGREE TO HOST A TEA PARTY THIS COMING WEEKEND.

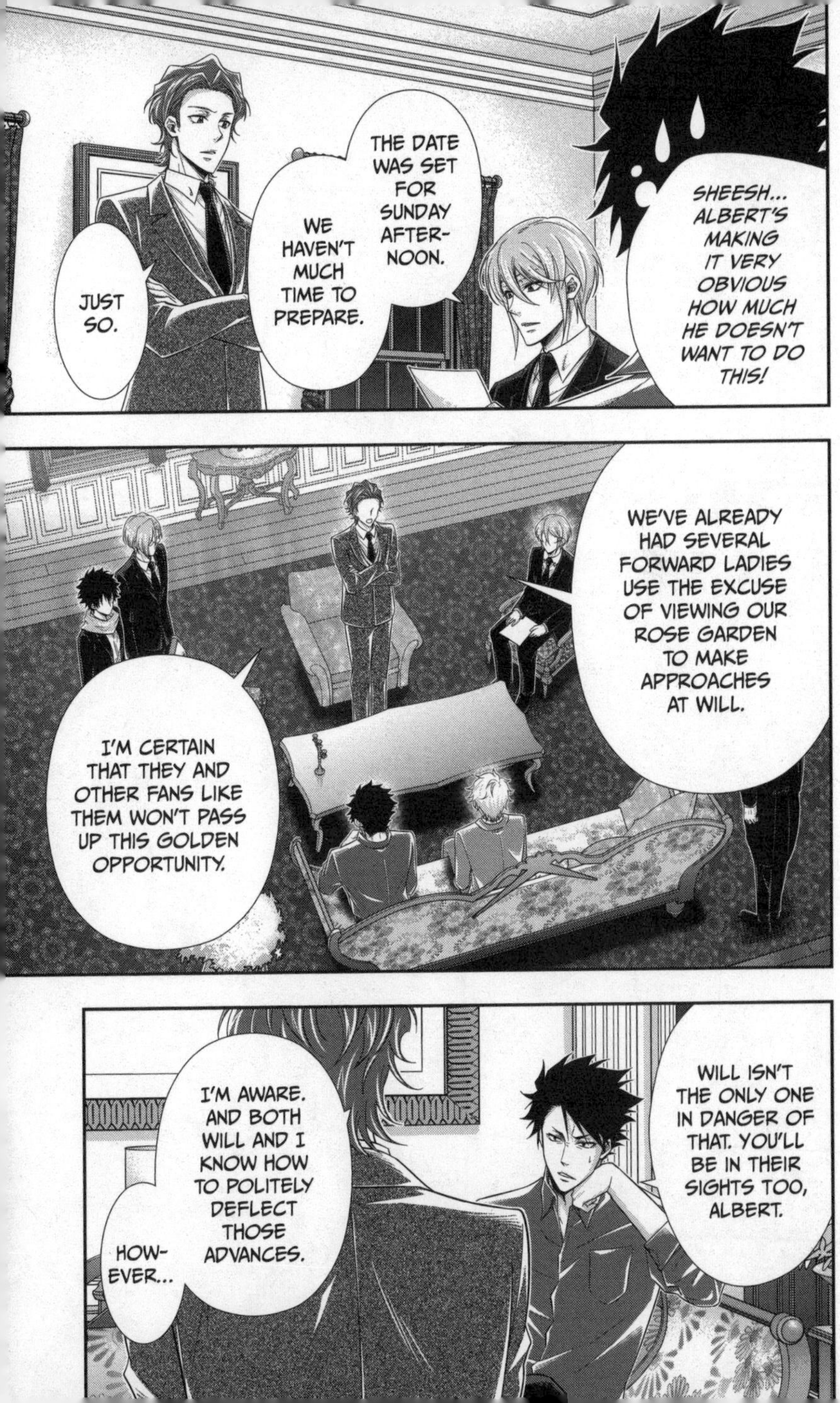
SHEESH... ALBERT'S MAKING IT VERY OBVIOUS HOW MUCH HE DOESN'T WANT TO DO THIS!
THE DATE WAS SET FOR SUNDAY AFTER-NOON.
WE HAVEN'T MUCH TIME TO PREPARE.
JUST SO.
WE'VE ALREADY HAD SEVERAL FORWARD LADIES USE THE EXCUSE OF VIEWING OUR ROSE GARDEN TO MAKE APPROACHES AT WILL.
I'M CERTAIN THAT THEY AND OTHER FANS LIKE THEM WON'T PASS UP THIS GOLDEN OPPORTUNITY.
WILL ISN'T THE ONLY ONE IN DANGER OF THAT. YOU'LL BE IN THEIR SIGHTS TOO, ALBERT.
I'M AWARE. AND BOTH WILL AND I KNOW HOW TO POLITELY DEFLECT THOSE ADVANCES.
HOW-EVER...

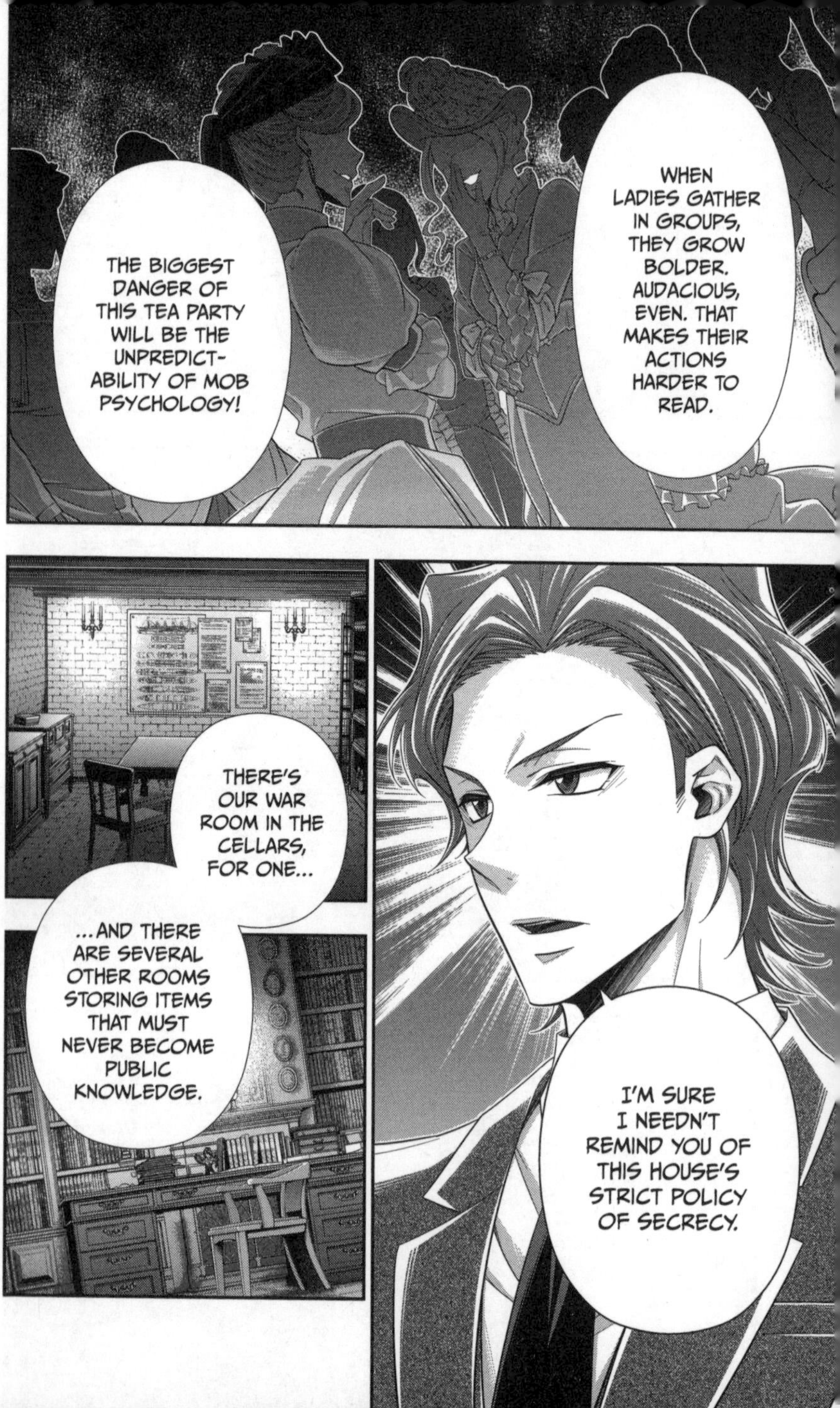
WHEN LADIES GATHER IN GROUPS, THEY GROW BOLDER. AUDACIOUS, EVEN. THAT MAKES THEIR ACTIONS HARDER TO READ.
THE BIGGEST DANGER OF THIS TEA PARTY WILL BE THE UNPREDICT-ABILITY OF MOB PSYCHOLOGY!
I'M SURE I NEEDN'T REMIND YOU OF THIS HOUSE'S STRICT POLICY OF SECRECY.
THERE'S OUR WAR ROOM IN THE CELLARS, FOR ONE...
...AND THERE ARE SEVERAL OTHER ROOMS STORING ITEMS THAT MUST NEVER BECOME PUBLIC KNOWLEDGE.

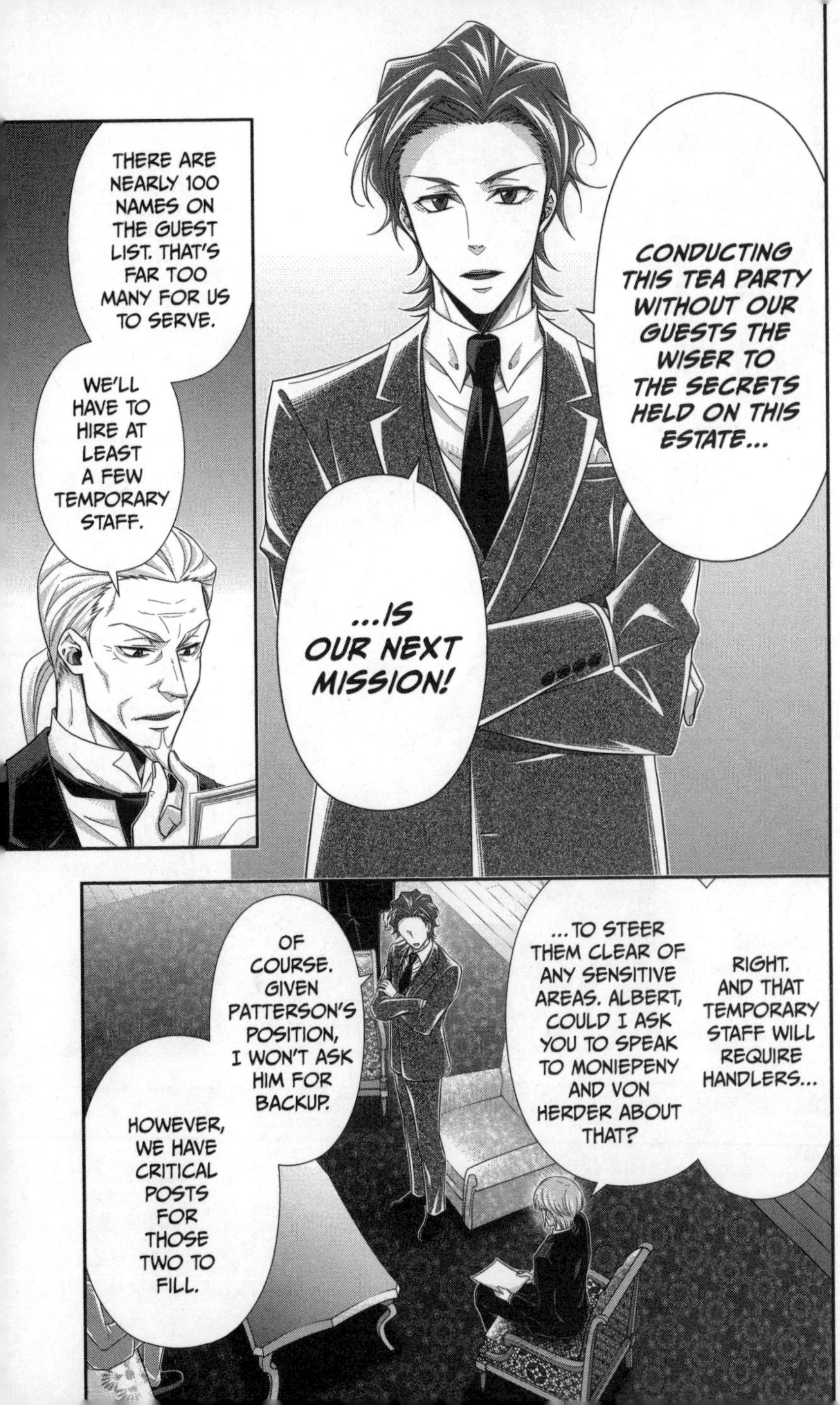
CONDUCTING THIS TEA PARTY WITHOUT OUR GUESTS THE WISER TO THE SECRETS HELD ON THIS ESTATE...
...IS OUR NEXT MISSION!
THERE ARE NEARLY 100 NAMES ON THE GUEST LIST. THAT'S FAR TOO MANY FOR US TO SERVE.
WE'LL HAVE TO HIRE AT LEAST A FEW TEMPORARY STAFF.
RIGHT. AND THAT TEMPORARY STAFF WILL REQUIRE HANDLERS...
...TO STEER THEM CLEAR OF ANY SENSITIVE AREAS. ALBERT, COULD I ASK YOU TO SPEAK TO MONIEPENY AND VON HERDER ABOUT THAT?
OF COURSE. GIVEN PATTERSON'S POSITION, I WON'T ASK HIM FOR BACKUP.
HOWEVER, WE HAVE CRITICAL POSTS FOR THOSE TWO TO FILL.

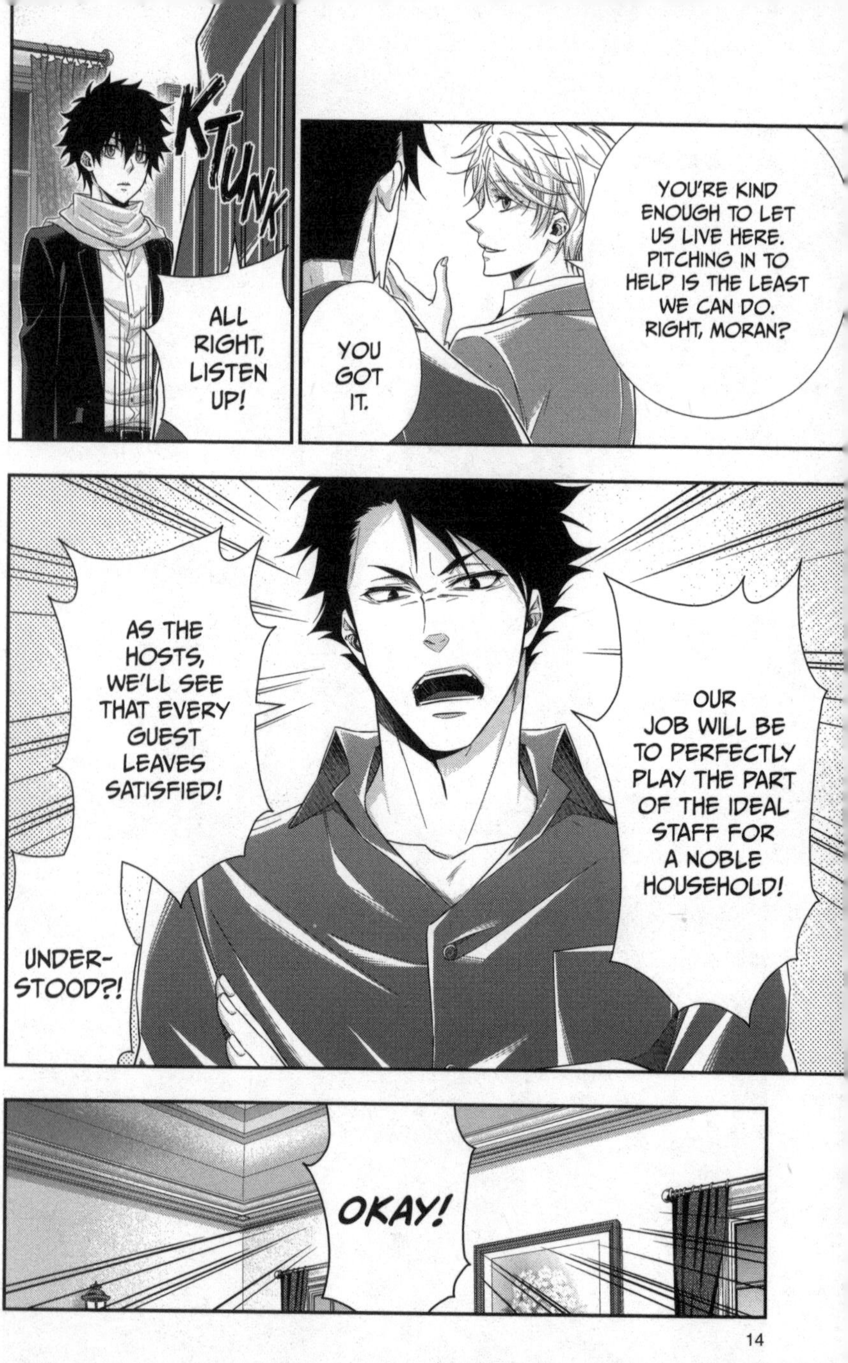
YOU'RE KIND ENOUGH TO LET US LIVE HERE. PITCHING IN TO HELP IS THE LEAST WE CAN DO. RIGHT, MORAN?
YOU GOT IT.
KTUNK
ALL RIGHT, LISTEN UP!
OUR JOB WILL BE TO PERFECTLY PLAY THE PART OF THE IDEAL STAFF FOR A NOBLE HOUSEHOLD!
AS THE HOSTS, WE'LL SEE THAT EVERY GUEST LEAVES SATISFIED!
UNDER-STOOD?!
OKAY!

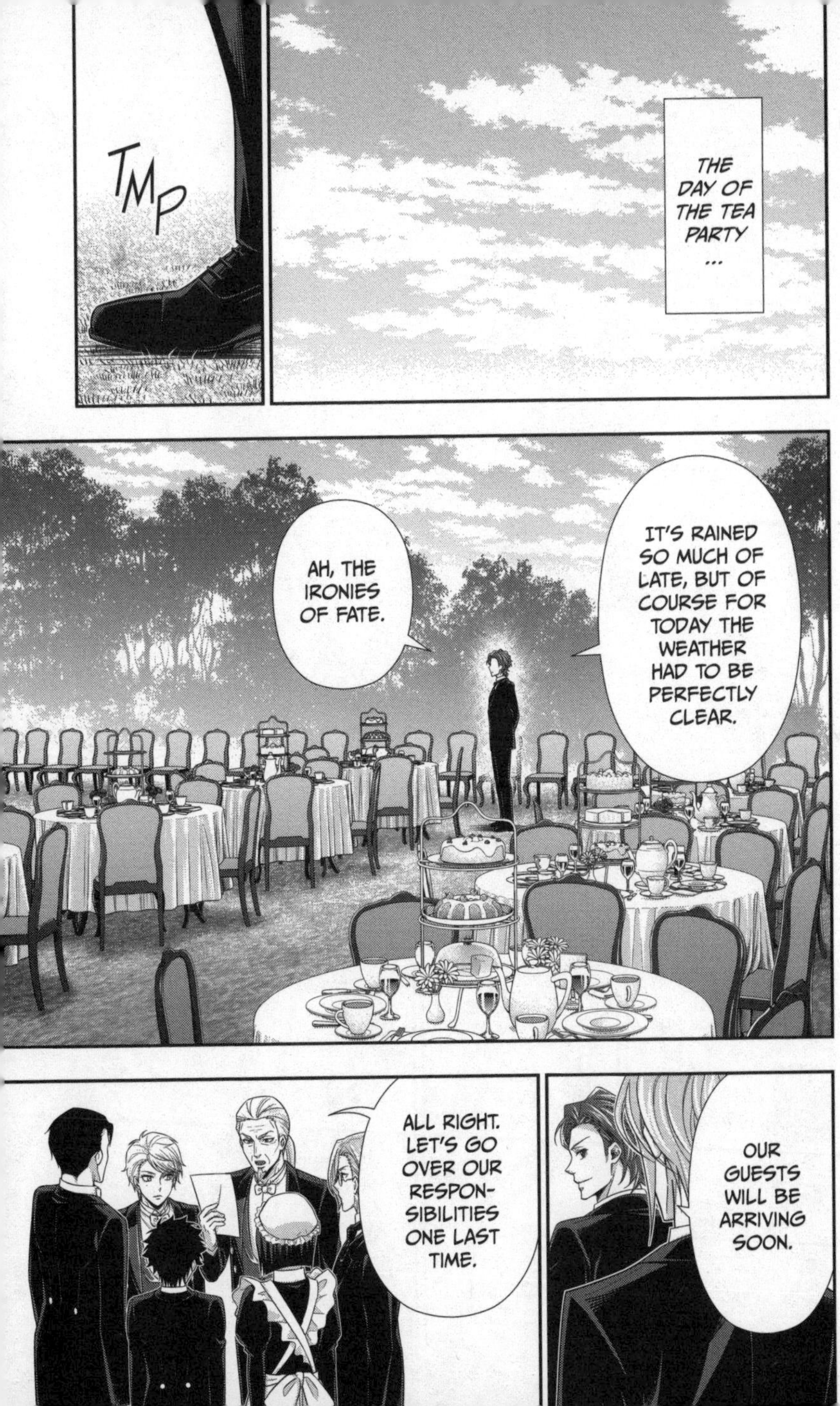
THE DAY OF THE TEA PARTY ...
TMP
IT'S RAINED SO MUCH OF LATE, BUT OF COURSE FOR TODAY THE WEATHER HAD TO BE PERFECTLY CLEAR.
AH, THE IRONIES OF FATE.
OUR GUESTS WILL BE ARRIVING SOON.
ALL RIGHT. LET'S GO OVER OUR RESPON-SIBILITIES ONE LAST TIME.

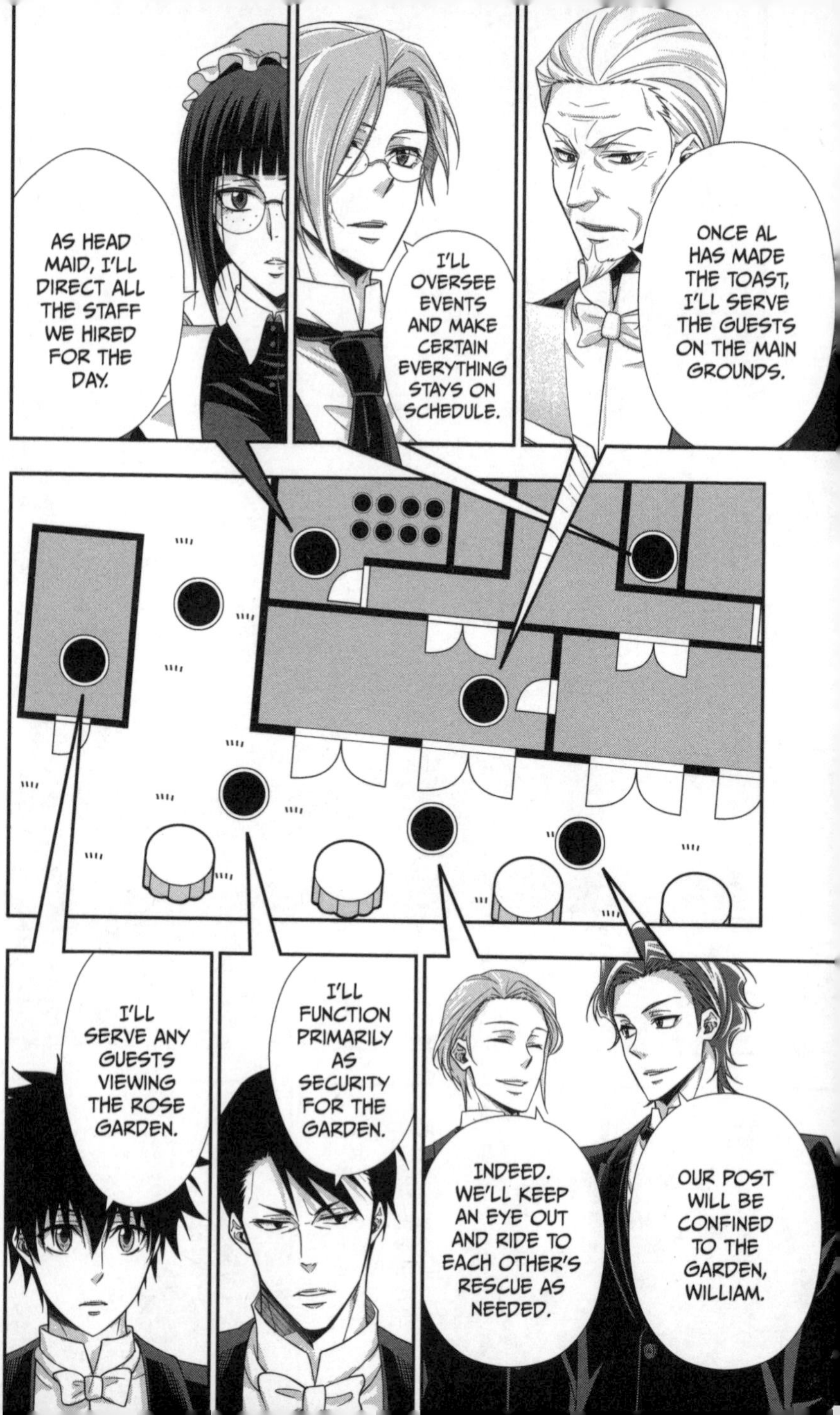
ONCE AL HAS MADE THE TOAST, I'LL SERVE THE GUESTS ON THE MAIN GROUNDS.
I'LL OVERSEE EVENTS AND MAKE CERTAIN EVERYTHING STAYS ON SCHEDULE.
AS HEAD MAID, I'LL DIRECT ALL THE STAFF WE HIRED FOR THE DAY.
OUR POST WILL BE CONFINED TO THE GARDEN, WILLIAM.
INDEED. WE'LL KEEP AN EYE OUT AND RIDE TO EACH OTHER'S RESCUE AS NEEDED.
I'LL FUNCTION PRIMARILY AS SECURITY FOR THE GARDEN.
I'LL SERVE ANY GUESTS VIEWING THE ROSE GARDEN.

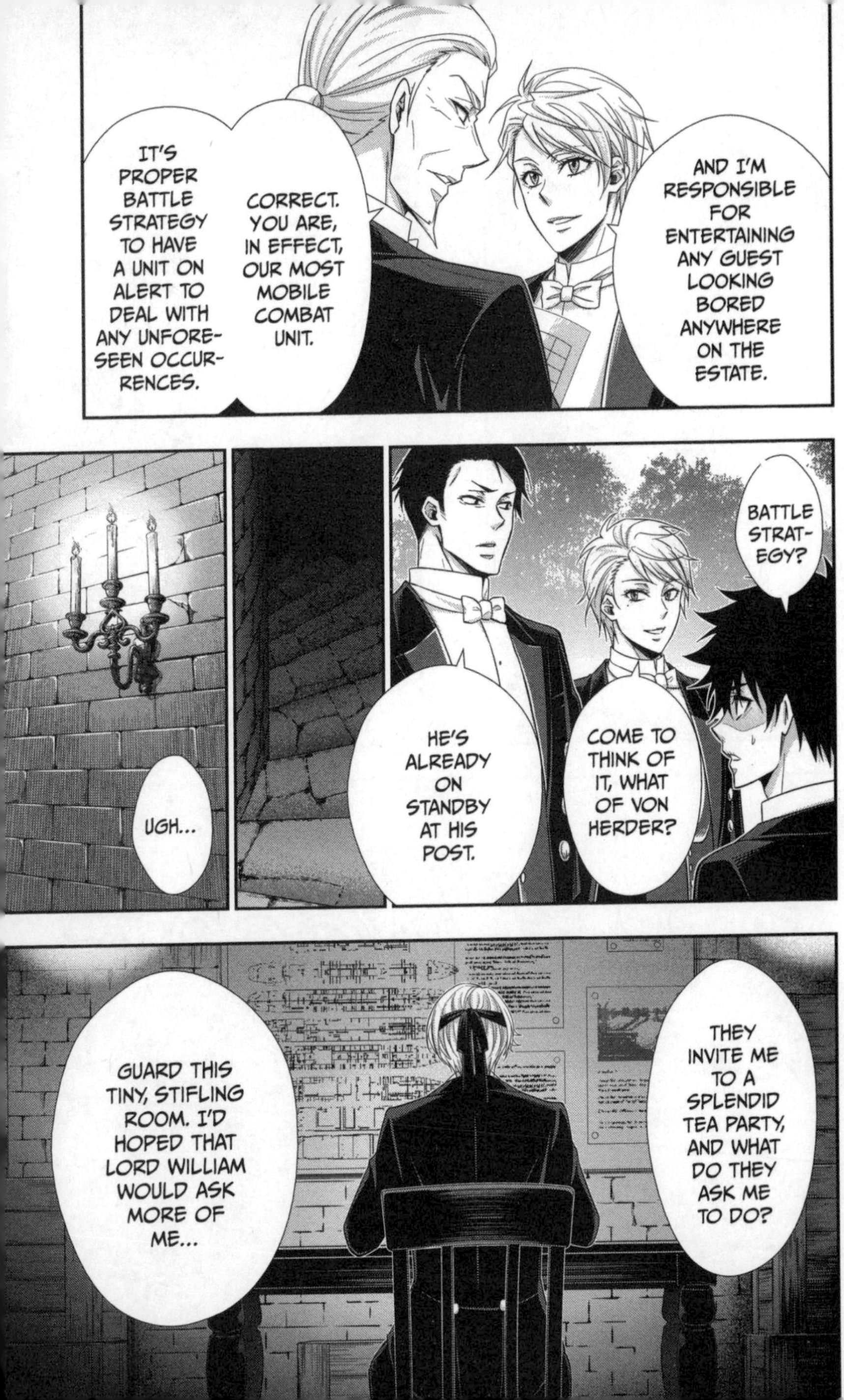
AND I'M RESPONSIBLE FOR ENTERTAINING ANY GUEST LOOKING BORED ANYWHERE ON THE ESTATE.
CORRECT. YOU ARE, IN EFFECT, OUR MOST MOBILE COMBAT UNIT.
IT'S PROPER BATTLE STRATEGY TO HAVE A UNIT ON ALERT TO DEAL WITH ANY UNFORESEEN OCCURRENCES.
BATTLE STRATEGY?
COME TO THINK OF IT, WHAT OF VON HERDER?
HE'S ALREADY ON STANDBY AT HIS POST.
UGH...
THEY INVITE ME TO A SPLENDID TEA PARTY, AND WHAT DO THEY ASK ME TO DO?
GUARD THIS TINY, STIFLING ROOM. I'D HOPED THAT LORD WILLIAM WOULD ASK MORE OF ME...

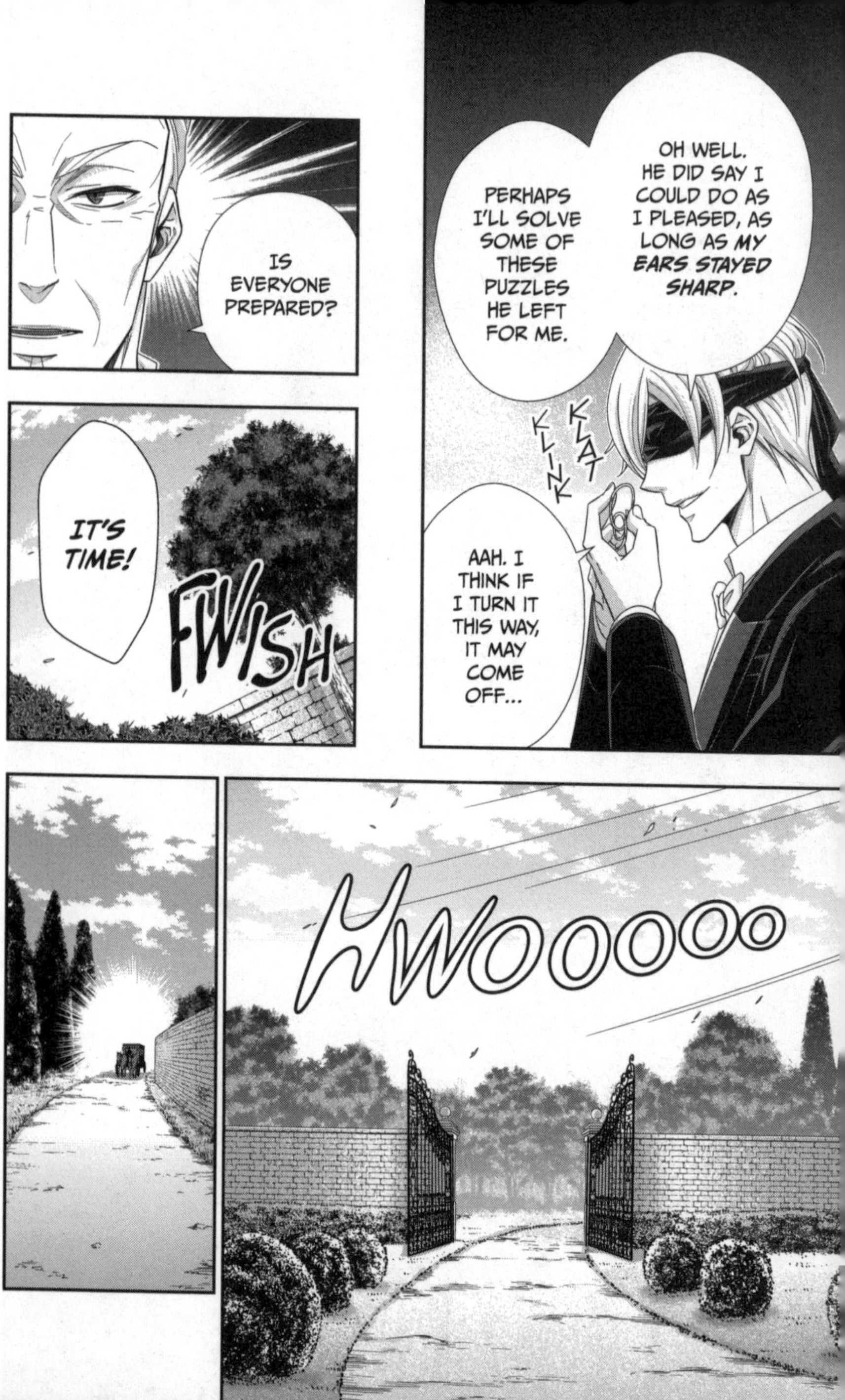
OH WELL. HE DID SAY I COULD DO AS I PLEASED, AS LONG AS MY EARS STAYED SHARP.
PERHAPS I'LL SOLVE SOME OF THESE PUZZLES HE LEFT FOR ME.
KLAT
KLINK
AAH. I THINK IF I TURN IT THIS WAY, IT MAY COME OFF...
IS EVERYONE PREPARED?
IT'S TIME!
FWISH
HWOOOOOO

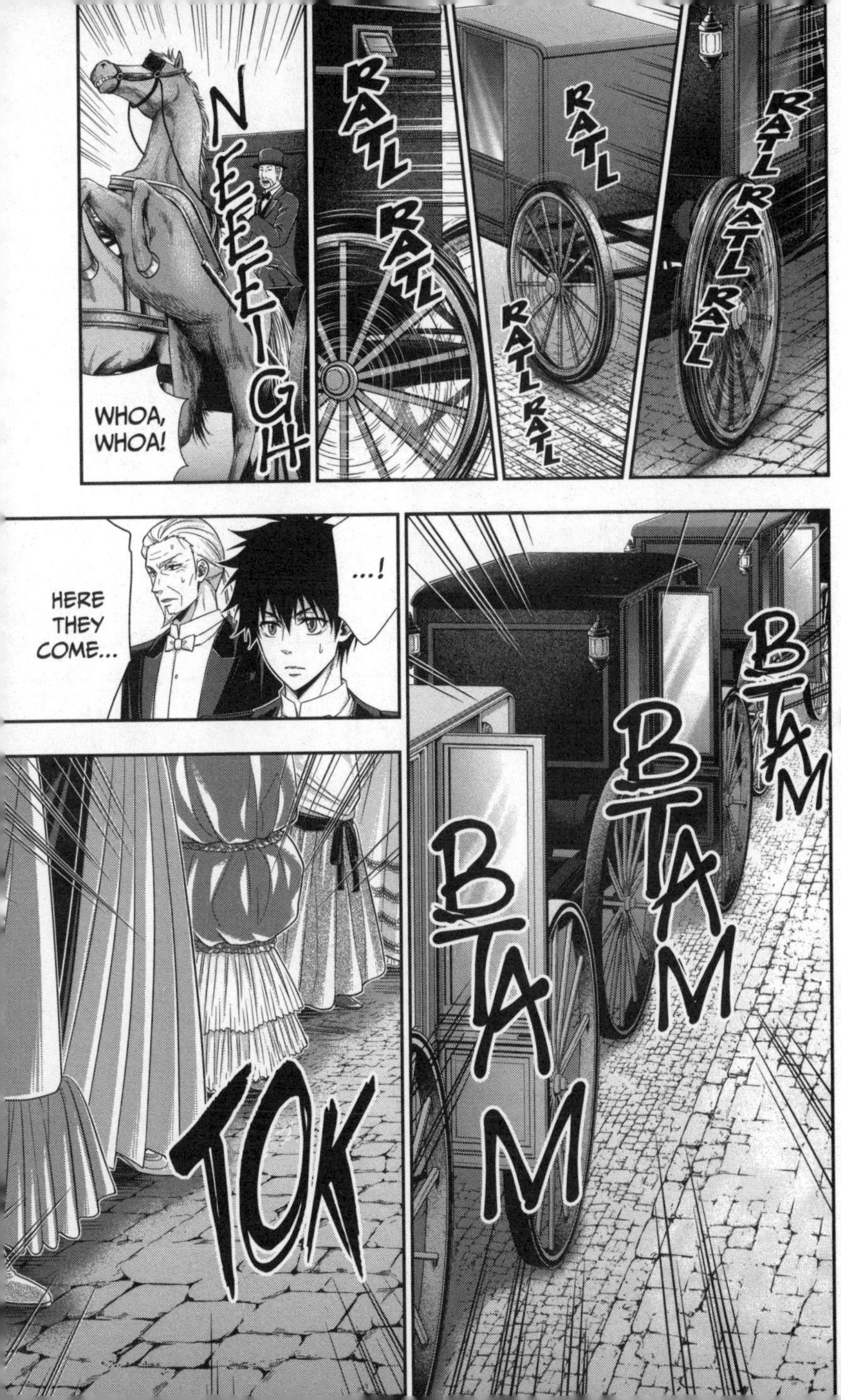

RATL RATL RATL RATL
RATL
RATL RATL
RATL
RATL
NEEEIGH
WHOA, WHOA!
BTAM
BTAM
BTAM
...!
HERE THEY COME...
TOK

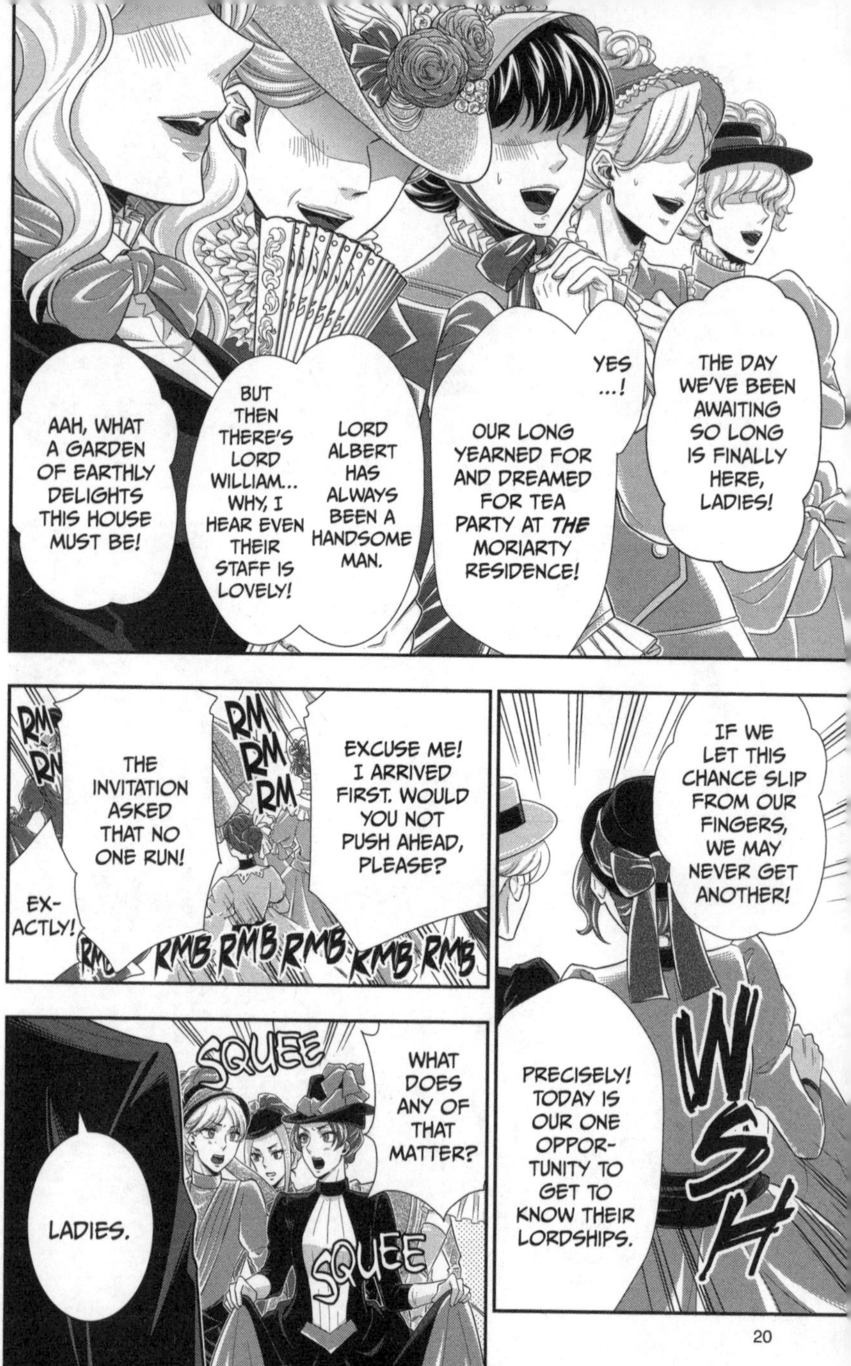
THE DAY WE'VE BEEN AWAITING SO LONG IS FINALLY HERE, LADIES!
YES ...!
OUR LONG YEARNED FOR AND DREAMED FOR TEA PARTY AT *THE* MORIARTY RESIDENCE!
LORD ALBERT HAS ALWAYS BEEN A HANDSOME MAN.
BUT THEN THERE'S LORD WILLIAM... WHY, I HEAR EVEN THEIR STAFF IS LOVELY!
AAH, WHAT A GARDEN OF EARTHLY DELIGHTS THIS HOUSE MUST BE!
IF WE LET THIS CHANCE SLIP FROM OUR FINGERS, WE MAY NEVER GET ANOTHER!
PRECISELY! TODAY IS OUR ONE OPPOR-TUNITY TO GET TO KNOW THEIR LORDSHIPS.
WSH
RM RM RM RM
EXCUSE ME! I ARRIVED FIRST. WOULD YOU NOT PUSH AHEAD, PLEASE?
THE INVITATION ASKED THAT NO ONE RUN!
RMB RMB RMB RMB RMB RMB
EX-ACTLY!
SQUEE
WHAT DOES ANY OF THAT MATTER?
SQUEE
LADIES.

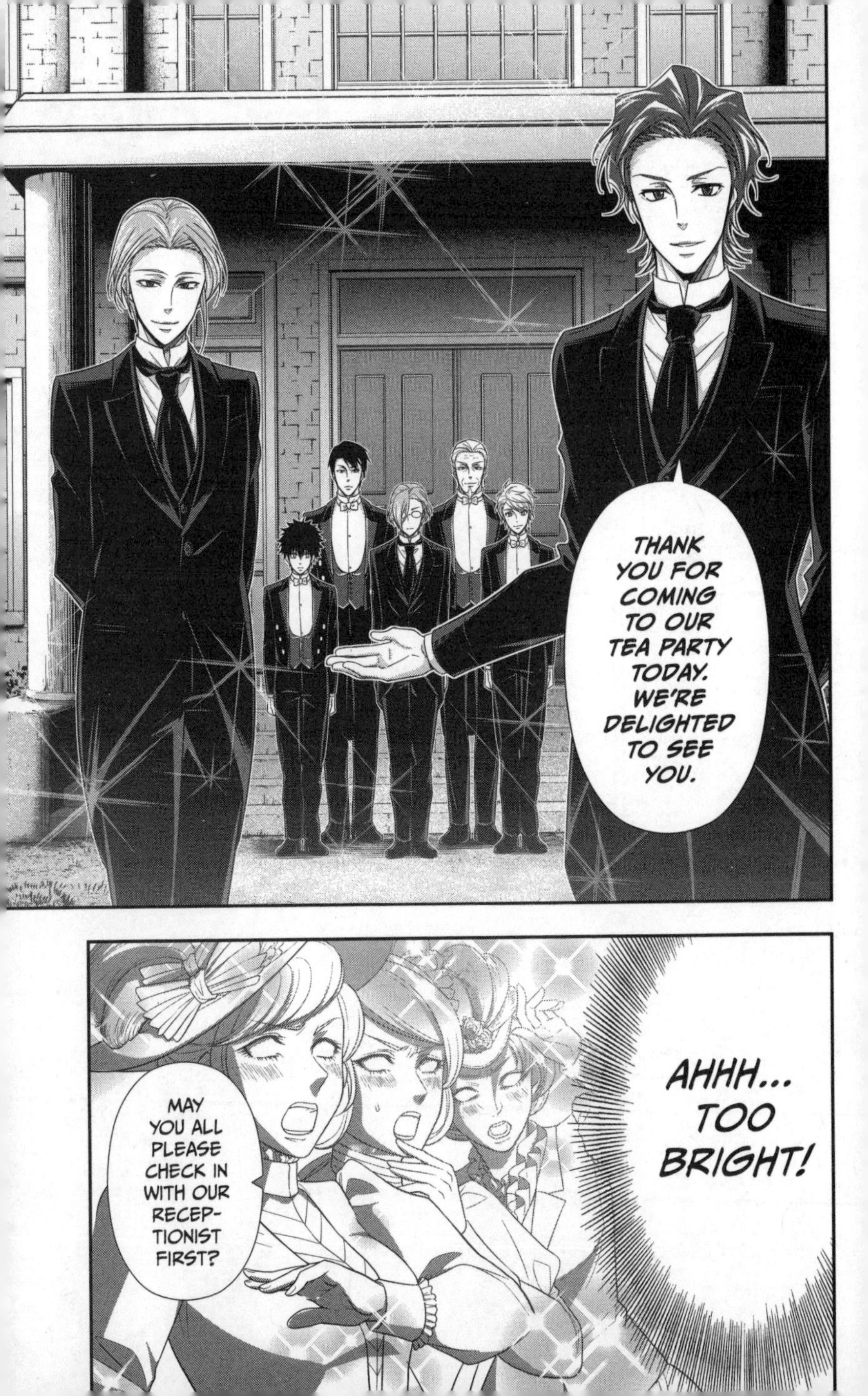
THANK YOU FOR COMING TO OUR TEA PARTY TODAY. WE'RE DELIGHTED TO SEE YOU.
AHHH... TOO BRIGHT!
MAY YOU ALL PLEASE CHECK IN WITH OUR RECEP-TIONIST FIRST?

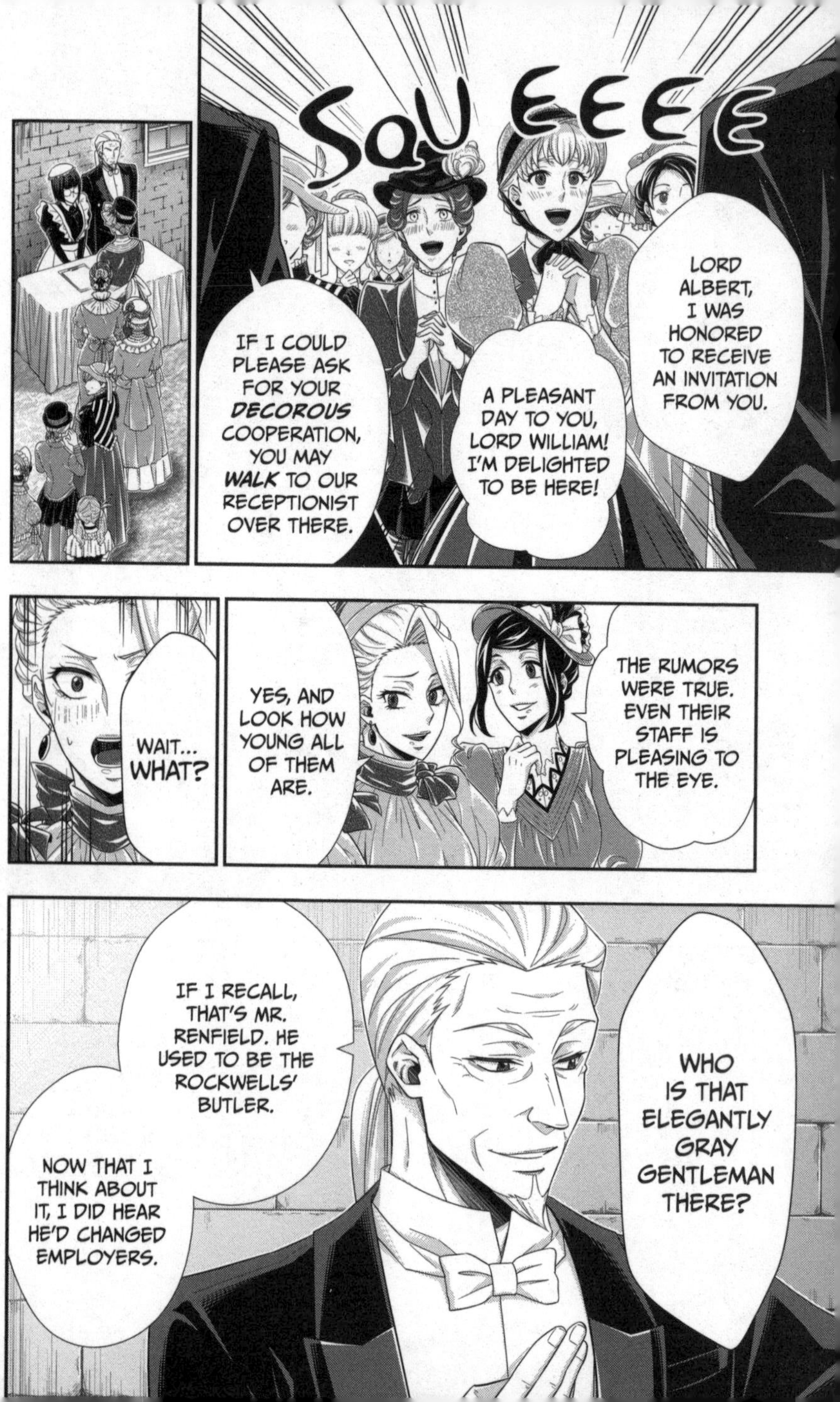
SQUEEEE
LORD ALBERT, I WAS HONORED TO RECEIVE AN INVITATION FROM YOU.
A PLEASANT DAY TO YOU, LORD WILLIAM! I'M DELIGHTED TO BE HERE!
IF I COULD PLEASE ASK FOR YOUR *DECOROUS* COOPERATION, YOU MAY *WALK* TO OUR RECEPTIONIST OVER THERE.
THE RUMORS WERE TRUE. EVEN THEIR STAFF IS PLEASING TO THE EYE.
YES, AND LOOK HOW YOUNG ALL OF THEM ARE.
WAIT... WHAT?
WHO IS THAT ELEGANTLY GRAY GENTLEMAN THERE?
IF I RECALL, THAT'S MR. RENFIELD. HE USED TO BE THE ROCKWELLS' BUTLER.
NOW THAT I THINK ABOUT IT, I DID HEAR HE'D CHANGED EMPLOYERS.

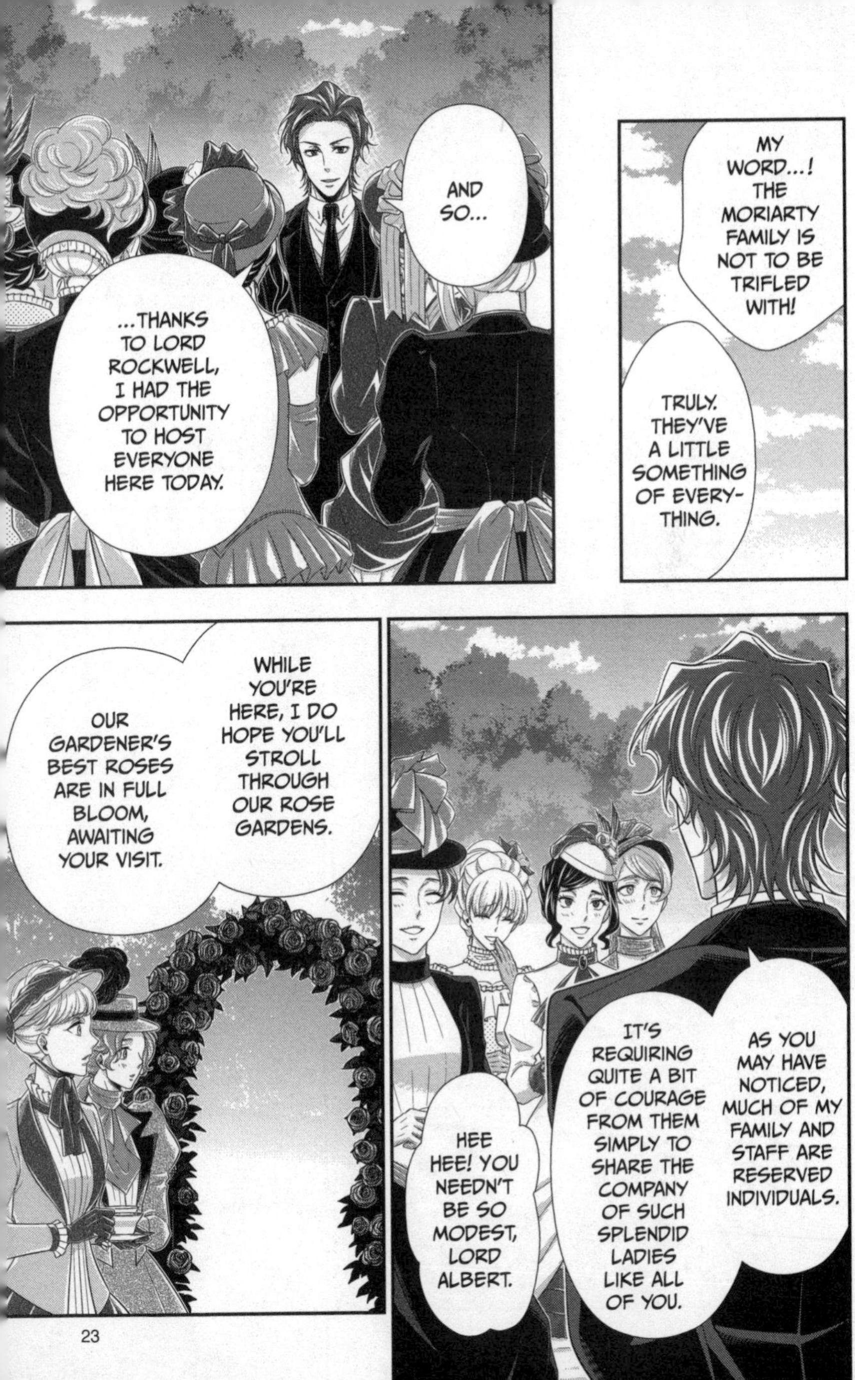
MY WORD...! THE MORIARTY FAMILY IS NOT TO BE TRIFLED WITH!
TRULY. THEY'VE A LITTLE SOMETHING OF EVERY-THING.
AND SO...
...THANKS TO LORD ROCKWELL, I HAD THE OPPORTUNITY TO HOST EVERYONE HERE TODAY.
AS YOU MAY HAVE NOTICED, MUCH OF MY FAMILY AND STAFF ARE RESERVED INDIVIDUALS.
IT'S REQUIRING QUITE A BIT OF COURAGE FROM THEM SIMPLY TO SHARE THE COMPANY OF SUCH SPLENDID LADIES LIKE ALL OF YOU.
HEE HEE! YOU NEEDN'T BE SO MODEST, LORD ALBERT.
WHILE YOU'RE HERE, I DO HOPE YOU'LL STROLL THROUGH OUR ROSE GARDENS.
OUR GARDENER'S BEST ROSES ARE IN FULL BLOOM, AWAITING YOUR VISIT.

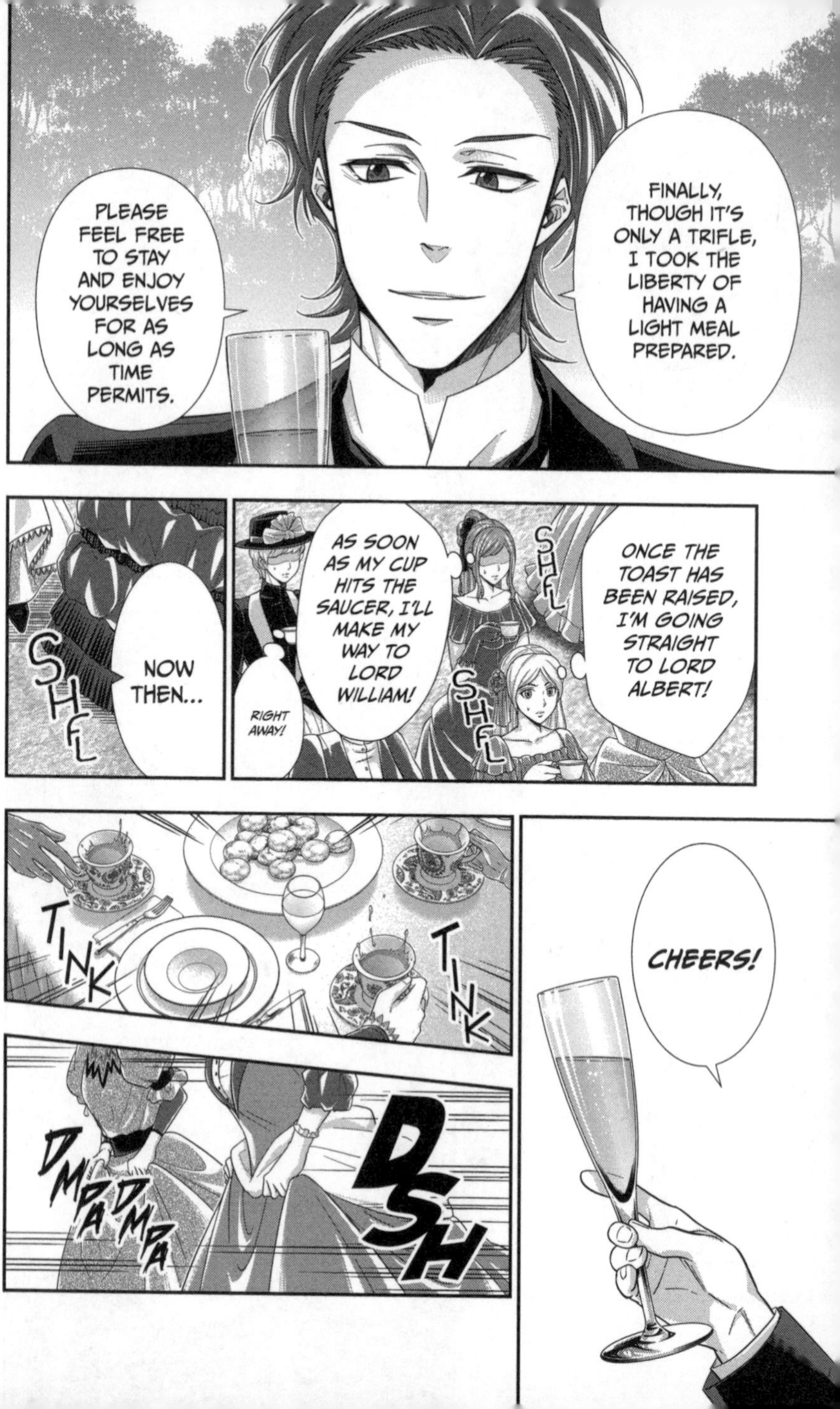
FINALLY, THOUGH IT'S ONLY A TRIFLE, I TOOK THE LIBERTY OF HAVING A LIGHT MEAL PREPARED.
PLEASE FEEL FREE TO STAY AND ENJOY YOURSELVES FOR AS LONG AS TIME PERMITS.
ONCE THE TOAST HAS BEEN RAISED, I'M GOING STRAIGHT TO LORD ALBERT!
SHFL
SHFL
AS SOON AS MY CUP HITS THE SAUCER, I'LL MAKE MY WAY TO LORD WILLIAM!
RIGHT AWAY!
NOW THEN...
SHFL
CHEERS!
TINK
TINK
DSH
DMPA DMPA

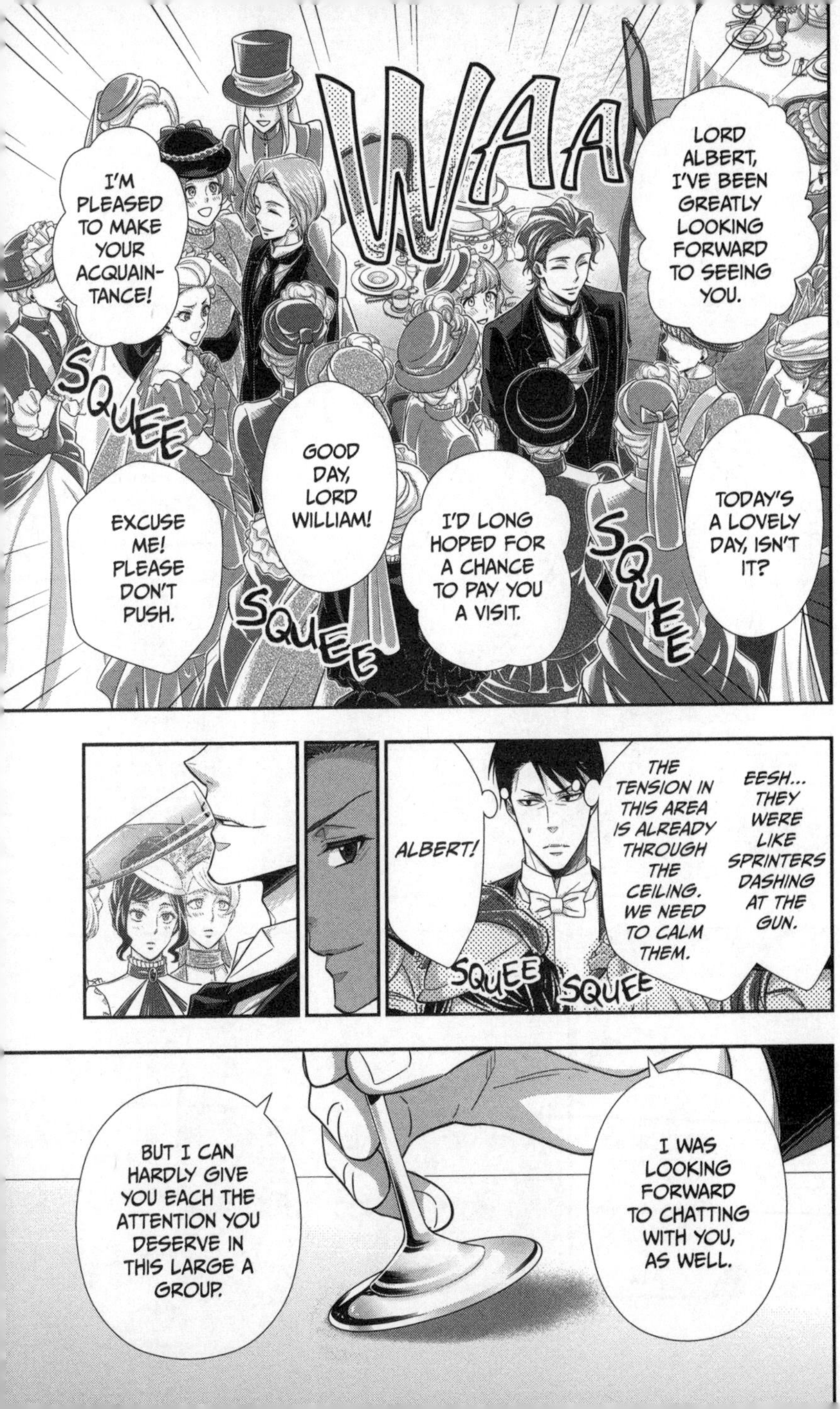
LORD ALBERT, I'VE BEEN GREATLY LOOKING FORWARD TO SEEING YOU.
WAA
I'M PLEASED TO MAKE YOUR ACQUAIN-TANCE!
SQUEE
TODAY'S A LOVELY DAY, ISN'T IT?
SQUEE
I'D LONG HOPED FOR A CHANCE TO PAY YOU A VISIT.
GOOD DAY, LORD WILLIAM!
SQUEE
EXCUSE ME! PLEASE DON'T PUSH.
EESH... THEY WERE LIKE SPRINTERS DASHING AT THE GUN.
THE TENSION IN THIS AREA IS ALREADY THROUGH THE CEILING. WE NEED TO CALM THEM.
ALBERT!
SQUEE
SQUEE
I WAS LOOKING FORWARD TO CHATTING WITH YOU, AS WELL.
BUT I CAN HARDLY GIVE YOU EACH THE ATTENTION YOU DESERVE IN THIS LARGE A GROUP.

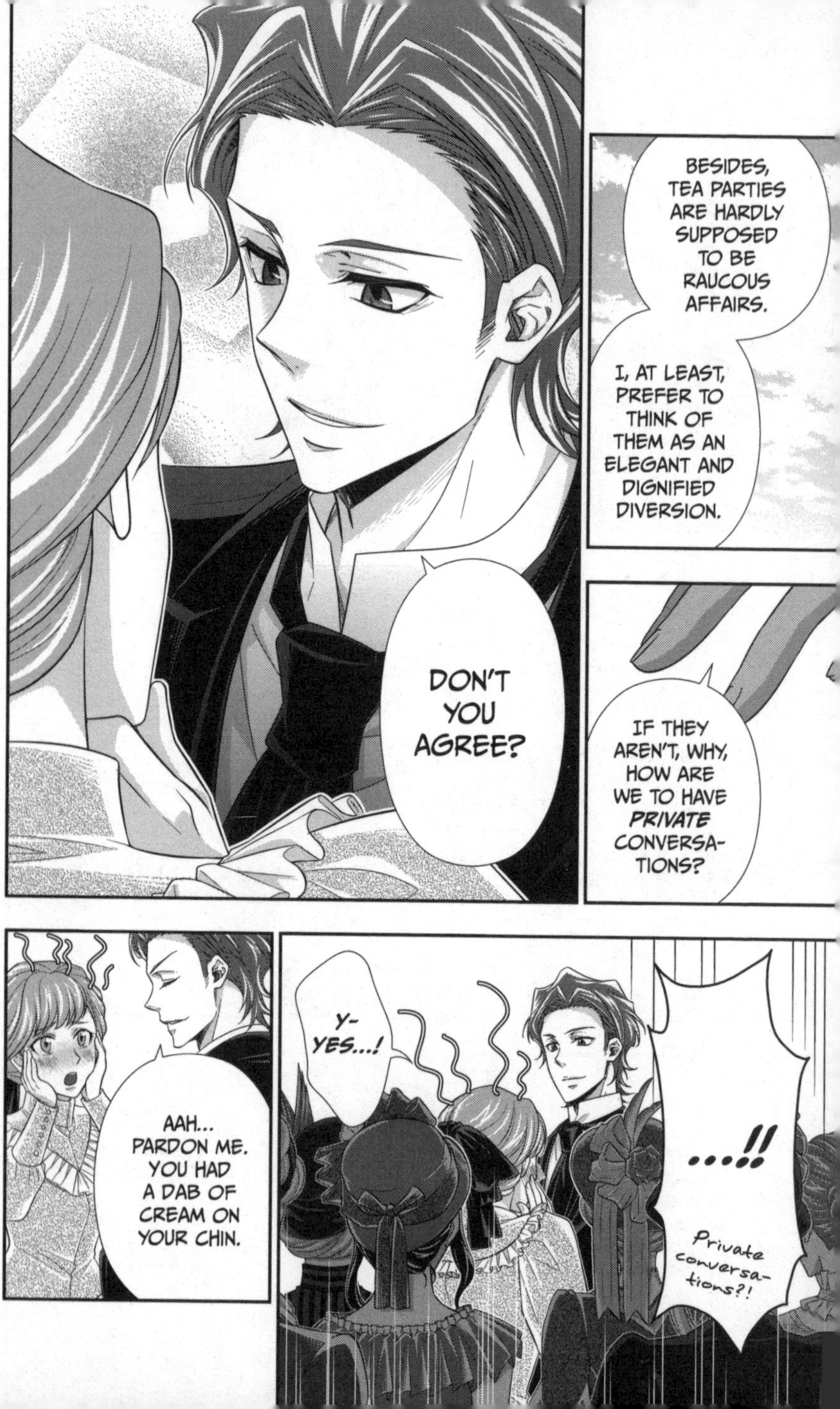
BESIDES, TEA PARTIES ARE HARDLY SUPPOSED TO BE RAUCOUS AFFAIRS.
I, AT LEAST, PREFER TO THINK OF THEM AS AN ELEGANT AND DIGNIFIED DIVERSION.
IF THEY AREN'T, WHY, HOW ARE WE TO HAVE *PRIVATE* CONVERSA-TIONS?
DON'T YOU AGREE?
...!!
Private conversa-tions?!
Y-YES...!
AAH... PARDON ME. YOU HAD A DAB OF CREAM ON YOUR CHIN.

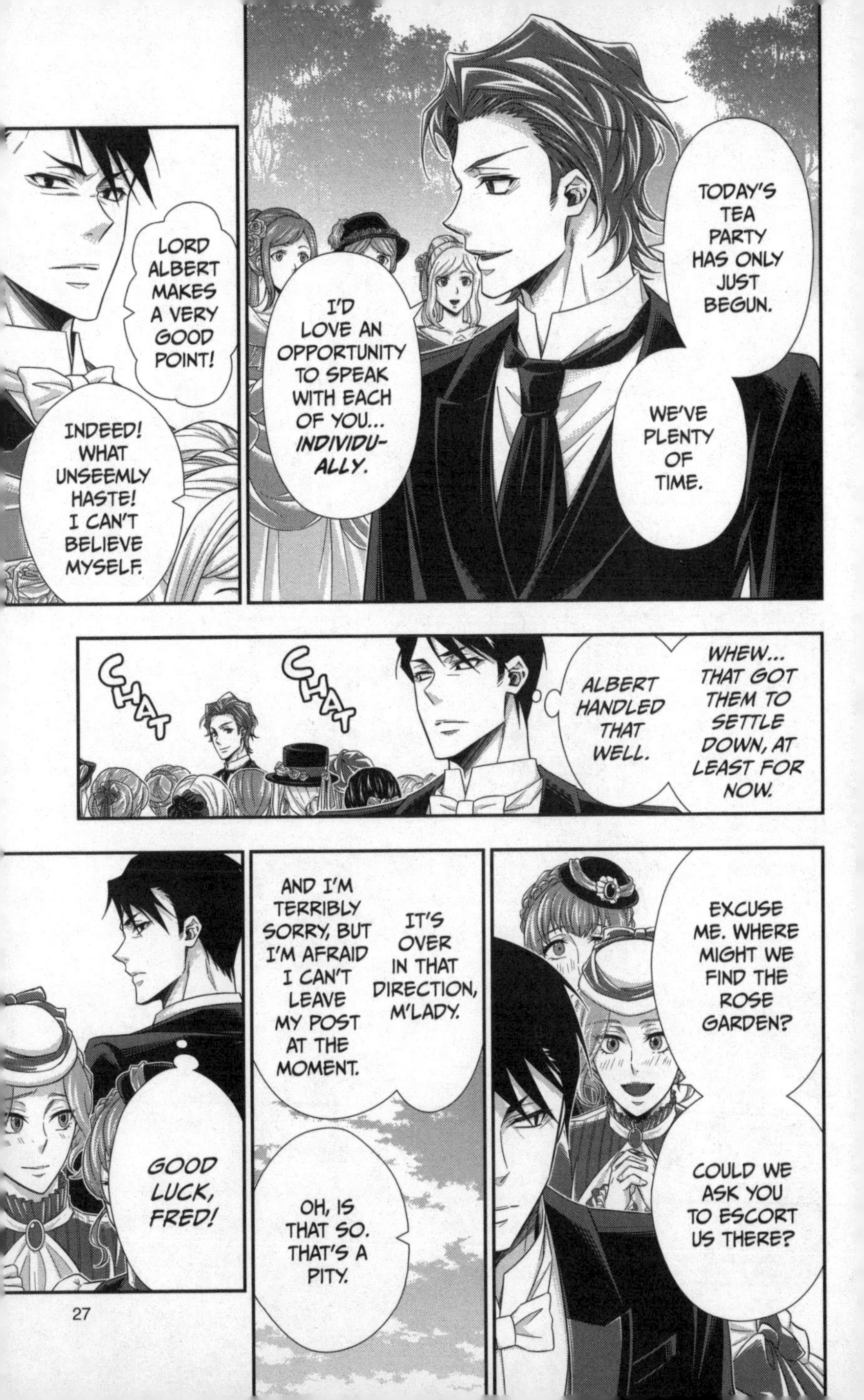
TODAY'S TEA PARTY HAS ONLY JUST BEGUN.
WE'VE PLENTY OF TIME.
I'D LOVE AN OPPORTUNITY TO SPEAK WITH EACH OF YOU... *INDIVIDUALLY*.
LORD ALBERT MAKES A VERY GOOD POINT!
INDEED! WHAT UNSEEMLY HASTE! I CAN'T BELIEVE MYSELF.
WHEW... THAT GOT THEM TO SETTLE DOWN, AT LEAST FOR NOW.
ALBERT HANDLED THAT WELL.
CHAT
CHAT
EXCUSE ME. WHERE MIGHT WE FIND THE ROSE GARDEN?
COULD WE ASK YOU TO ESCORT US THERE?
IT'S OVER IN THAT DIRECTION, M'LADY.
AND I'M TERRIBLY SORRY, BUT I'M AFRAID I CAN'T LEAVE MY POST AT THE MOMENT.
OH, IS THAT SO. THAT'S A PITY.
GOOD LUCK, FRED!

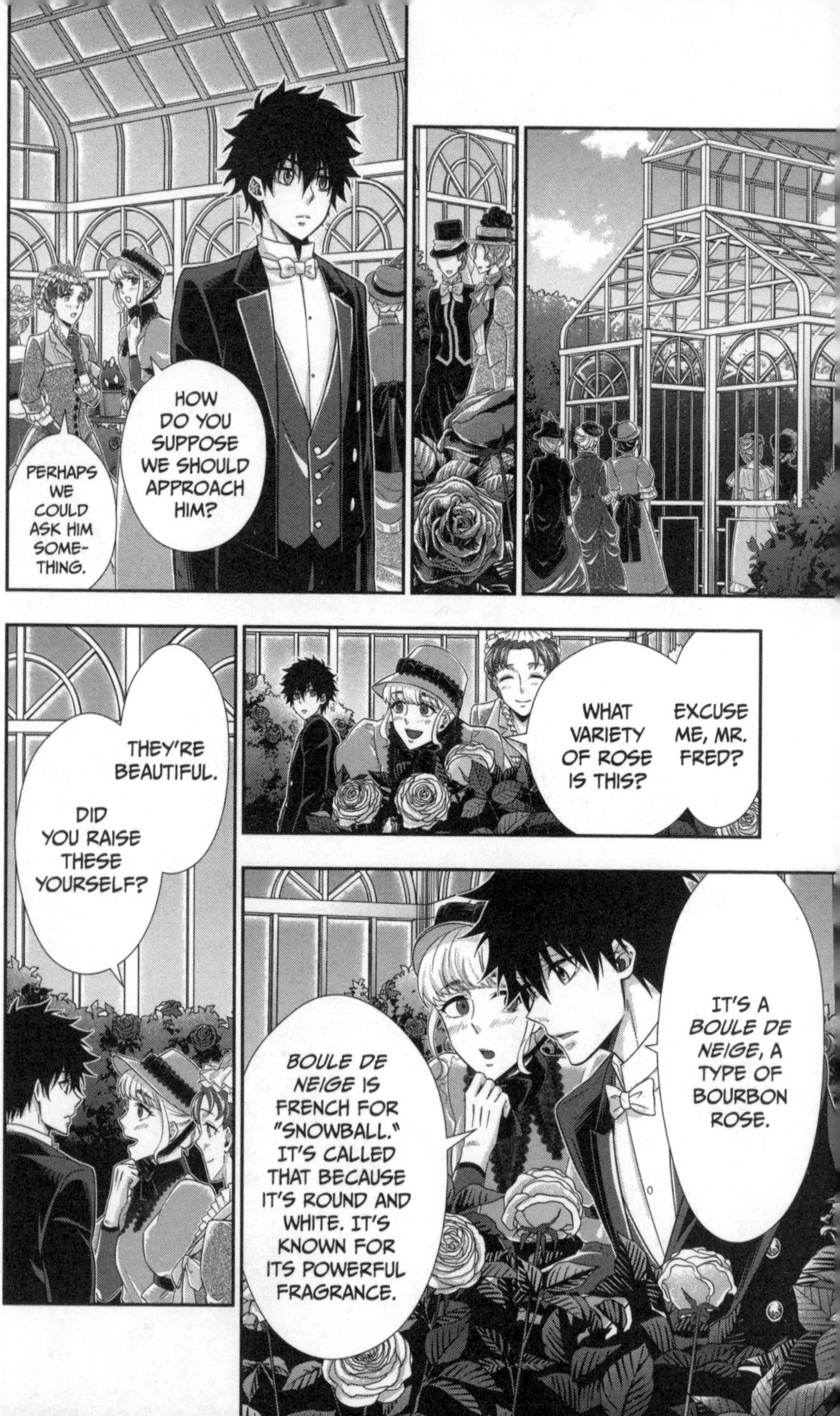
HOW DO YOU SUPPOSE WE SHOULD APPROACH HIM?
PERHAPS WE COULD ASK HIM SOME-THING.
EXCUSE ME, MR. FRED?
WHAT VARIETY OF ROSE IS THIS?
IT'S A *BOULE DE NEIGE*, A TYPE OF BOURBON ROSE.
BOULE DE NEIGE IS FRENCH FOR "SNOWBALL." IT'S CALLED THAT BECAUSE IT'S ROUND AND WHITE. IT'S KNOWN FOR ITS POWERFUL FRAGRANCE.
THEY'RE BEAUTIFUL.
DID YOU RAISE THESE YOURSELF?

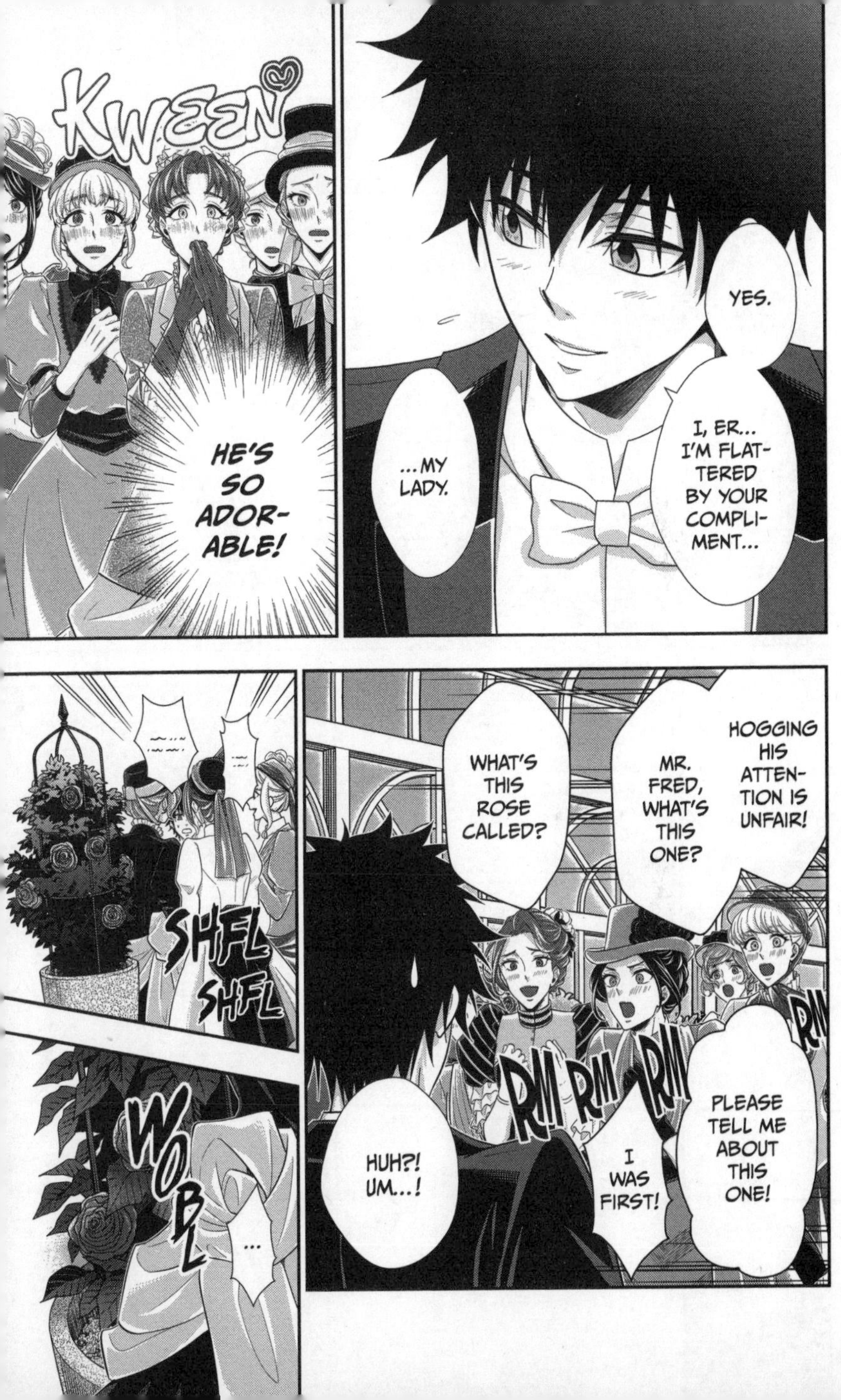
YES.
I, ER... I'M FLATTERED BY YOUR COMPLIMENT...
...MY LADY.
KWEEN
HE'S SO ADORABLE!
HOGGING HIS ATTENTION IS UNFAIR!
MR. FRED, WHAT'S THIS ONE?
WHAT'S THIS ROSE CALLED?
RM RM RM RM
PLEASE TELL ME ABOUT THIS ONE!
I WAS FIRST!
HUH?! UM...!
SHFL SHFL
WOBL
...

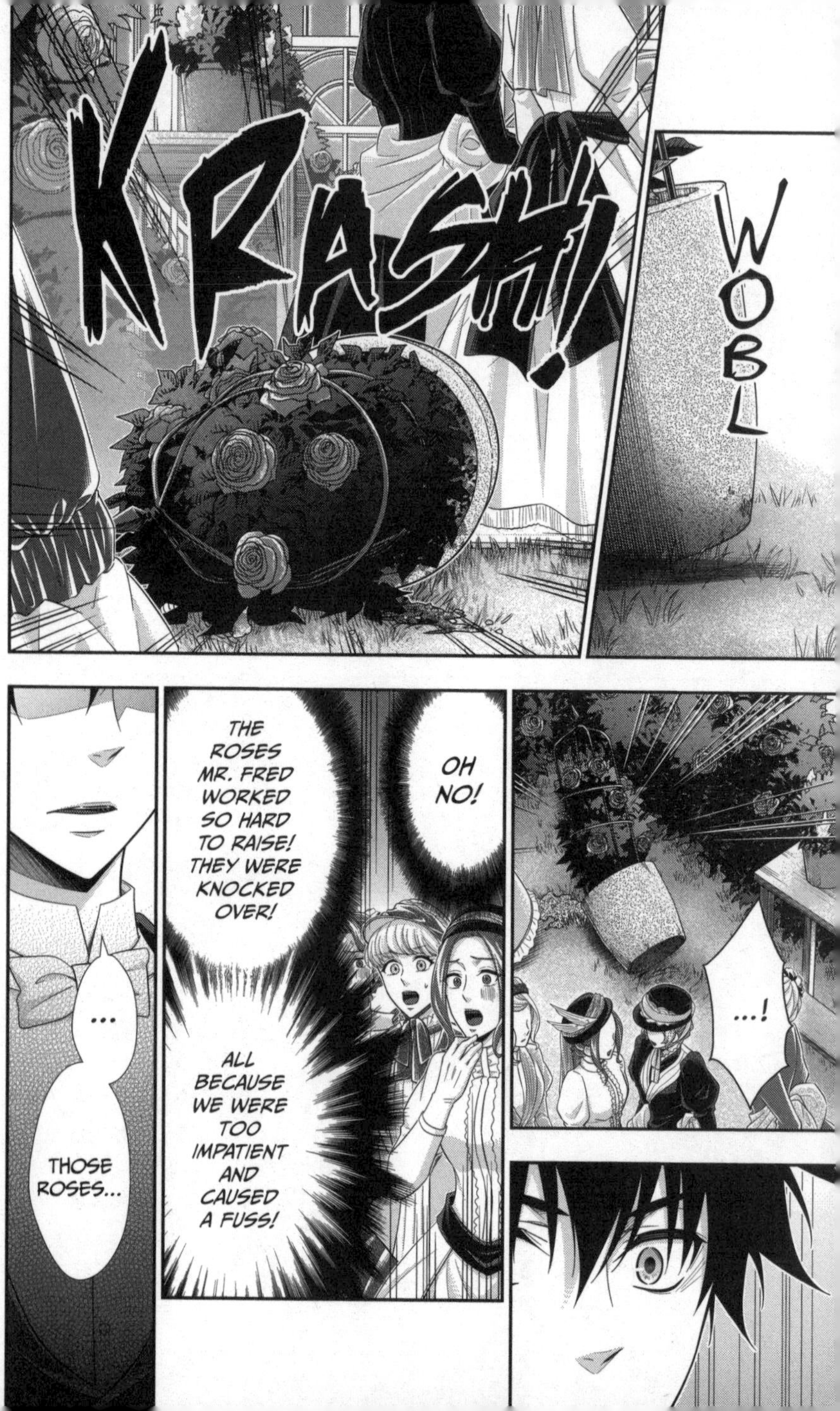
WOBL
KRASH!
...!
OH NO!
THE ROSES MR. FRED WORKED SO HARD TO RAISE! THEY WERE KNOCKED OVER!
ALL BECAUSE WE WERE TOO IMPATIENT AND CAUSED A FUSS!
...
THOSE ROSES...

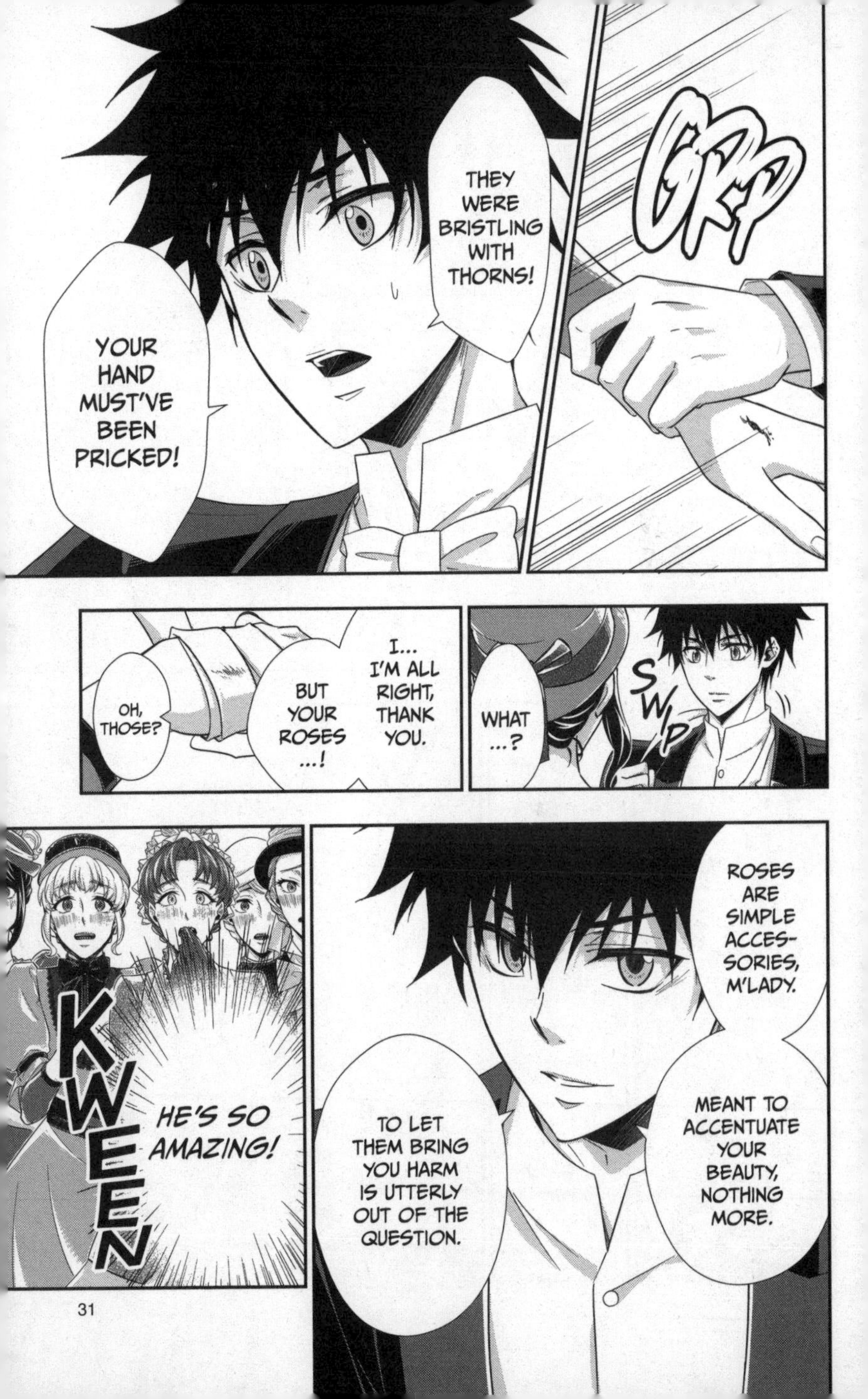
GRP
THEY WERE BRISTLING WITH THORNS!
YOUR HAND MUST'VE BEEN PRICKED!
SWIP
WHAT ...?
I... I'M ALL RIGHT, THANK YOU.
BUT YOUR ROSES ...!
OH, THOSE?
ROSES ARE SIMPLE ACCES-SORIES, M'LADY.
MEANT TO ACCENTUATE YOUR BEAUTY, NOTHING MORE.
TO LET THEM BRING YOU HARM IS UTTERLY OUT OF THE QUESTION.
HE'S SO AMAZING!
KWEEN

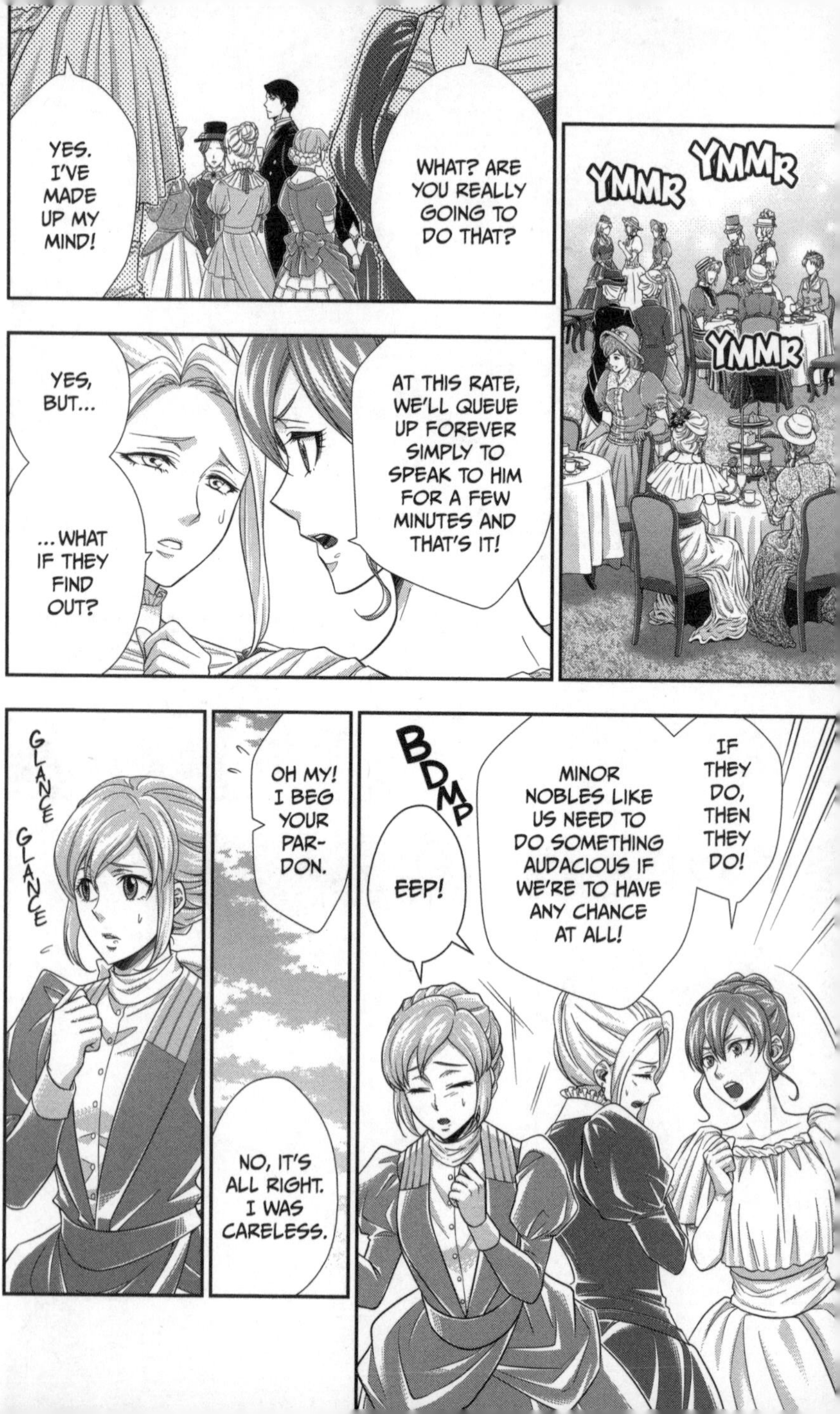
YMMR
YMMR
YMMR
WHAT? ARE YOU REALLY GOING TO DO THAT?
YES. I'VE MADE UP MY MIND!
AT THIS RATE, WE'LL QUEUE UP FOREVER SIMPLY TO SPEAK TO HIM FOR A FEW MINUTES AND THAT'S IT!
YES, BUT...
...WHAT IF THEY FIND OUT?
IF THEY DO, THEN THEY DO!
MINOR NOBLES LIKE US NEED TO DO SOMETHING AUDACIOUS IF WE'RE TO HAVE ANY CHANCE AT ALL!
BDMP
EEP!
OH MY! I BEG YOUR PAR-DON.
NO, IT'S ALL RIGHT. I WAS CARELESS.
GLANCE GLANCE

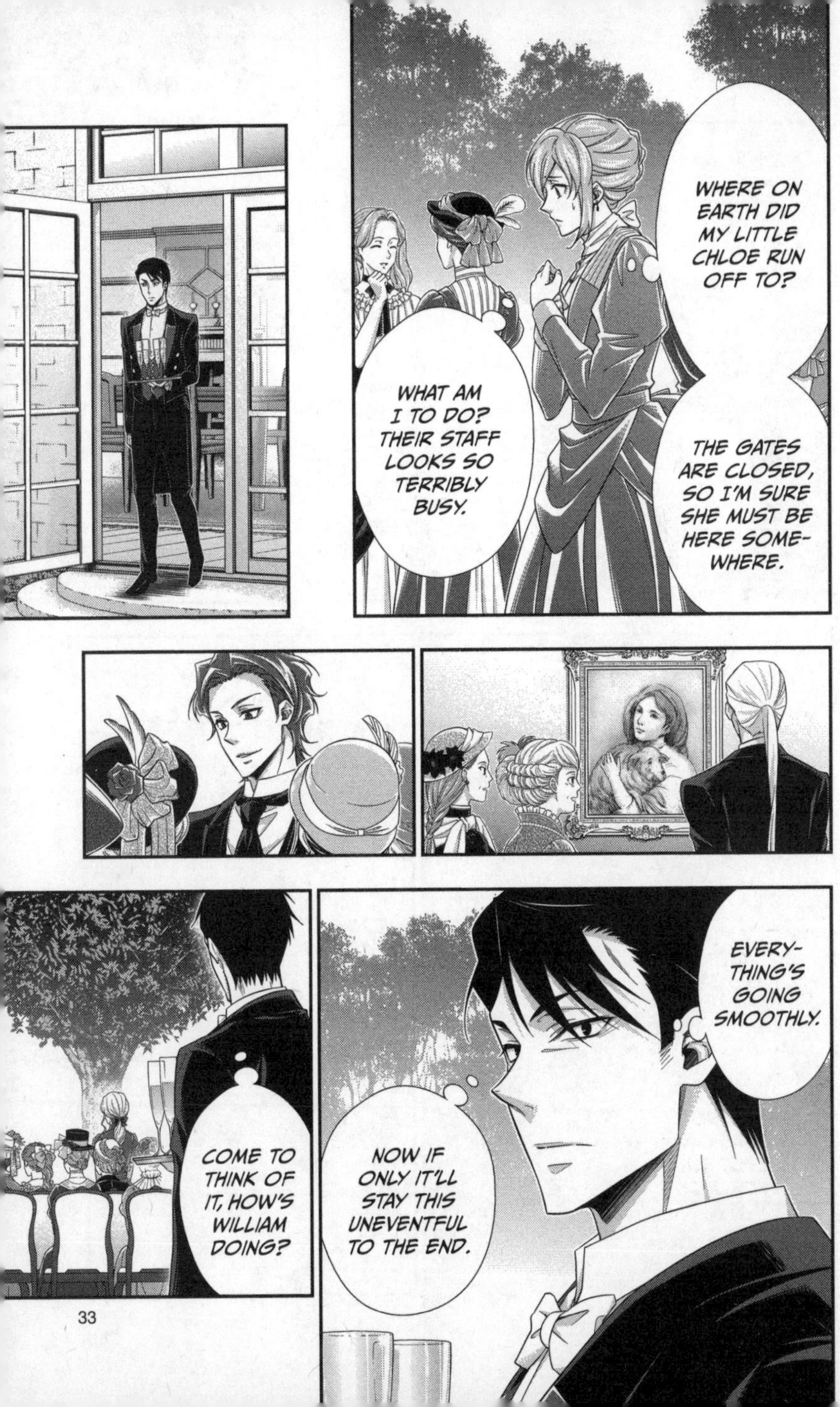
WHERE ON EARTH DID MY LITTLE CHLOE RUN OFF TO?
THE GATES ARE CLOSED, SO I'M SURE SHE MUST BE HERE SOME-WHERE.
WHAT AM I TO DO? THEIR STAFF LOOKS SO TERRIBLY BUSY.
EVERY-THING'S GOING SMOOTHLY.
NOW IF ONLY IT'LL STAY THIS UNEVENTFUL TO THE END.
COME TO THINK OF IT, HOW'S WILLIAM DOING?

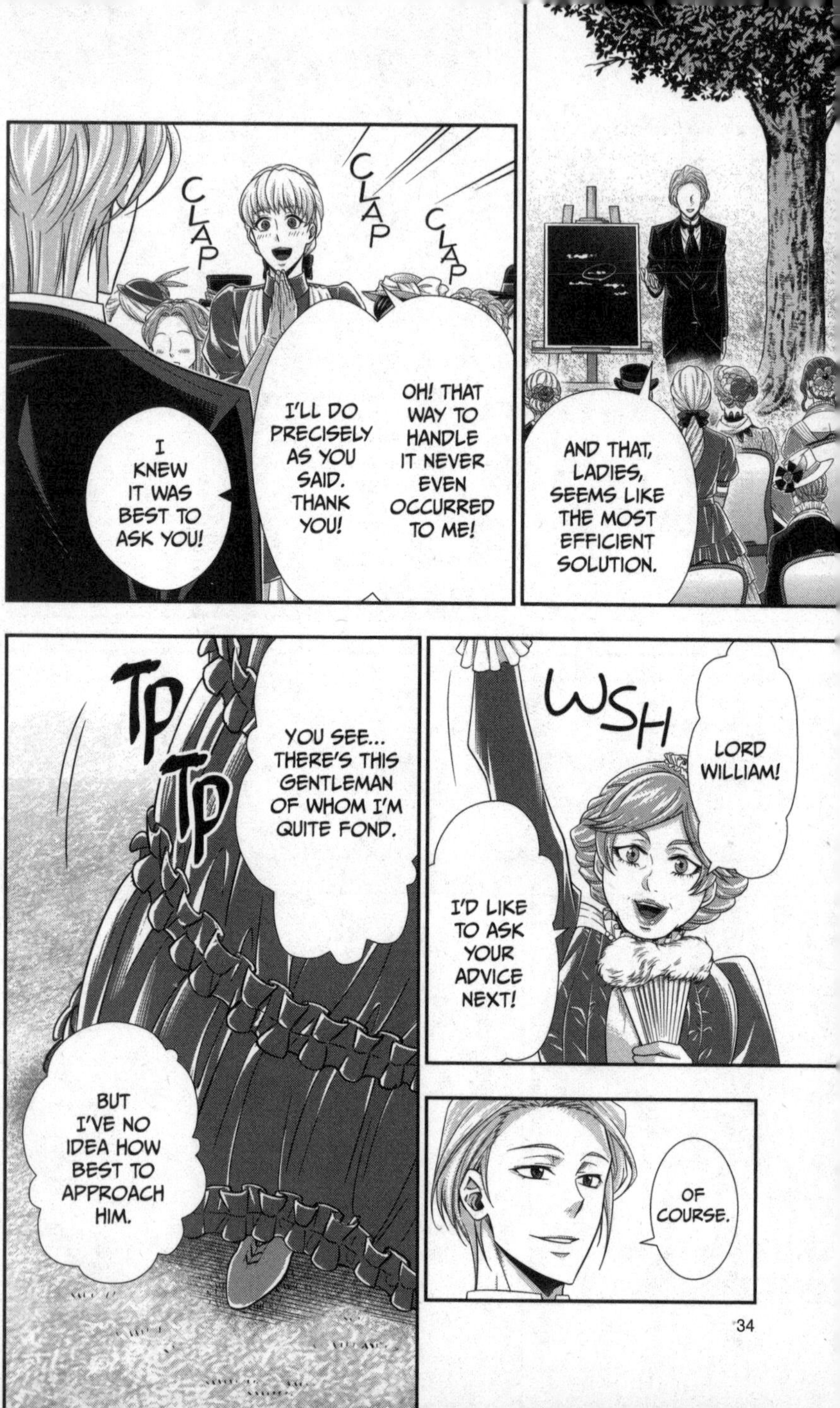
AND THAT, LADIES, SEEMS LIKE THE MOST EFFICIENT SOLUTION.
CLAP
CLAP
CLAP
CLAP
OH! THAT WAY TO HANDLE IT NEVER EVEN OCCURRED TO ME!
I'LL DO PRECISELY AS YOU SAID. THANK YOU!
I KNEW IT WAS BEST TO ASK YOU!
WSH
LORD WILLIAM!
I'D LIKE TO ASK YOUR ADVICE NEXT!
OF COURSE.
TP
TP
YOU SEE... THERE'S THIS GENTLEMAN OF WHOM I'M QUITE FOND.
BUT I'VE NO IDEA HOW BEST TO APPROACH HIM.

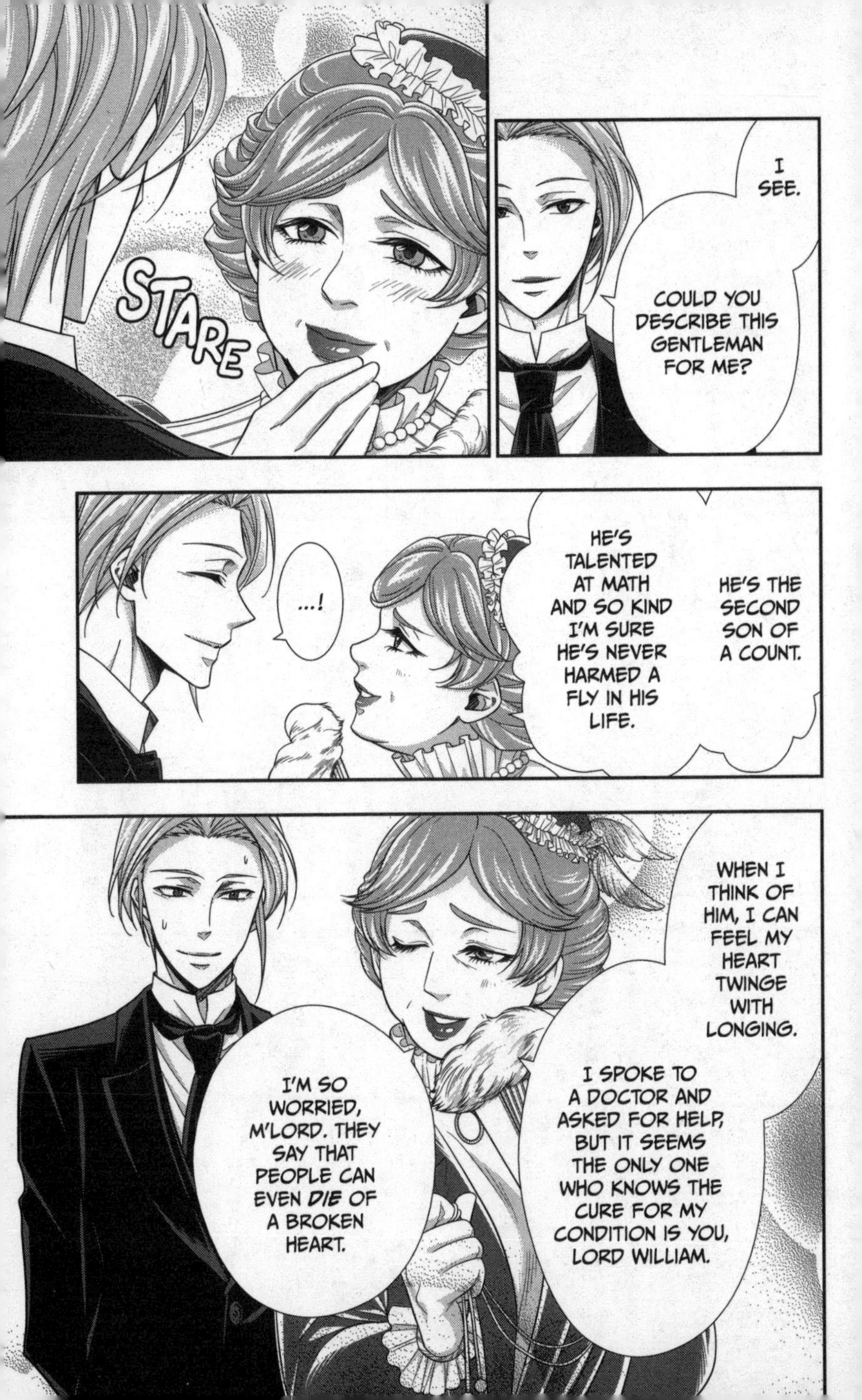
I SEE.
COULD YOU DESCRIBE THIS GENTLEMAN FOR ME?
STARE
HE'S THE SECOND SON OF A COUNT.
HE'S TALENTED AT MATH AND SO KIND I'M SURE HE'S NEVER HARMED A FLY IN HIS LIFE.
...!
WHEN I THINK OF HIM, I CAN FEEL MY HEART TWINGE WITH LONGING.
I SPOKE TO A DOCTOR AND ASKED FOR HELP, BUT IT SEEMS THE ONLY ONE WHO KNOWS THE CURE FOR MY CONDITION IS YOU, LORD WILLIAM.
I'M SO WORRIED, M'LORD. THEY SAY THAT PEOPLE CAN EVEN *DIE* OF A BROKEN HEART.

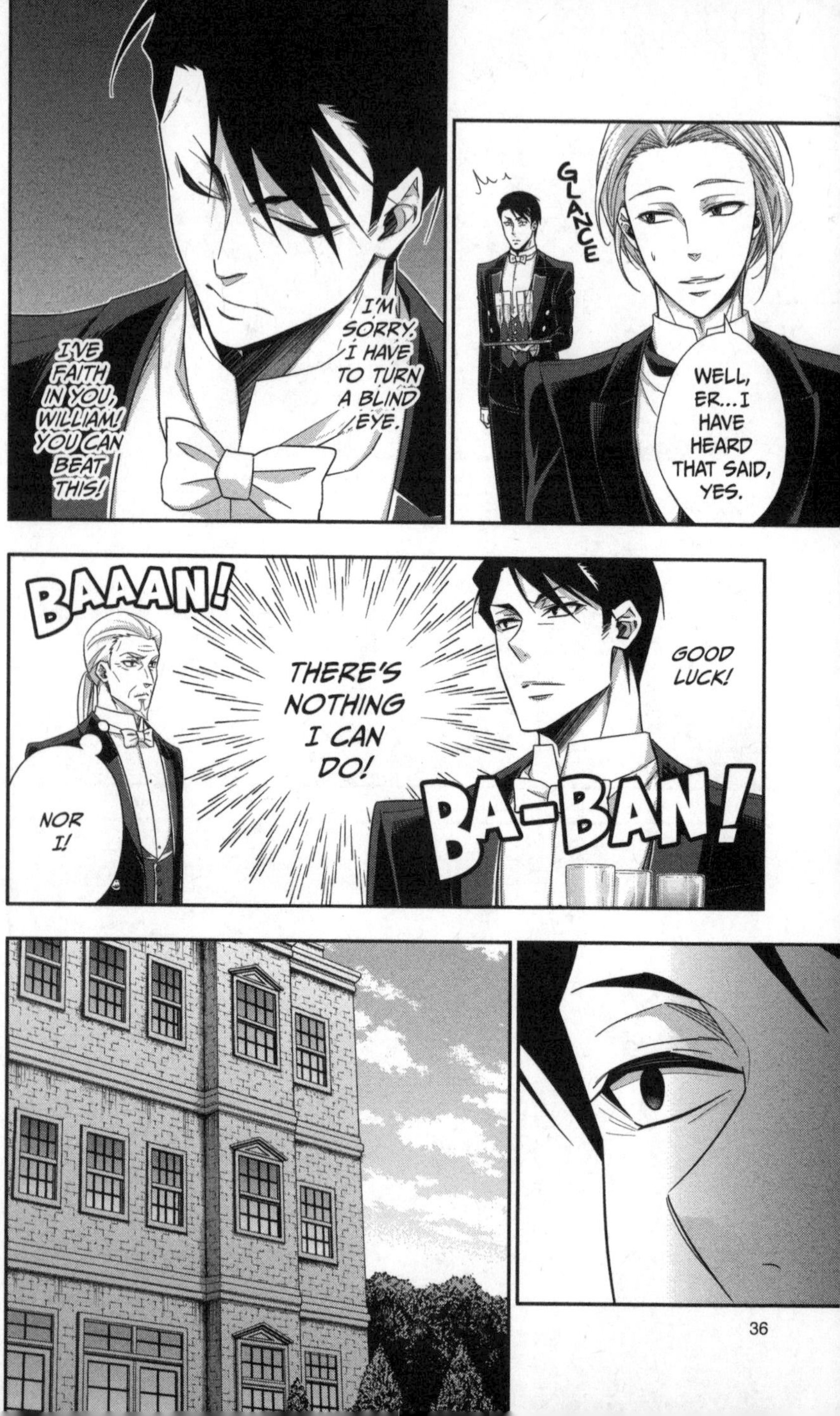
GLANCE
WELL, ER...I HAVE HEARD THAT SAID, YES.
I'M SORRY. I HAVE TO TURN A BLIND EYE.
I'VE FAITH IN YOU, WILLIAM! YOU CAN BEAT THIS!
GOOD LUCK!
BAAAN!
THERE'S NOTHING I CAN DO!
BA-BAN!
NOR I!

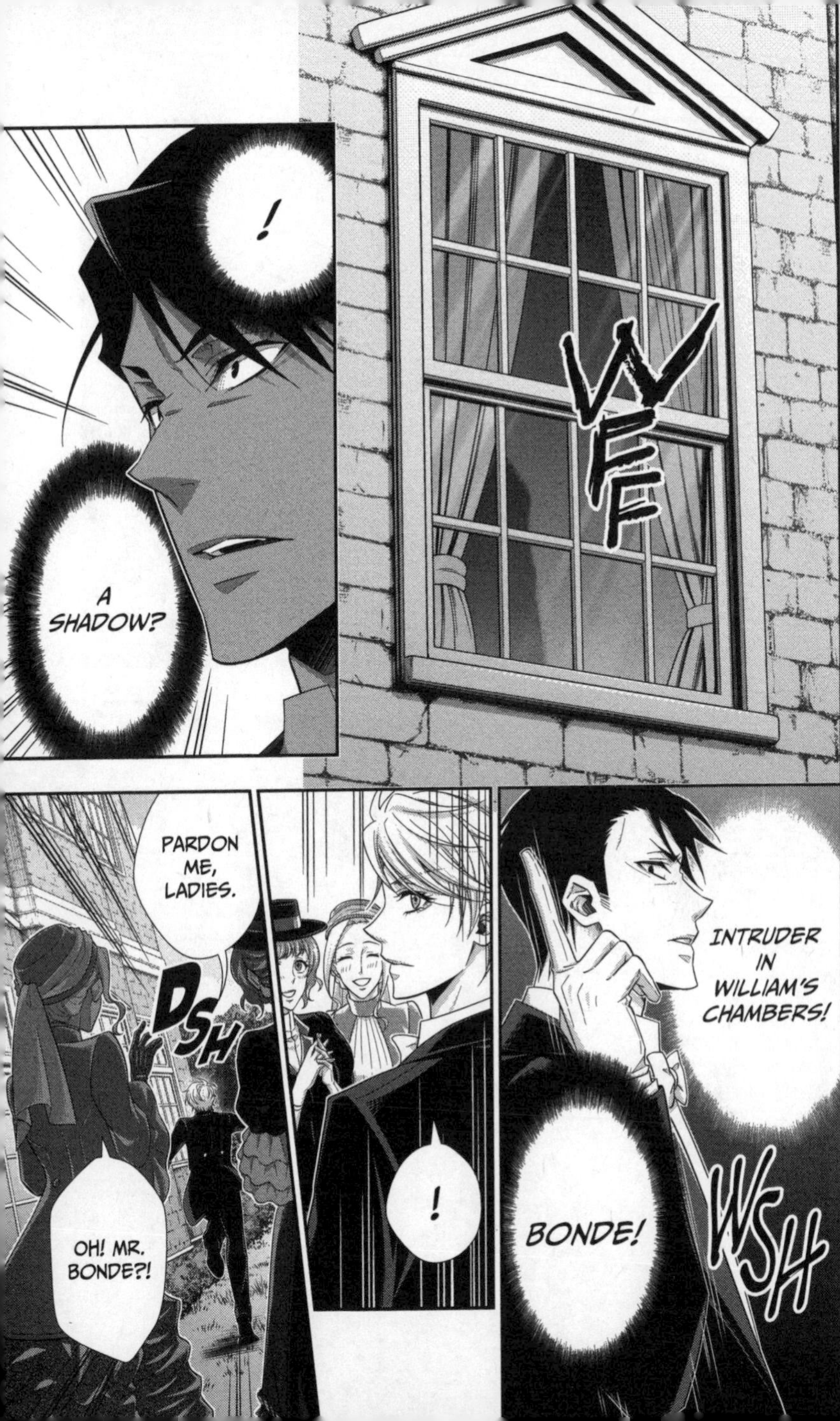
WFF
!
A SHADOW?
INTRUDER IN WILLIAM'S CHAMBERS!
BONDE!
WSH
!
PARDON ME, LADIES.
DSH
OH! MR. BONDE?!

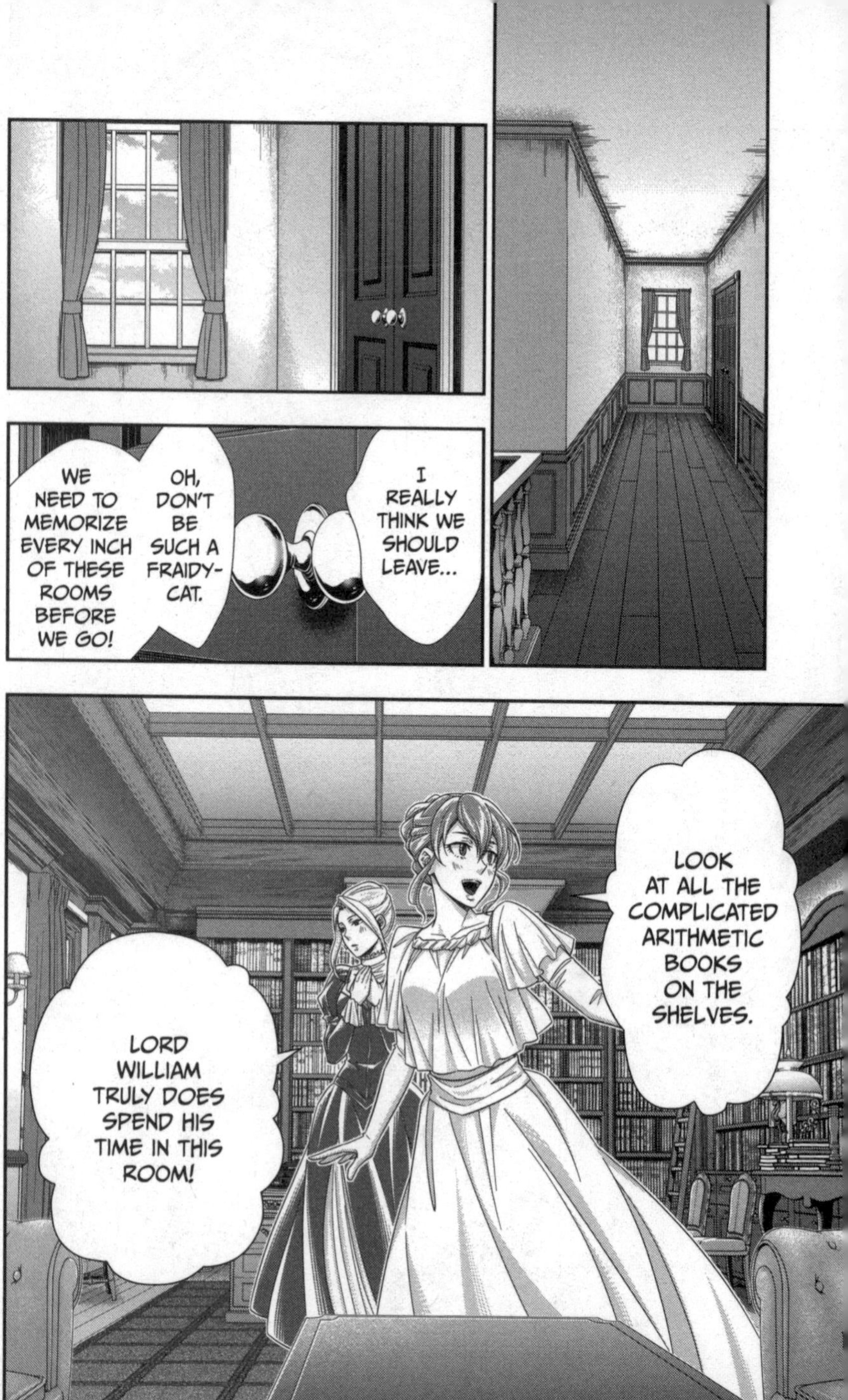
I REALLY THINK WE SHOULD LEAVE...
OH, DON'T BE SUCH A FRAIDY-CAT.
WE NEED TO MEMORIZE EVERY INCH OF THESE ROOMS BEFORE WE GO!
LOOK AT ALL THE COMPLICATED ARITHMETIC BOOKS ON THE SHELVES.
LORD WILLIAM TRULY DOES SPEND HIS TIME IN THIS ROOM!

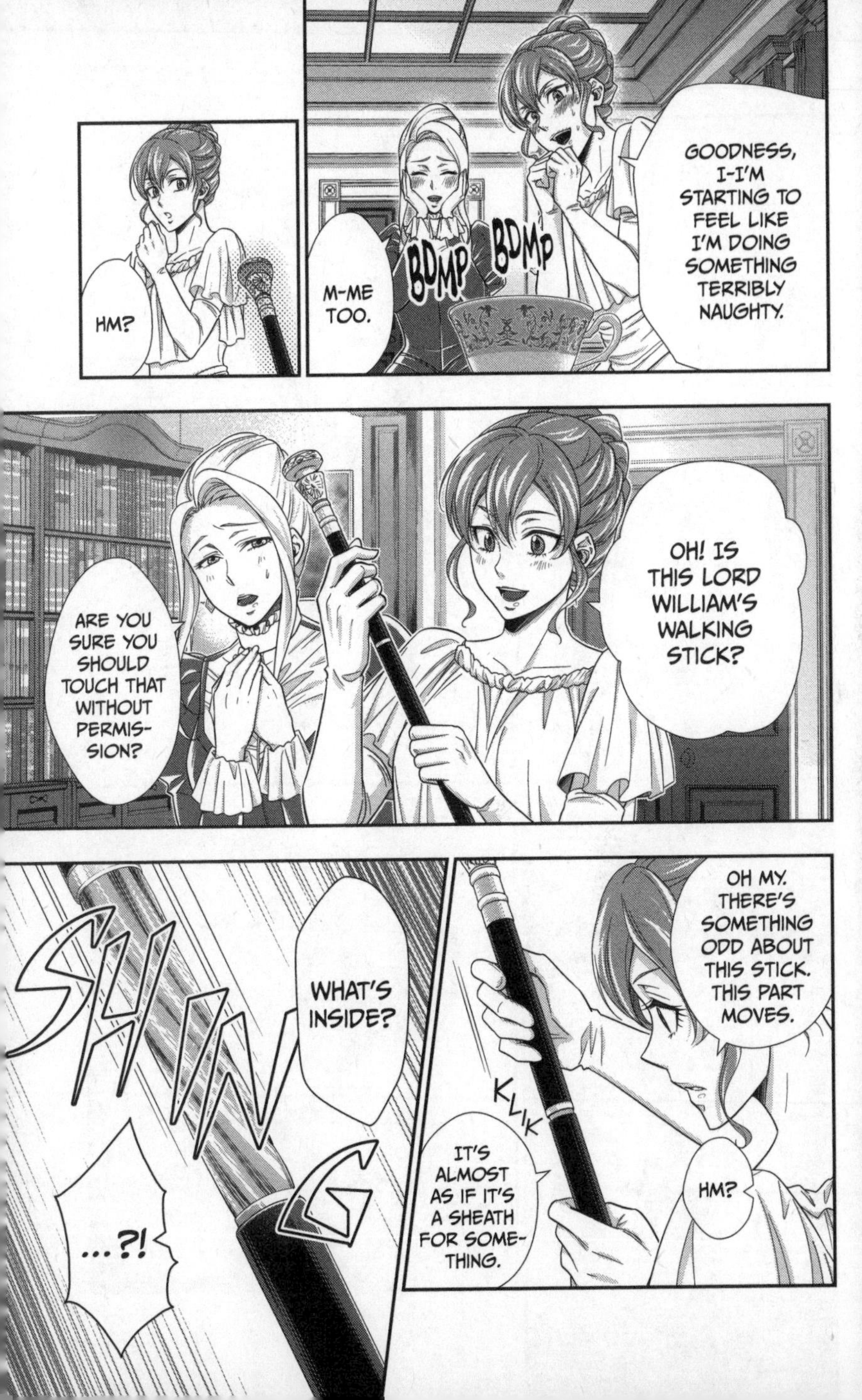
GOODNESS, I-I'M STARTING TO FEEL LIKE I'M DOING SOMETHING TERRIBLY NAUGHTY.
BDMP BDMP
M-ME TOO.
HM?
OH! IS THIS LORD WILLIAM'S WALKING STICK?
ARE YOU SURE YOU SHOULD TOUCH THAT WITHOUT PERMIS-SION?
OH MY. THERE'S SOMETHING ODD ABOUT THIS STICK. THIS PART MOVES.
HM?
KLIK
IT'S ALMOST AS IF IT'S A SHEATH FOR SOME-THING.
WHAT'S INSIDE?
SHING
...?!

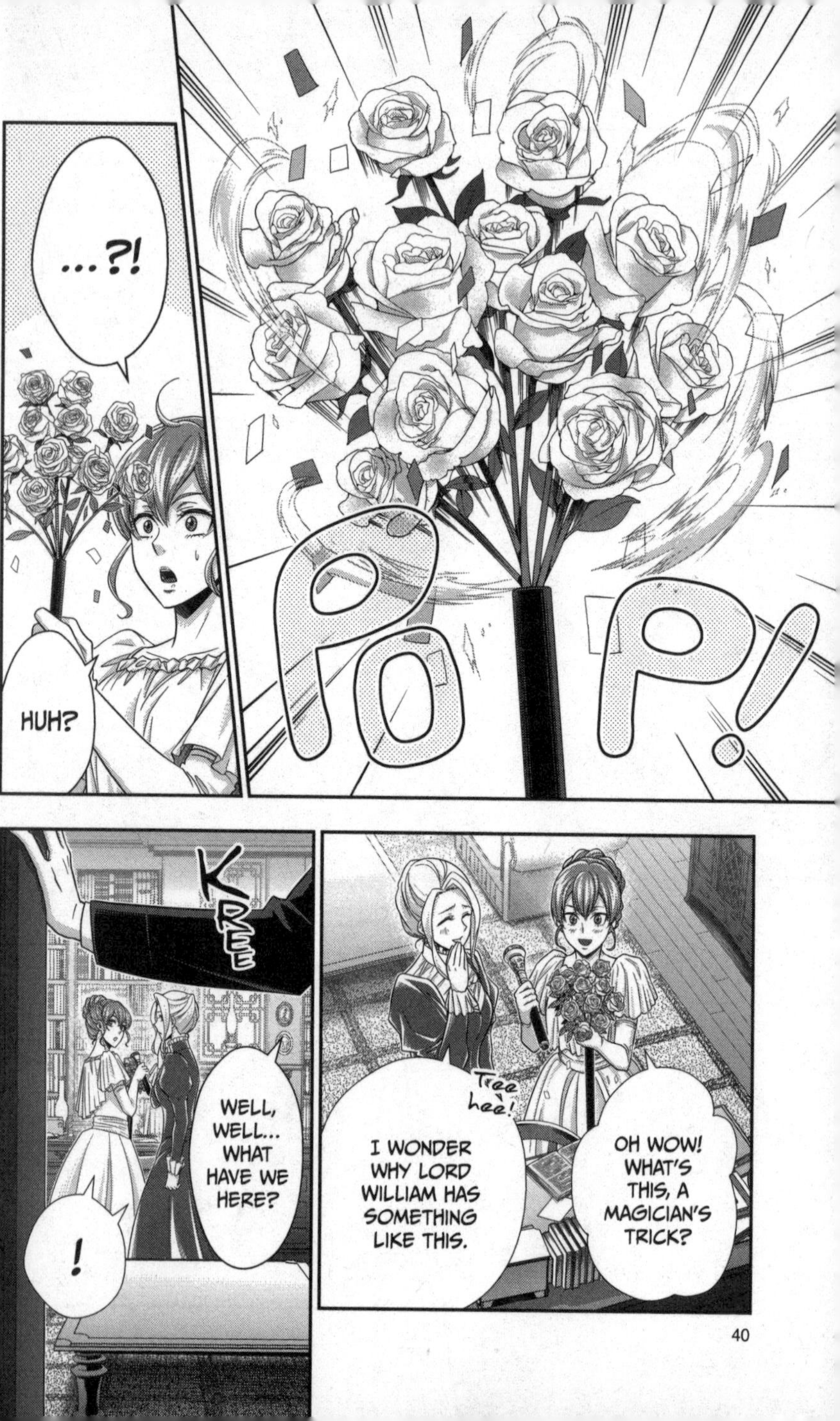
POP!
...?!
HUH?
OH WOW! WHAT'S THIS, A MAGICIAN'S TRICK?
Tee hee!
I WONDER WHY LORD WILLIAM HAS SOMETHING LIKE THIS.
KREE
WELL, WELL... WHAT HAVE WE HERE?
!

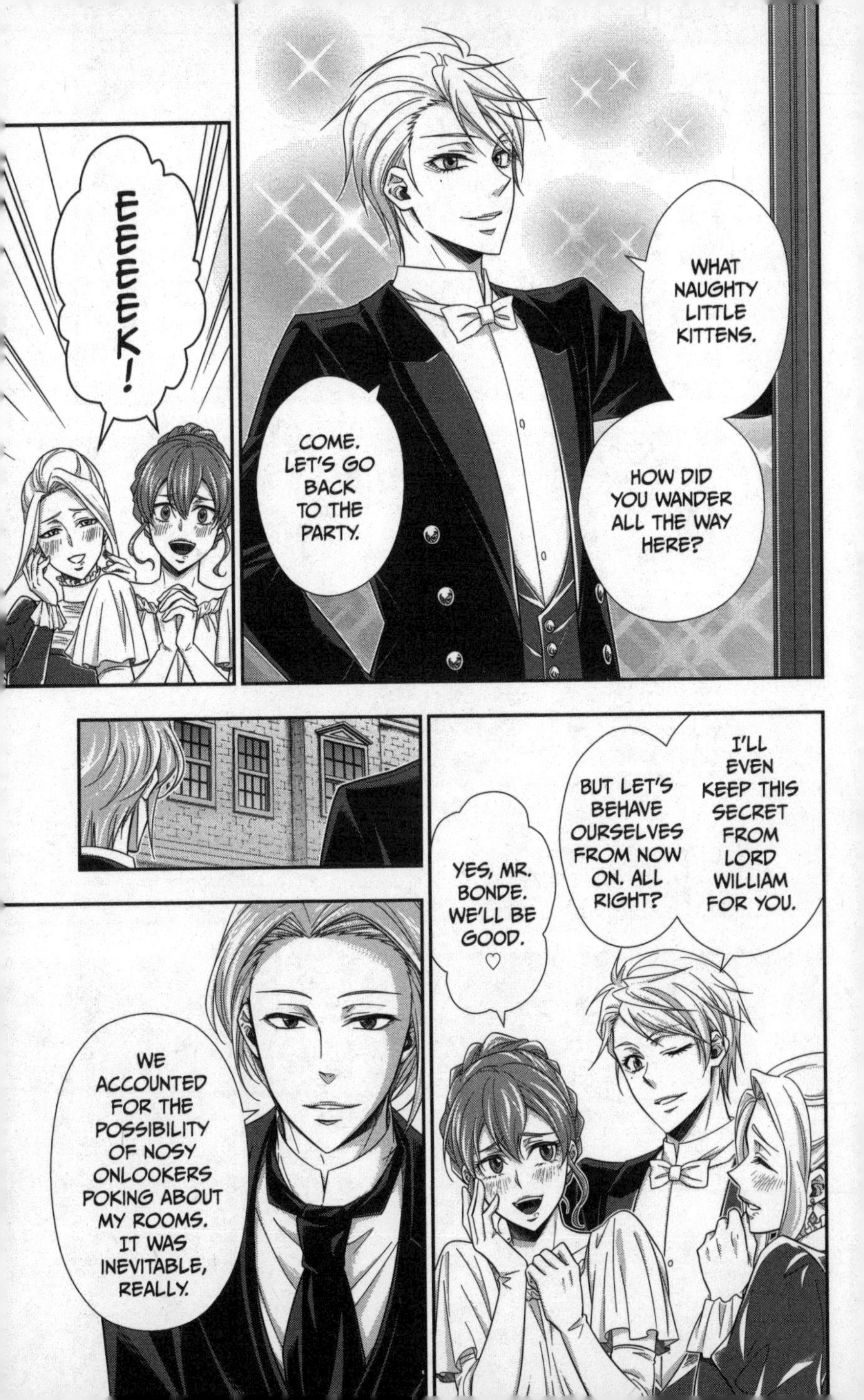
WHAT NAUGHTY LITTLE KITTENS.
HOW DID YOU WANDER ALL THE WAY HERE?
COME. LET'S GO BACK TO THE PARTY.
EEEEK!
I'LL EVEN KEEP THIS SECRET FROM LORD WILLIAM FOR YOU.
BUT LET'S BEHAVE OURSELVES FROM NOW ON. ALL RIGHT?
YES, MR. BONDE. WE'LL BE GOOD. ♡
WE ACCOUNTED FOR THE POSSIBILITY OF NOSY ONLOOKERS POKING ABOUT MY ROOMS. IT WAS INEVITABLE, REALLY.

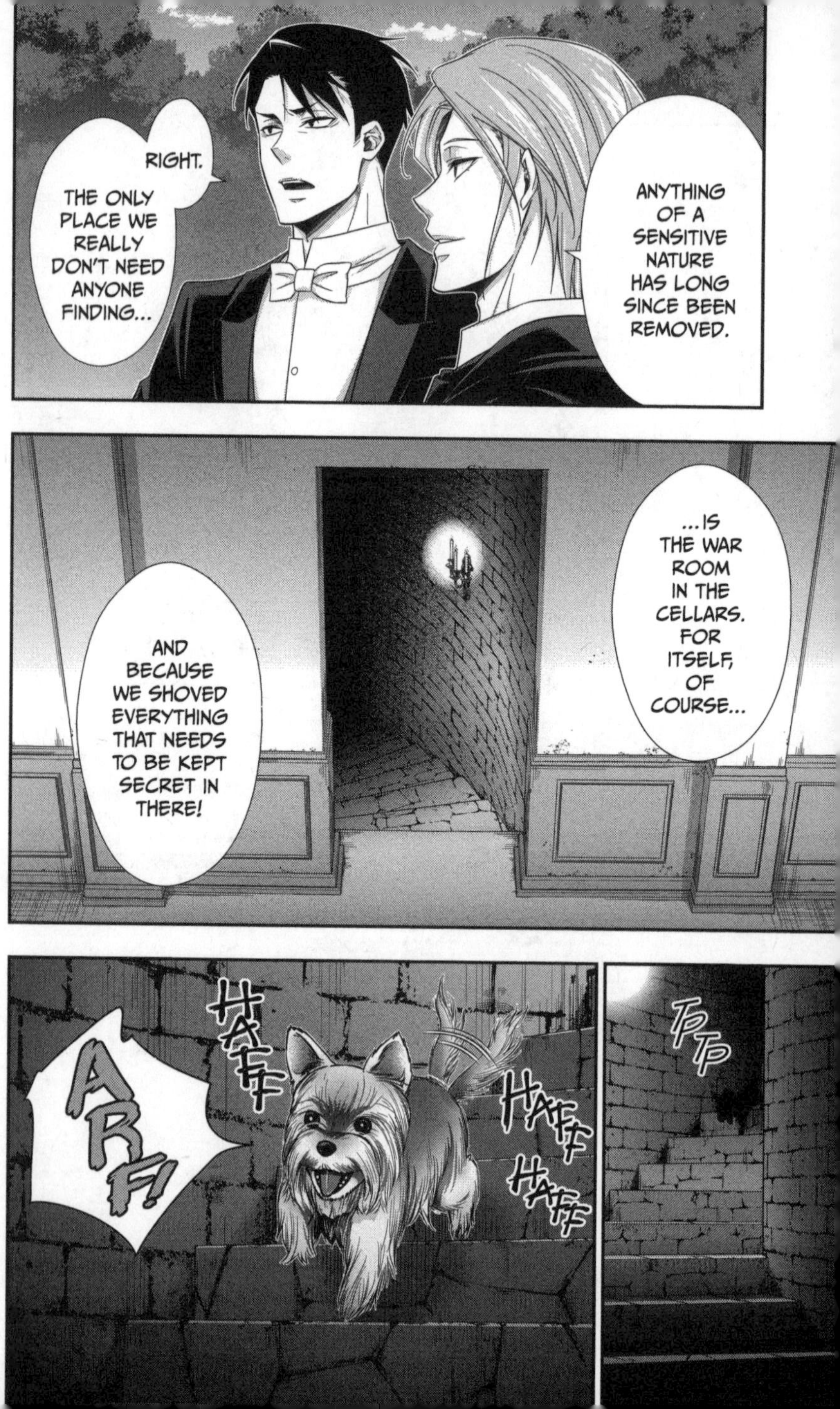
ANYTHING OF A SENSITIVE NATURE HAS LONG SINCE BEEN REMOVED.
RIGHT.
THE ONLY PLACE WE REALLY DON'T NEED ANYONE FINDING...
...IS THE WAR ROOM IN THE CELLARS. FOR ITSELF, OF COURSE...
AND BECAUSE WE SHOVED EVERYTHING THAT NEEDS TO BE KEPT SECRET IN THERE!
TPTP
HAFF
HAFF
HAFF
ARF!

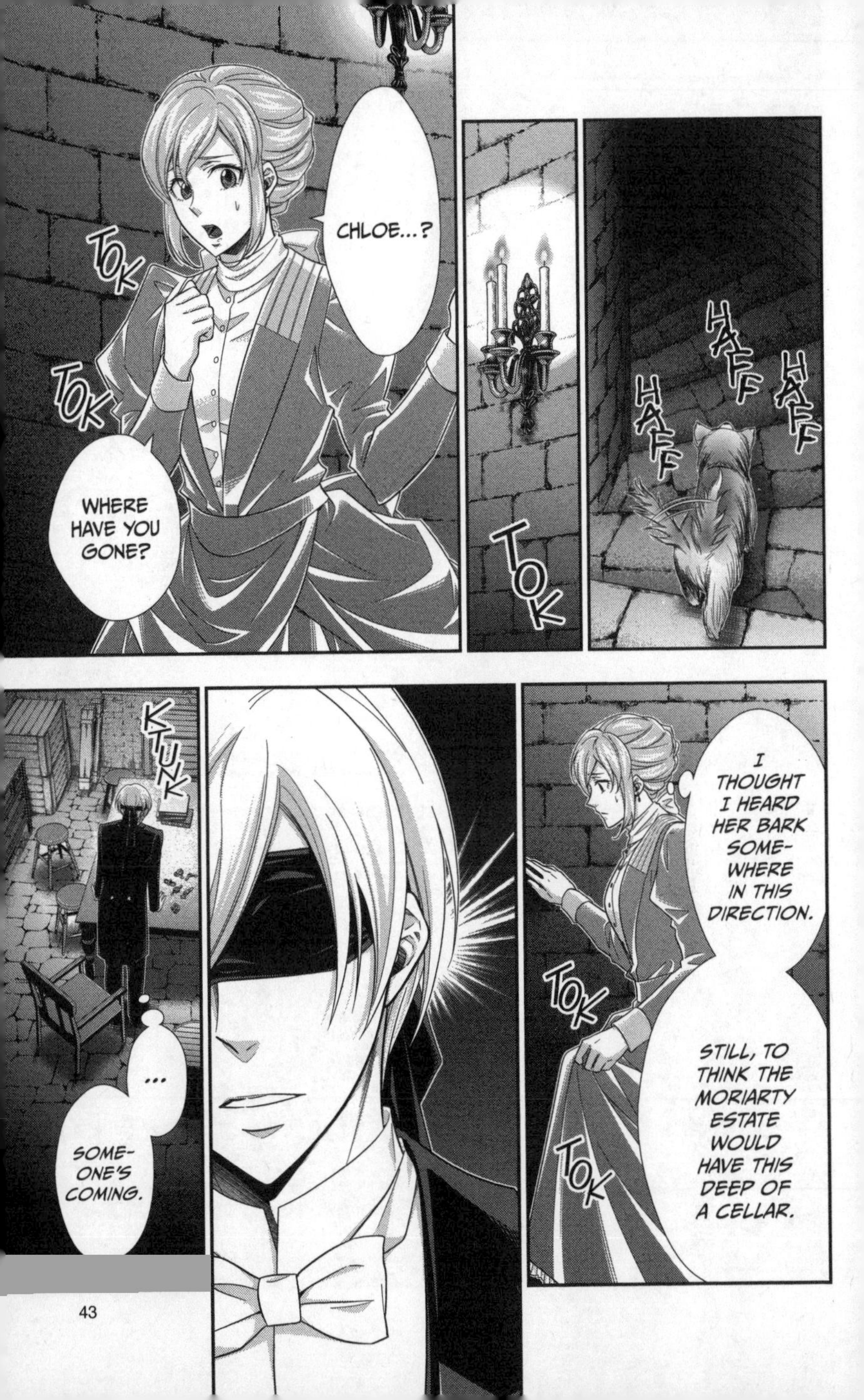
HAFF HAFF
HAFF HAFF
TOK
CHLOE...?
TOK
TOK
WHERE HAVE YOU GONE?
I THOUGHT I HEARD HER BARK SOME-WHERE IN THIS DIRECTION.
TOK
STILL, TO THINK THE MORIARTY ESTATE WOULD HAVE THIS DEEP OF A CELLAR.
TOK
KTUNK
...
SOME-ONE'S COMING.

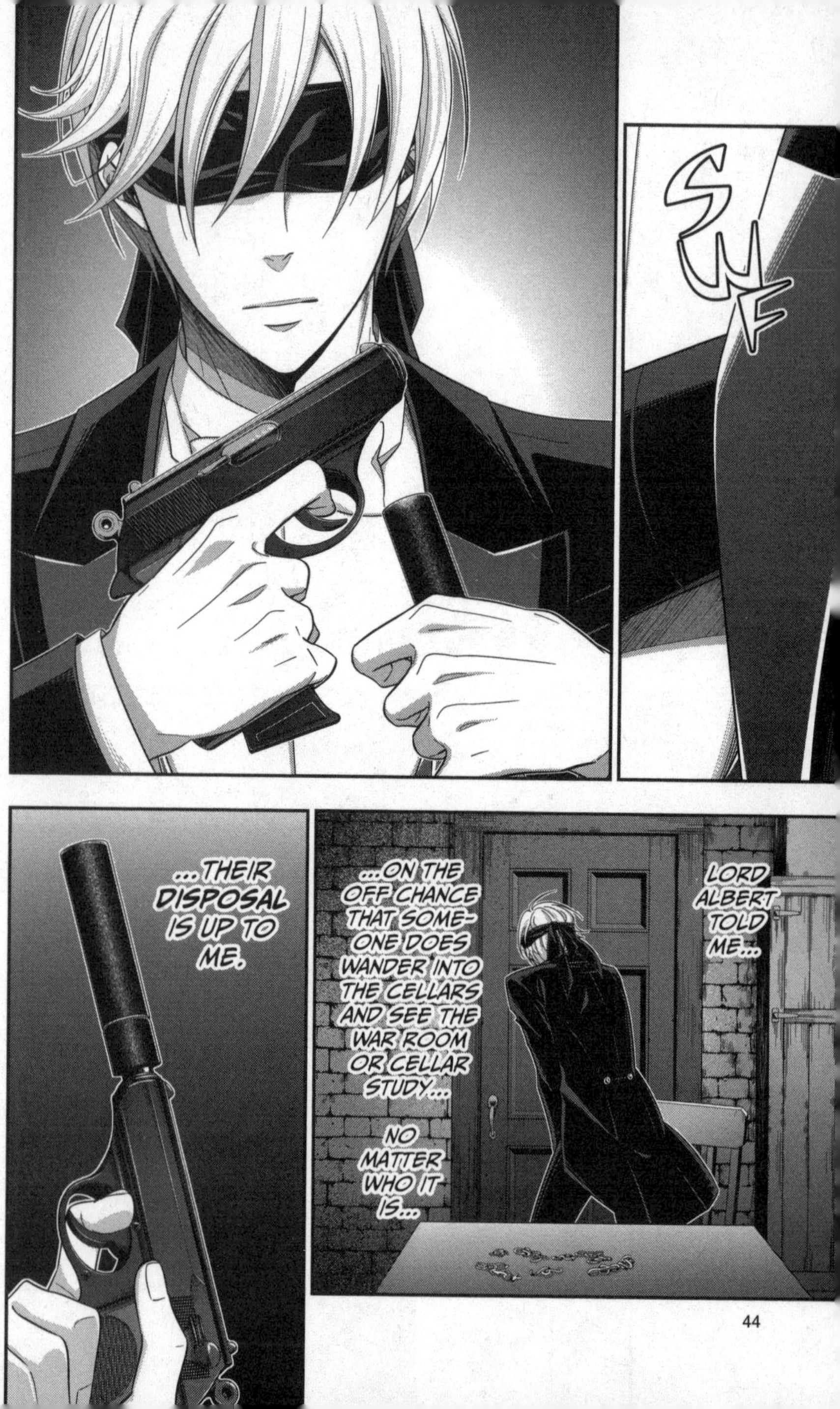
SWF
LORD ALBERT TOLD ME...
...ON THE OFF CHANCE THAT SOME-ONE DOES WANDER INTO THE CELLARS AND SEE THE WAR ROOM OR CELLAR STUDY...
NO MATTER WHO IT IS...
...THEIR DISPOSAL IS UP TO ME.

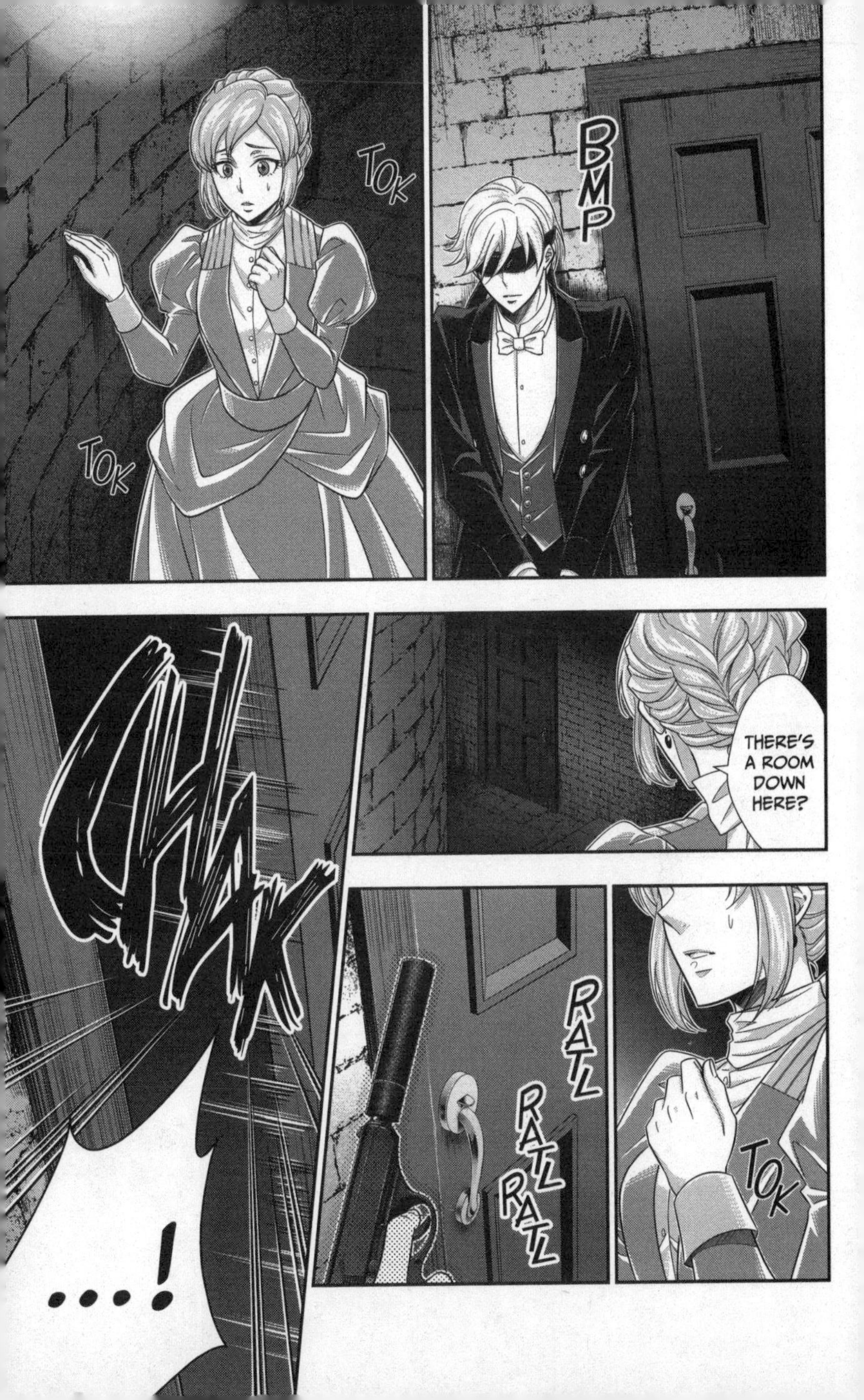
BMMP
TOK
TOK
THERE'S A ROOM DOWN HERE?
TOK
RATL
RATL
RATL
...!

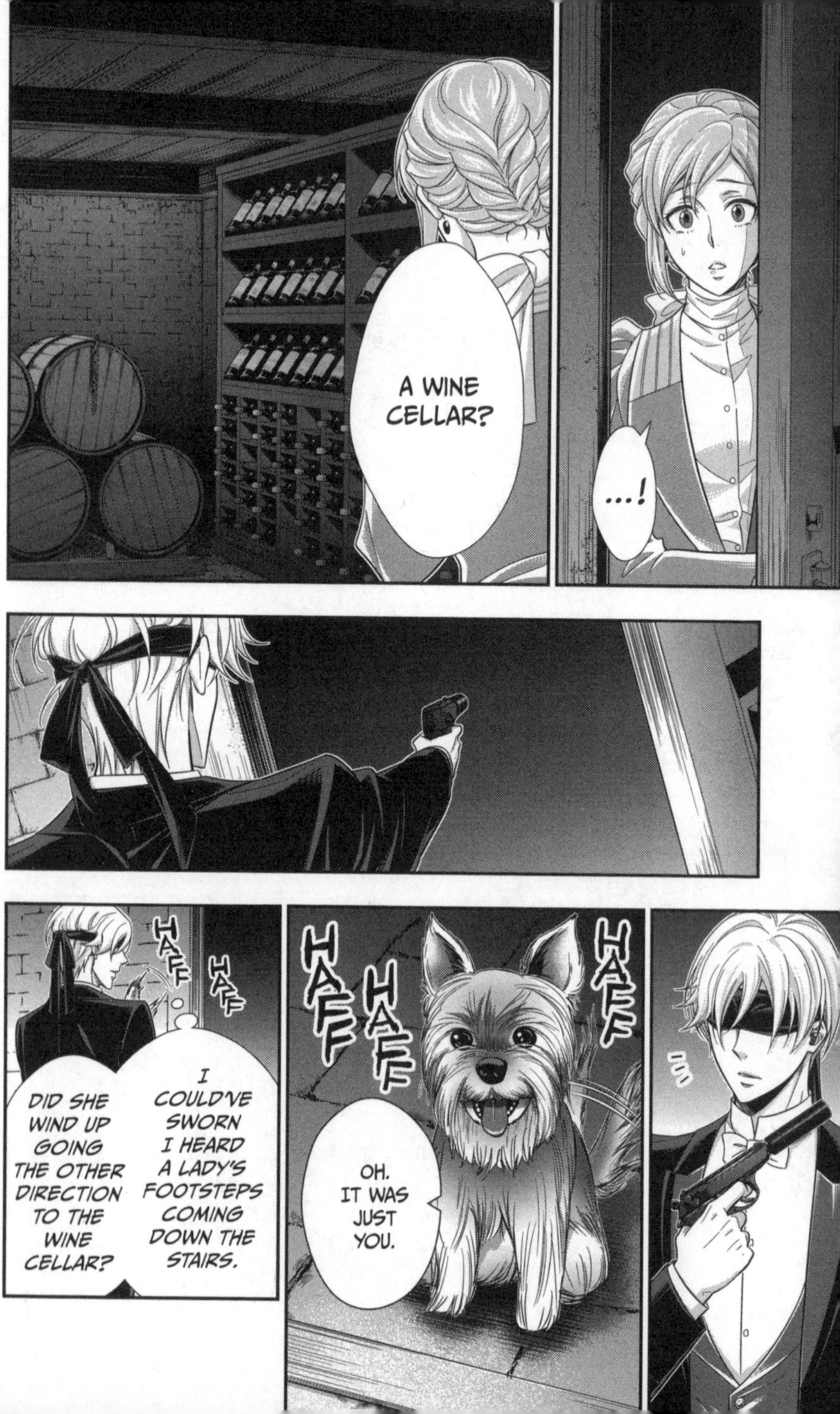
...!
A WINE CELLAR?
HAFF
HAFF
HAFF
OH. IT WAS JUST YOU.
HAFF
HAFF
I COULD'VE SWORN I HEARD A LADY'S FOOTSTEPS COMING DOWN THE STAIRS.
DID SHE WIND UP GOING THE OTHER DIRECTION TO THE WINE CELLAR?

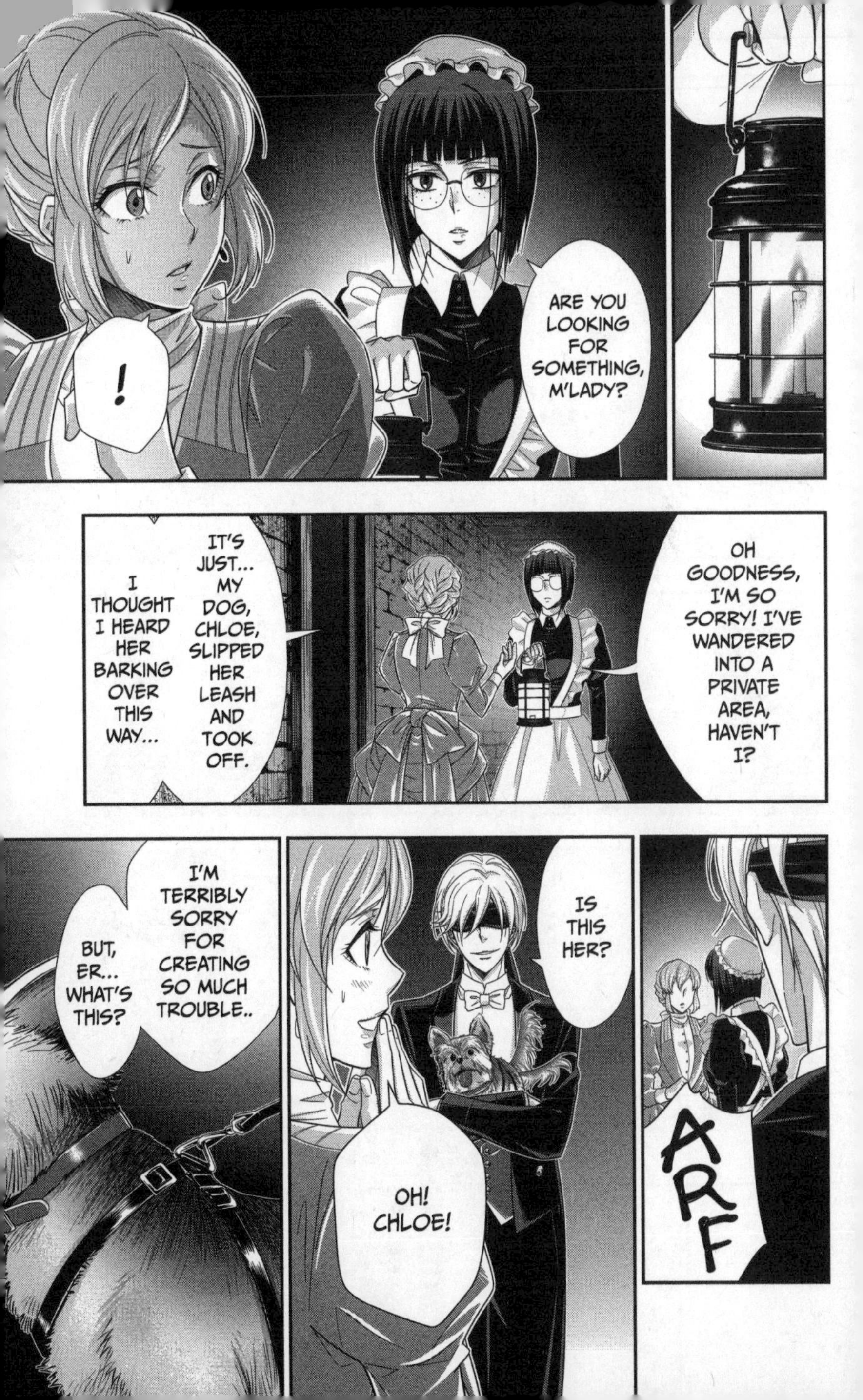
ARE YOU LOOKING FOR SOMETHING, M'LADY?
!
OH GOODNESS, I'M SO SORRY! I'VE WANDERED INTO A PRIVATE AREA, HAVEN'T I?
IT'S JUST... MY DOG, CHLOE, SLIPPED HER LEASH AND TOOK OFF.
I THOUGHT I HEARD HER BARKING OVER THIS WAY...
ARF
IS THIS HER?
OH! CHLOE!
I'M TERRIBLY SORRY FOR CREATING SO MUCH TROUBLE..
BUT, ER... WHAT'S THIS?

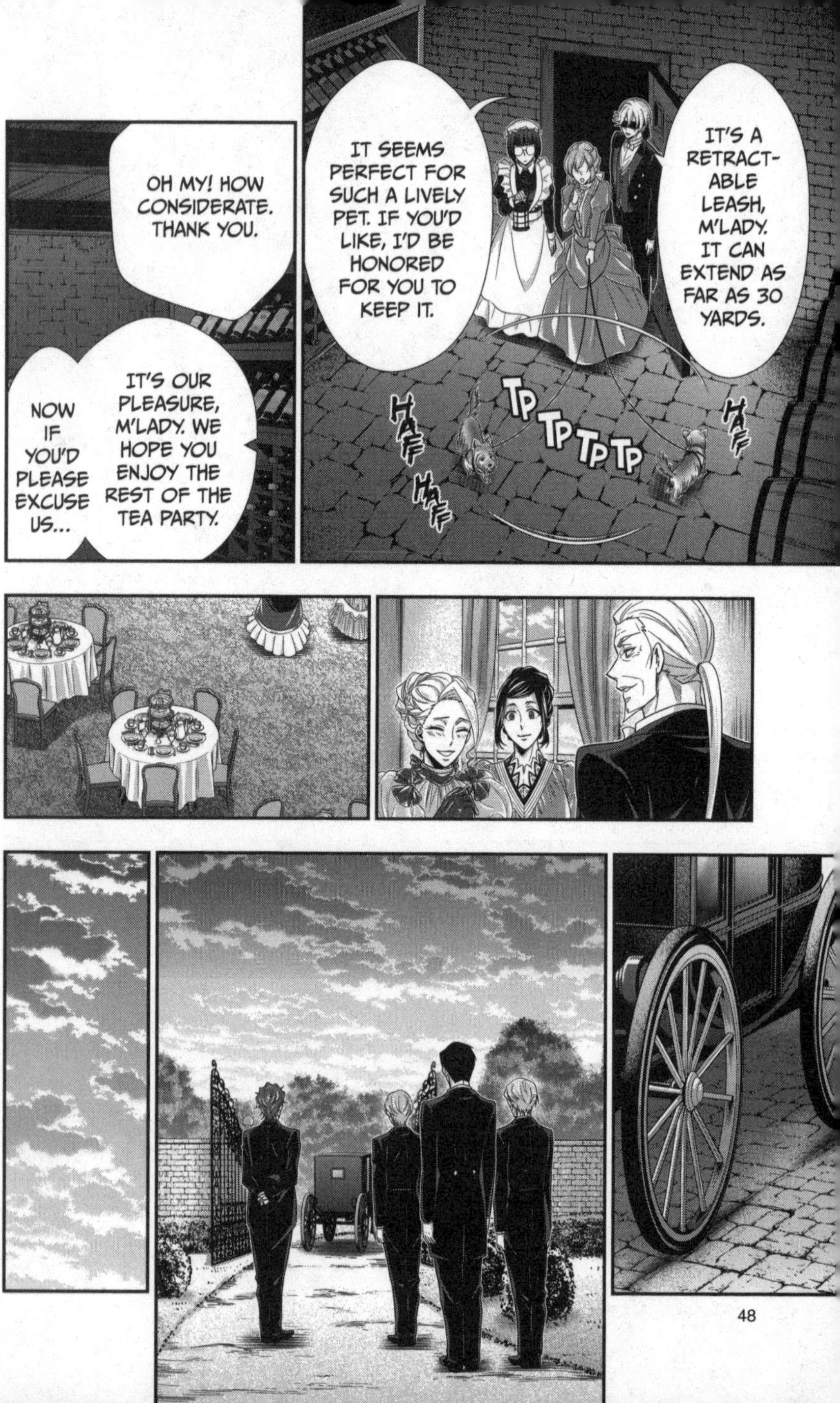
IT'S A RETRACT-ABLE LEASH, M'LADY. IT CAN EXTEND AS FAR AS 30 YARDS.
IT SEEMS PERFECT FOR SUCH A LIVELY PET. IF YOU'D LIKE, I'D BE HONORED FOR YOU TO KEEP IT.
HAFF
TP TP TP TP
HAFF HAFF
OH MY! HOW CONSIDERATE. THANK YOU.
IT'S OUR PLEASURE, M'LADY. WE HOPE YOU ENJOY THE REST OF THE TEA PARTY.
NOW IF YOU'D PLEASE EXCUSE US...

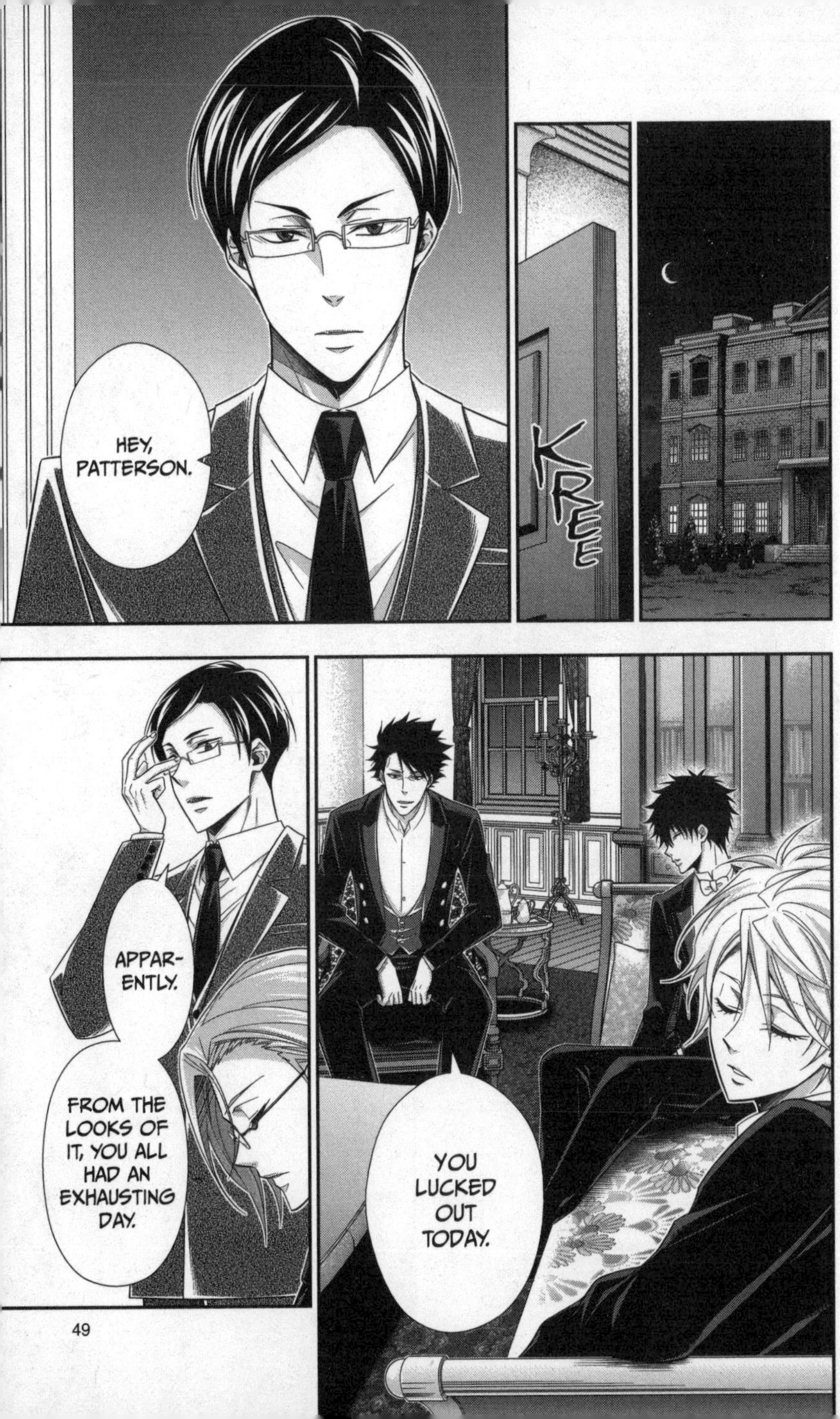
KREE
HEY, PATTERSON.
YOU LUCKED OUT TODAY.
APPAR-ENTLY.
FROM THE LOOKS OF IT, YOU ALL HAD AN EXHAUSTING DAY.

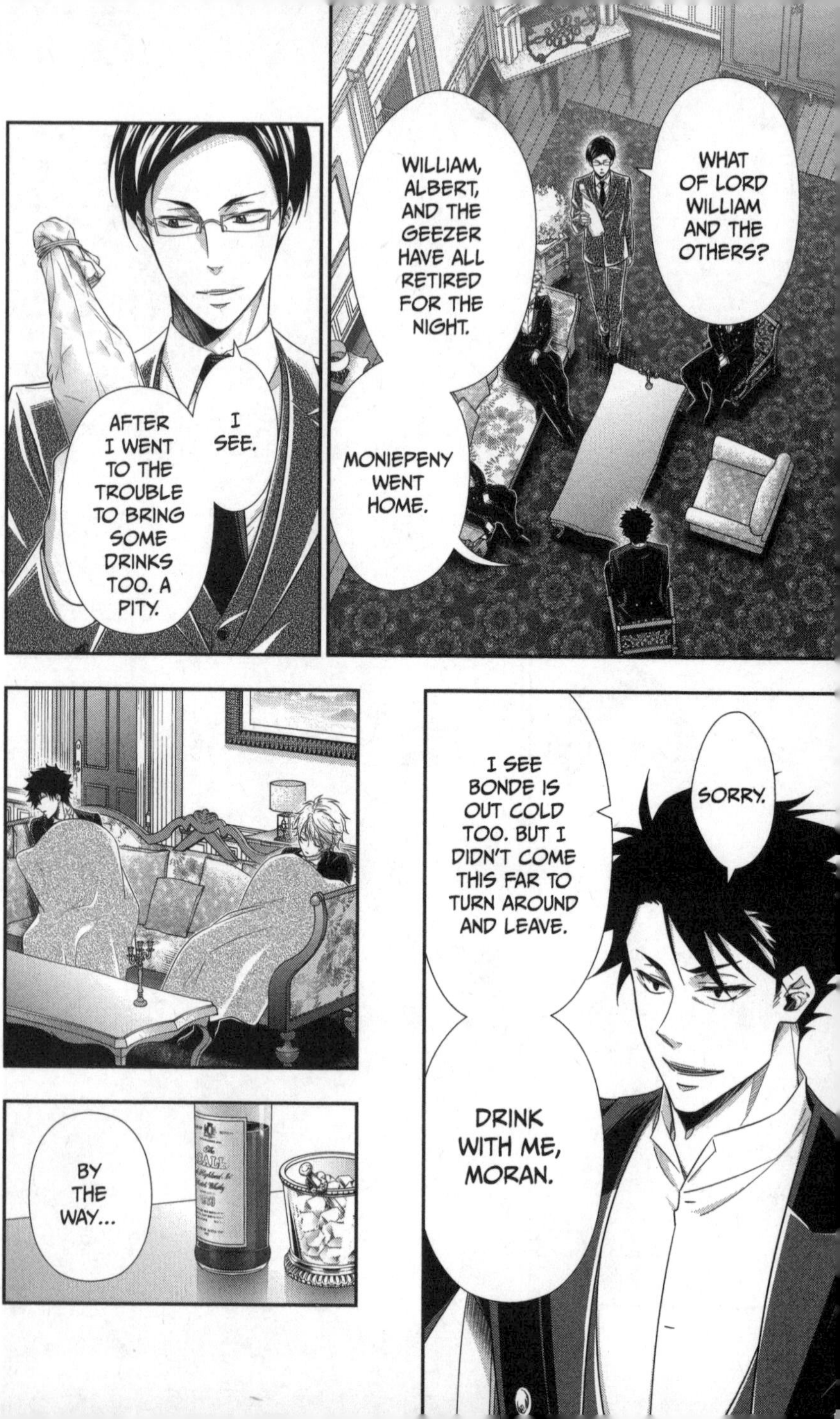
WHAT OF LORD WILLIAM AND THE OTHERS?
WILLIAM, ALBERT, AND THE GEEZER HAVE ALL RETIRED FOR THE NIGHT.
MONIEPENY WENT HOME.
I SEE.
AFTER I WENT TO THE TROUBLE TO BRING SOME DRINKS TOO. A PITY.
SORRY.
I SEE BONDE IS OUT COLD TOO. BUT I DIDN'T COME THIS FAR TO TURN AROUND AND LEAVE.
DRINK WITH ME, MORAN.
BY THE WAY...

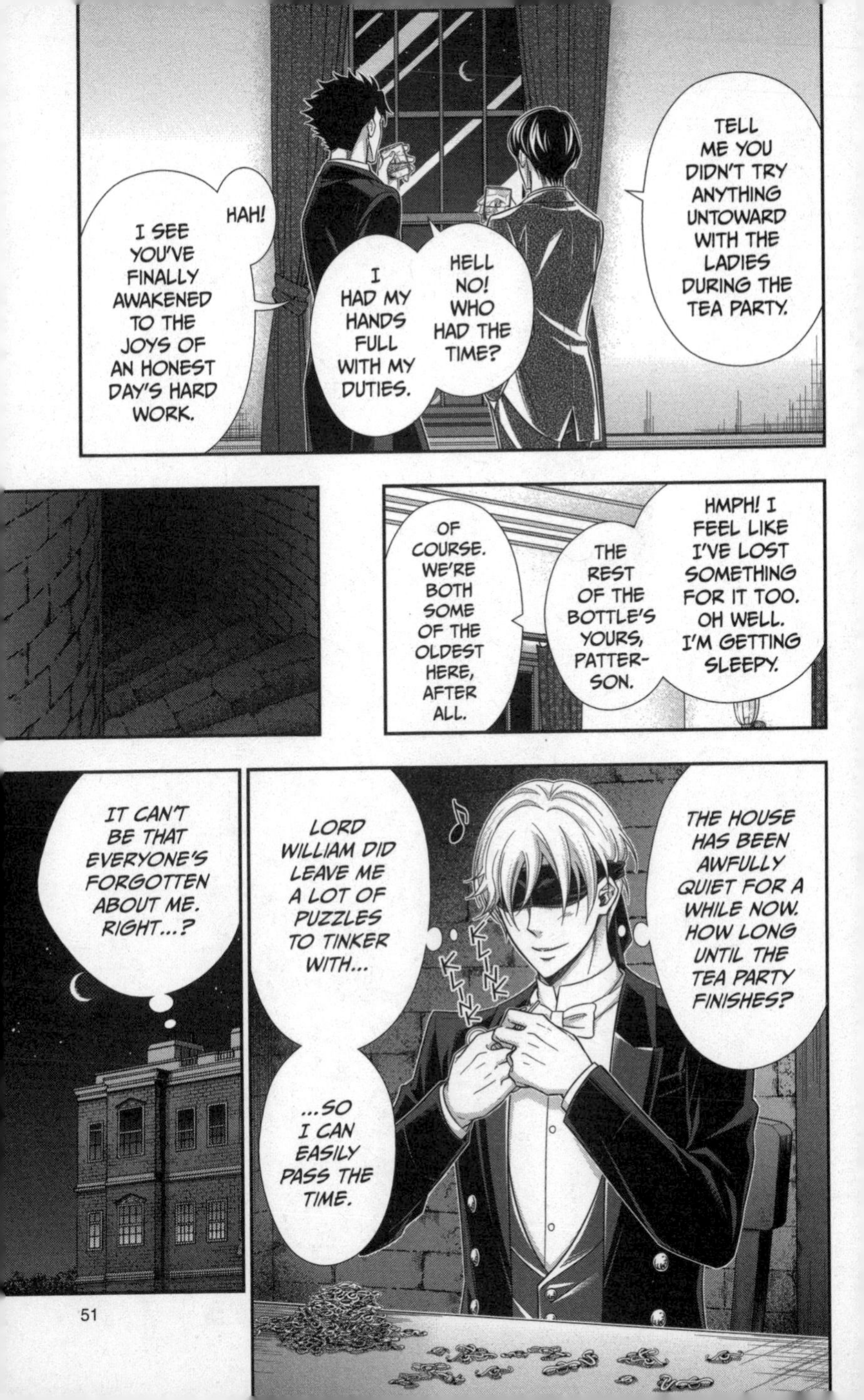
TELL ME YOU DIDN'T TRY ANYTHING UNTOWARD WITH THE LADIES DURING THE TEA PARTY.
HELL NO! WHO HAD THE TIME?
I HAD MY HANDS FULL WITH MY DUTIES.
HAH! I SEE YOU'VE FINALLY AWAKENED TO THE JOYS OF AN HONEST DAY'S HARD WORK.
HMPH! I FEEL LIKE I'VE LOST SOMETHING FOR IT TOO. OH WELL. I'M GETTING SLEEPY.
THE REST OF THE BOTTLE'S YOURS, PATTERSON.
OF COURSE. WE'RE BOTH SOME OF THE OLDEST HERE, AFTER ALL.
THE HOUSE HAS BEEN AWFULLY QUIET FOR A WHILE NOW. HOW LONG UNTIL THE TEA PARTY FINISHES?
LORD WILLIAM DID LEAVE ME A LOT OF PUZZLES TO TINKER WITH...
KLINK KLINK
...SO I CAN EASILY PASS THE TIME.
IT CAN'T BE THAT EVERYONE'S FORGOTTEN ABOUT ME. RIGHT...?

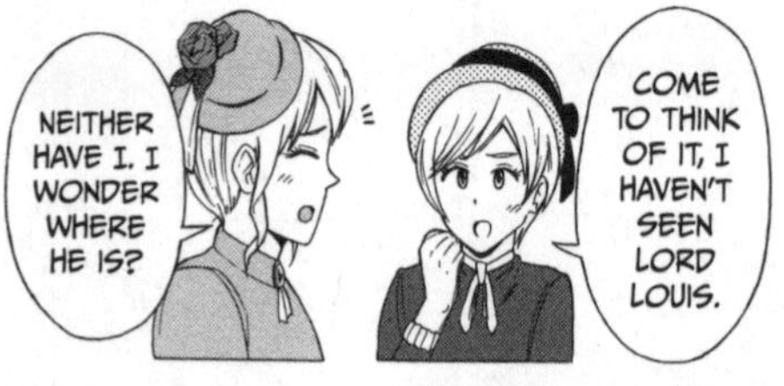
COME TO THINK OF IT, I HAVEN'T SEEN LORD LOUIS.
NEITHER HAVE I. I WONDER WHERE HE IS?

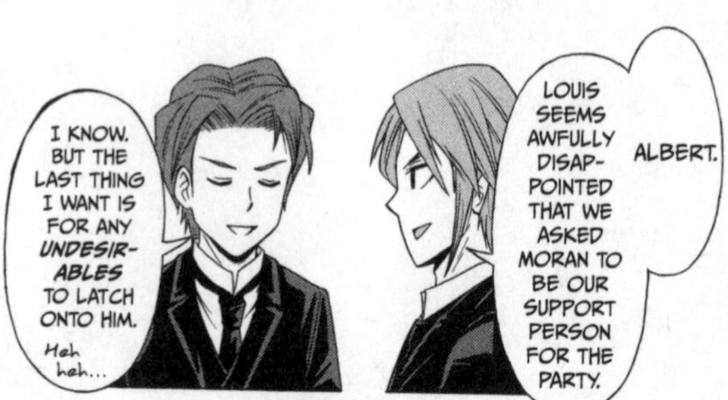
ALBERT.
LOUIS SEEMS AWFULLY DISAP-POINTED THAT WE ASKED MORAN TO BE OUR SUPPORT PERSON FOR THE PARTY.
I KNOW. BUT THE LAST THING I WANT IS FOR ANY *UNDESIR-ABLES* TO LATCH ONTO HIM.
Heh heh...

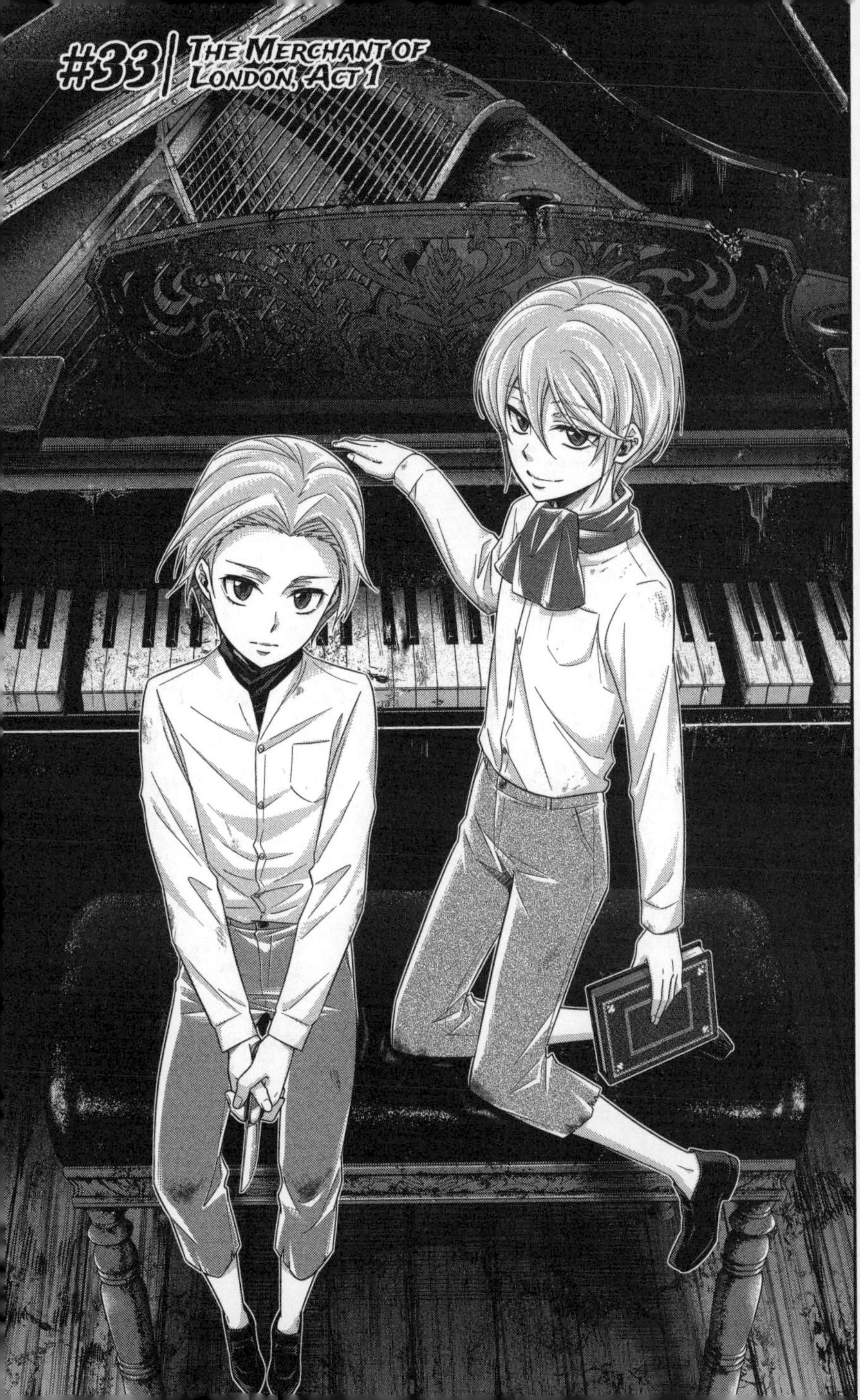
#33
The Merchant of London, Act 1

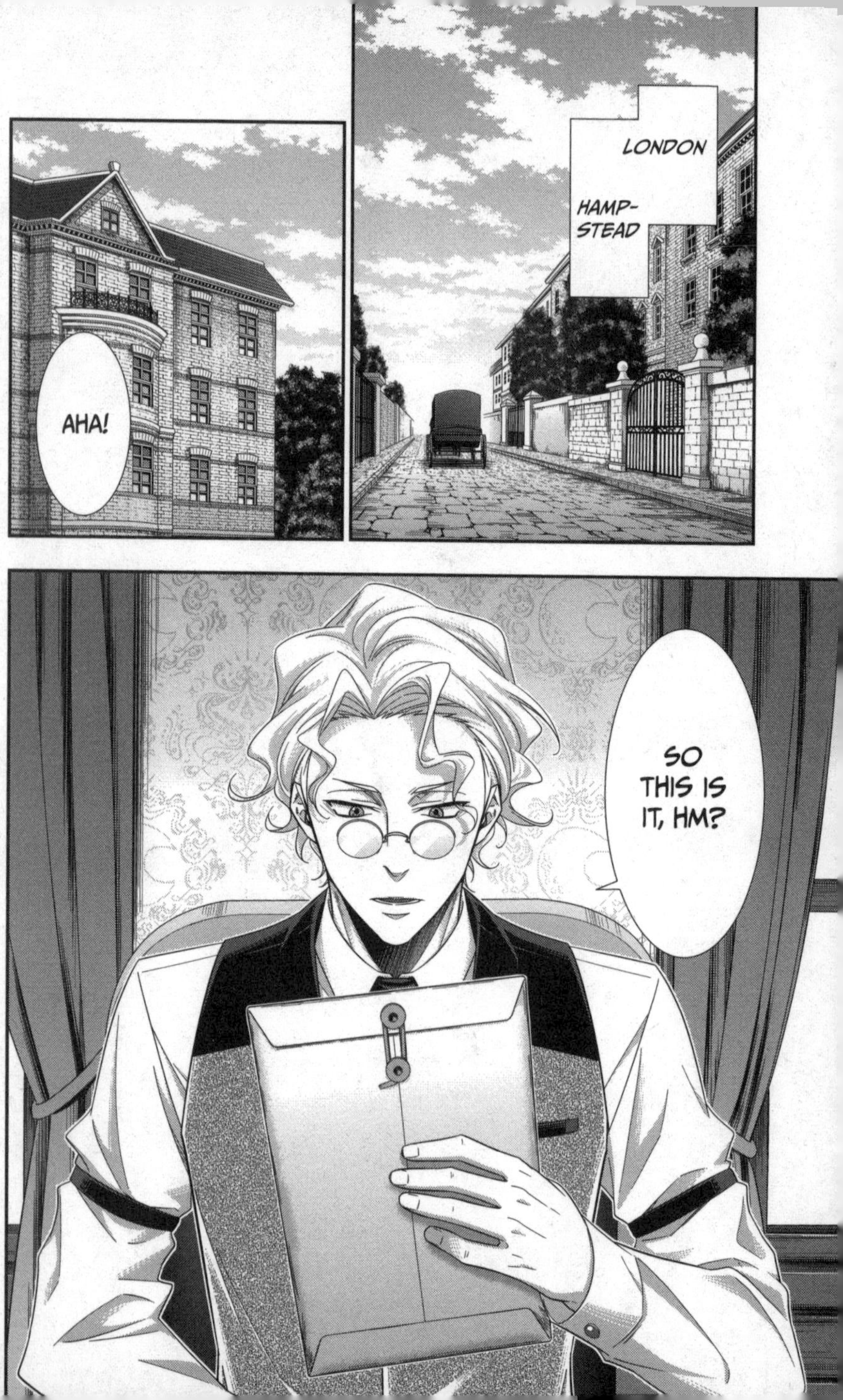
LONDON
HAMP-
STEAD
AHA!
SO THIS IS IT, HM?

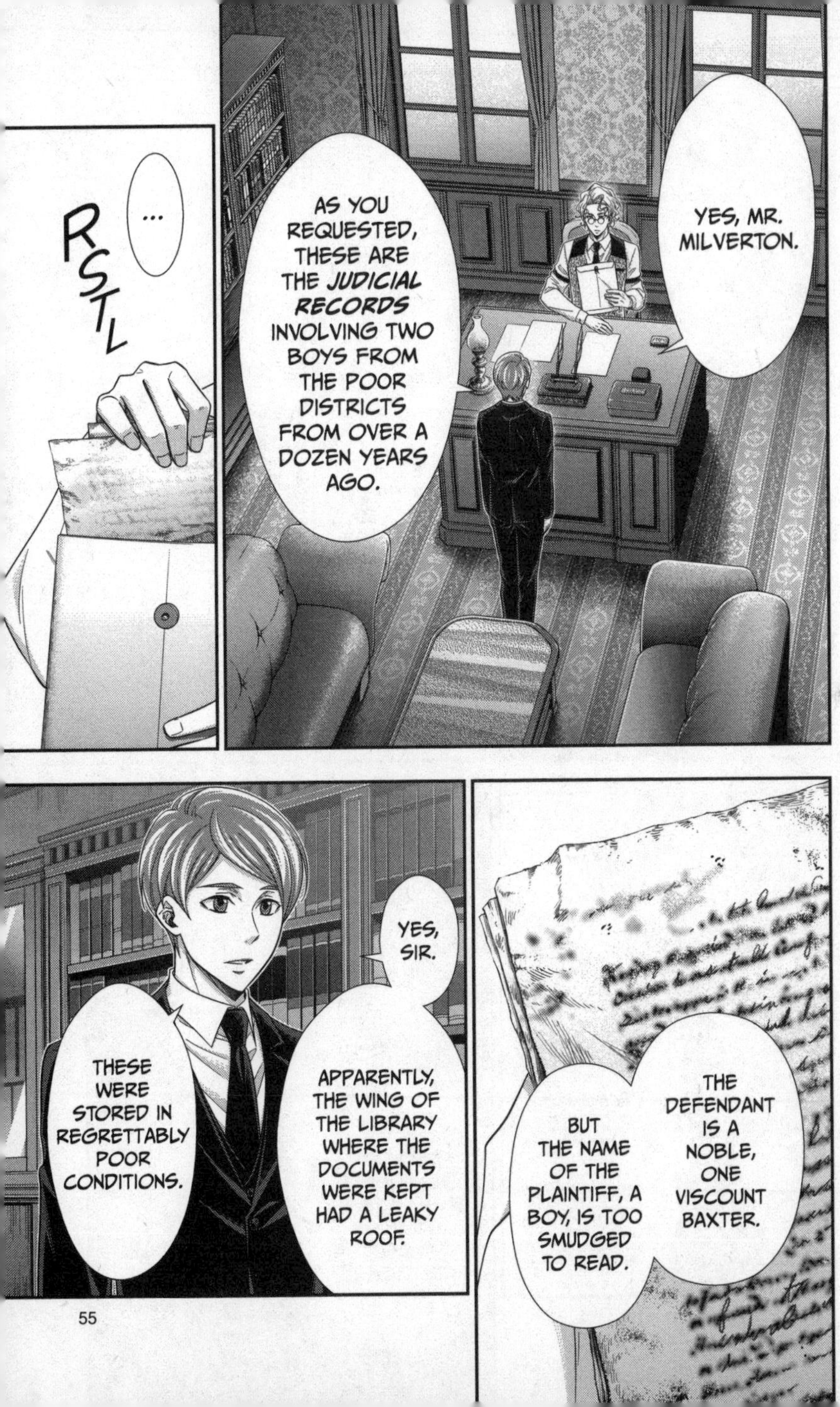

YES, MR. MILVERTON.
AS YOU REQUESTED, THESE ARE THE *JUDICIAL RECORDS* INVOLVING TWO BOYS FROM THE POOR DISTRICTS FROM OVER A DOZEN YEARS AGO.
...
RSTL
THE DEFENDANT IS A NOBLE, ONE VISCOUNT BAXTER.
BUT THE NAME OF THE PLAINTIFF, A BOY, IS TOO SMUDGED TO READ.
YES, SIR.
APPARENTLY, THE WING OF THE LIBRARY WHERE THE DOCUMENTS WERE KEPT HAD A LEAKY ROOF.
THESE WERE STORED IN REGRETTABLY POOR CONDITIONS.

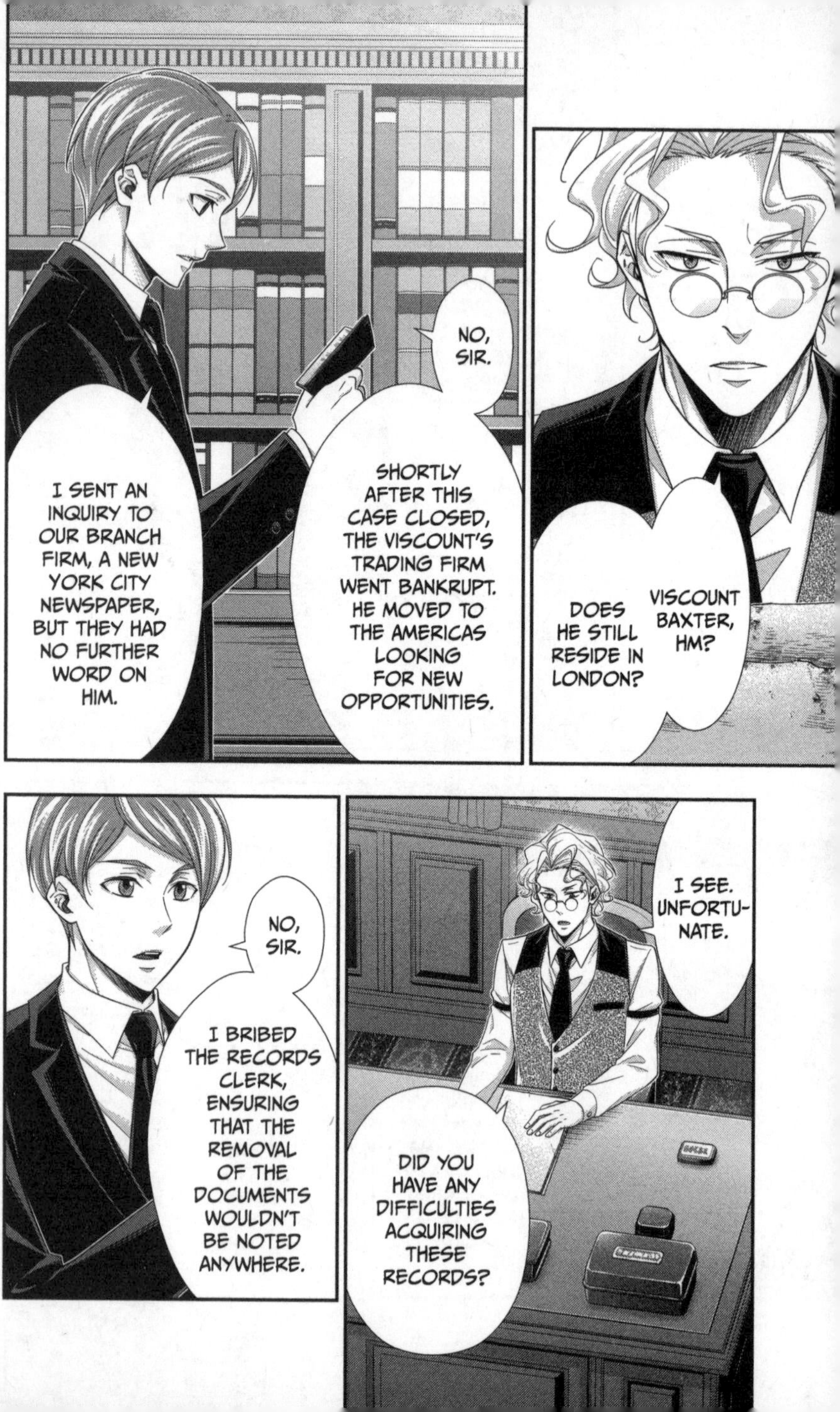
VISCOUNT BAXTER, HM?
DOES HE STILL RESIDE IN LONDON?
NO, SIR.
SHORTLY AFTER THIS CASE CLOSED, THE VISCOUNT'S TRADING FIRM WENT BANKRUPT. HE MOVED TO THE AMERICAS LOOKING FOR NEW OPPORTUNITIES.
I SENT AN INQUIRY TO OUR BRANCH FIRM, A NEW YORK CITY NEWSPAPER, BUT THEY HAD NO FURTHER WORD ON HIM.
I SEE. UNFORTU-NATE.
DID YOU HAVE ANY DIFFICULTIES ACQUIRING THESE RECORDS?
NO, SIR.
I BRIBED THE RECORDS CLERK, ENSURING THAT THE REMOVAL OF THE DOCUMENTS WOULDN'T BE NOTED ANYWHERE.

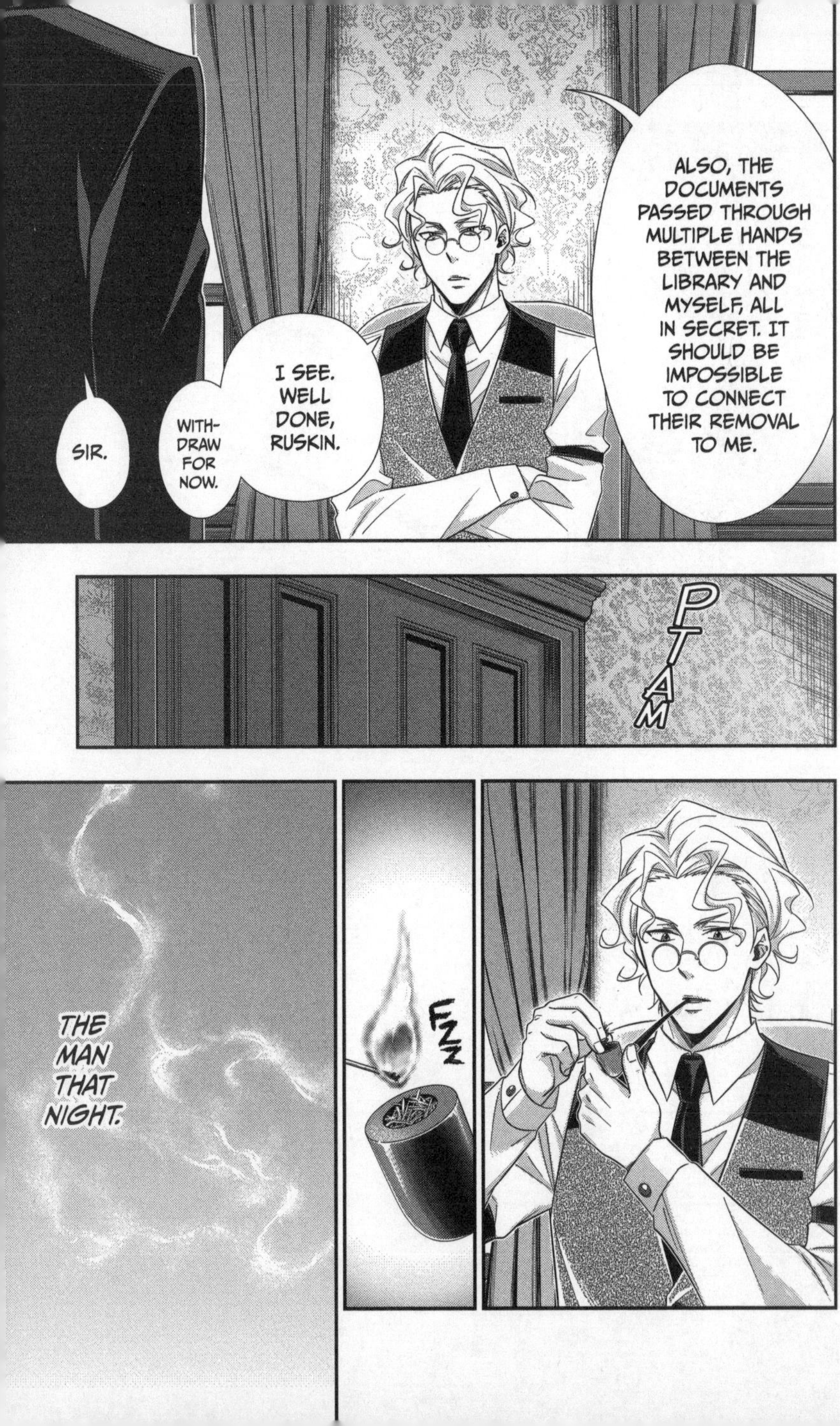
ALSO, THE DOCUMENTS PASSED THROUGH MULTIPLE HANDS BETWEEN THE LIBRARY AND MYSELF, ALL IN SECRET. IT SHOULD BE IMPOSSIBLE TO CONNECT THEIR REMOVAL TO ME.
I SEE. WELL DONE, RUSKIN.
WITH-DRAW FOR NOW.
SIR.
PTAM
FZZ
THE MAN THAT NIGHT.

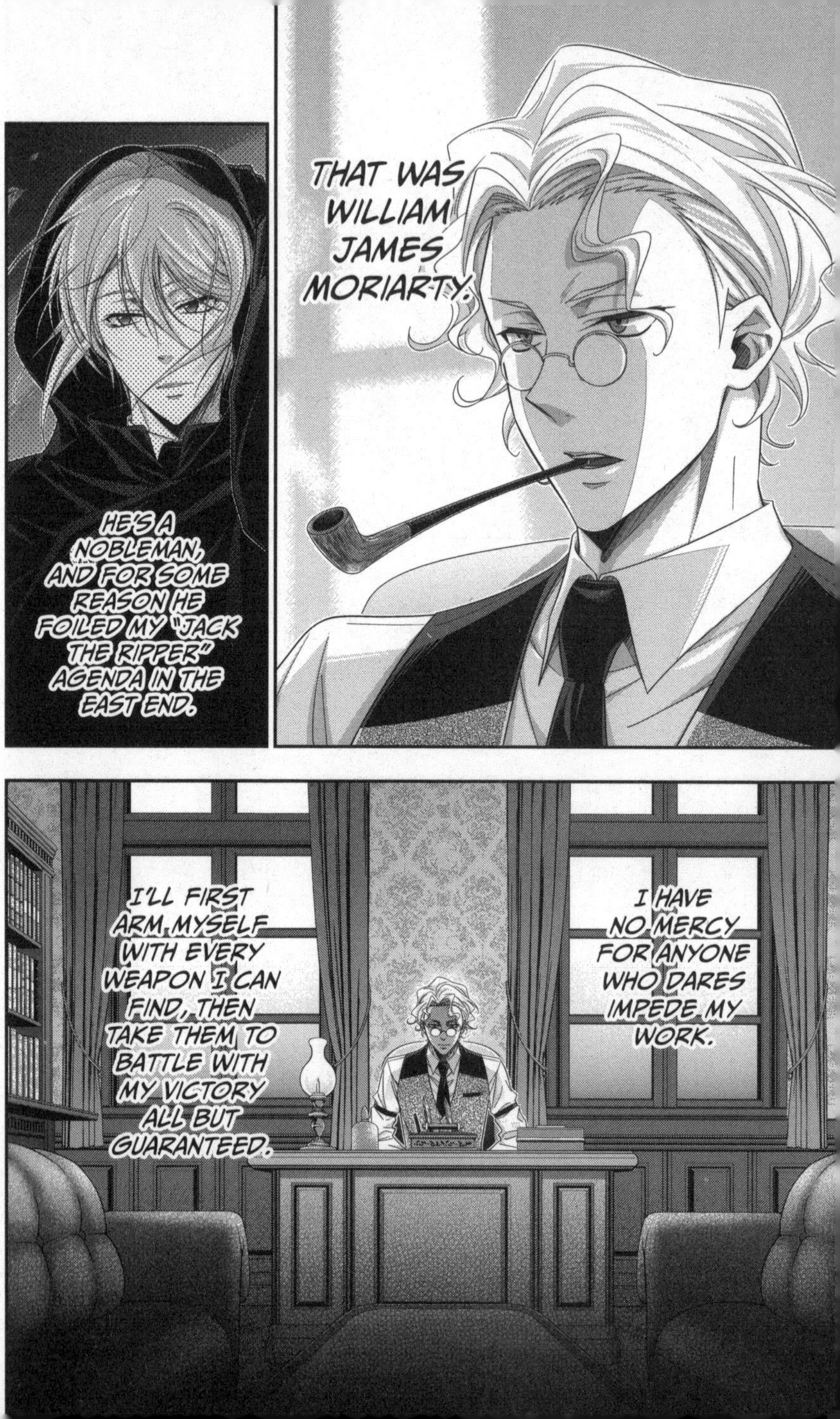
THAT WAS WILLIAM JAMES MORIARTY.
HE'S A NOBLEMAN, AND FOR SOME REASON HE FOILED MY "JACK THE RIPPER" AGENDA IN THE EAST END.
I HAVE NO MERCY FOR ANYONE WHO DARES IMPEDE MY WORK.
I'LL FIRST ARM MYSELF WITH EVERY WEAPON I CAN FIND, THEN TAKE THEM TO BATTLE WITH MY VICTORY ALL BUT GUARANTEED.

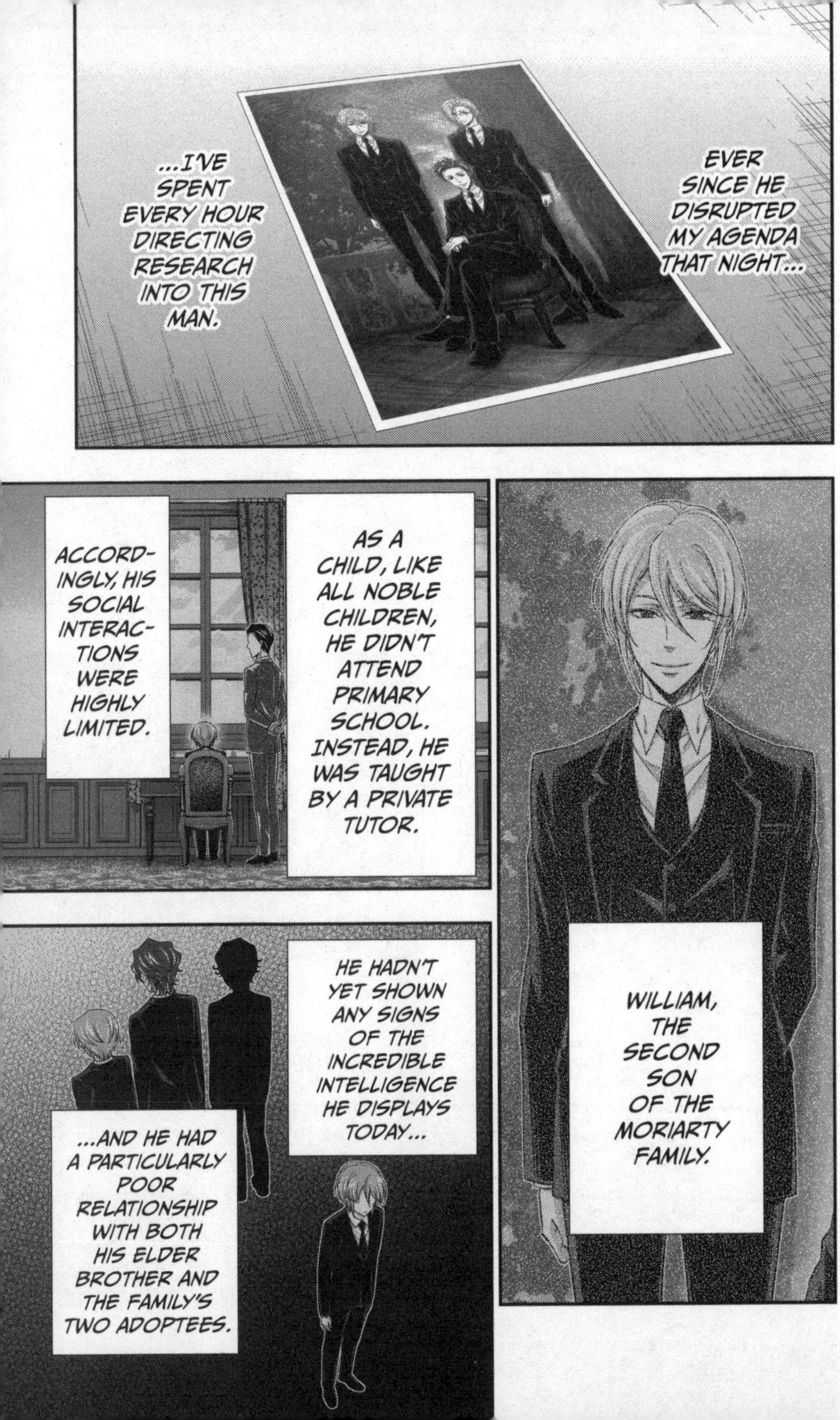
EVER SINCE HE DISRUPTED MY AGENDA THAT NIGHT...
...I'VE SPENT EVERY HOUR DIRECTING RESEARCH INTO THIS MAN.
WILLIAM, THE SECOND SON OF THE MORIARTY FAMILY.
AS A CHILD, LIKE ALL NOBLE CHILDREN, HE DIDN'T ATTEND PRIMARY SCHOOL. INSTEAD, HE WAS TAUGHT BY A PRIVATE TUTOR.
ACCORD-INGLY, HIS SOCIAL INTERAC-TIONS WERE HIGHLY LIMITED.
HE HADN'T YET SHOWN ANY SIGNS OF THE INCREDIBLE INTELLIGENCE HE DISPLAYS TODAY...
...AND HE HAD A PARTICULARLY POOR RELATIONSHIP WITH BOTH HIS ELDER BROTHER AND THE FAMILY'S TWO ADOPTEES.

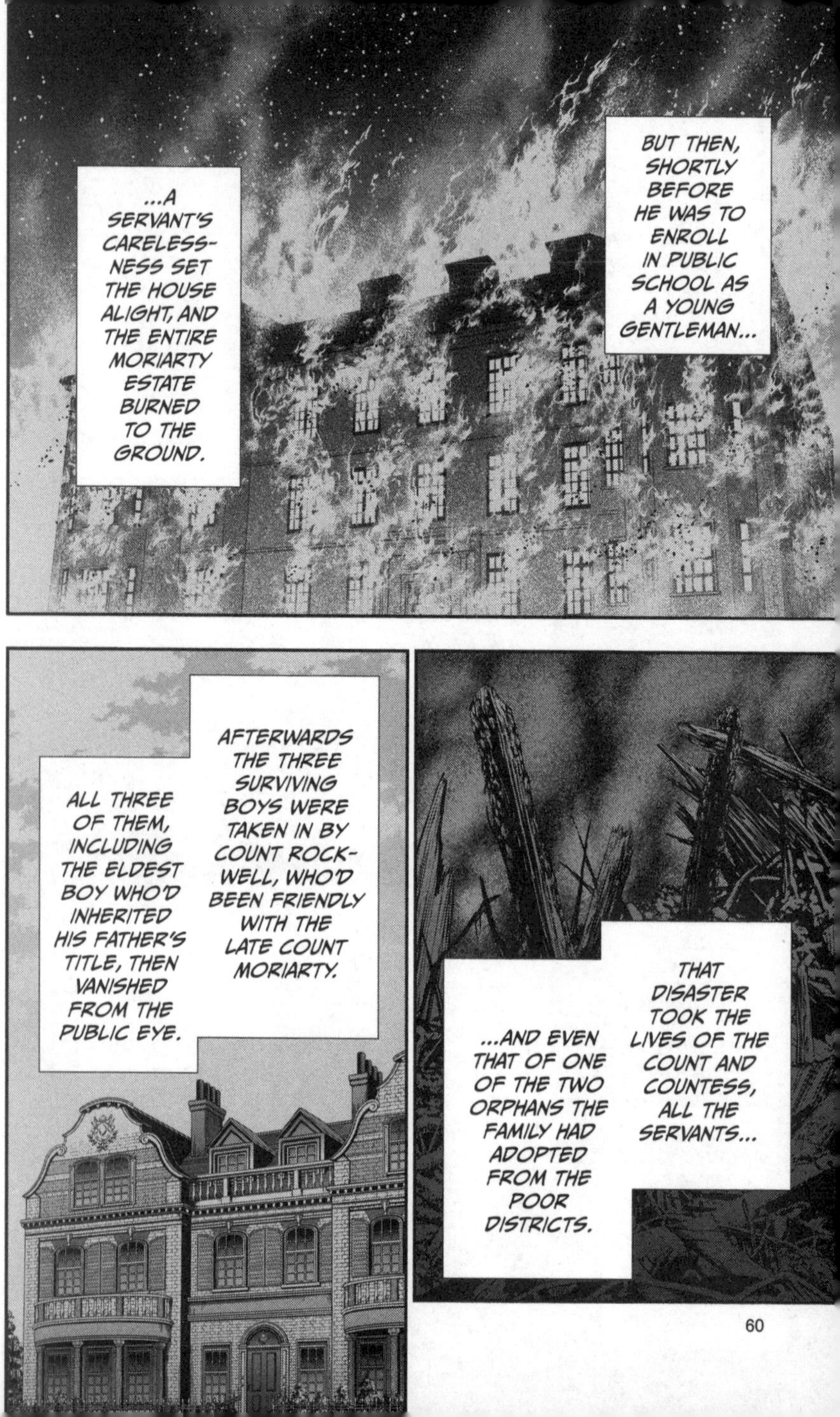
BUT THEN, SHORTLY BEFORE HE WAS TO ENROLL IN PUBLIC SCHOOL AS A YOUNG GENTLEMAN...
...A SERVANT'S CARELESS-NESS SET THE HOUSE ALIGHT, AND THE ENTIRE MORIARTY ESTATE BURNED TO THE GROUND.
THAT DISASTER TOOK THE LIVES OF THE COUNT AND COUNTESS, ALL THE SERVANTS...
...AND EVEN THAT OF ONE OF THE TWO ORPHANS THE FAMILY HAD ADOPTED FROM THE POOR DISTRICTS.
AFTERWARDS THE THREE SURVIVING BOYS WERE TAKEN IN BY COUNT ROCK-WELL, WHO'D BEEN FRIENDLY WITH THE LATE COUNT MORIARTY.
ALL THREE OF THEM, INCLUDING THE ELDEST BOY WHO'D INHERITED HIS FATHER'S TITLE, THEN VANISHED FROM THE PUBLIC EYE.

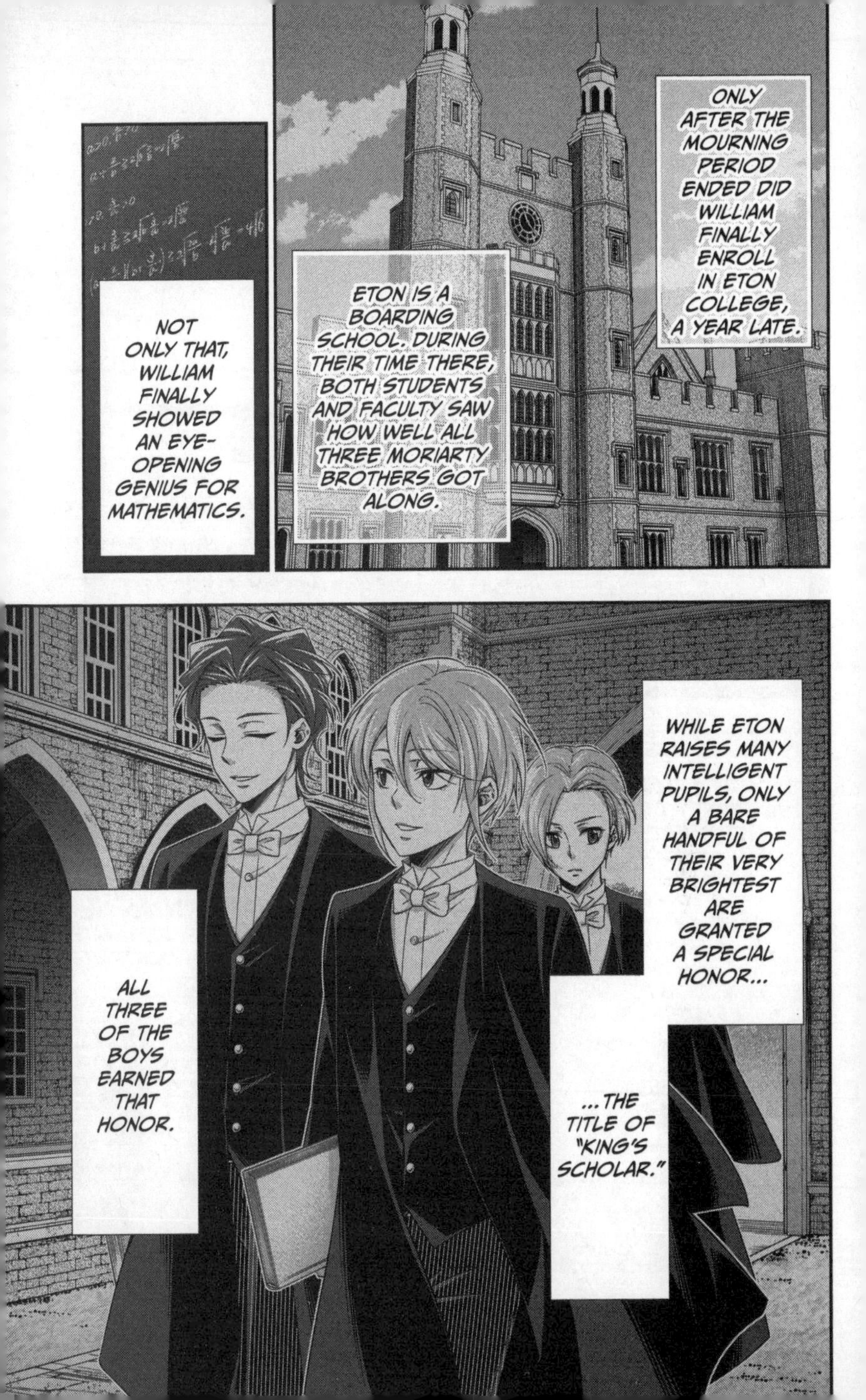
ONLY AFTER THE MOURNING PERIOD ENDED DID WILLIAM FINALLY ENROLL IN ETON COLLEGE, A YEAR LATE.
ETON IS A BOARDING SCHOOL. DURING THEIR TIME THERE, BOTH STUDENTS AND FACULTY SAW HOW WELL ALL THREE MORIARTY BROTHERS GOT ALONG.
NOT ONLY THAT, WILLIAM FINALLY SHOWED AN EYE-OPENING GENIUS FOR MATHEMATICS.
WHILE ETON RAISES MANY INTELLIGENT PUPILS, ONLY A BARE HANDFUL OF THEIR VERY BRIGHTEST ARE GRANTED A SPECIAL HONOR...
...THE TITLE OF "KING'S SCHOLAR."
ALL THREE OF THE BOYS EARNED THAT HONOR.

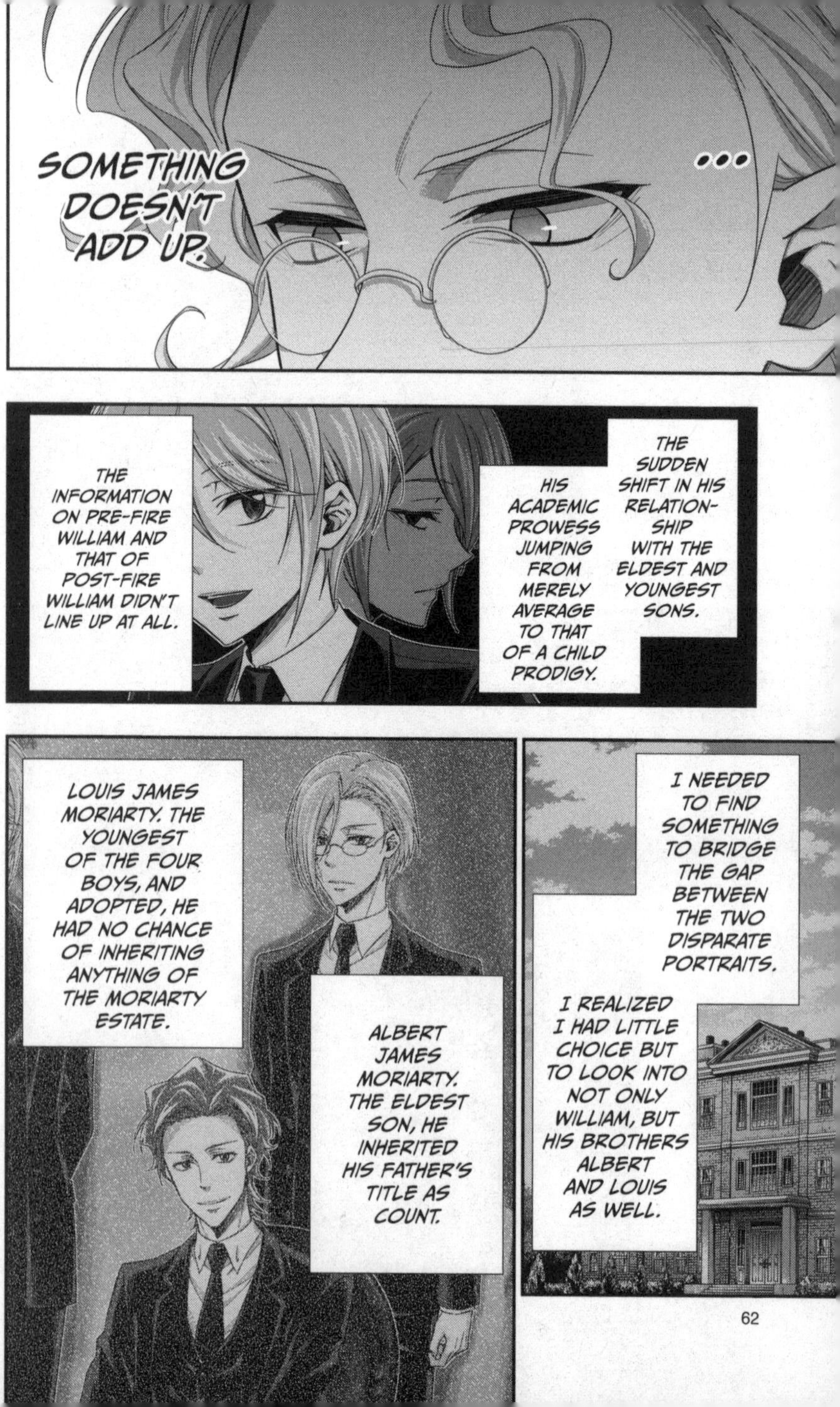
...
SOMETHING DOESN'T ADD UP.
THE SUDDEN SHIFT IN HIS RELATION-SHIP WITH THE ELDEST AND YOUNGEST SONS.
HIS ACADEMIC PROWESS JUMPING FROM MERELY AVERAGE TO THAT OF A CHILD PRODIGY.
THE INFORMATION ON PRE-FIRE WILLIAM AND THAT OF POST-FIRE WILLIAM DIDN'T LINE UP AT ALL.
I NEEDED TO FIND SOMETHING TO BRIDGE THE GAP BETWEEN THE TWO DISPARATE PORTRAITS.
I REALIZED I HAD LITTLE CHOICE BUT TO LOOK INTO NOT ONLY WILLIAM, BUT HIS BROTHERS ALBERT AND LOUIS AS WELL.
LOUIS JAMES MORIARTY. THE YOUNGEST OF THE FOUR BOYS, AND ADOPTED, HE HAD NO CHANCE OF INHERITING ANYTHING OF THE MORIARTY ESTATE.
ALBERT JAMES MORIARTY. THE ELDEST SON, HE INHERITED HIS FATHER'S TITLE AS COUNT.

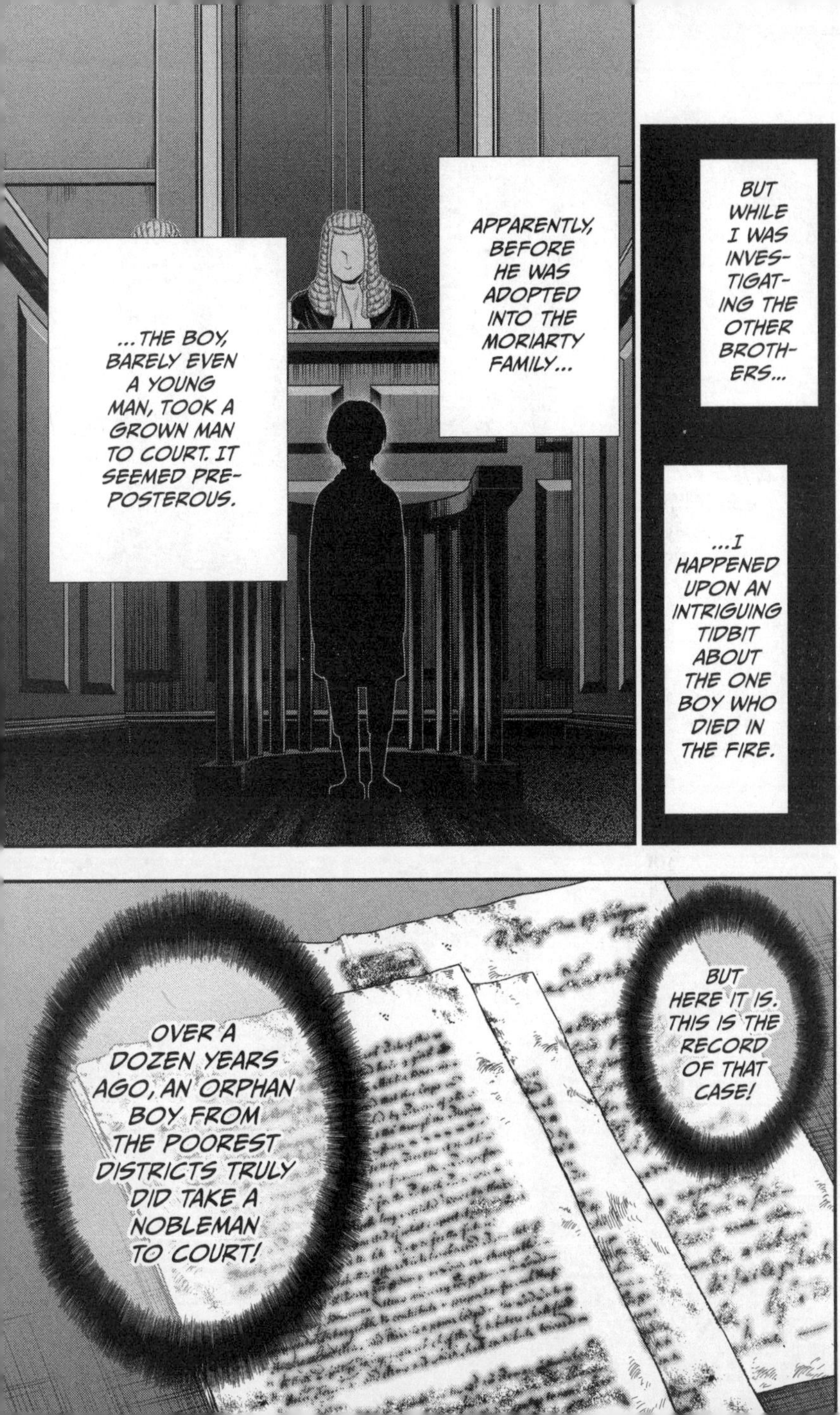
BUT WHILE I WAS INVES-TIGAT-ING THE OTHER BROTH-ERS...
...I HAPPENED UPON AN INTRIGUING TIDBIT ABOUT THE ONE BOY WHO DIED IN THE FIRE.
APPARENTLY, BEFORE HE WAS ADOPTED INTO THE MORIARTY FAMILY...
...THE BOY, BARELY EVEN A YOUNG MAN, TOOK A GROWN MAN TO COURT. IT SEEMED PRE-POSTEROUS.
BUT HERE IT IS. THIS IS THE RECORD OF THAT CASE!
OVER A DOZEN YEARS AGO, AN ORPHAN BOY FROM THE POOREST DISTRICTS TRULY DID TAKE A NOBLEMAN TO COURT!

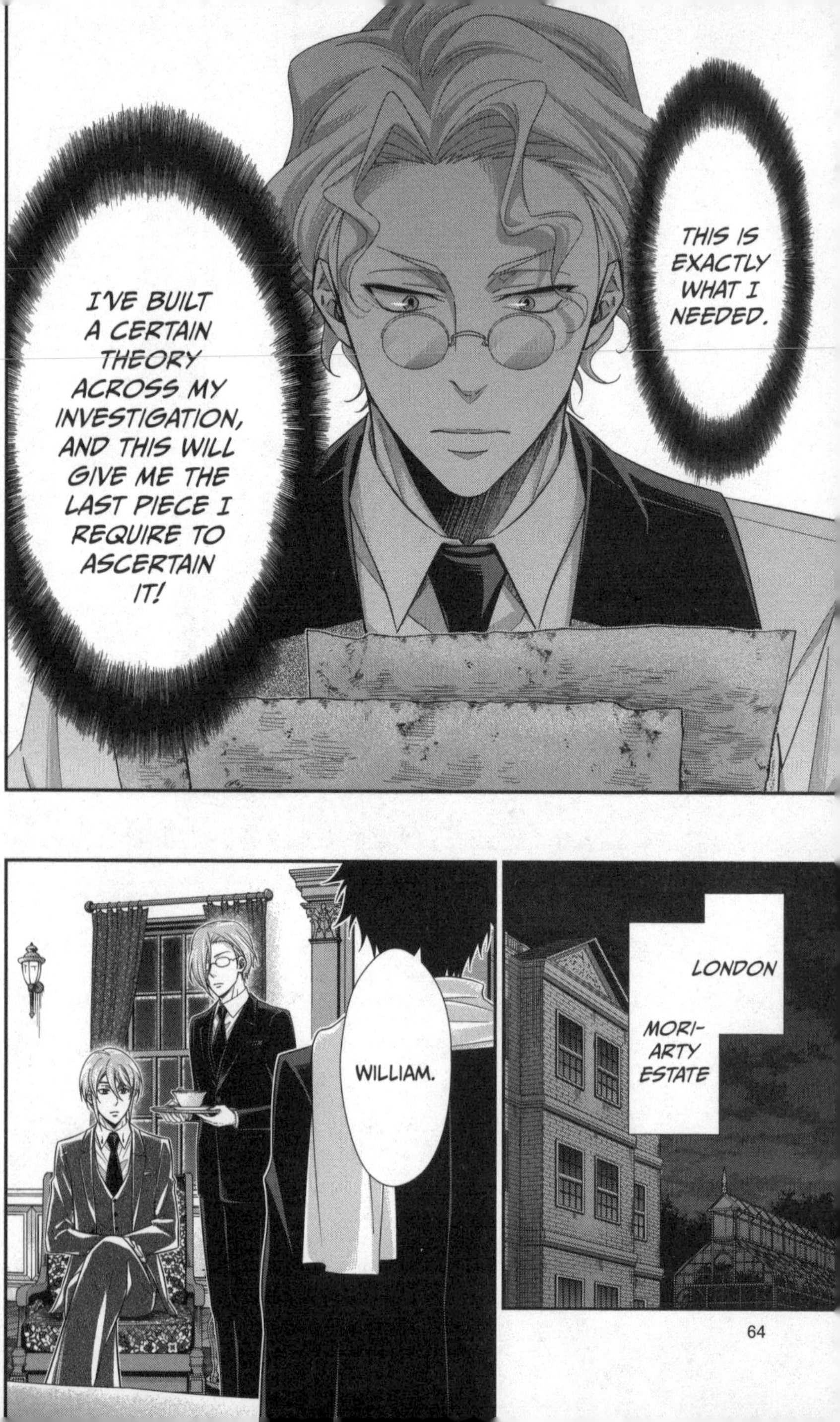

THIS IS EXACTLY WHAT I NEEDED.
I'VE BUILT A CERTAIN THEORY ACROSS MY INVESTIGATION, AND THIS WILL GIVE ME THE LAST PIECE I REQUIRE TO ASCERTAIN IT!
LONDON
MORI-ARTY ESTATE
WILLIAM.

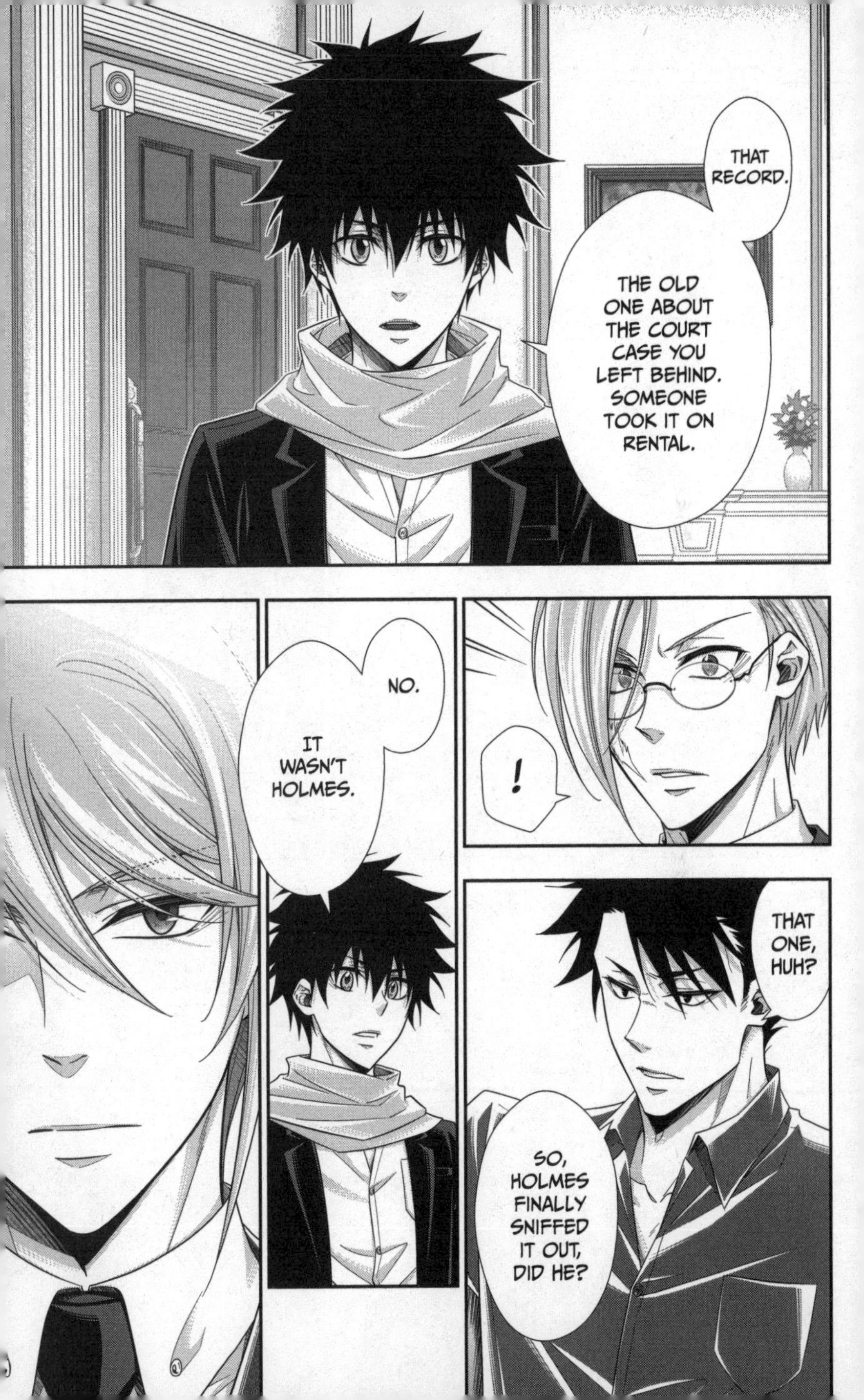
THAT RECORD.
THE OLD ONE ABOUT THE COURT CASE YOU LEFT BEHIND. SOMEONE TOOK IT ON RENTAL.
!
THAT ONE, HUH?
SO, HOLMES FINALLY SNIFFED IT OUT, DID HE?
NO.
IT WASN'T HOLMES.

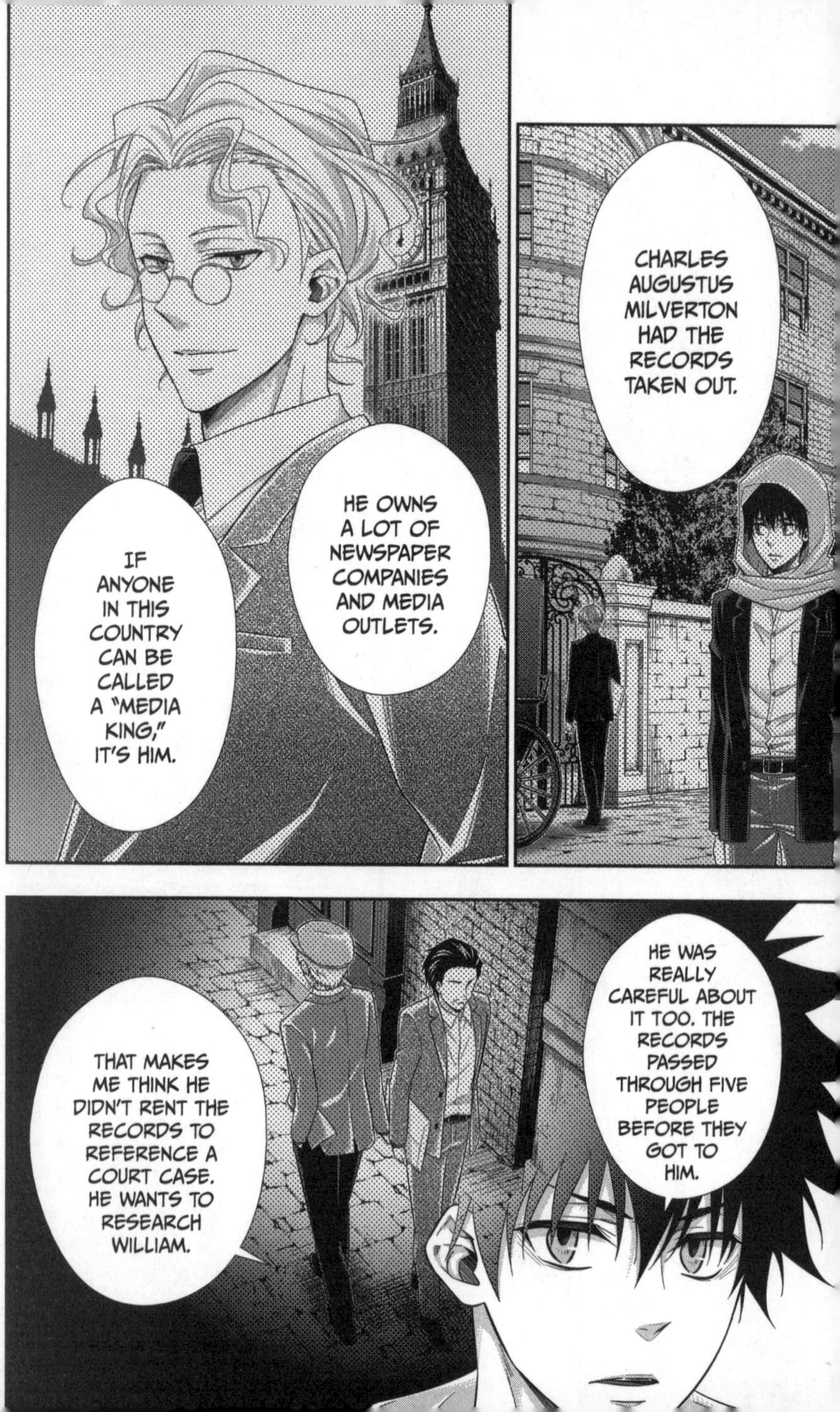
CHARLES AUGUSTUS MILVERTON HAD THE RECORDS TAKEN OUT.
HE OWNS A LOT OF NEWSPAPER COMPANIES AND MEDIA OUTLETS.
IF ANYONE IN THIS COUNTRY CAN BE CALLED A "MEDIA KING," IT'S HIM.
HE WAS REALLY CAREFUL ABOUT IT TOO. THE RECORDS PASSED THROUGH FIVE PEOPLE BEFORE THEY GOT TO HIM.
THAT MAKES ME THINK HE DIDN'T RENT THE RECORDS TO REFERENCE A COURT CASE. HE WANTS TO RESEARCH WILLIAM.

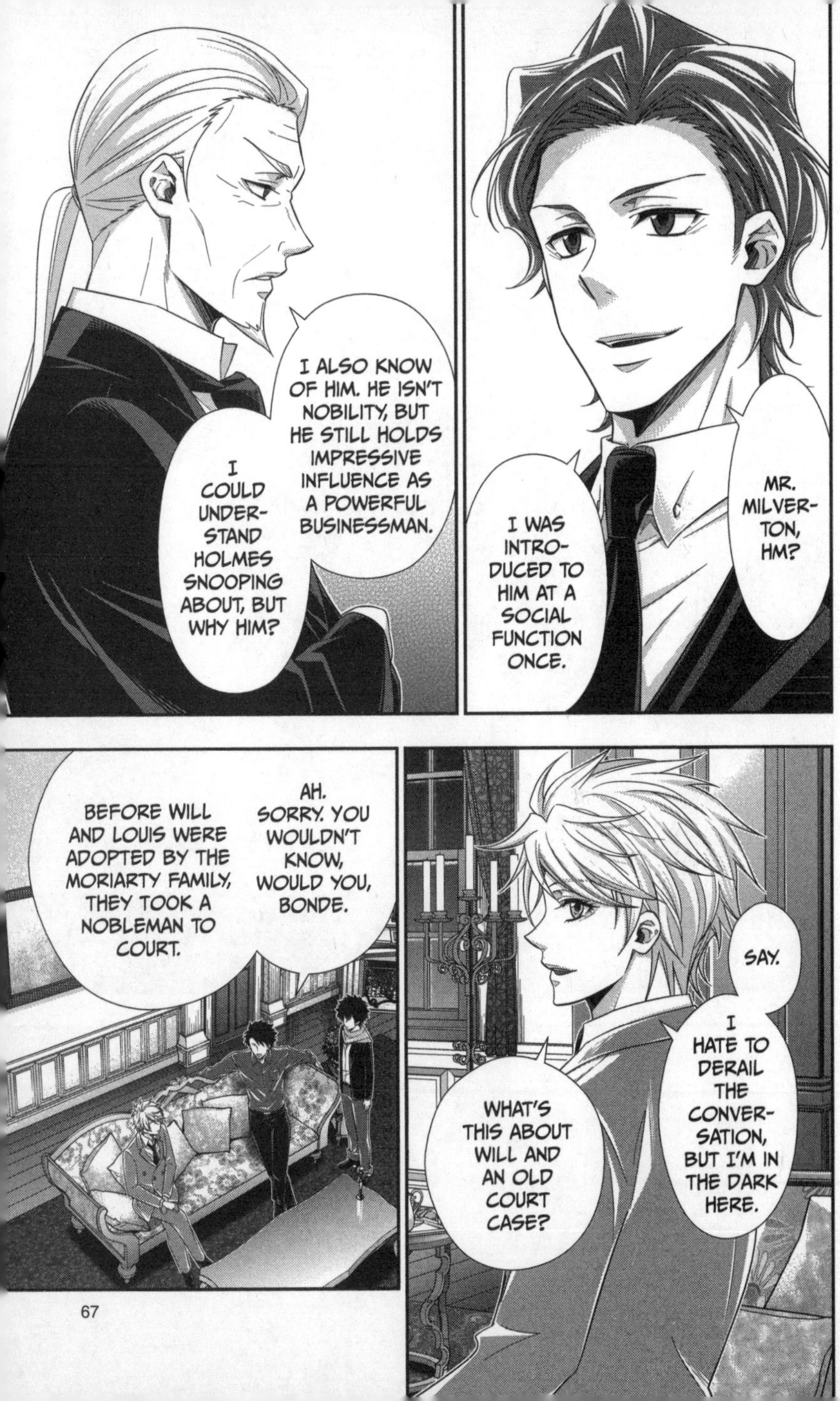
MR. MILVER-TON, HM?
I WAS INTRO-DUCED TO HIM AT A SOCIAL FUNCTION ONCE.
I ALSO KNOW OF HIM. HE ISN'T NOBILITY, BUT HE STILL HOLDS IMPRESSIVE INFLUENCE AS A POWERFUL BUSINESSMAN.
I COULD UNDER-STAND HOLMES SNOOPING ABOUT, BUT WHY HIM?
SAY.
I HATE TO DERAIL THE CONVER-SATION, BUT I'M IN THE DARK HERE.
WHAT'S THIS ABOUT WILL AND AN OLD COURT CASE?
AH. SORRY. YOU WOULDN'T KNOW, WOULD YOU, BONDE.
BEFORE WILL AND LOUIS WERE ADOPTED BY THE MORIARTY FAMILY, THEY TOOK A NOBLEMAN TO COURT.

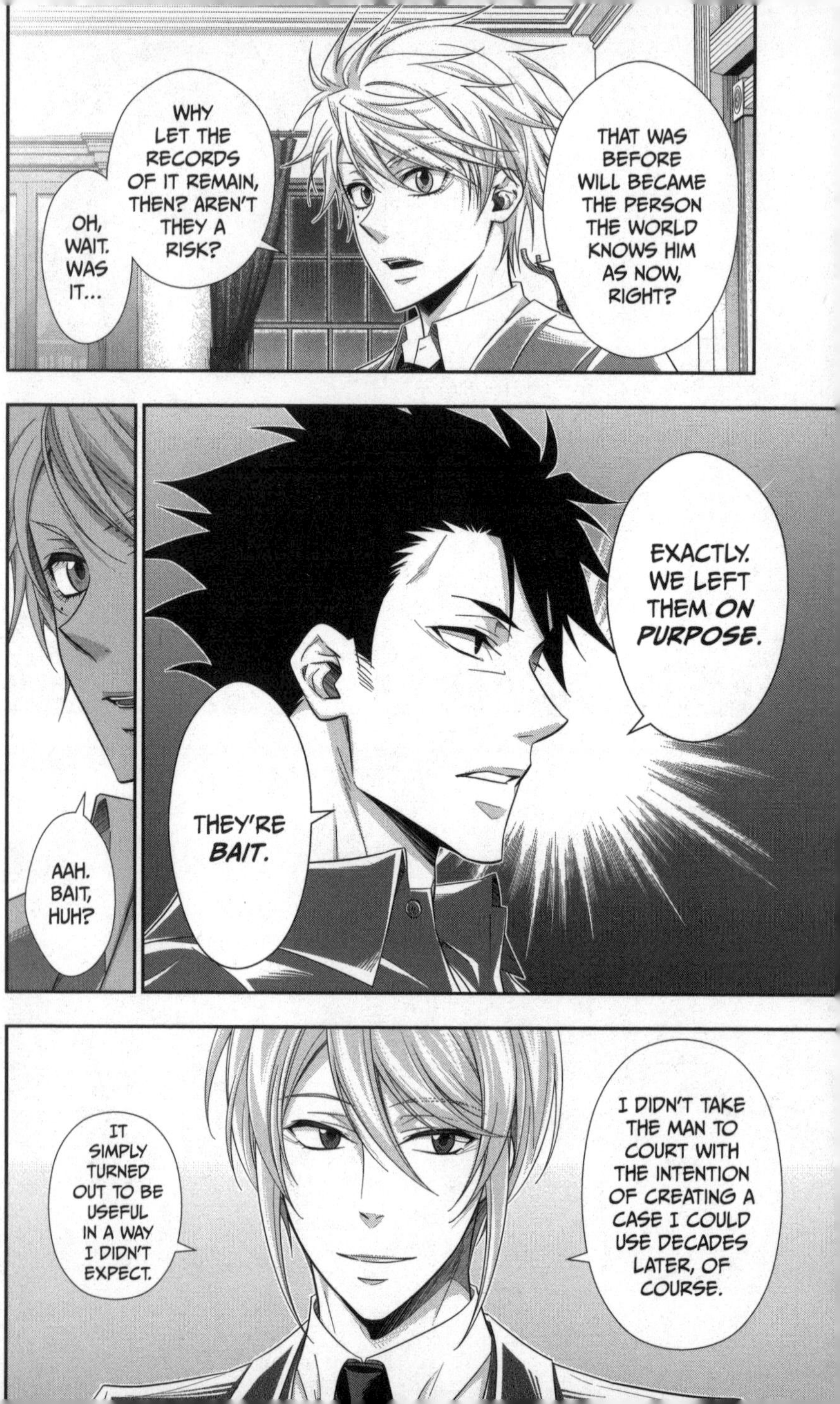
THAT WAS BEFORE WILL BECAME THE PERSON THE WORLD KNOWS HIM AS NOW, RIGHT?
WHY LET THE RECORDS OF IT REMAIN, THEN? AREN'T THEY A RISK?
OH, WAIT. WAS IT...
EXACTLY. WE LEFT THEM *ON PURPOSE*.
THEY'RE *BAIT*.
AAH. BAIT, HUH?
I DIDN'T TAKE THE MAN TO COURT WITH THE INTENTION OF CREATING A CASE I COULD USE DECADES LATER, OF COURSE.
IT SIMPLY TURNED OUT TO BE USEFUL IN A WAY I DIDN'T EXPECT.

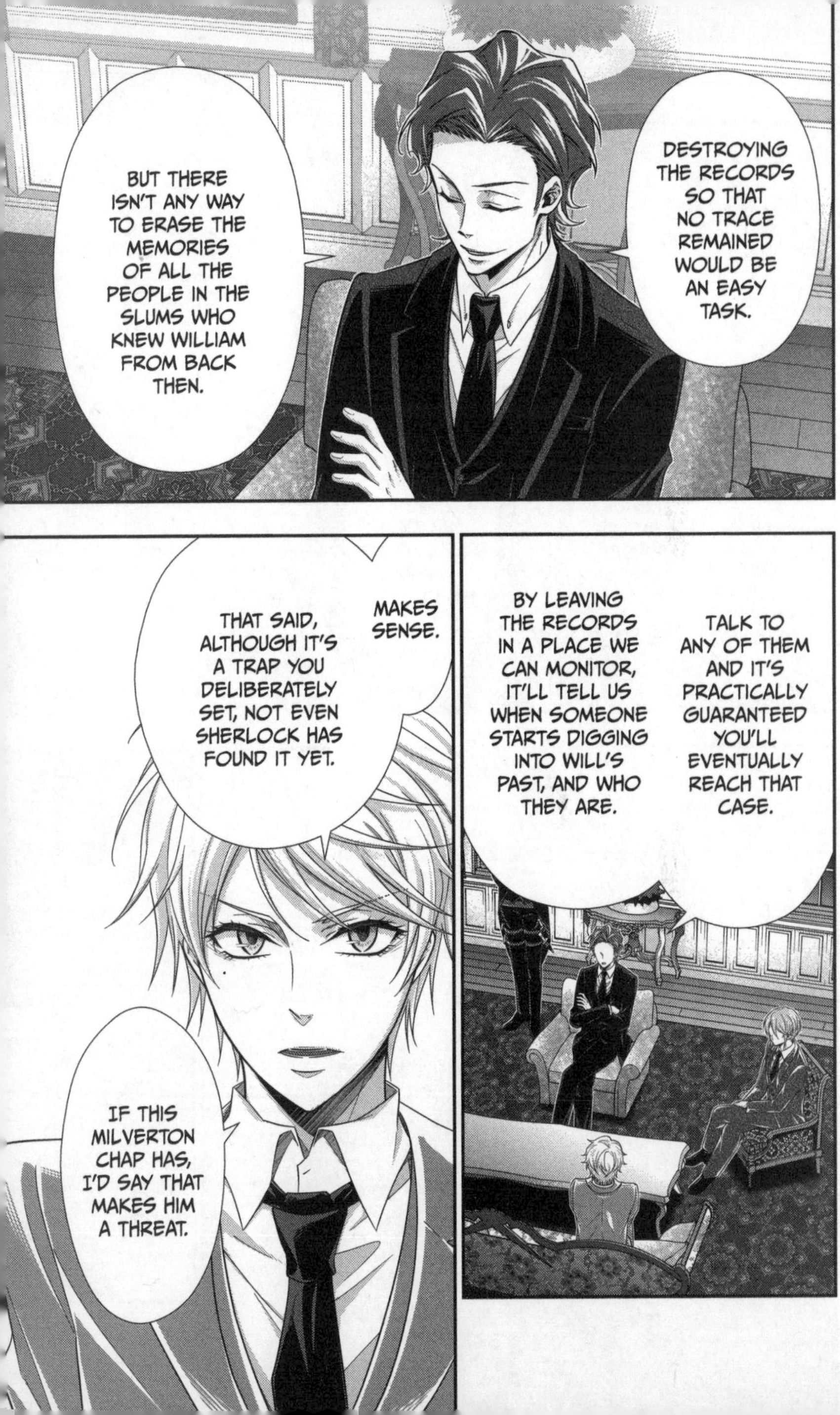
DESTROYING THE RECORDS SO THAT NO TRACE REMAINED WOULD BE AN EASY TASK.
BUT THERE ISN'T ANY WAY TO ERASE THE MEMORIES OF ALL THE PEOPLE IN THE SLUMS WHO KNEW WILLIAM FROM BACK THEN.
TALK TO ANY OF THEM AND IT'S PRACTICALLY GUARANTEED YOU'LL EVENTUALLY REACH THAT CASE.
BY LEAVING THE RECORDS IN A PLACE WE CAN MONITOR, IT'LL TELL US WHEN SOMEONE STARTS DIGGING INTO WILL'S PAST, AND WHO THEY ARE.
MAKES SENSE.
THAT SAID, ALTHOUGH IT'S A TRAP YOU DELIBERATELY SET, NOT EVEN SHERLOCK HAS FOUND IT YET.
IF THIS MILVERTON CHAP HAS, I'D SAY THAT MAKES HIM A THREAT.

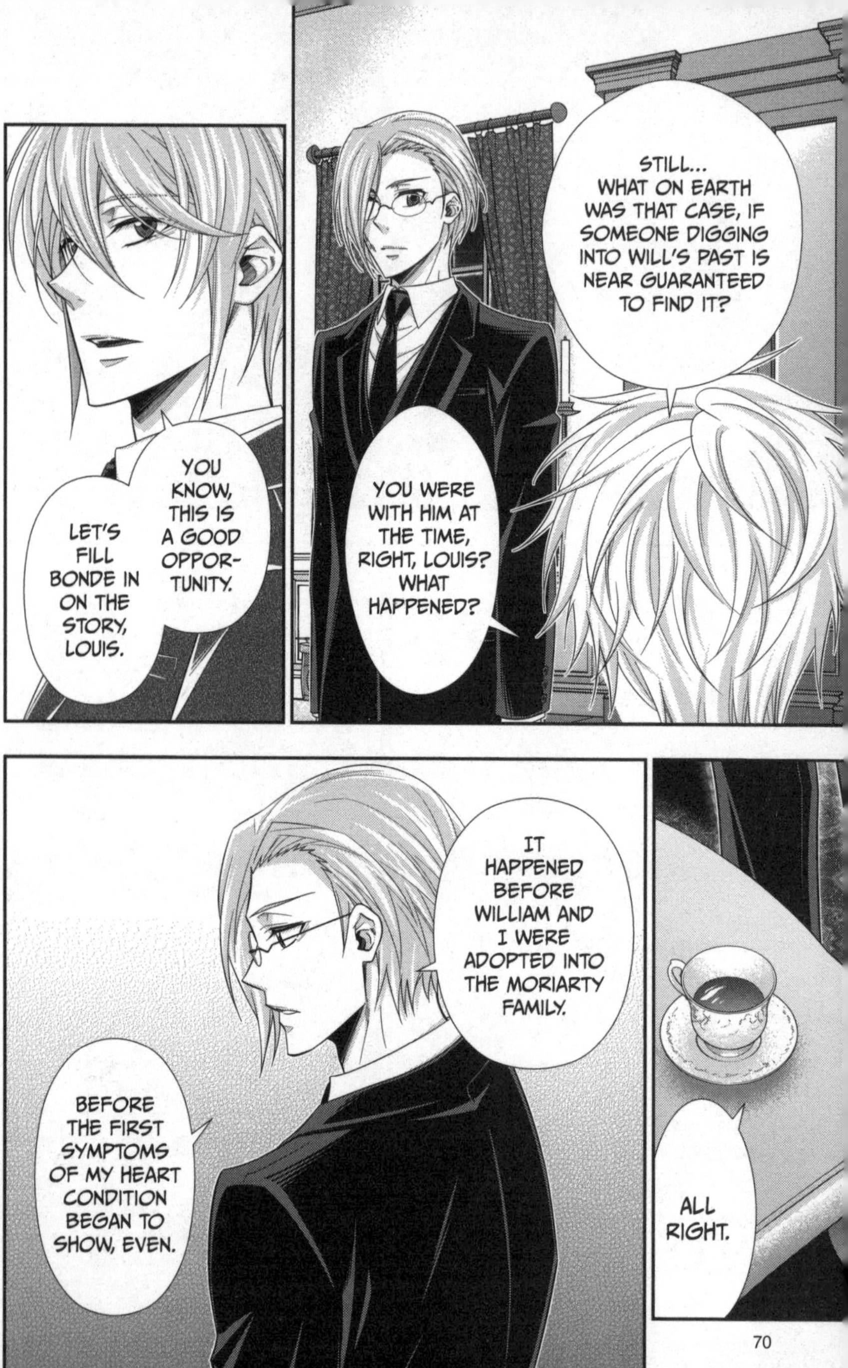
STILL... WHAT ON EARTH WAS THAT CASE, IF SOMEONE DIGGING INTO WILL'S PAST IS NEAR GUARANTEED TO FIND IT?
YOU WERE WITH HIM AT THE TIME, RIGHT, LOUIS? WHAT HAPPENED?
YOU KNOW, THIS IS A GOOD OPPOR-TUNITY.
LET'S FILL BONDE IN ON THE STORY, LOUIS.
ALL RIGHT.
IT HAPPENED BEFORE WILLIAM AND I WERE ADOPTED INTO THE MORIARTY FAMILY.
BEFORE THE FIRST SYMPTOMS OF MY HEART CONDITION BEGAN TO SHOW, EVEN.

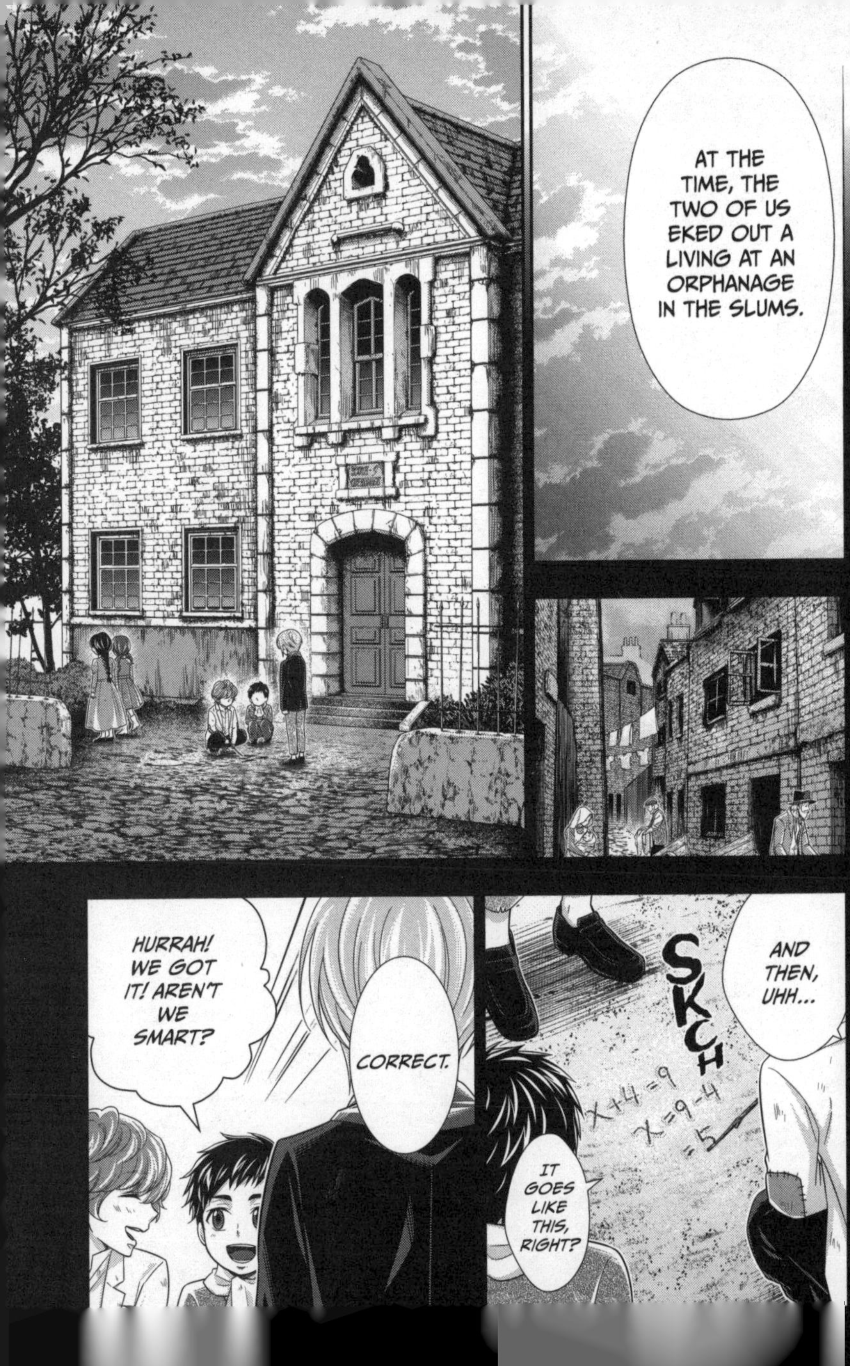

AT THE TIME, THE TWO OF US EKED OUT A LIVING AT AN ORPHANAGE IN THE SLUMS.
AND THEN, UHH...
SKCH
x+4=9
x=9-4
=5
IT GOES LIKE THIS, RIGHT?
CORRECT.
HURRAH! WE GOT IT! AREN'T WE SMART?

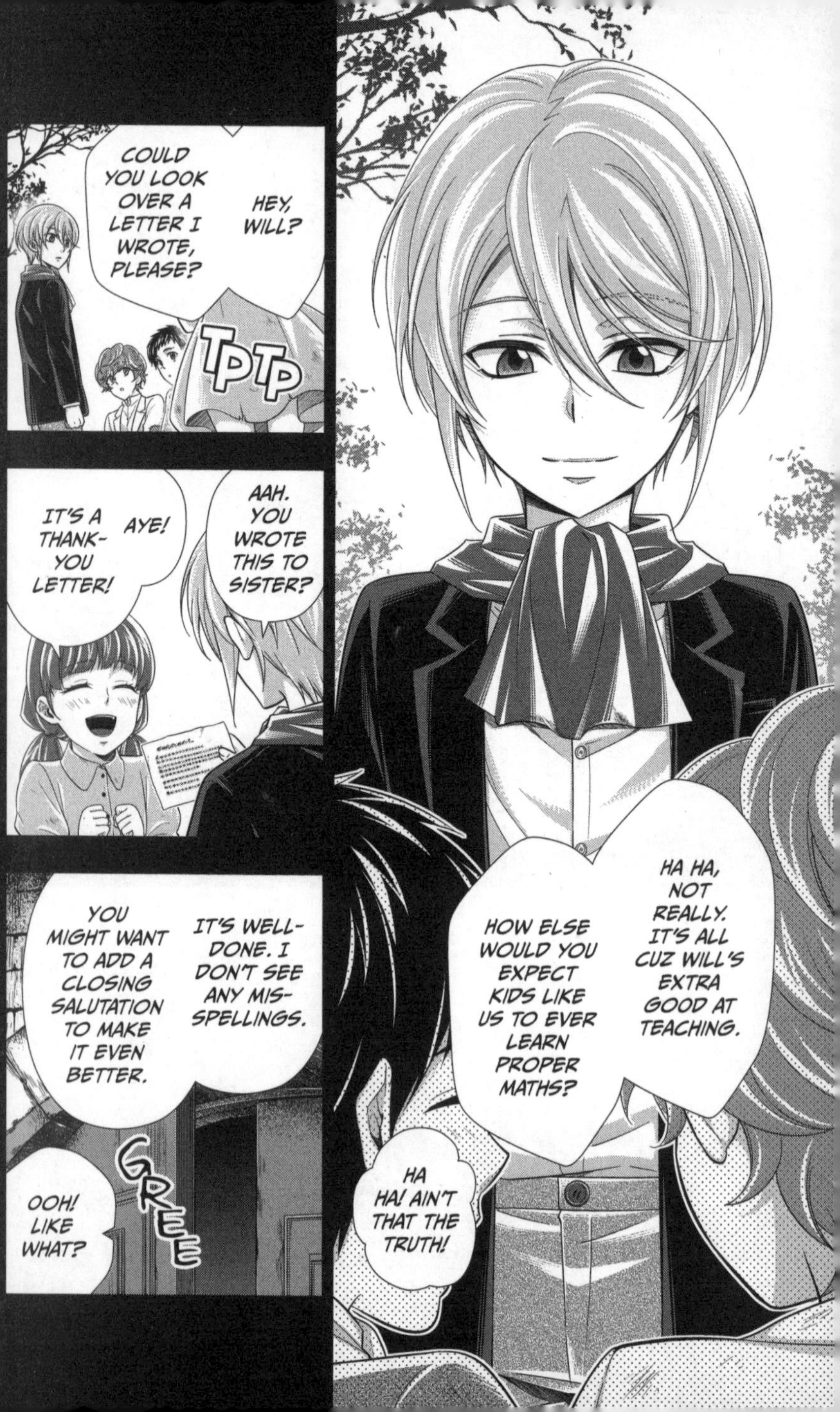
HA HA, NOT REALLY. IT'S ALL CUZ WILL'S EXTRA GOOD AT TEACHING.
HOW ELSE WOULD YOU EXPECT KIDS LIKE US TO EVER LEARN PROPER MATHS?
HA HA! AIN'T THAT THE TRUTH!
HEY, WILL?
COULD YOU LOOK OVER A LETTER I WROTE, PLEASE?
TPTP
AAH. YOU WROTE THIS TO SISTER?
AYE!
IT'S A THANK-YOU LETTER!
IT'S WELL-DONE. I DON'T SEE ANY MIS-SPELLINGS.
YOU MIGHT WANT TO ADD A CLOSING SALUTATION TO MAKE IT EVEN BETTER.
GREE
OOH! LIKE WHAT?

EVERY-ONE.
IT'S ALMOST SUPPER-TIME. COME HELP SET THE TABLE.
AH! HI, LOUIS!
COM-ING!
LET'S GO OVER YOUR LETTER MORE AFTER SUPPER. OKAY?
OKAY!
I'M HUNGRY!
DSH
CHAT
CHAT
TNK
TNK
BREAD. THIN PEASE POR-RIDGE.
AND MILK. THAT OUGHT TO BE IT.
SNIF

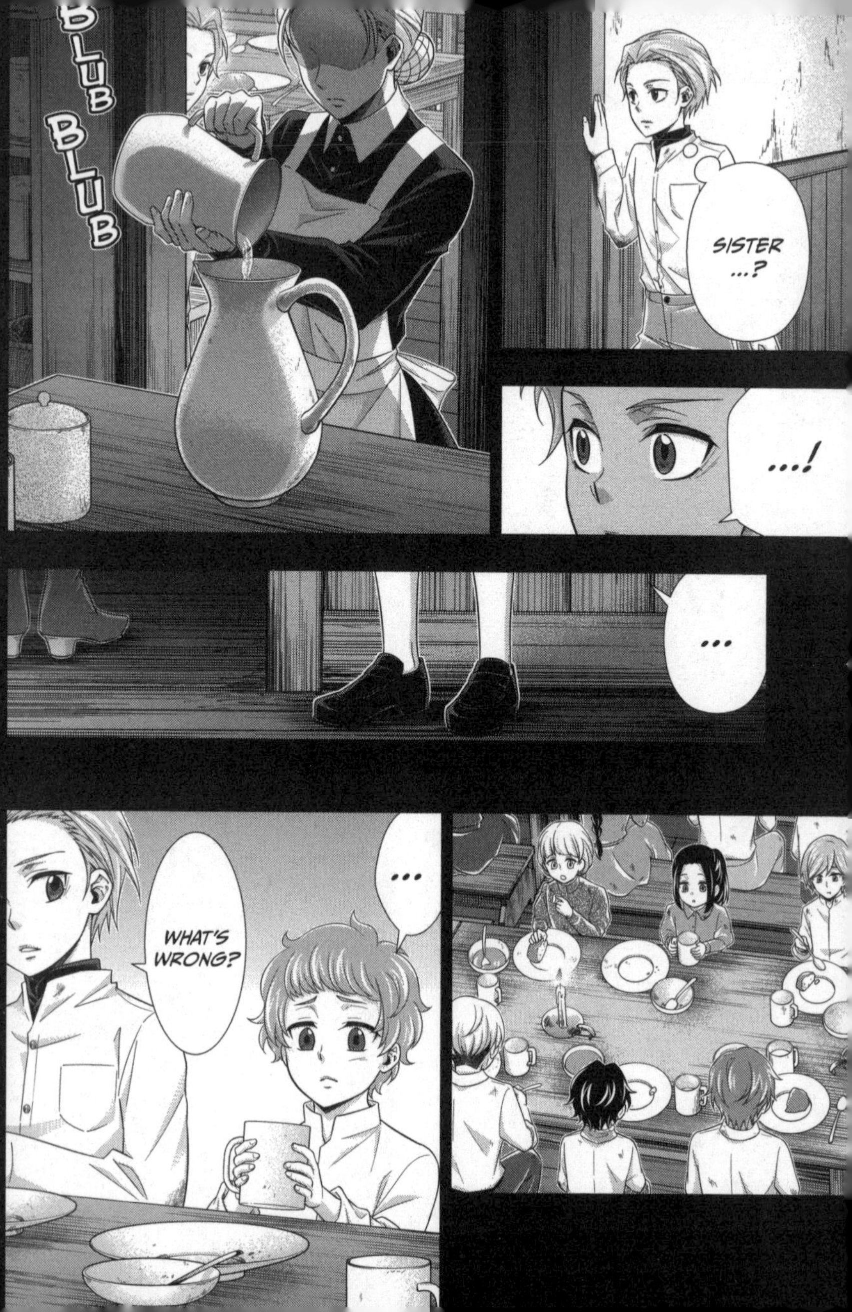
SISTER ...?
...!
BLUB BLUB
...
...
WHAT'S WRONG?

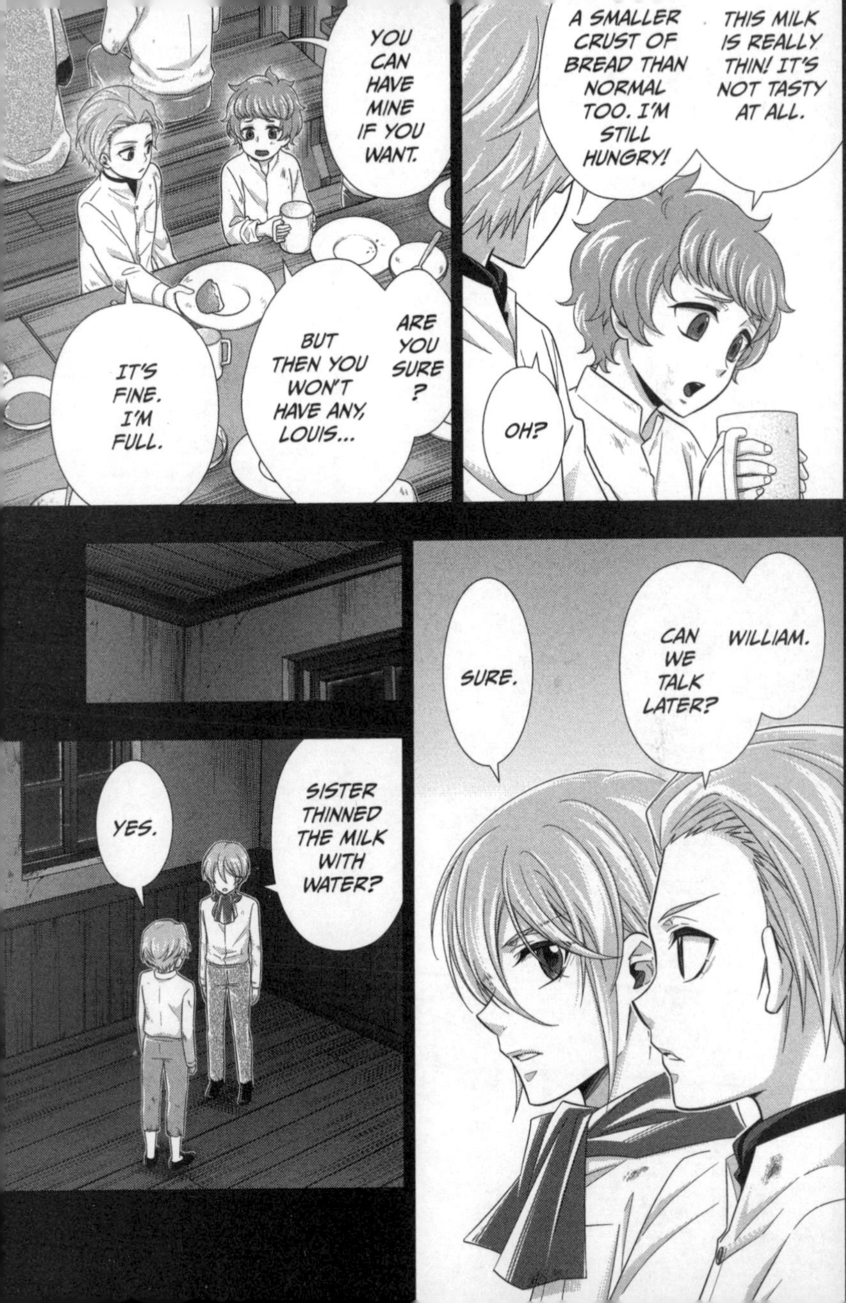
THIS MILK IS REALLY THIN! IT'S NOT TASTY AT ALL.
A SMALLER CRUST OF BREAD THAN NORMAL TOO. I'M STILL HUNGRY!
OH?
YOU CAN HAVE MINE IF YOU WANT.
ARE YOU SURE?
BUT THEN YOU WON'T HAVE ANY, LOUIS...
IT'S FINE. I'M FULL.
WILLIAM.
CAN WE TALK LATER?
SURE.
SISTER THINNED THE MILK WITH WATER?
YES.

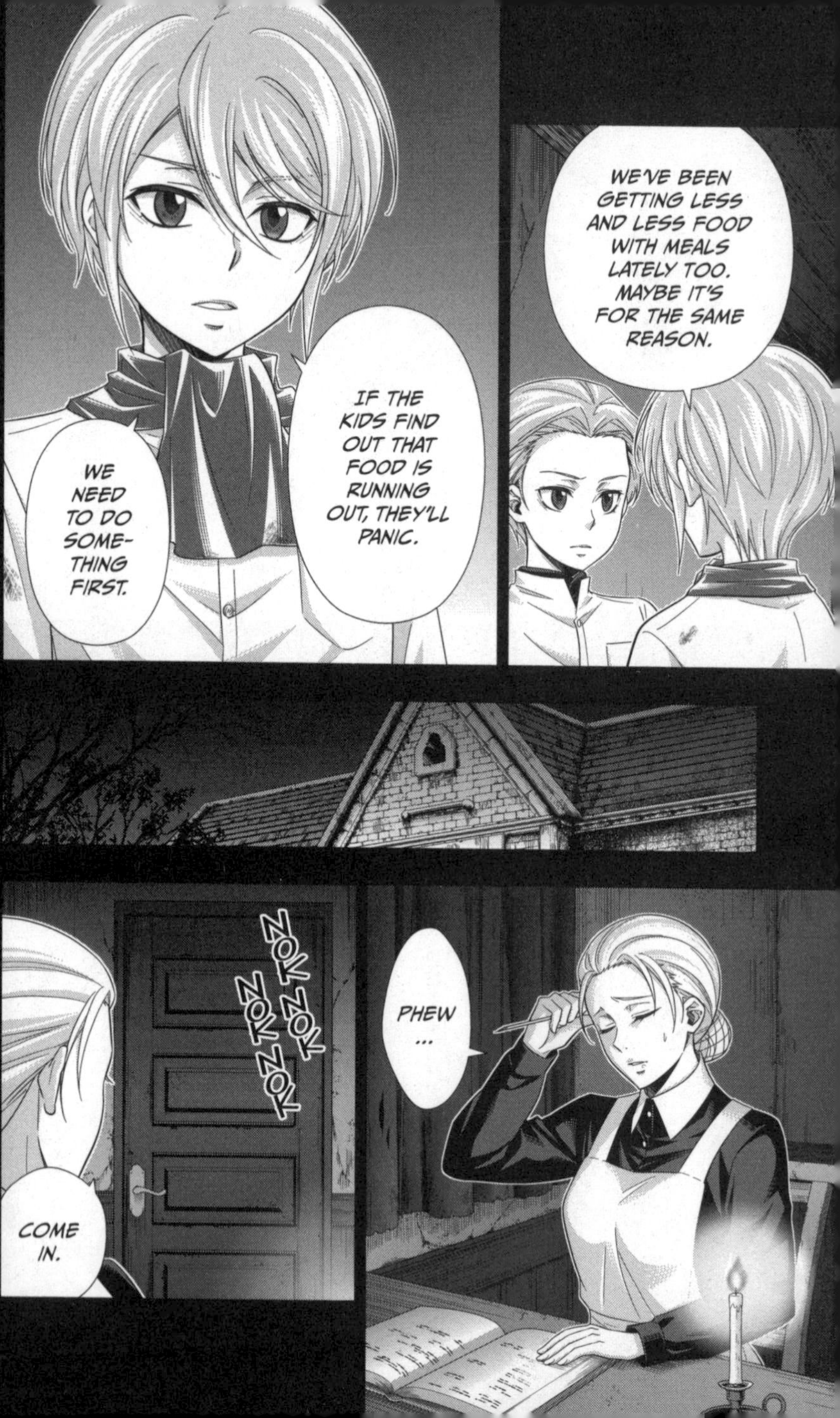
WE'VE BEEN GETTING LESS AND LESS FOOD WITH MEALS LATELY TOO. MAYBE IT'S FOR THE SAME REASON.
IF THE KIDS FIND OUT THAT FOOD IS RUNNING OUT, THEY'LL PANIC.
WE NEED TO DO SOME-THING FIRST.
PHEW ...
KON KON
KON KON
COME IN.

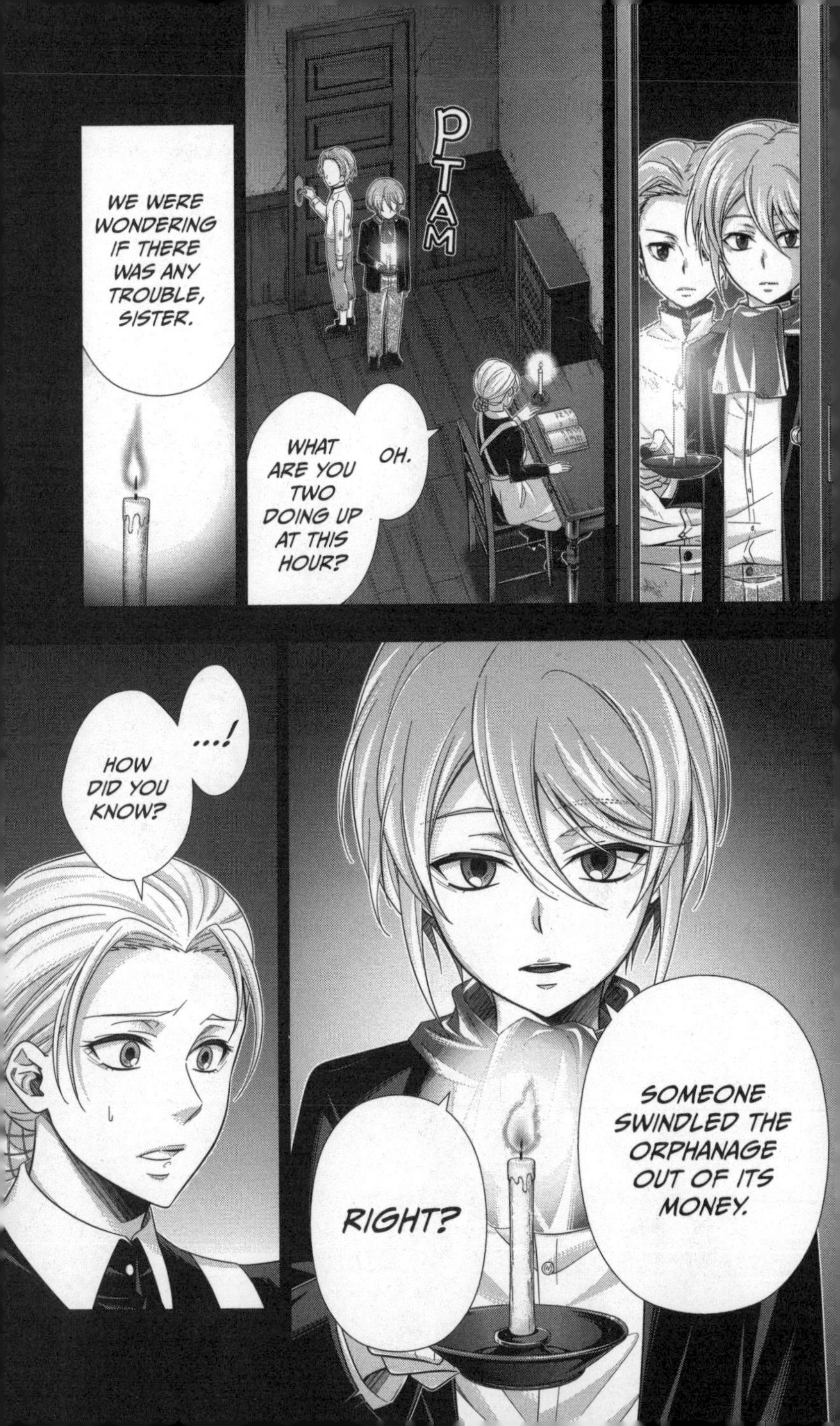
PTAM
OH.
WHAT ARE YOU TWO DOING UP AT THIS HOUR?
WE WERE WONDERING IF THERE WAS ANY TROUBLE, SISTER.
SOMEONE SWINDLED THE ORPHANAGE OUT OF ITS MONEY.
RIGHT?
...!
HOW DID YOU KNOW?

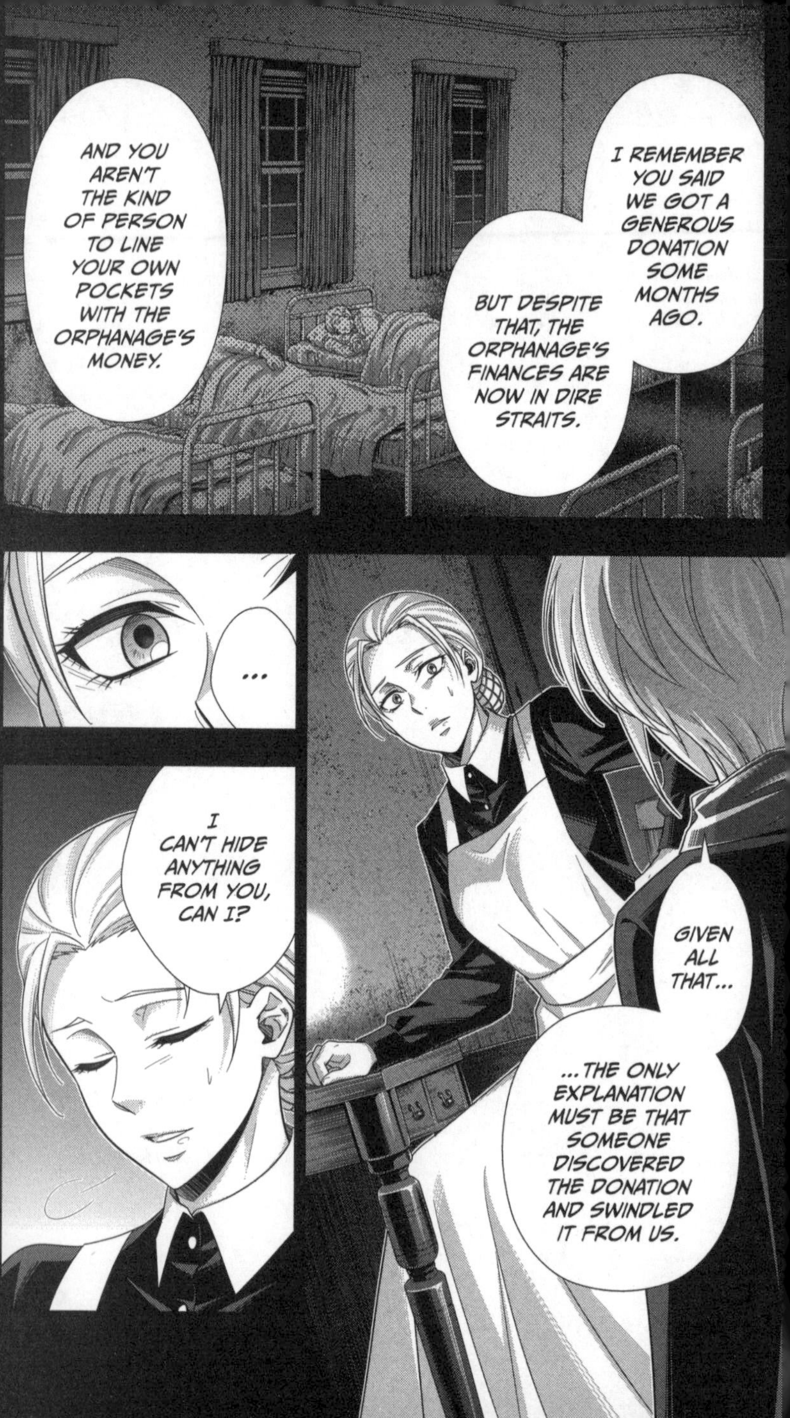
I REMEMBER YOU SAID WE GOT A GENEROUS DONATION SOME MONTHS AGO.
BUT DESPITE THAT, THE ORPHANAGE'S FINANCES ARE NOW IN DIRE STRAITS.
AND YOU AREN'T THE KIND OF PERSON TO LINE YOUR OWN POCKETS WITH THE ORPHANAGE'S MONEY.
GIVEN ALL THAT...
...THE ONLY EXPLANATION MUST BE THAT SOMEONE DISCOVERED THE DONATION AND SWINDLED IT FROM US.
...
I CAN'T HIDE ANYTHING FROM YOU, CAN I?

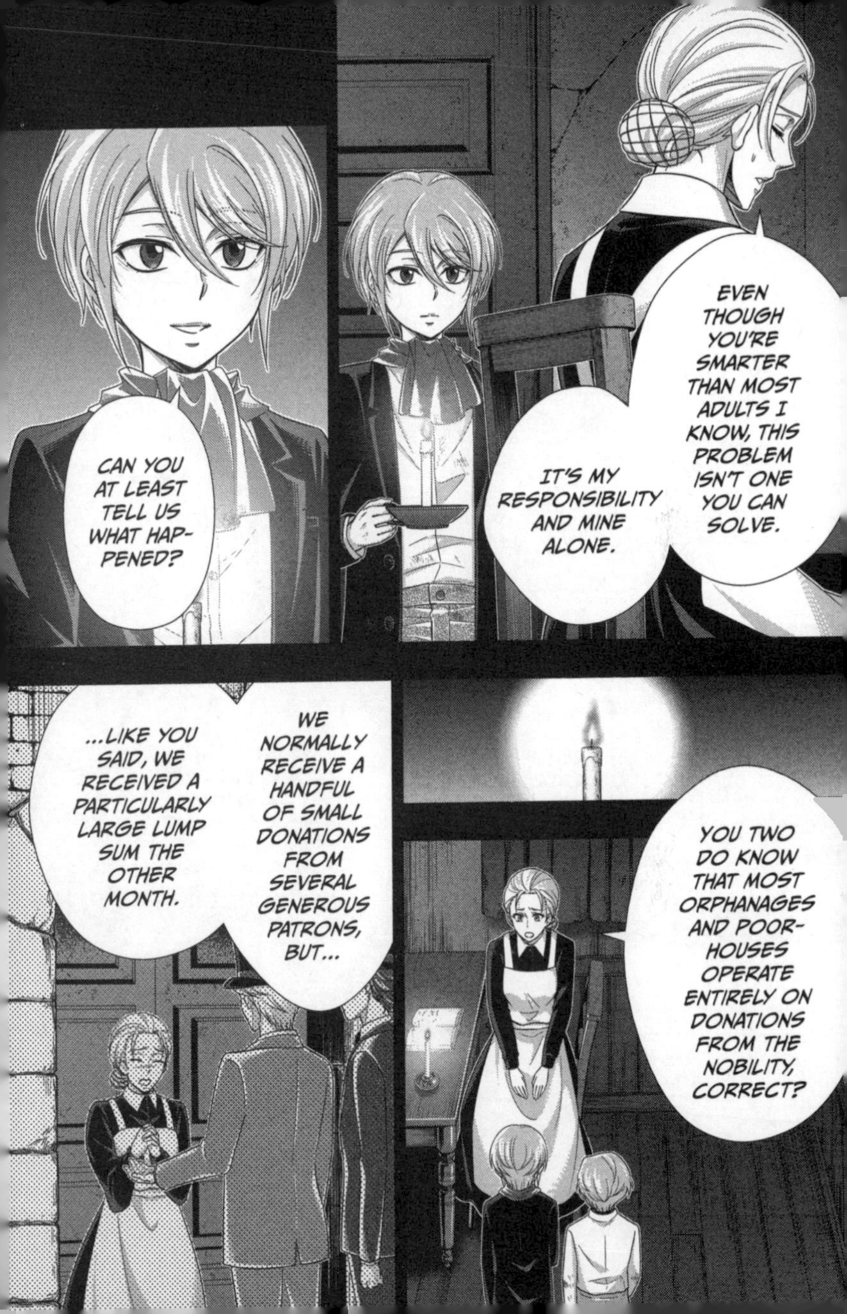
EVEN THOUGH YOU'RE SMARTER THAN MOST ADULTS I KNOW, THIS PROBLEM ISN'T ONE YOU CAN SOLVE.
IT'S MY RESPONSIBILITY AND MINE ALONE.
CAN YOU AT LEAST TELL US WHAT HAP-PENED?
YOU TWO DO KNOW THAT MOST ORPHANAGES AND POOR-HOUSES OPERATE ENTIRELY ON DONATIONS FROM THE NOBILITY, CORRECT?
WE NORMALLY RECEIVE A HANDFUL OF SMALL DONATIONS FROM SEVERAL GENEROUS PATRONS, BUT...
...LIKE YOU SAID, WE RECEIVED A PARTICULARLY LARGE LUMP SUM THE OTHER MONTH.

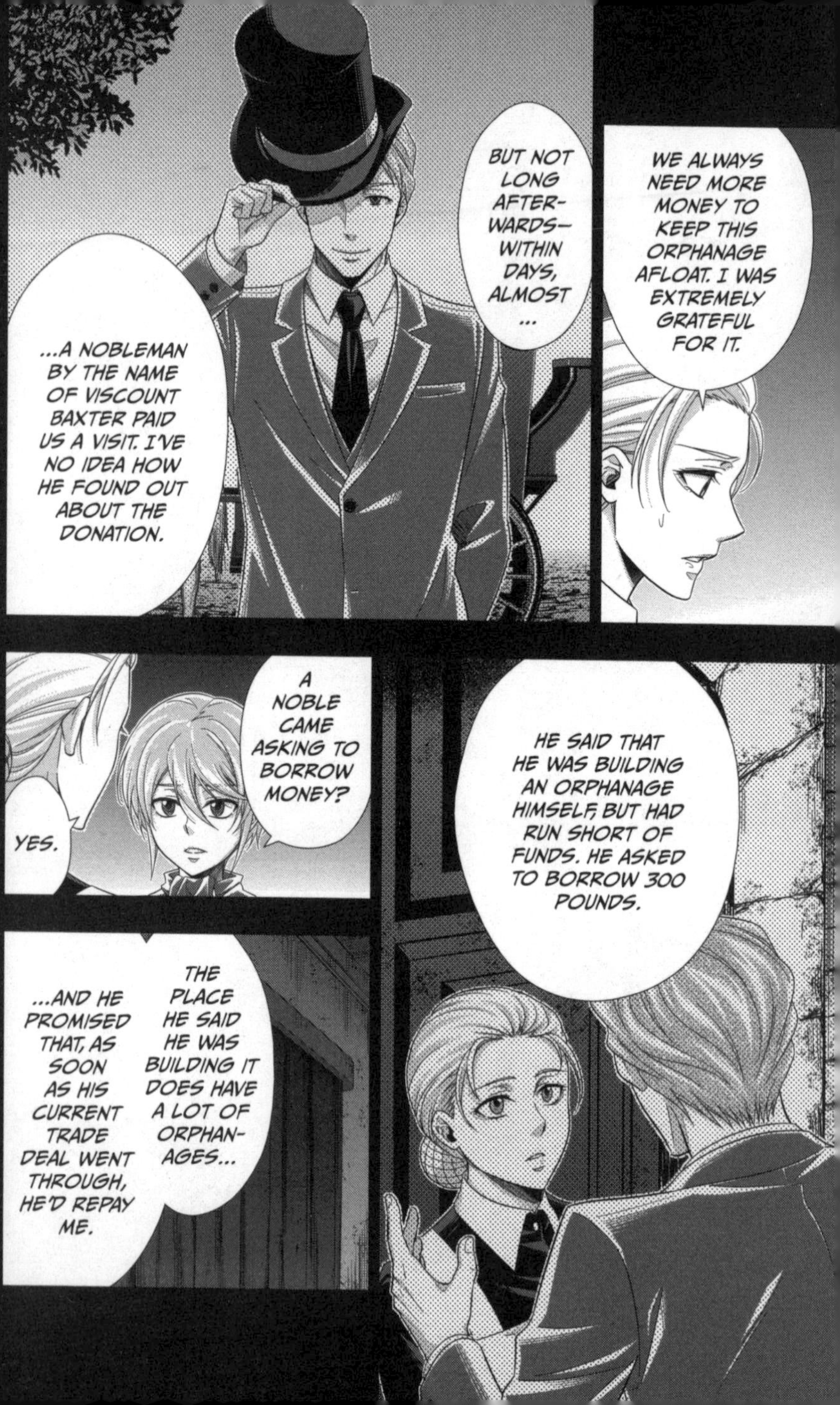
WE ALWAYS NEED MORE MONEY TO KEEP THIS ORPHANAGE AFLOAT. I WAS EXTREMELY GRATEFUL FOR IT.
BUT NOT LONG AFTER-WARDS—WITHIN DAYS, ALMOST...
...A NOBLEMAN BY THE NAME OF VISCOUNT BAXTER PAID US A VISIT. I'VE NO IDEA HOW HE FOUND OUT ABOUT THE DONATION.
HE SAID THAT HE WAS BUILDING AN ORPHANAGE HIMSELF, BUT HAD RUN SHORT OF FUNDS. HE ASKED TO BORROW 300 POUNDS.
A NOBLE CAME ASKING TO BORROW MONEY?
YES.
THE PLACE HE SAID HE WAS BUILDING IT DOES HAVE A LOT OF ORPHAN-AGES...
...AND HE PROMISED THAT, AS SOON AS HIS CURRENT TRADE DEAL WENT THROUGH, HE'D REPAY ME.

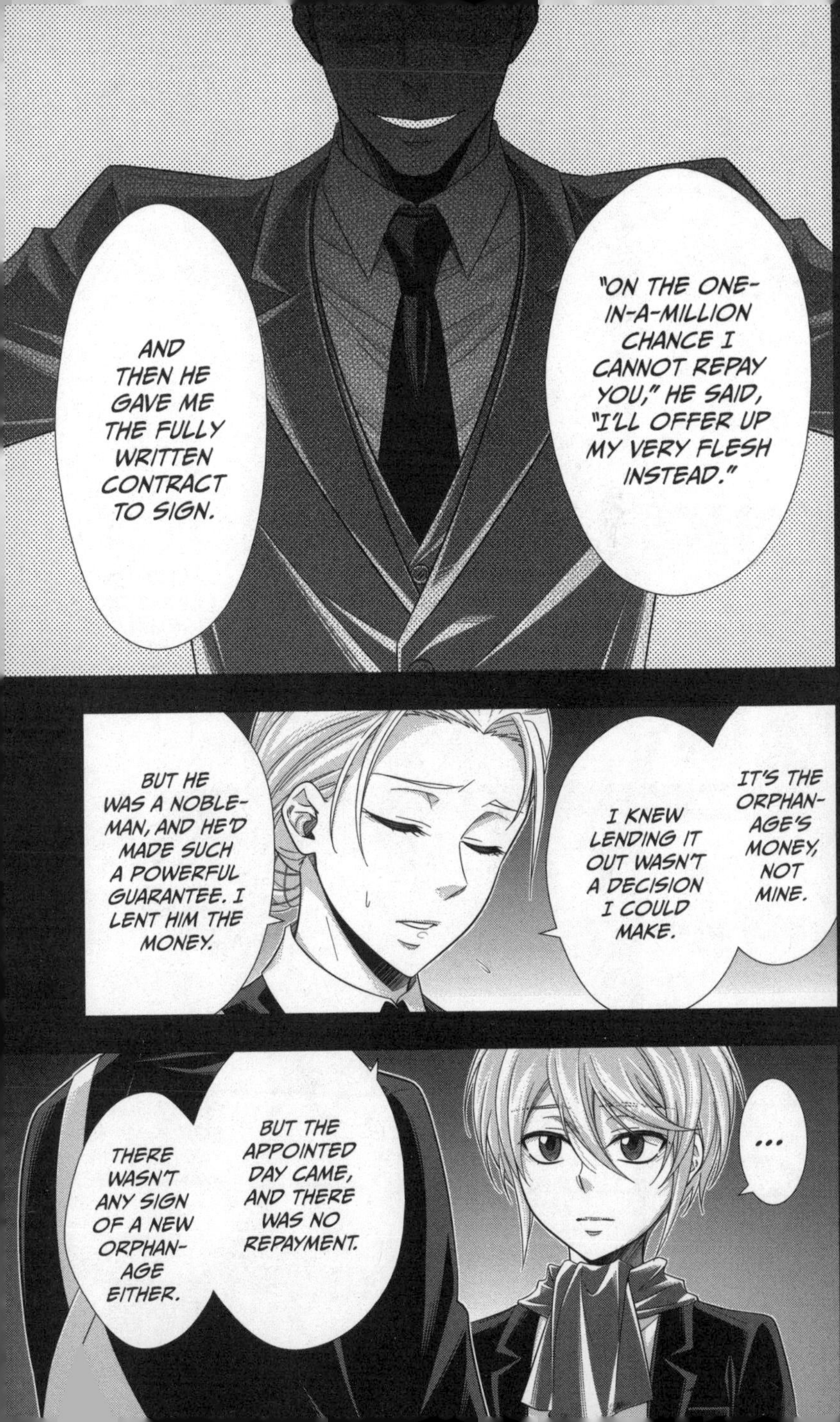
"ON THE ONE-IN-A-MILLION CHANCE I CANNOT REPAY YOU," HE SAID, "I'LL OFFER UP MY VERY FLESH INSTEAD."
AND THEN HE GAVE ME THE FULLY WRITTEN CONTRACT TO SIGN.
IT'S THE ORPHAN-AGE'S MONEY, NOT MINE.
I KNEW LENDING IT OUT WASN'T A DECISION I COULD MAKE.
BUT HE WAS A NOBLE-MAN, AND HE'D MADE SUCH A POWERFUL GUARANTEE. I LENT HIM THE MONEY.
...
BUT THE APPOINTED DAY CAME, AND THERE WAS NO REPAYMENT.
THERE WASN'T ANY SIGN OF A NEW ORPHAN-AGE EITHER.

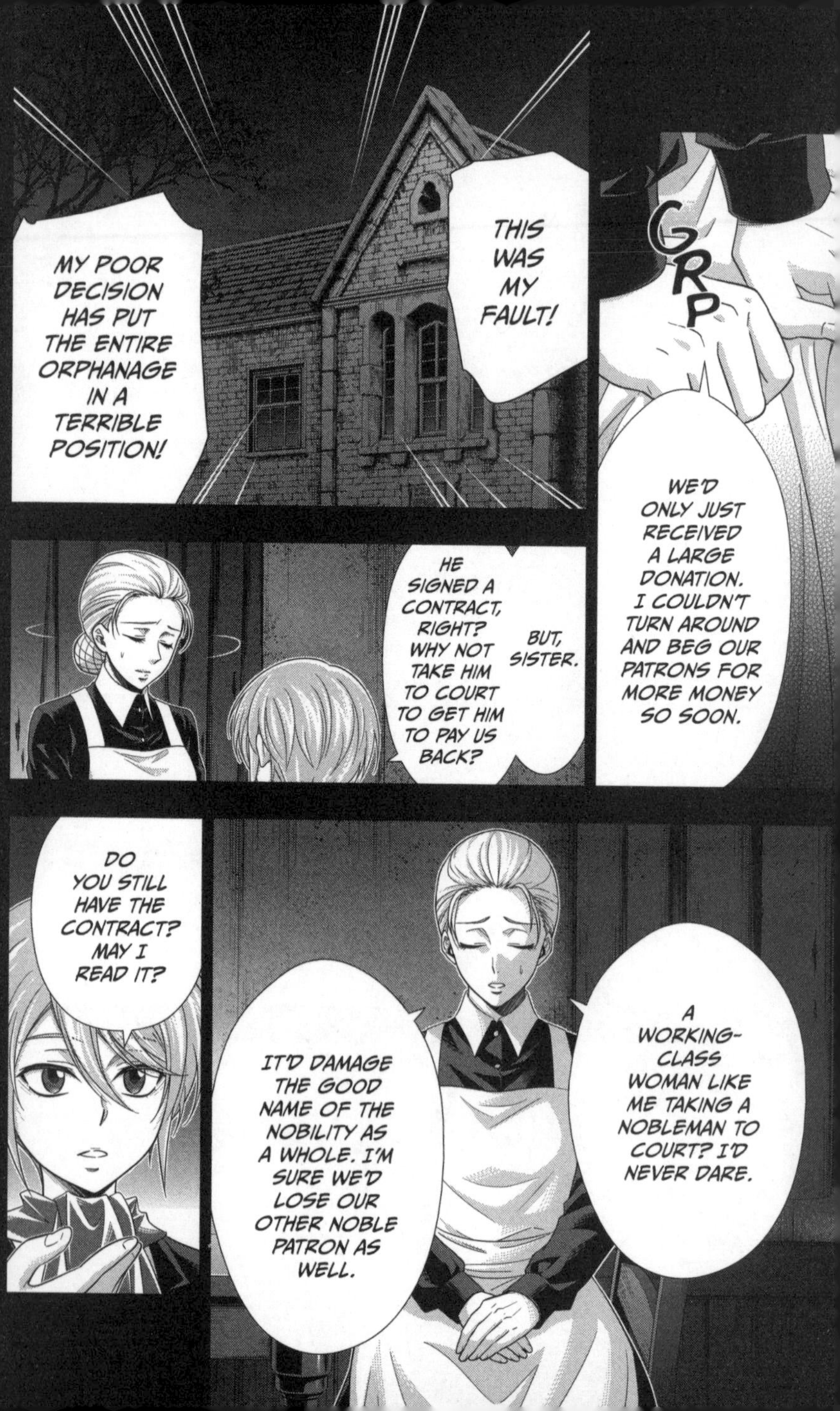
THIS WAS MY FAULT!
MY POOR DECISION HAS PUT THE ENTIRE ORPHANAGE IN A TERRIBLE POSITION!
GRP
WE'D ONLY JUST RECEIVED A LARGE DONATION. I COULDN'T TURN AROUND AND BEG OUR PATRONS FOR MORE MONEY SO SOON.
BUT, SISTER.
HE SIGNED A CONTRACT, RIGHT? WHY NOT TAKE HIM TO COURT TO GET HIM TO PAY US BACK?
A WORKING-CLASS WOMAN LIKE ME TAKING A NOBLEMAN TO COURT? I'D NEVER DARE.
IT'D DAMAGE THE GOOD NAME OF THE NOBILITY AS A WHOLE. I'M SURE WE'D LOSE OUR OTHER NOBLE PATRON AS WELL.
DO YOU STILL HAVE THE CONTRACT? MAY I READ IT?

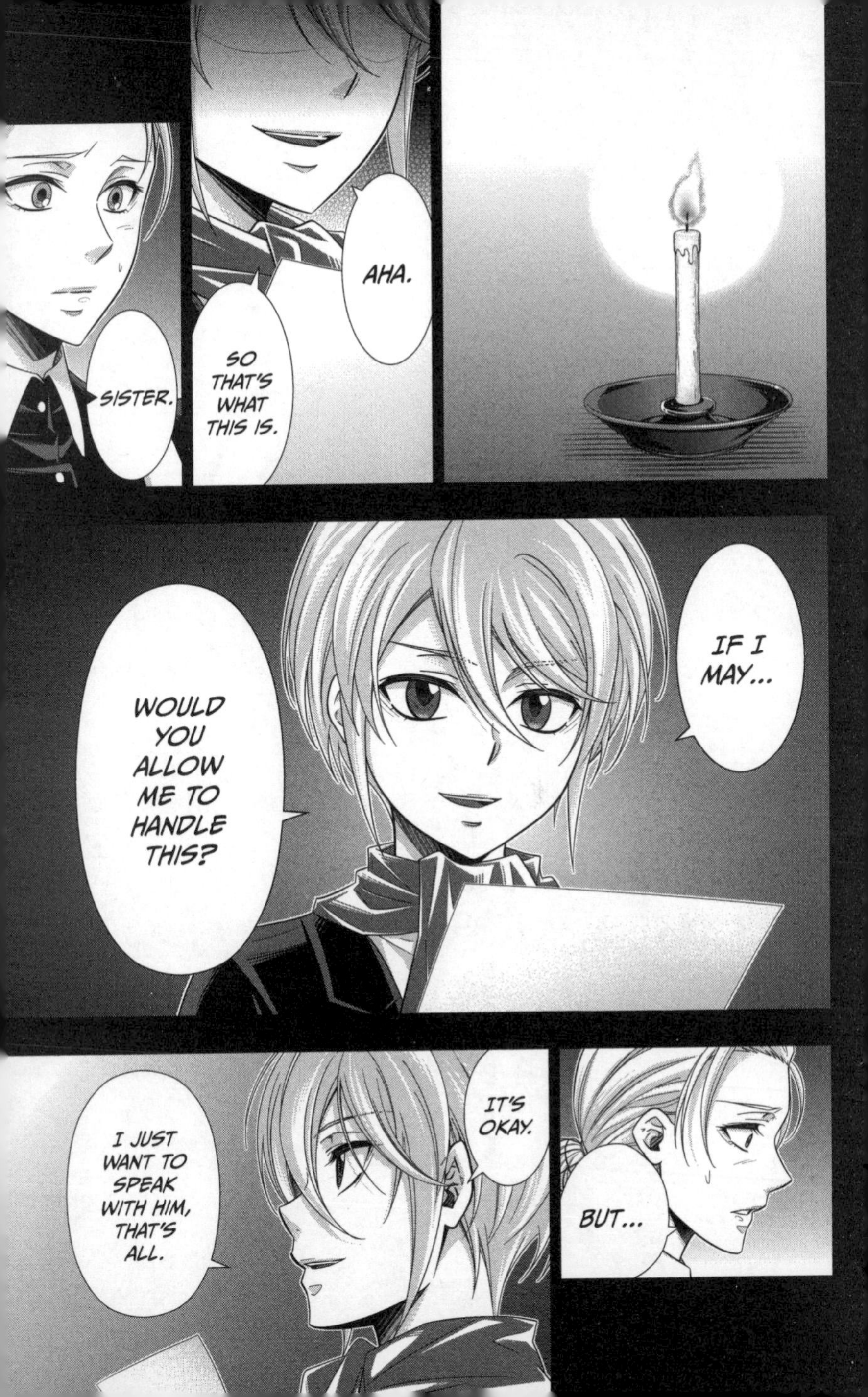
AHA.
SO THAT'S WHAT THIS IS.
SISTER.
IF I MAY...
WOULD YOU ALLOW ME TO HANDLE THIS?
BUT...
IT'S OKAY.
I JUST WANT TO SPEAK WITH HIM, THAT'S ALL.

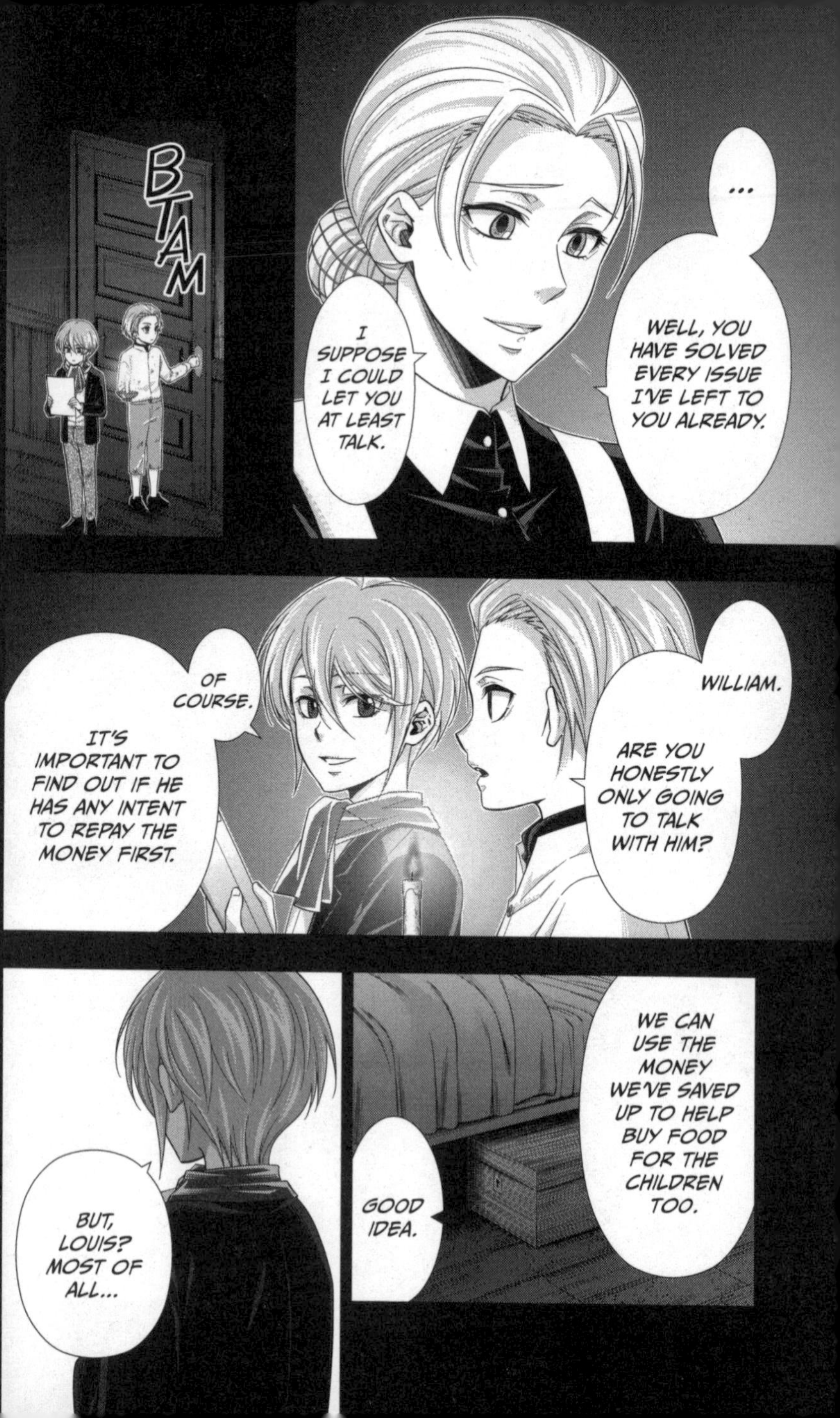
...
WELL, YOU HAVE SOLVED EVERY ISSUE I'VE LEFT TO YOU ALREADY.
I SUPPOSE I COULD LET YOU AT LEAST TALK.
BTAM
WILLIAM.
ARE YOU HONESTLY ONLY GOING TO TALK WITH HIM?
OF COURSE.
IT'S IMPORTANT TO FIND OUT IF HE HAS ANY INTENT TO REPAY THE MONEY FIRST.
WE CAN USE THE MONEY WE'VE SAVED UP TO HELP BUY FOOD FOR THE CHILDREN TOO.
GOOD IDEA.
BUT, LOUIS? MOST OF ALL...

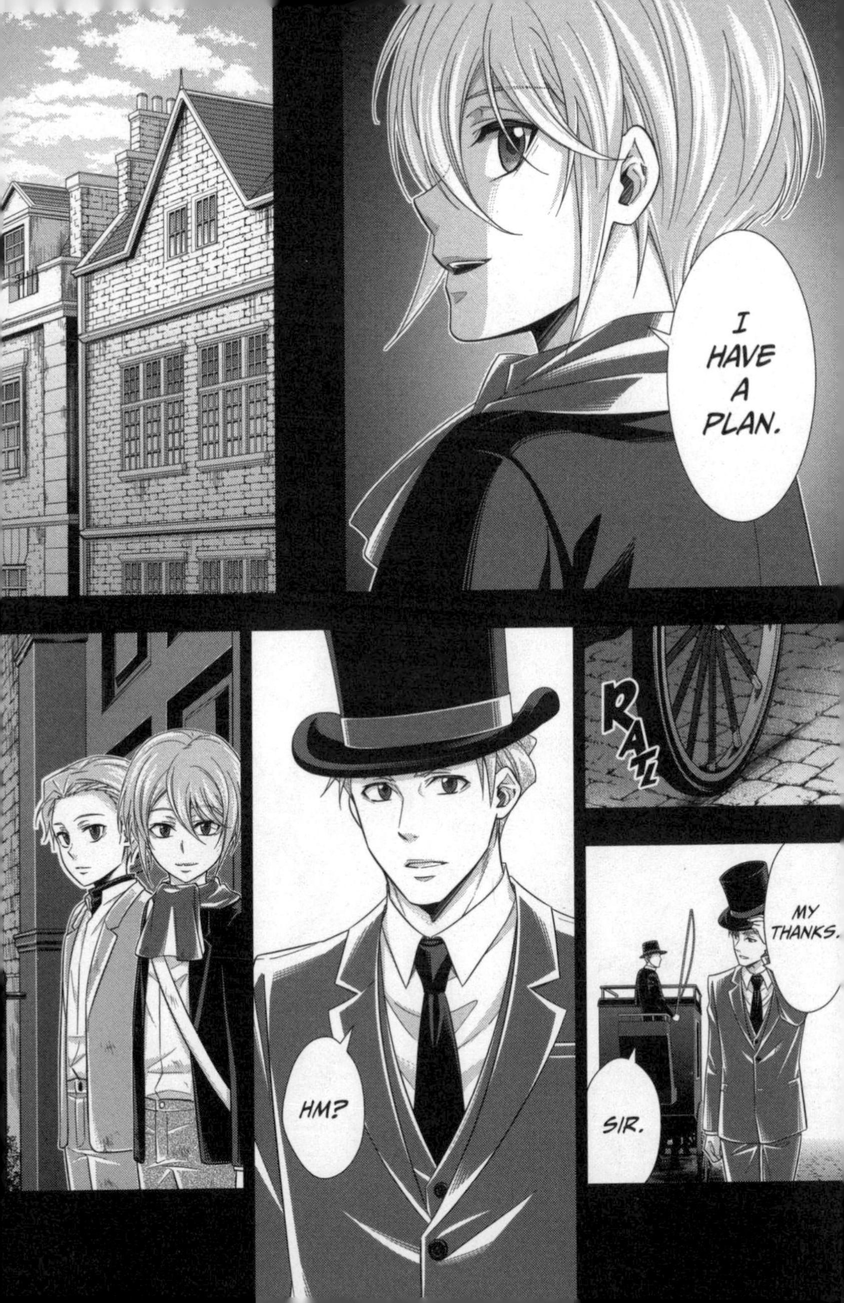
I HAVE A PLAN.
RATTL
MY THANKS.
SIR.
HM?

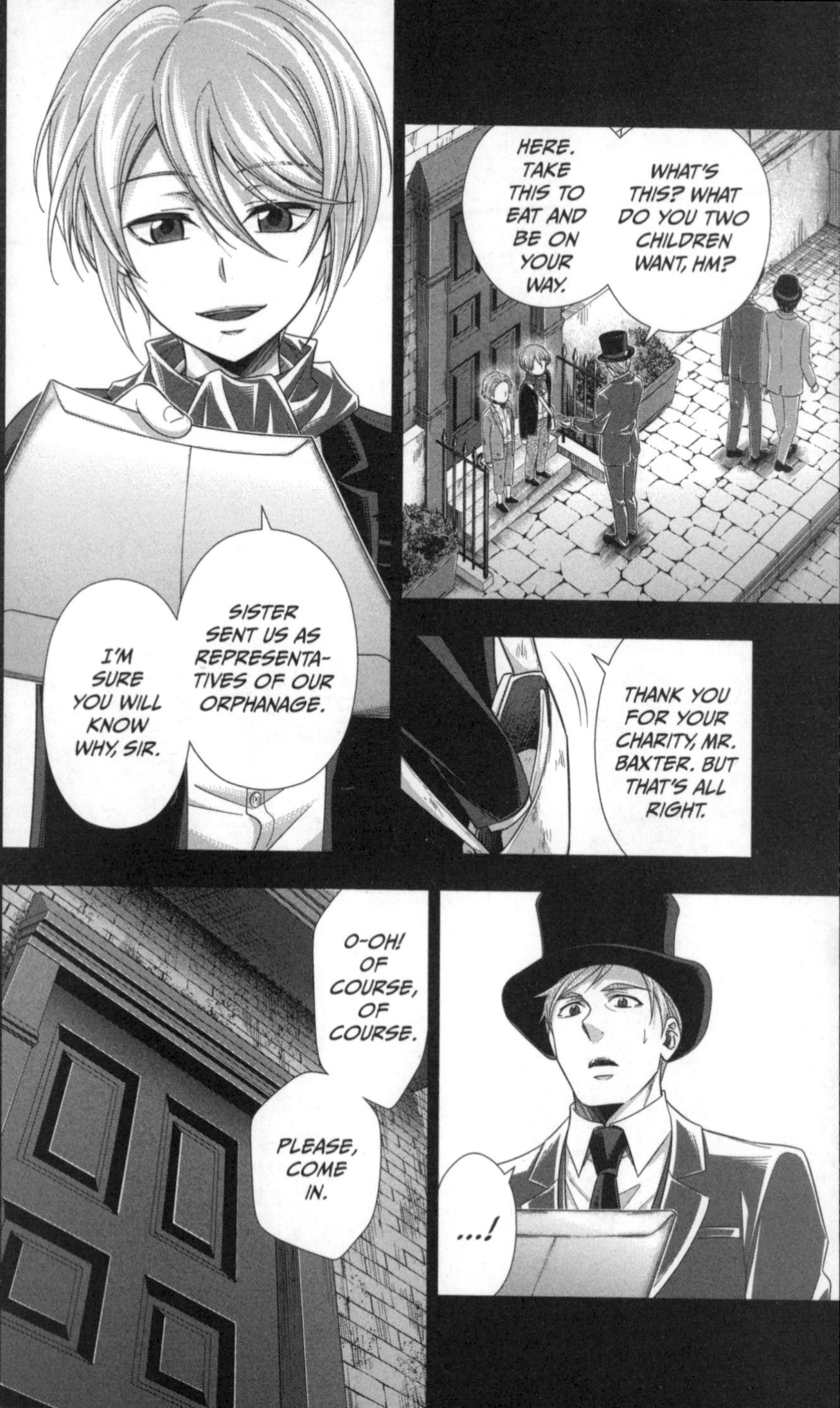
WHAT'S THIS? WHAT DO YOU TWO CHILDREN WANT, HM?
HERE. TAKE THIS TO EAT AND BE ON YOUR WAY.
THANK YOU FOR YOUR CHARITY, MR. BAXTER. BUT THAT'S ALL RIGHT.
SISTER SENT US AS REPRESENTATIVES OF OUR ORPHANAGE.
I'M SURE YOU WILL KNOW WHY, SIR.
...!
O-OH! OF COURSE, OF COURSE.
PLEASE, COME IN.

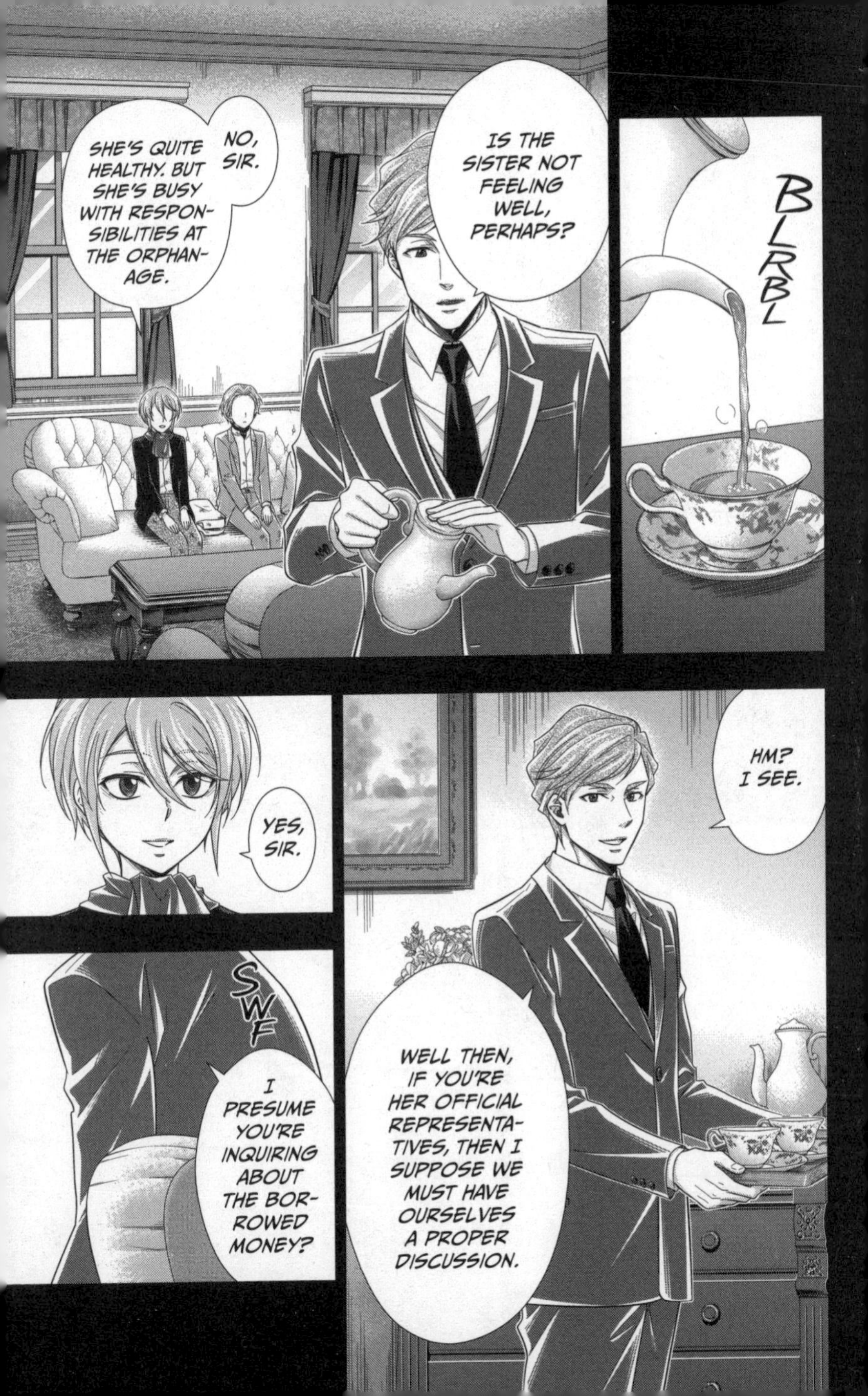
BLRBL
IS THE SISTER NOT FEELING WELL, PERHAPS?
NO, SIR.
SHE'S QUITE HEALTHY. BUT SHE'S BUSY WITH RESPON-SIBILITIES AT THE ORPHAN-AGE.
HM? I SEE.
WELL THEN, IF YOU'RE HER OFFICIAL REPRESENTA-TIVES, THEN I SUPPOSE WE MUST HAVE OURSELVES A PROPER DISCUSSION.
YES, SIR.
SWF
I PRESUME YOU'RE INQUIRING ABOUT THE BOR-ROWED MONEY?

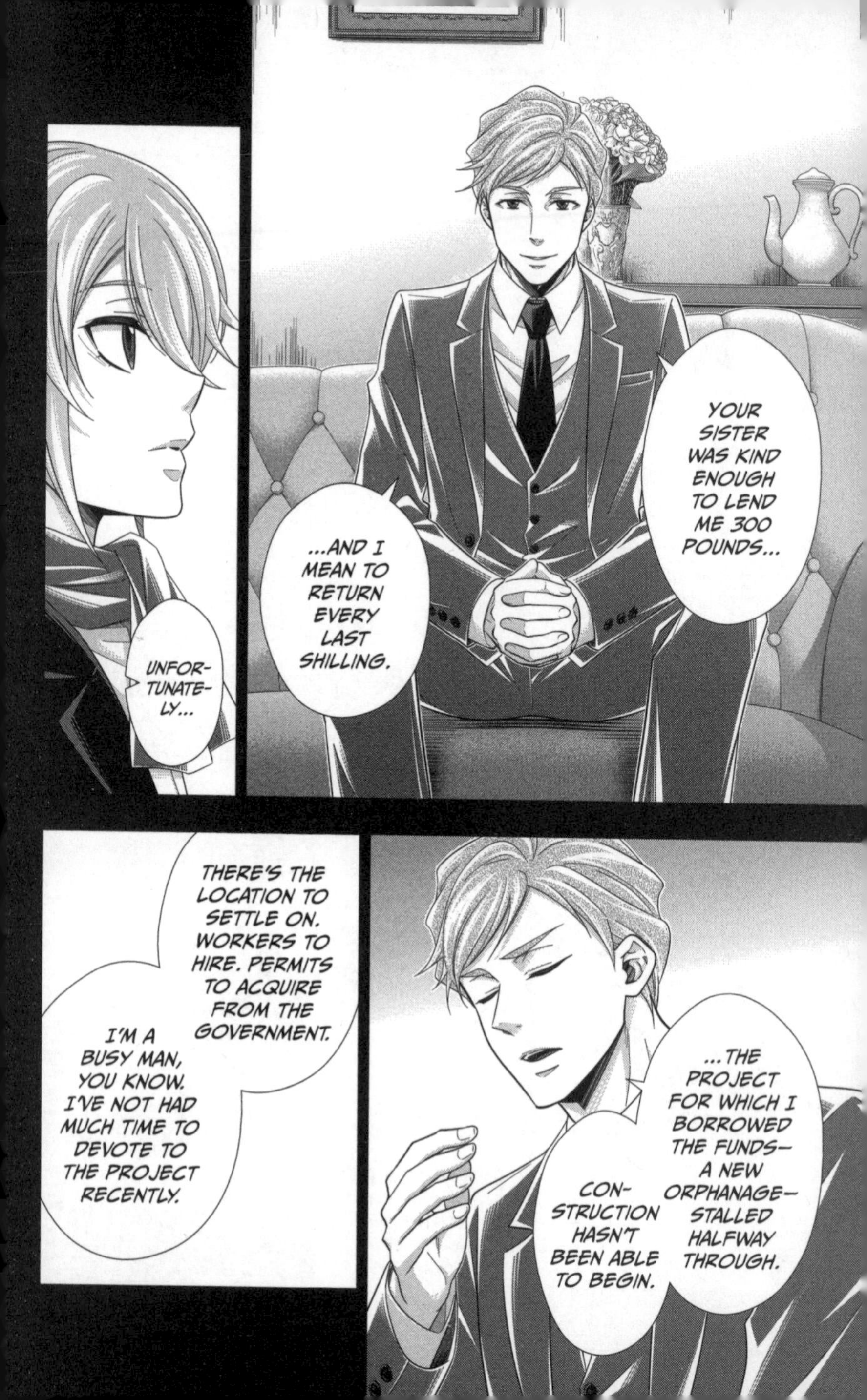
YOUR SISTER WAS KIND ENOUGH TO LEND ME 300 POUNDS...
...AND I MEAN TO RETURN EVERY LAST SHILLING.
UNFOR-TUNATE-LY...
...THE PROJECT FOR WHICH I BORROWED THE FUNDS—A NEW ORPHANAGE—STALLED HALFWAY THROUGH.
CON-STRUCTION HASN'T BEEN ABLE TO BEGIN.
THERE'S THE LOCATION TO SETTLE ON. WORKERS TO HIRE. PERMITS TO ACQUIRE FROM THE GOVERNMENT.
I'M A BUSY MAN, YOU KNOW. I'VE NOT HAD MUCH TIME TO DEVOTE TO THE PROJECT RECENTLY.

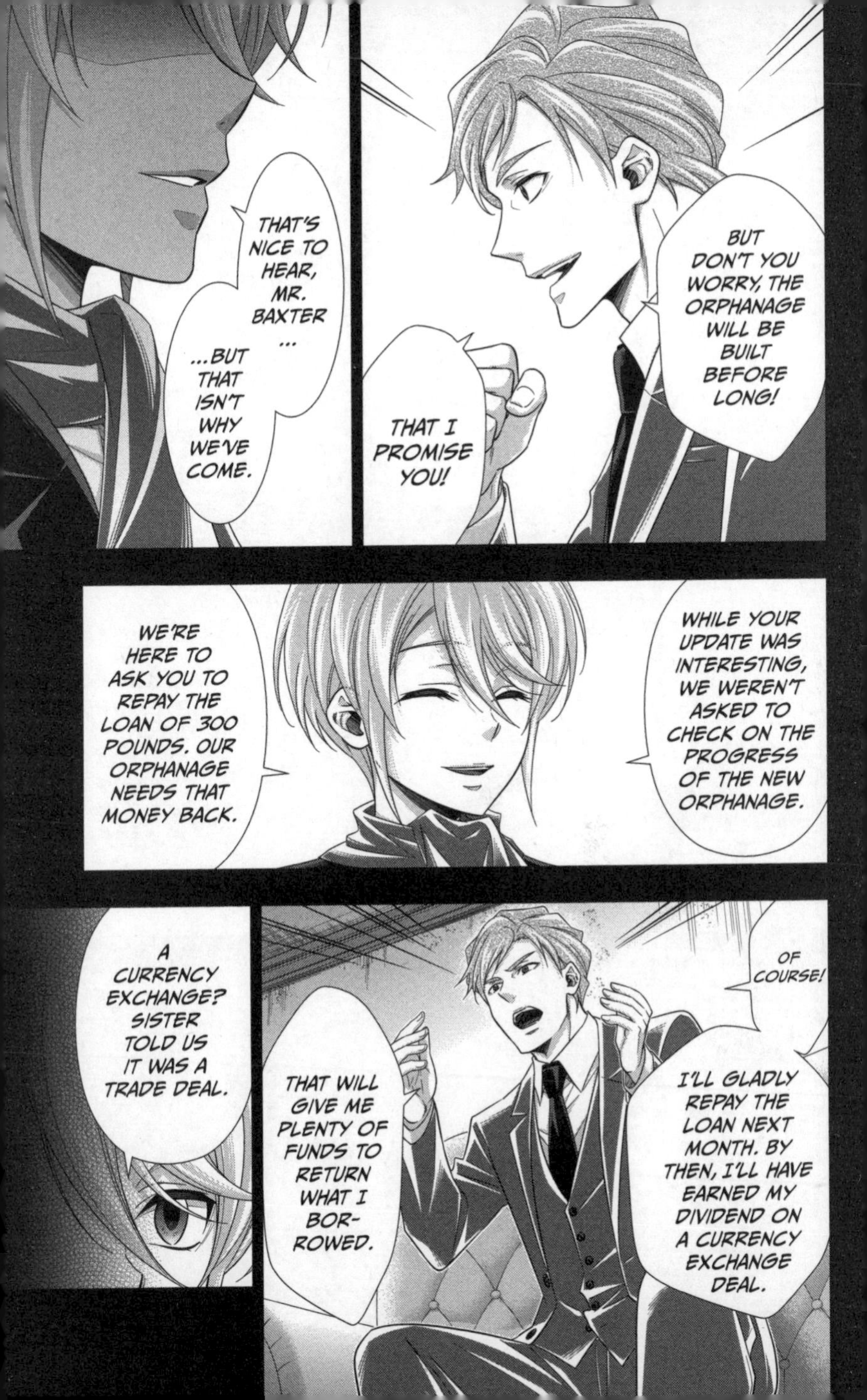
BUT DON'T YOU WORRY, THE ORPHANAGE WILL BE BUILT BEFORE LONG!
THAT I PROMISE YOU!
THAT'S NICE TO HEAR, MR. BAXTER ...
...BUT THAT ISN'T WHY WE'VE COME.
WHILE YOUR UPDATE WAS INTERESTING, WE WEREN'T ASKED TO CHECK ON THE PROGRESS OF THE NEW ORPHANAGE.
WE'RE HERE TO ASK YOU TO REPAY THE LOAN OF 300 POUNDS. OUR ORPHANAGE NEEDS THAT MONEY BACK.
OF COURSE!
I'LL GLADLY REPAY THE LOAN NEXT MONTH. BY THEN, I'LL HAVE EARNED MY DIVIDEND ON A CURRENCY EXCHANGE DEAL.
THAT WILL GIVE ME PLENTY OF FUNDS TO RETURN WHAT I BOR-ROWED.
A CURRENCY EXCHANGE? SISTER TOLD US IT WAS A TRADE DEAL.

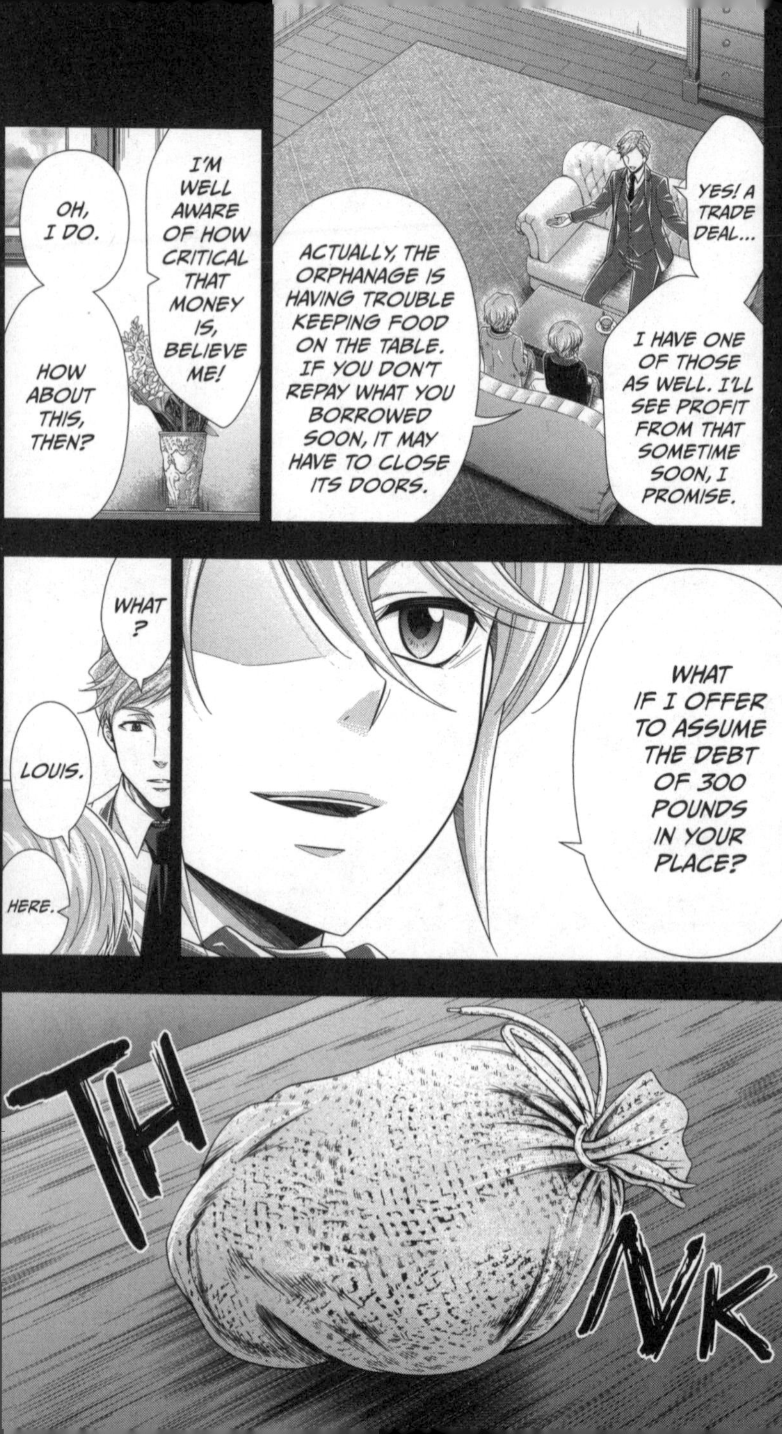
YES! A TRADE DEAL...
I HAVE ONE OF THOSE AS WELL. I'LL SEE PROFIT FROM THAT SOMETIME SOON, I PROMISE.
ACTUALLY, THE ORPHANAGE IS HAVING TROUBLE KEEPING FOOD ON THE TABLE. IF YOU DON'T REPAY WHAT YOU BORROWED SOON, IT MAY HAVE TO CLOSE ITS DOORS.
I'M WELL AWARE OF HOW CRITICAL THAT MONEY IS, BELIEVE ME!
OH, I DO.
HOW ABOUT THIS, THEN?
WHAT IF I OFFER TO ASSUME THE DEBT OF 300 POUNDS IN YOUR PLACE?
WHAT?
LOUIS.
HERE.
THUNK

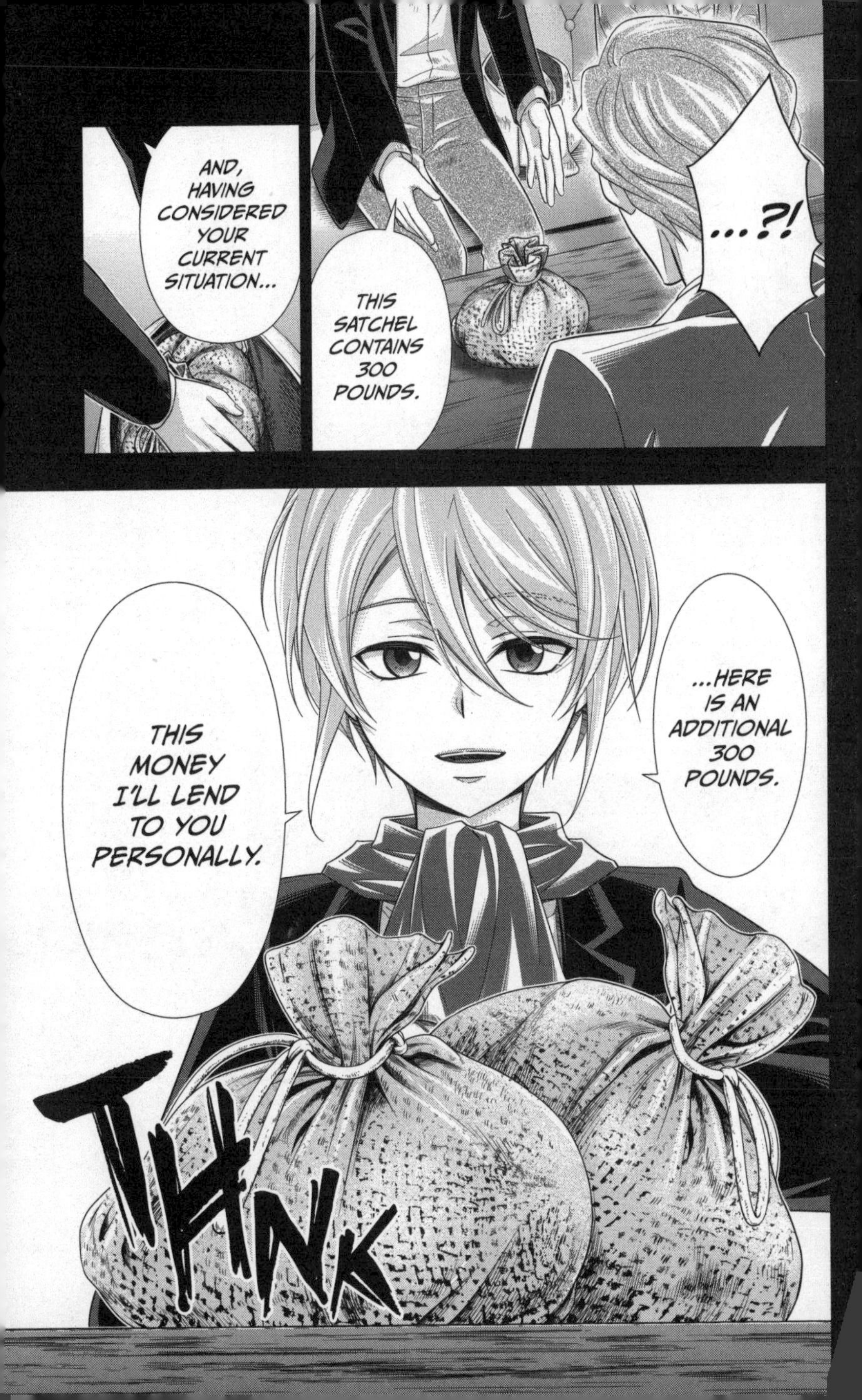
...?!
THIS SATCHEL CONTAINS 300 POUNDS.
AND, HAVING CONSIDERED YOUR CURRENT SITUATION...
...HERE IS AN ADDITIONAL 300 POUNDS.
THIS MONEY I'LL LEND TO YOU PERSONALLY.
THNK

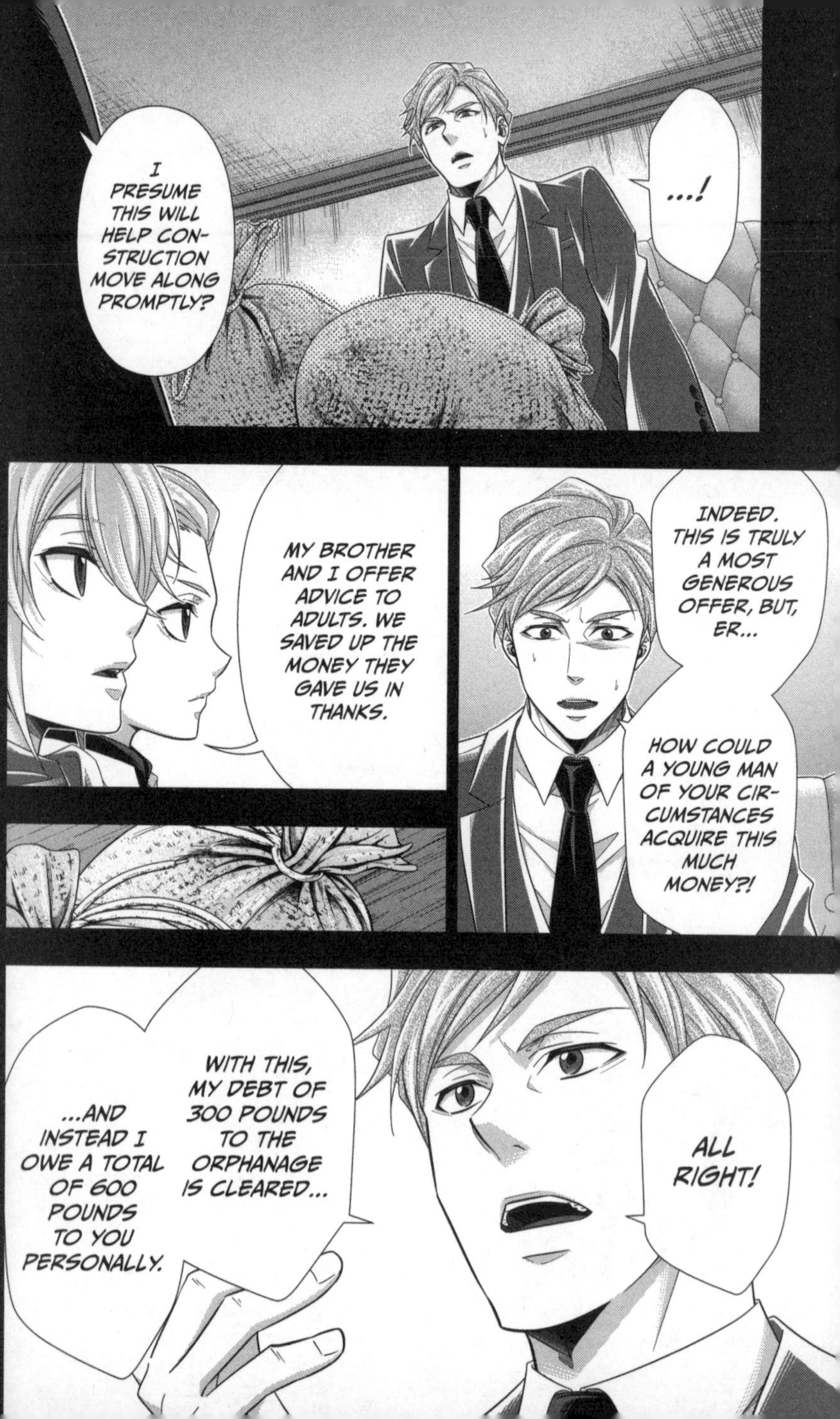

...!
I PRESUME THIS WILL HELP CON-STRUCTION MOVE ALONG PROMPTLY?
INDEED. THIS IS TRULY A MOST GENEROUS OFFER, BUT, ER...
HOW COULD A YOUNG MAN OF YOUR CIR-CUMSTANCES ACQUIRE THIS MUCH MONEY?!
MY BROTHER AND I OFFER ADVICE TO ADULTS. WE SAVED UP THE MONEY THEY GAVE US IN THANKS.
ALL RIGHT!
WITH THIS, MY DEBT OF 300 POUNDS TO THE ORPHANAGE IS CLEARED...
...AND INSTEAD I OWE A TOTAL OF 600 POUNDS TO YOU PERSONALLY.

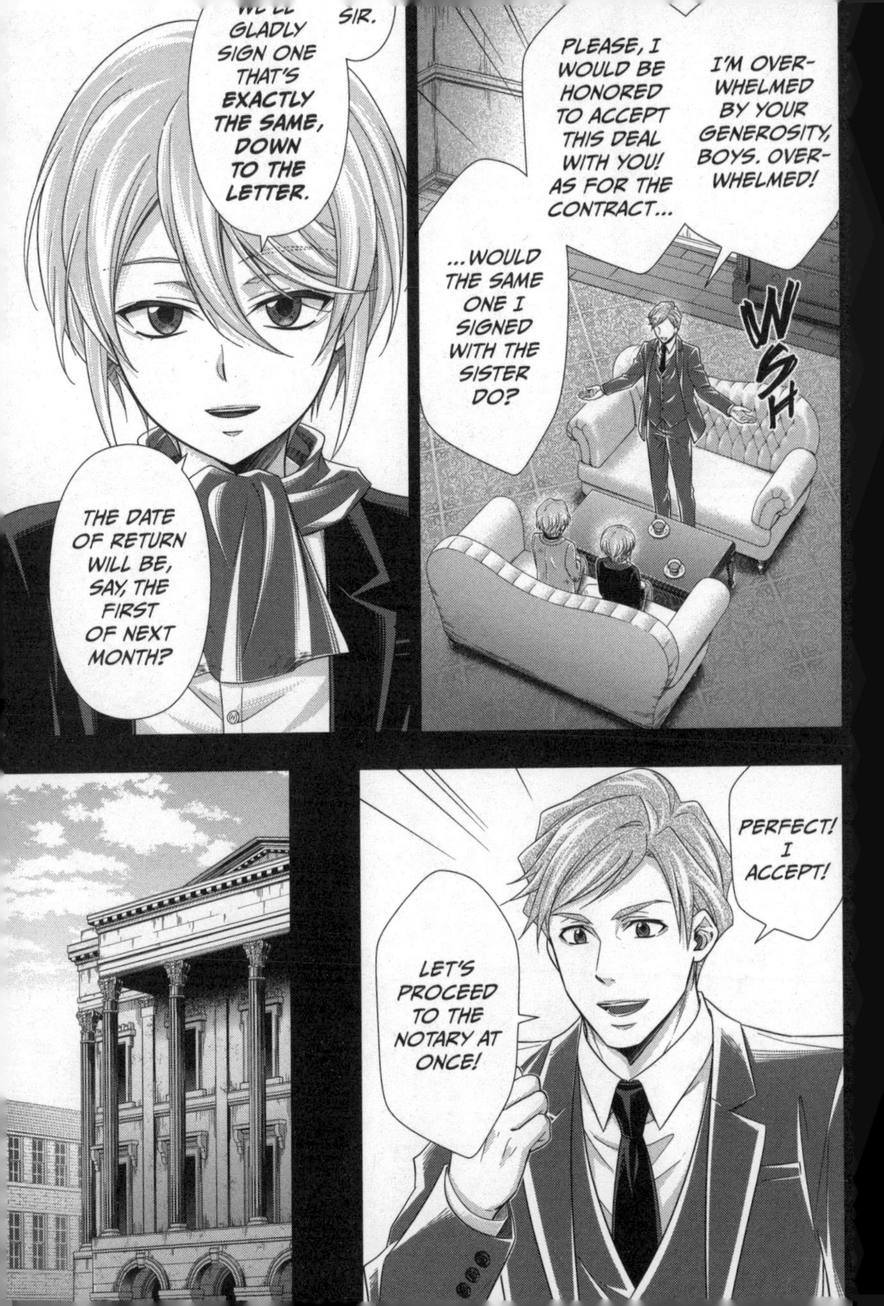
I'M OVER-WHELMED BY YOUR GENEROSITY, BOYS. OVER-WHELMED!
PLEASE, I WOULD BE HONORED TO ACCEPT THIS DEAL WITH YOU! AS FOR THE CONTRACT...
...WOULD THE SAME ONE I SIGNED WITH THE SISTER DO?
WSH
SIR.
GLADLY SIGN ONE THAT'S EXACTLY THE SAME, DOWN TO THE LETTER.
THE DATE OF RETURN WILL BE, SAY, THE FIRST OF NEXT MONTH?
PERFECT! I ACCEPT!
LET'S PROCEED TO THE NOTARY AT ONCE!

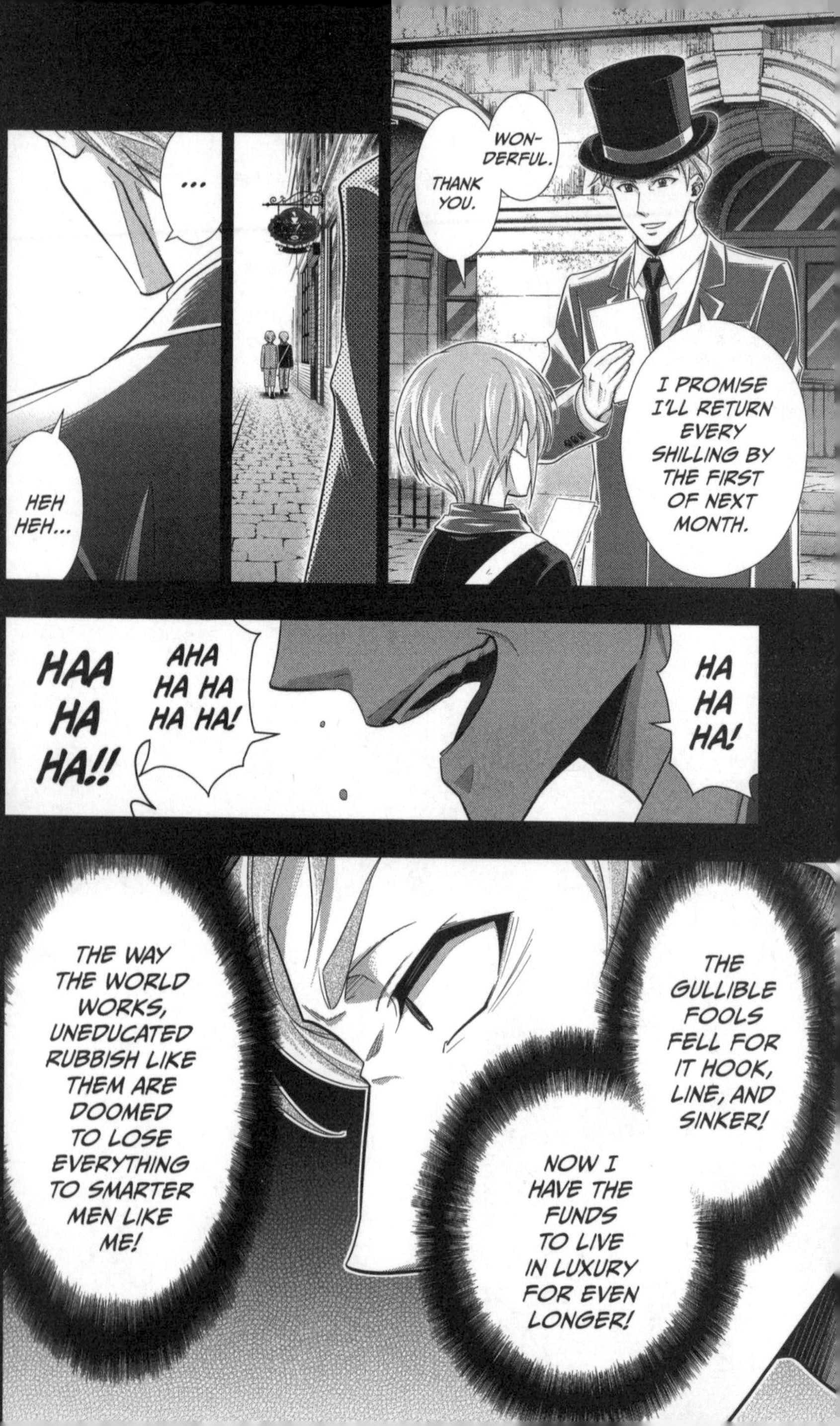
WON-DERFUL.
THANK YOU.
I PROMISE I'LL RETURN EVERY SHILLING BY THE FIRST OF NEXT MONTH.
...
HEH HEH...
HA HA HA!
AHA HA HA HA HA!
HAA HA HA!!
THE GULLIBLE FOOLS FELL FOR IT HOOK, LINE, AND SINKER!
NOW I HAVE THE FUNDS TO LIVE IN LUXURY FOR EVEN LONGER!
THE WAY THE WORLD WORKS, UNEDUCATED RUBBISH LIKE THEM ARE DOOMED TO LOSE EVERYTHING TO SMARTER MEN LIKE ME!

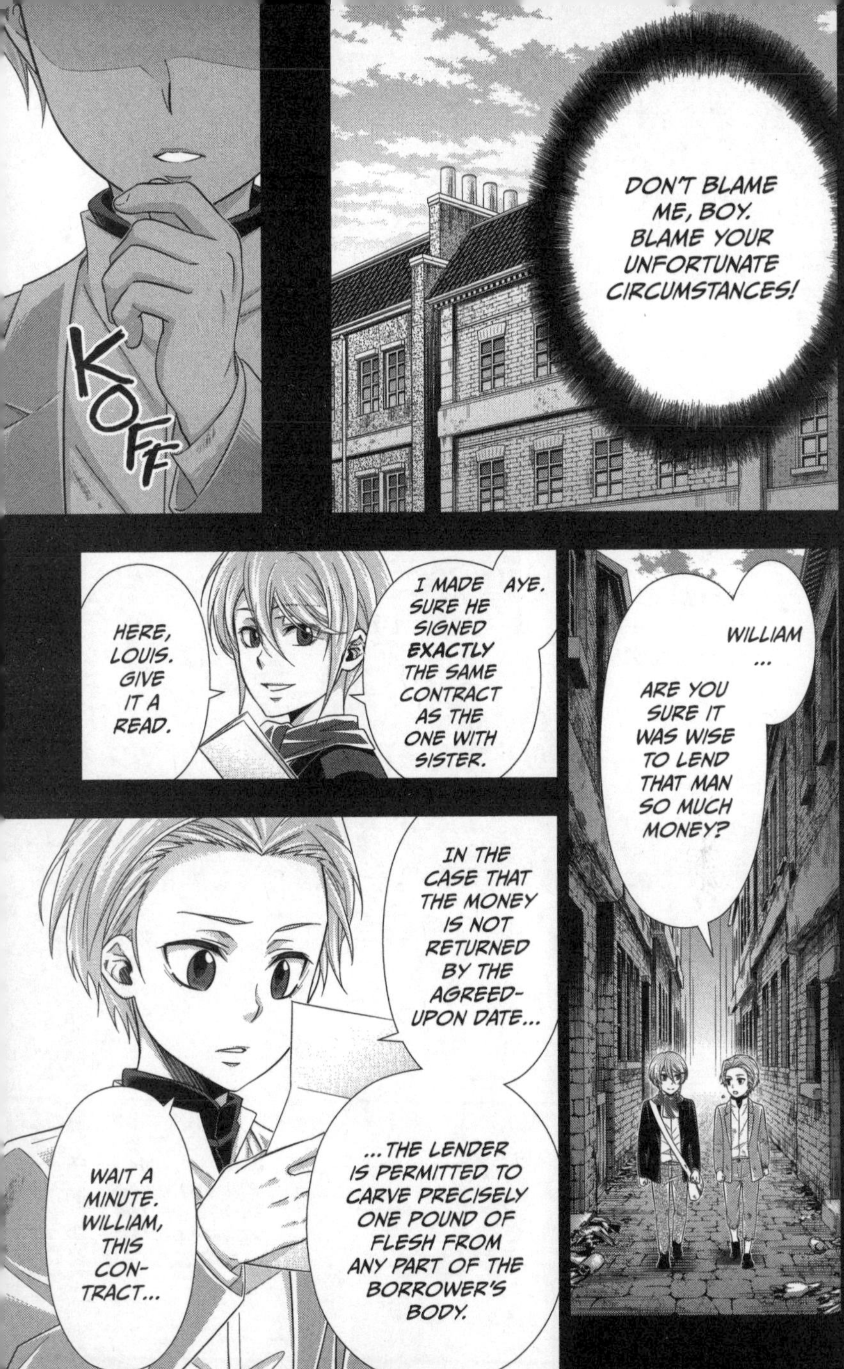
DON'T BLAME ME, BOY. BLAME YOUR UNFORTUNATE CIRCUMSTANCES!
KOFF
WILLIAM ...
ARE YOU SURE IT WAS WISE TO LEND THAT MAN SO MUCH MONEY?
AYE.
I MADE SURE HE SIGNED **EXACTLY** THE SAME CONTRACT AS THE ONE WITH SISTER.
HERE, LOUIS. GIVE IT A READ.
IN THE CASE THAT THE MONEY IS NOT RETURNED BY THE AGREED-UPON DATE...
...THE LENDER IS PERMITTED TO CARVE PRECISELY ONE POUND OF FLESH FROM ANY PART OF THE BORROWER'S BODY.
WAIT A MINUTE. WILLIAM, THIS CON-TRACT...

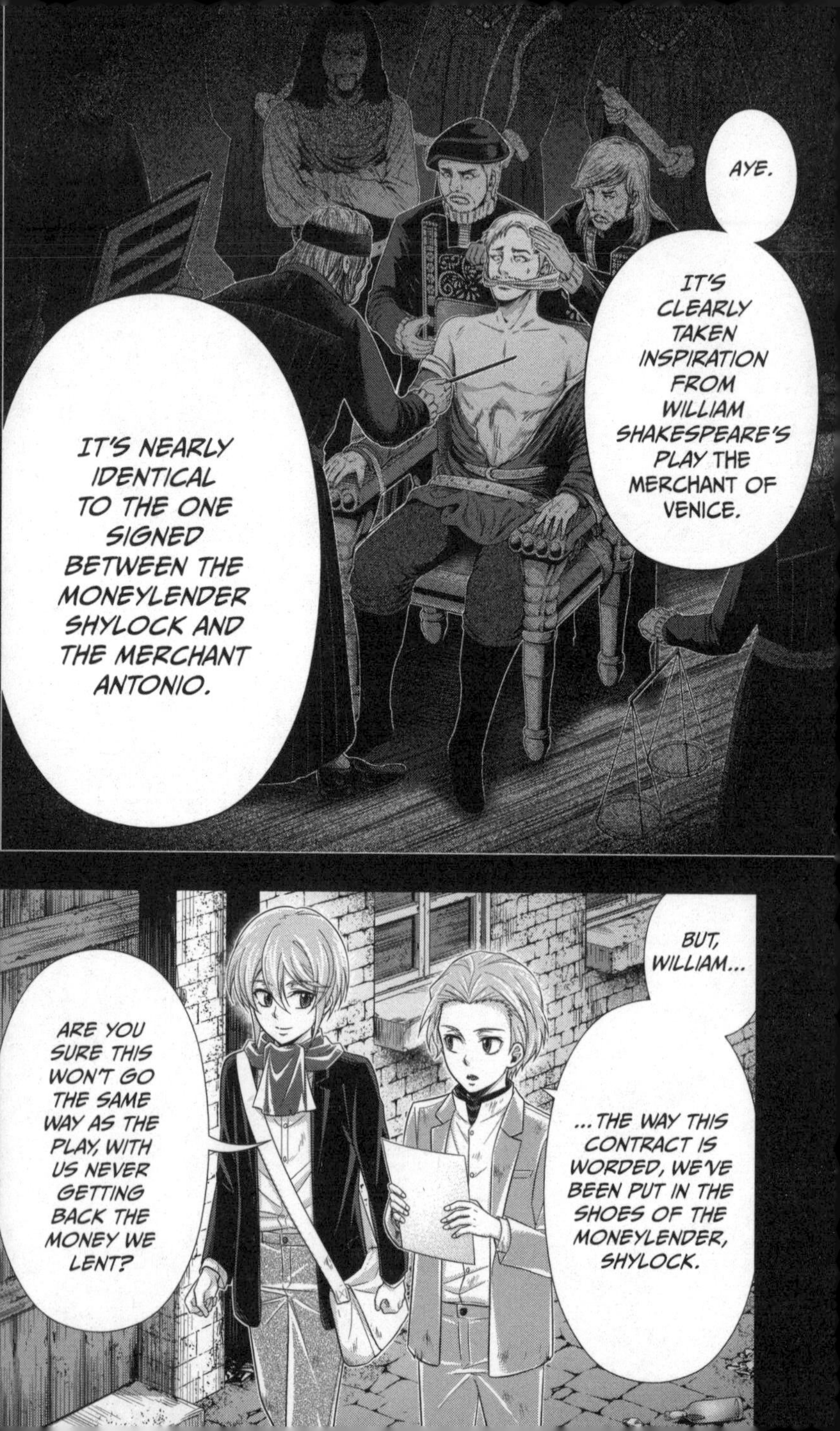
AYE.
IT'S CLEARLY TAKEN INSPIRATION FROM WILLIAM SHAKESPEARE'S PLAY THE MERCHANT OF VENICE.
IT'S NEARLY IDENTICAL TO THE ONE SIGNED BETWEEN THE MONEYLENDER SHYLOCK AND THE MERCHANT ANTONIO.
BUT, WILLIAM...
...THE WAY THIS CONTRACT IS WORDED, WE'VE BEEN PUT IN THE SHOES OF THE MONEYLENDER, SHYLOCK.
ARE YOU SURE THIS WON'T GO THE SAME WAY AS THE PLAY, WITH US NEVER GETTING BACK THE MONEY WE LENT?

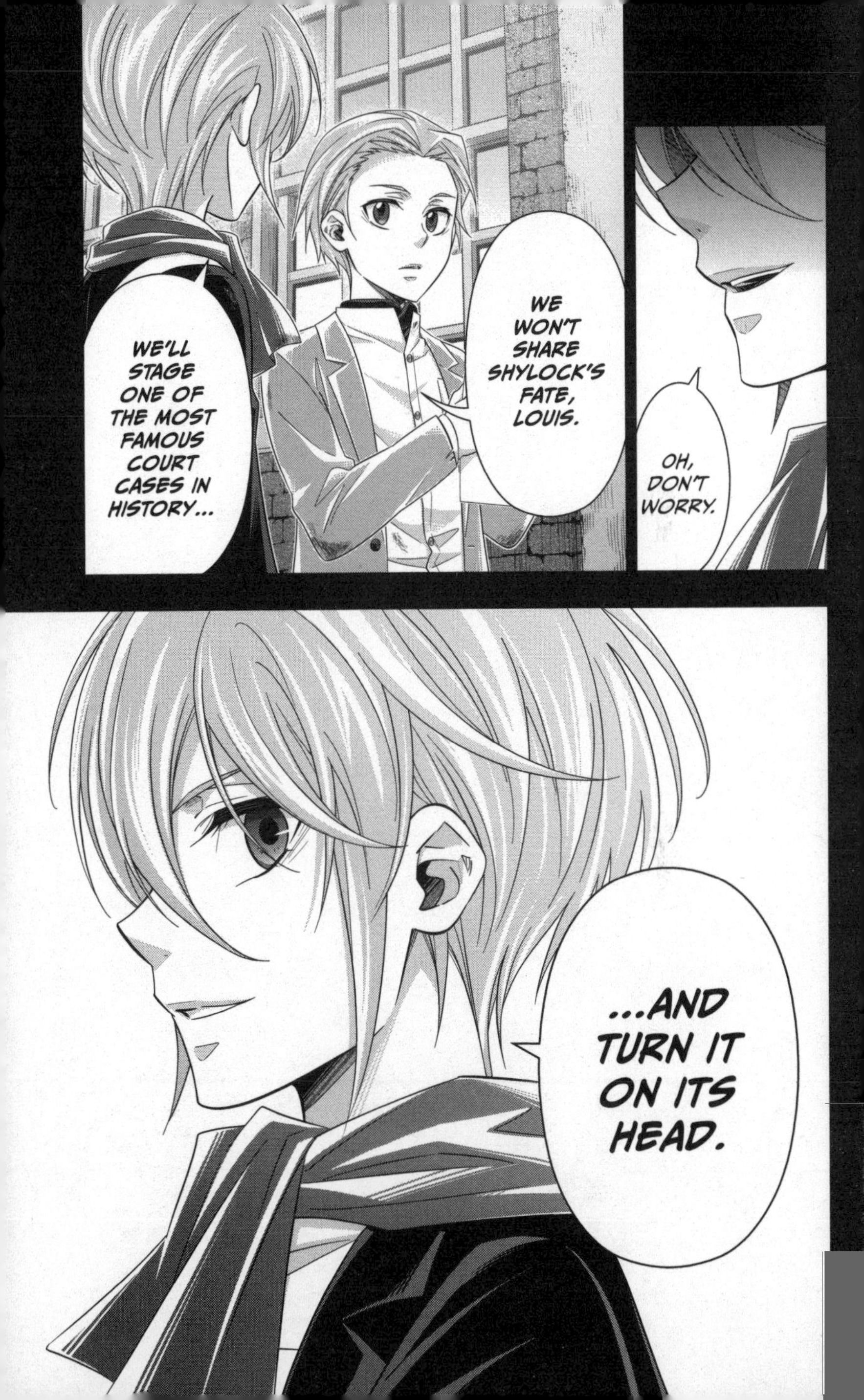
OH, DON'T WORRY.
WE WON'T SHARE SHYLOCK'S FATE, LOUIS.
WE'LL STAGE ONE OF THE MOST FAMOUS COURT CASES IN HISTORY...
...AND TURN IT ON ITS HEAD.

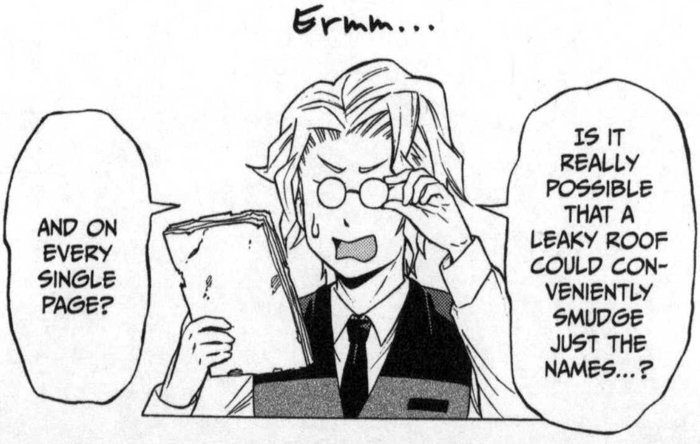
Ermm...
IS IT REALLY POSSIBLE THAT A LEAKY ROOF COULD CON-VENIENTLY SMUDGE JUST THE NAMES...?
AND ON EVERY SINGLE PAGE?

MORIARTY
THE PATRIOT

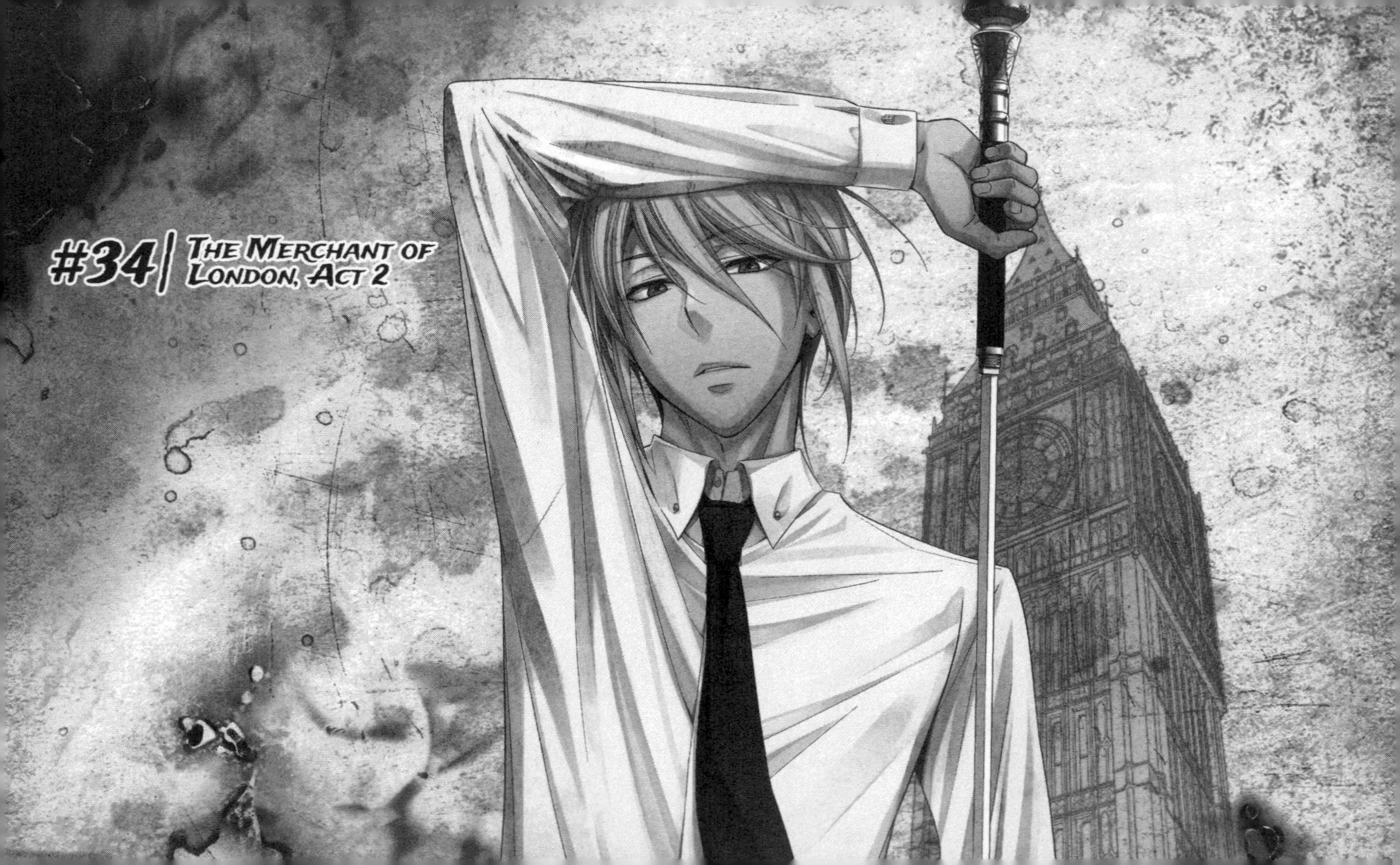
#34 The Merchant of London, Act 2

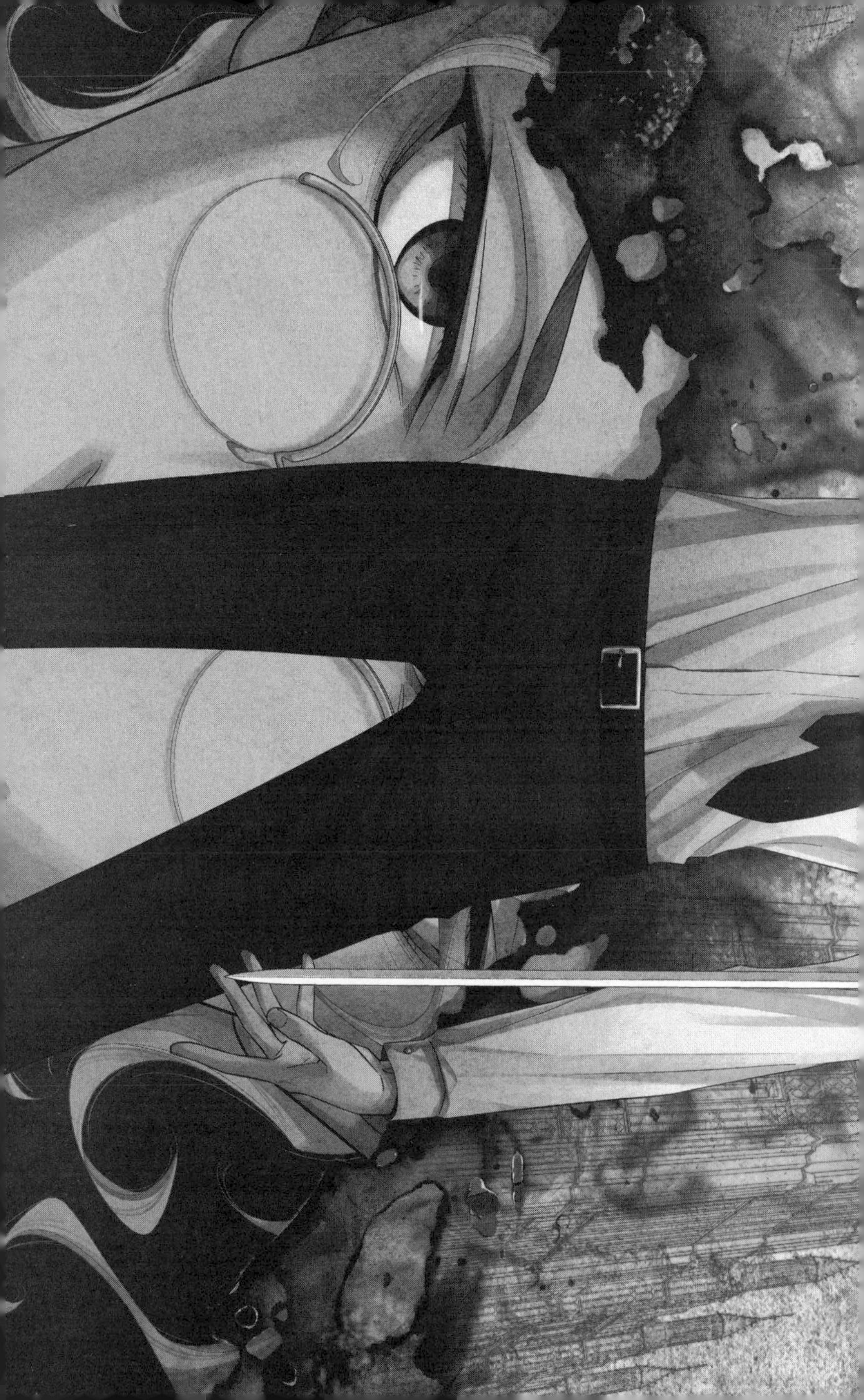

MORIARTY
THE PATRIOT

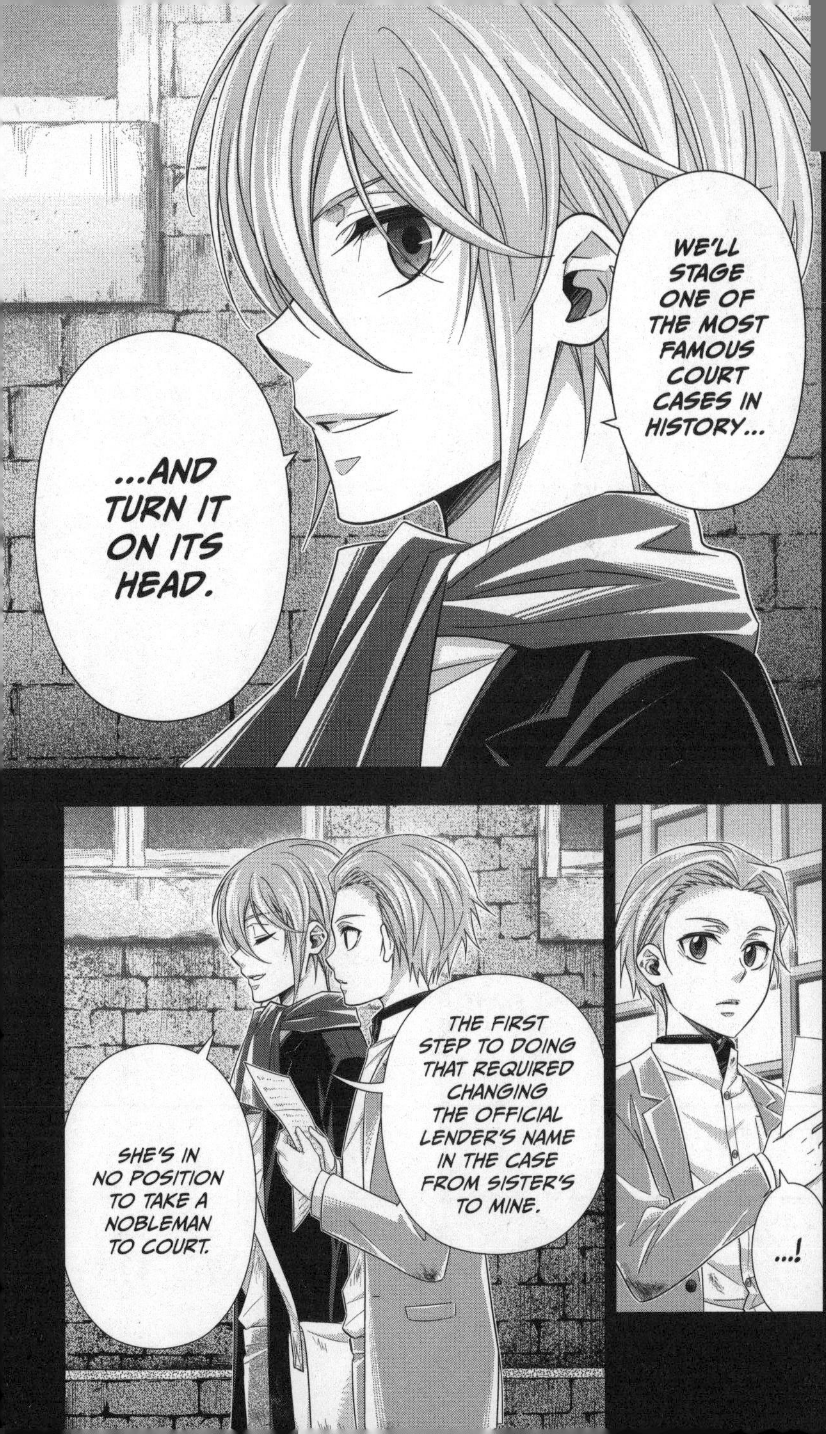
WE'LL STAGE ONE OF THE MOST FAMOUS COURT CASES IN HISTORY...
...AND TURN IT ON ITS HEAD.
...!
THE FIRST STEP TO DOING THAT REQUIRED CHANGING THE OFFICIAL LENDER'S NAME IN THE CASE FROM SISTER'S TO MINE.
SHE'S IN NO POSITION TO TAKE A NOBLEMAN TO COURT.

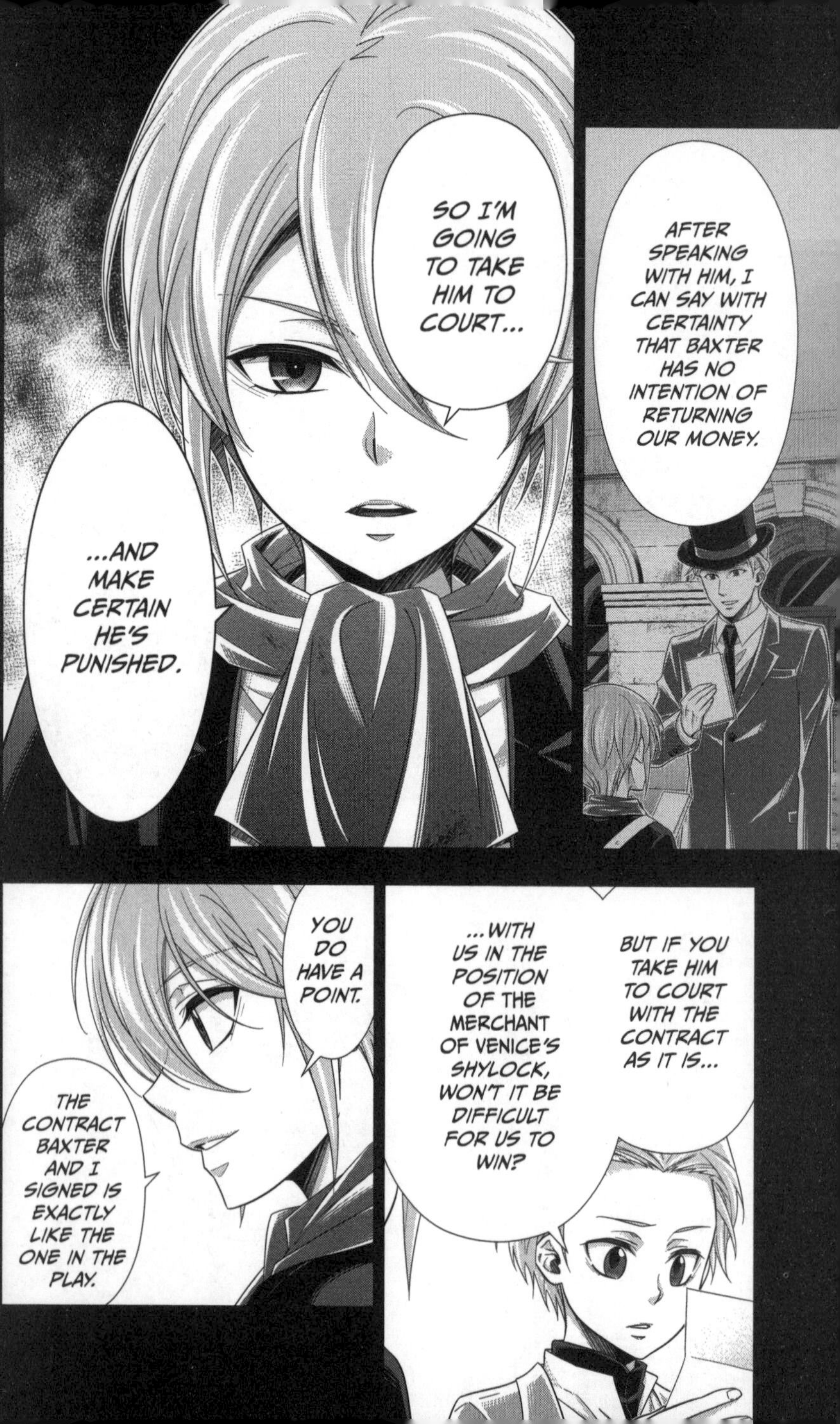
AFTER SPEAKING WITH HIM, I CAN SAY WITH CERTAINTY THAT BAXTER HAS NO INTENTION OF RETURNING OUR MONEY.
SO I'M GOING TO TAKE HIM TO COURT...
...AND MAKE CERTAIN HE'S PUNISHED.
BUT IF YOU TAKE HIM TO COURT WITH THE CONTRACT AS IT IS...
...WITH US IN THE POSITION OF THE MERCHANT OF VENICE'S SHYLOCK, WON'T IT BE DIFFICULT FOR US TO WIN?
YOU DO HAVE A POINT.
THE CONTRACT BAXTER AND I SIGNED IS EXACTLY LIKE THE ONE IN THE PLAY.

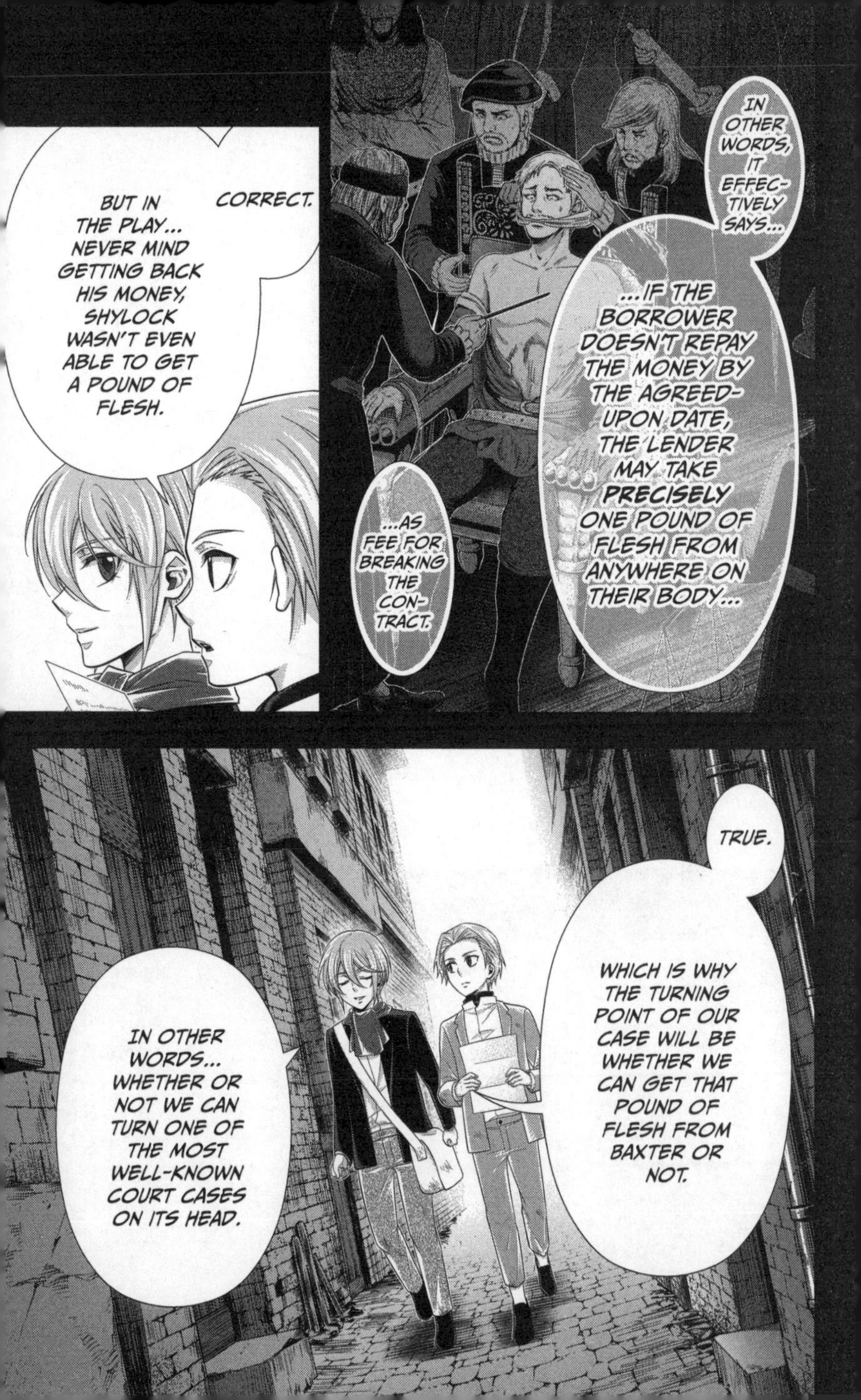
IN OTHER WORDS, IT EFFECTIVELY SAYS...
...IF THE BORROWER DOESN'T REPAY THE MONEY BY THE AGREED-UPON DATE, THE LENDER MAY TAKE **PRECISELY** ONE POUND OF FLESH FROM ANYWHERE ON THEIR BODY...
...AS FEE FOR BREAKING THE CON-TRACT.
CORRECT.
BUT IN THE PLAY... NEVER MIND GETTING BACK HIS MONEY, SHYLOCK WASN'T EVEN ABLE TO GET A POUND OF FLESH.
TRUE.
WHICH IS WHY THE TURNING POINT OF OUR CASE WILL BE WHETHER WE CAN GET THAT POUND OF FLESH FROM BAXTER OR NOT.
IN OTHER WORDS... WHETHER OR NOT WE CAN TURN ONE OF THE MOST WELL-KNOWN COURT CASES ON ITS HEAD.

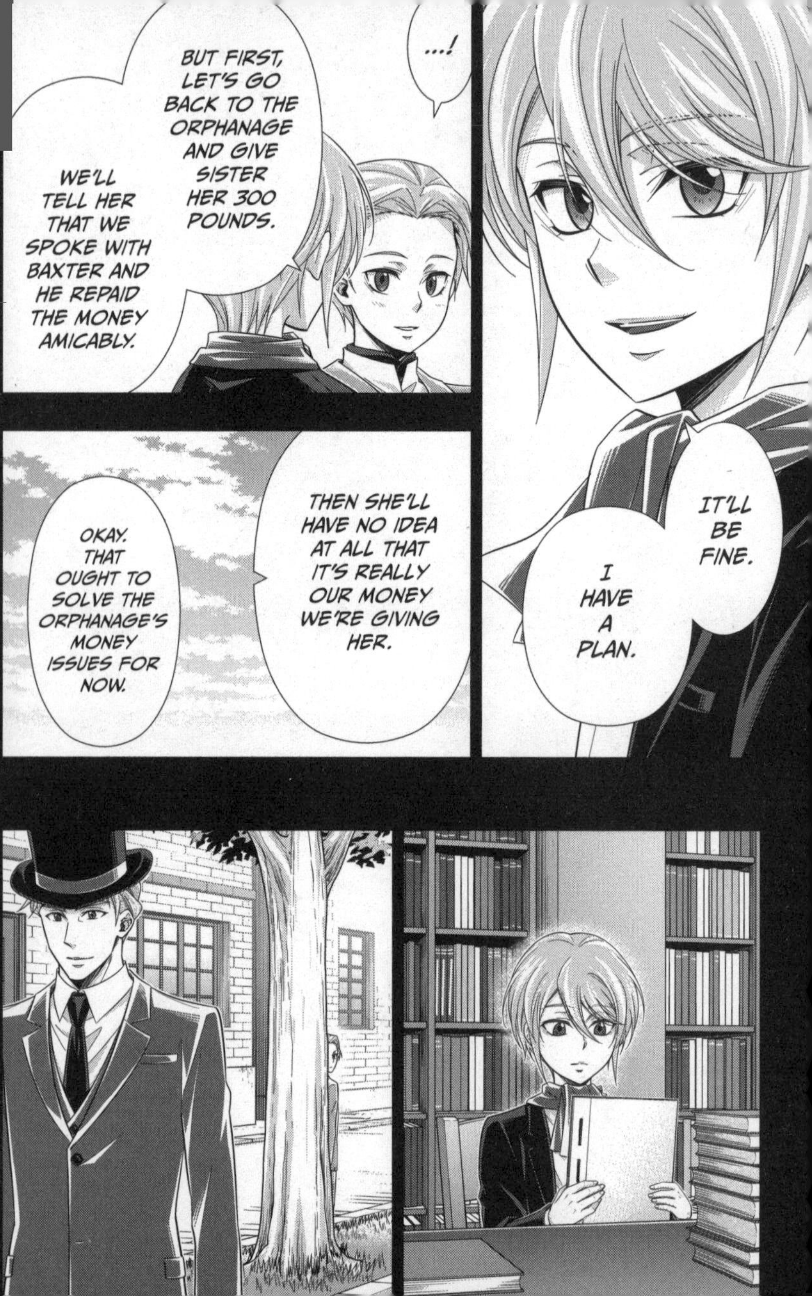
IT'LL BE FINE.
I HAVE A PLAN.
...!
BUT FIRST, LET'S GO BACK TO THE ORPHANAGE AND GIVE SISTER HER 300 POUNDS.
WE'LL TELL HER THAT WE SPOKE WITH BAXTER AND HE REPAID THE MONEY AMICABLY.
THEN SHE'LL HAVE NO IDEA AT ALL THAT IT'S REALLY OUR MONEY WE'RE GIVING HER.
OKAY. THAT OUGHT TO SOLVE THE ORPHANAGE'S MONEY ISSUES FOR NOW.

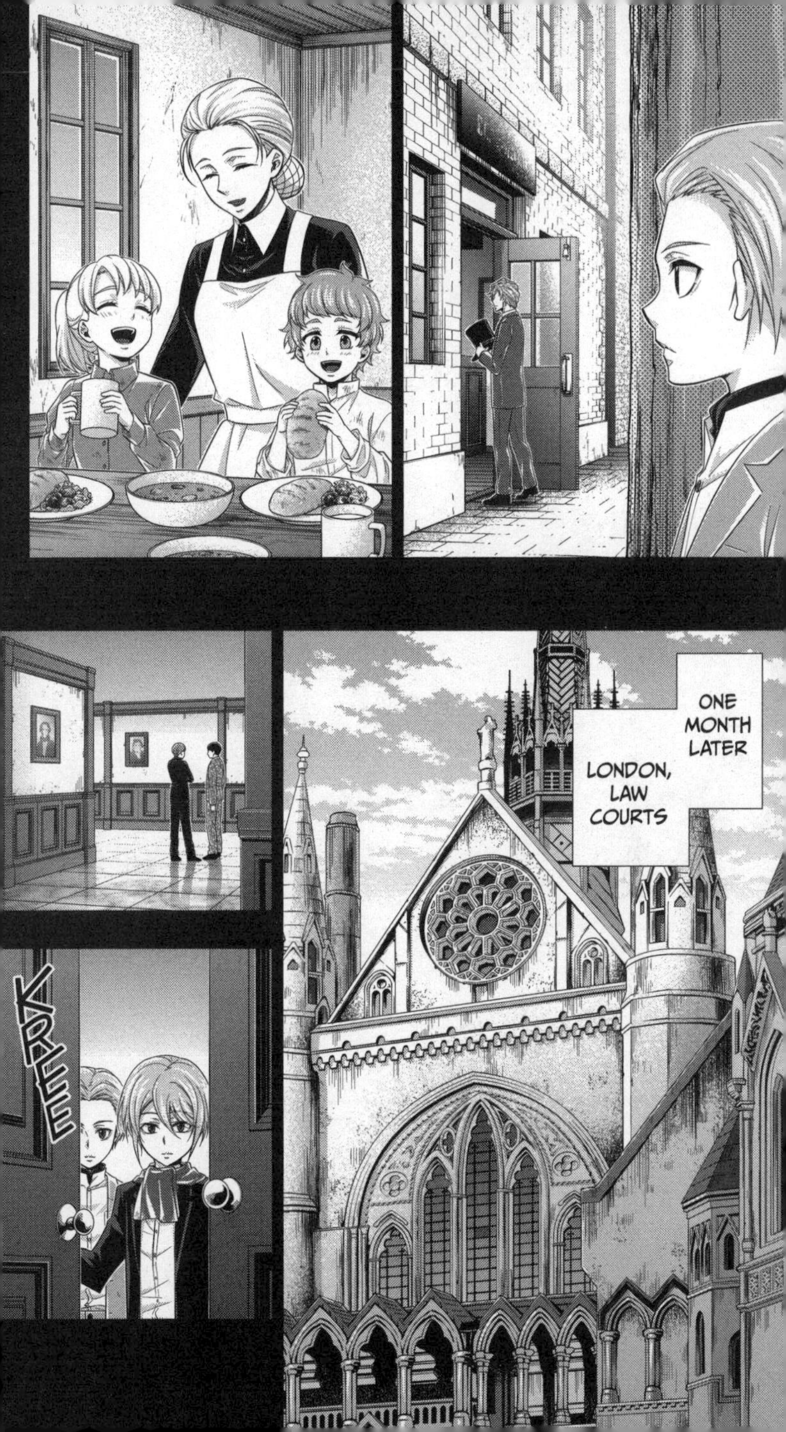
ONE MONTH LATER
LONDON, LAW COURTS
KREE

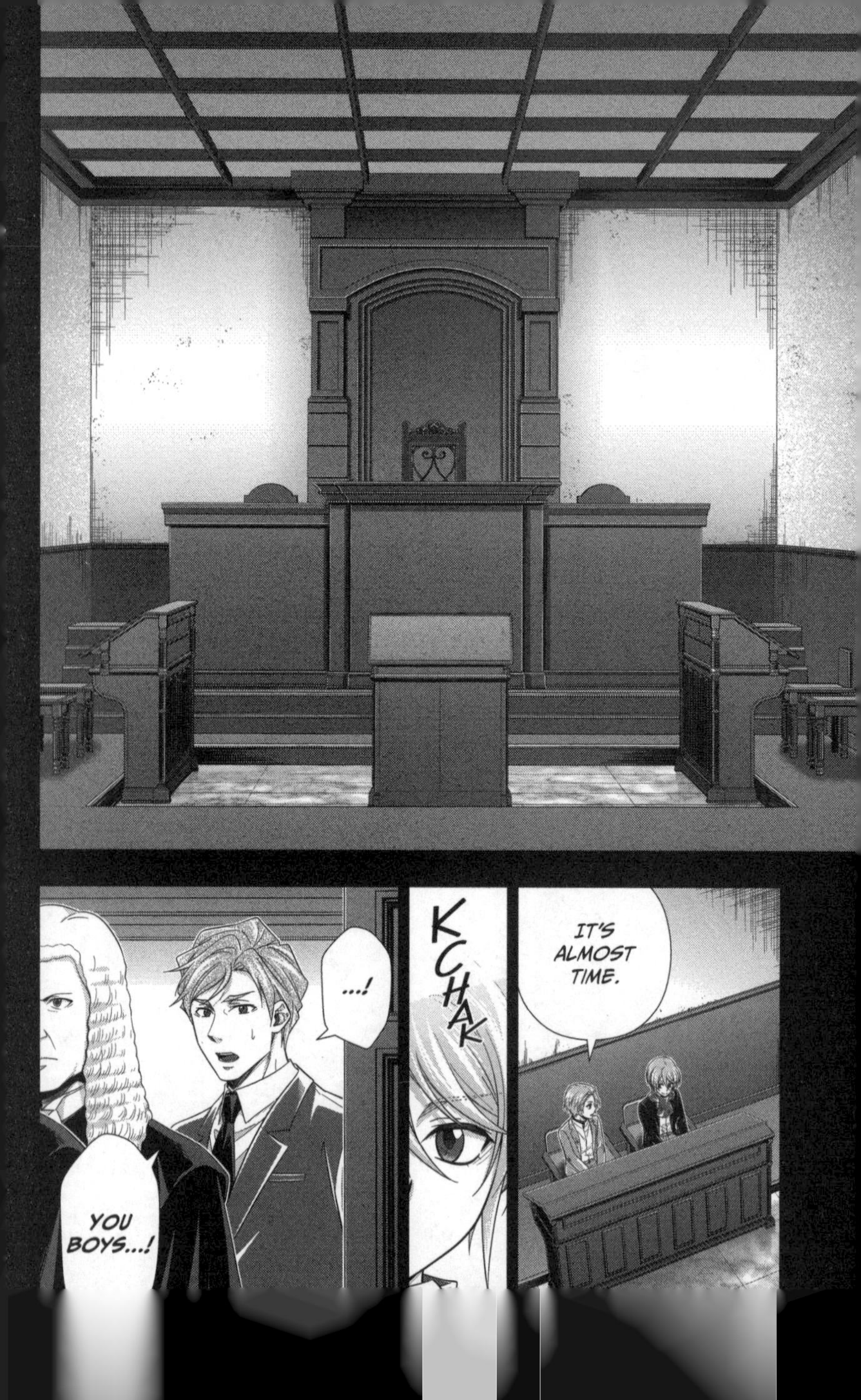
IT'S ALMOST TIME.
KCHAK
...!
YOU BOYS...!

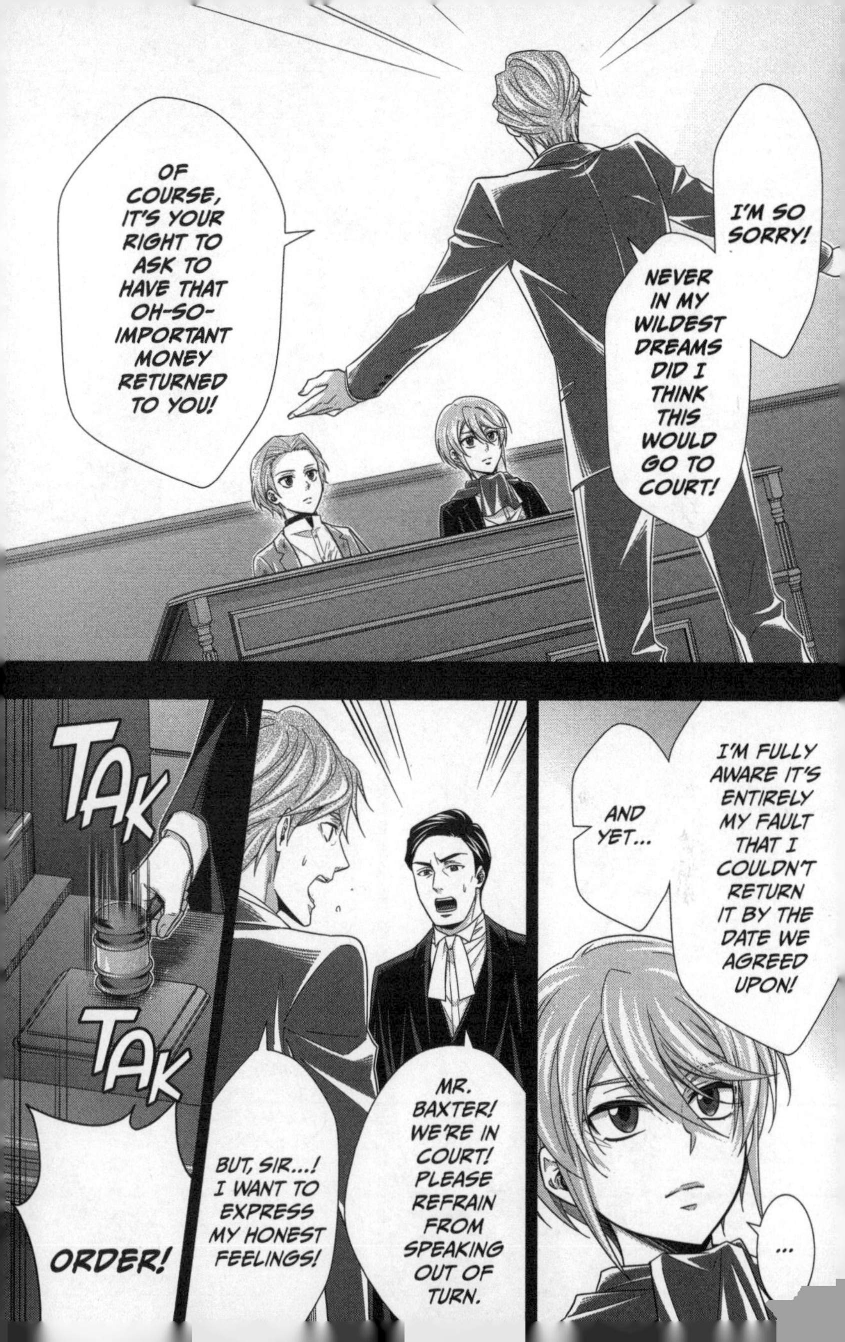
I'M SO SORRY!
NEVER IN MY WILDEST DREAMS DID I THINK THIS WOULD GO TO COURT!
OF COURSE, IT'S YOUR RIGHT TO ASK TO HAVE THAT OH-SO-IMPORTANT MONEY RETURNED TO YOU!
I'M FULLY AWARE IT'S ENTIRELY MY FAULT THAT I COULDN'T RETURN IT BY THE DATE WE AGREED UPON!
AND YET...
...
MR. BAXTER! WE'RE IN COURT! PLEASE REFRAIN FROM SPEAKING OUT OF TURN.
BUT, SIR...! I WANT TO EXPRESS MY HONEST FEELINGS!
TAK
TAK
ORDER!

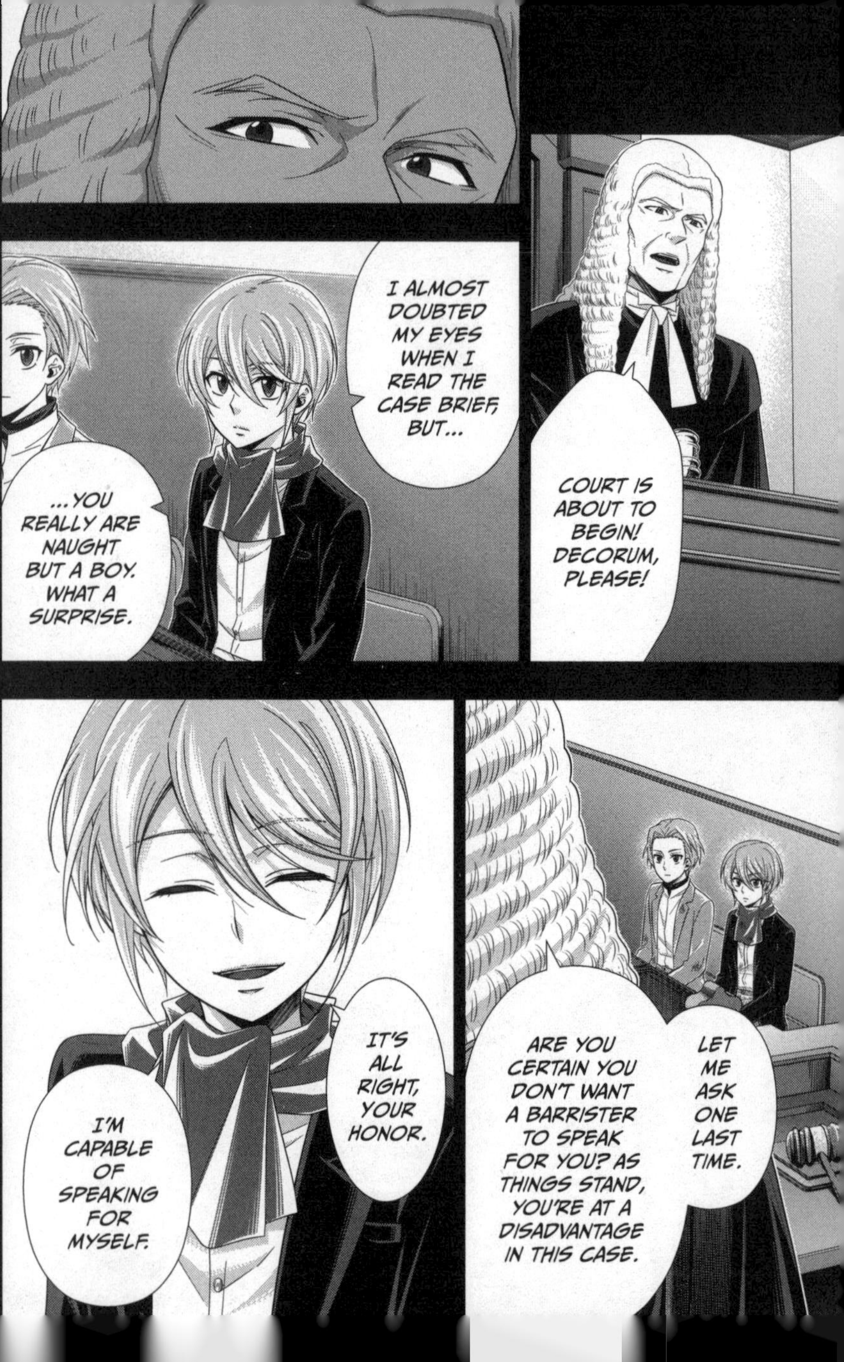
COURT IS ABOUT TO BEGIN! DECORUM, PLEASE!
I ALMOST DOUBTED MY EYES WHEN I READ THE CASE BRIEF, BUT...
...YOU REALLY ARE NAUGHT BUT A BOY. WHAT A SURPRISE.
LET ME ASK ONE LAST TIME.
ARE YOU CERTAIN YOU DON'T WANT A BARRISTER TO SPEAK FOR YOU? AS THINGS STAND, YOU'RE AT A DISADVANTAGE IN THIS CASE.
IT'S ALL RIGHT, YOUR HONOR.
I'M CAPABLE OF SPEAKING FOR MYSELF.

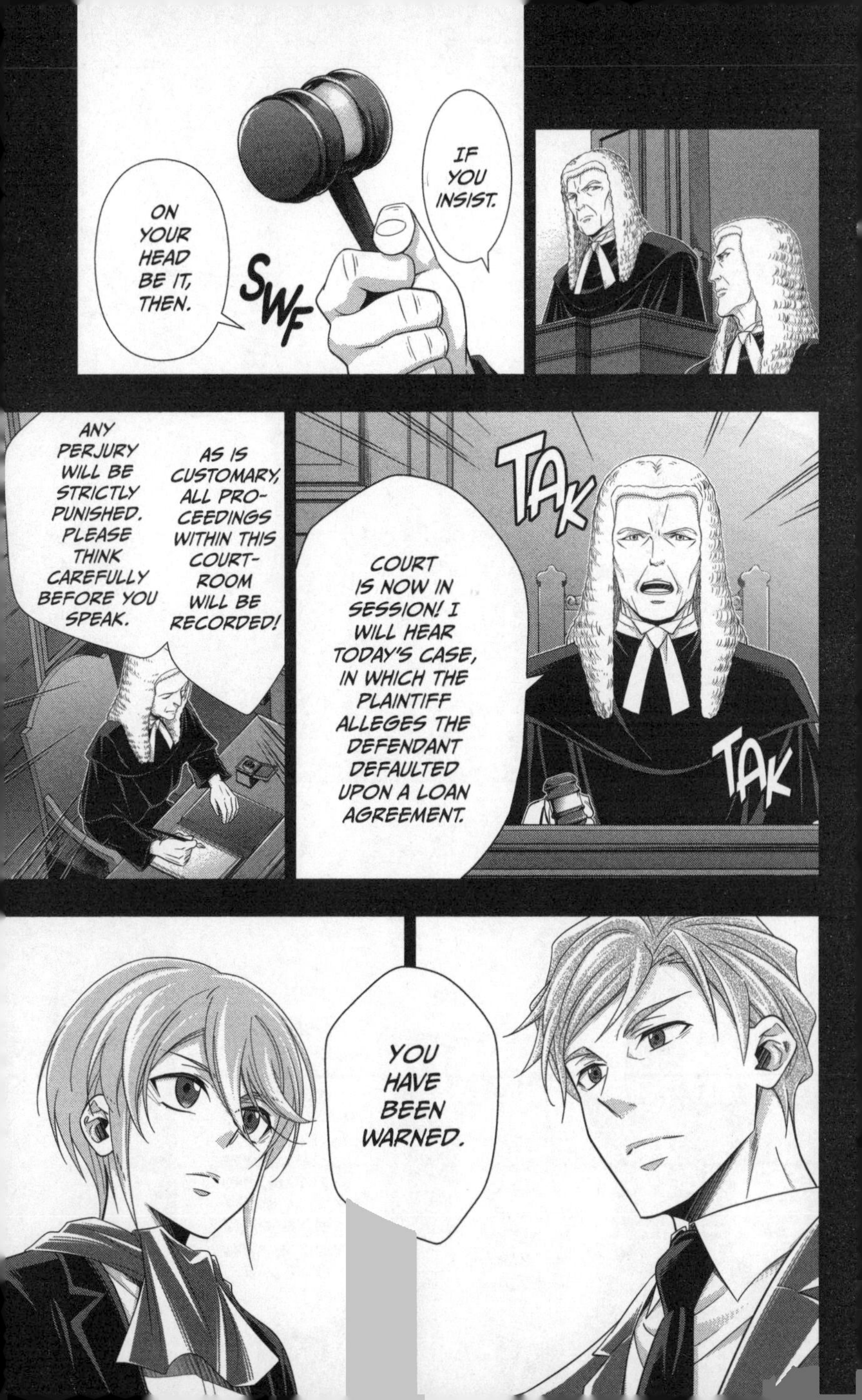
IF YOU INSIST.
ON YOUR HEAD BE IT, THEN.
SWF
TAK
COURT IS NOW IN SESSION! I WILL HEAR TODAY'S CASE, IN WHICH THE PLAINTIFF ALLEGES THE DEFENDANT DEFAULTED UPON A LOAN AGREEMENT.
TAK
AS IS CUSTOMARY, ALL PROCEEDINGS WITHIN THIS COURTROOM WILL BE RECORDED!
ANY PERJURY WILL BE STRICTLY PUNISHED. PLEASE THINK CAREFULLY BEFORE YOU SPEAK.
YOU HAVE BEEN WARNED.

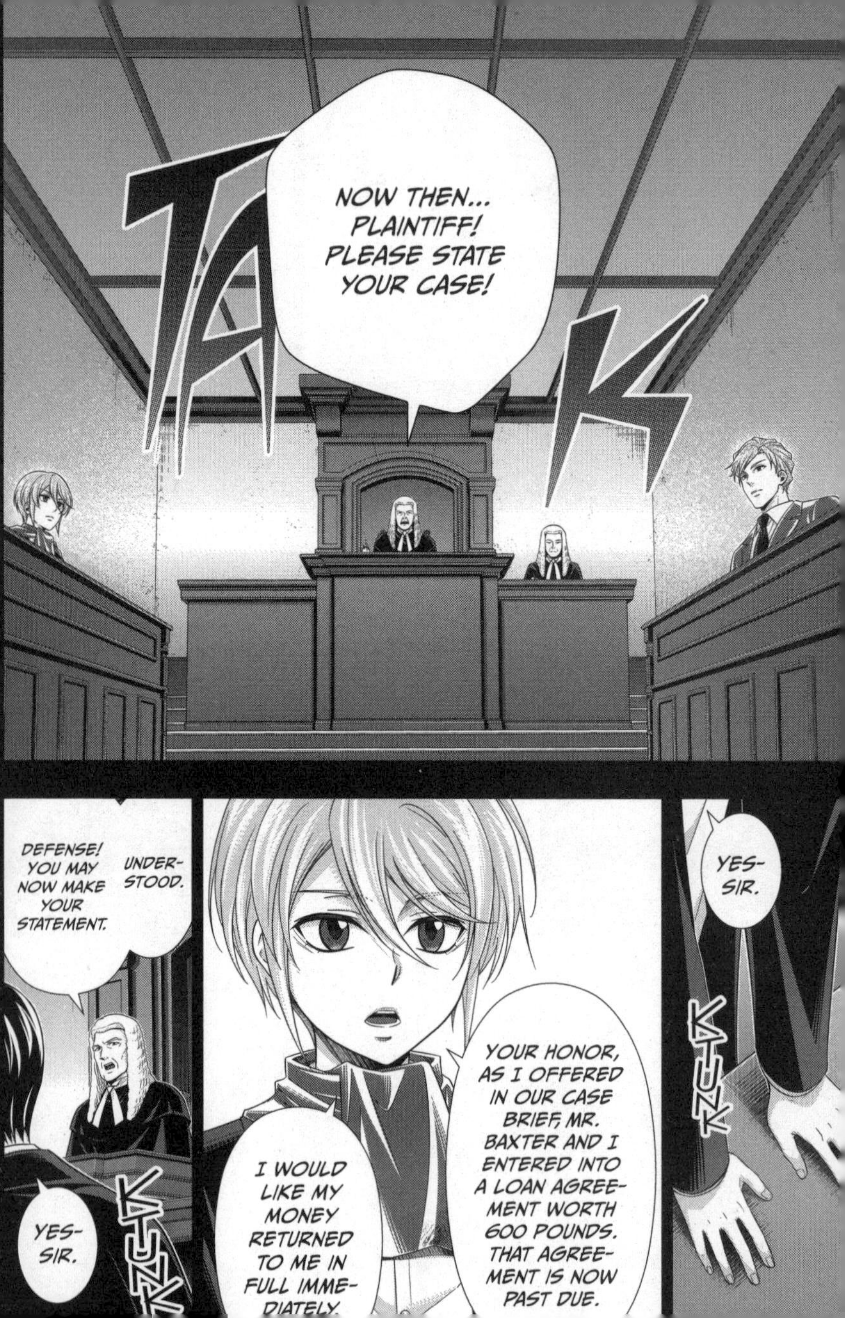
TAK
NOW THEN... PLAINTIFF! PLEASE STATE YOUR CASE!
YES-SIR.
KTUNK
YOUR HONOR, AS I OFFERED IN OUR CASE BRIEF, MR. BAXTER AND I ENTERED INTO A LOAN AGREE-MENT WORTH 600 POUNDS. THAT AGREE-MENT IS NOW PAST DUE.
I WOULD LIKE MY MONEY RETURNED TO ME IN FULL IMME-DIATELY.
DEFENSE! YOU MAY NOW MAKE YOUR STATEMENT.
UNDER-STOOD.
YES-SIR.
KTUNK

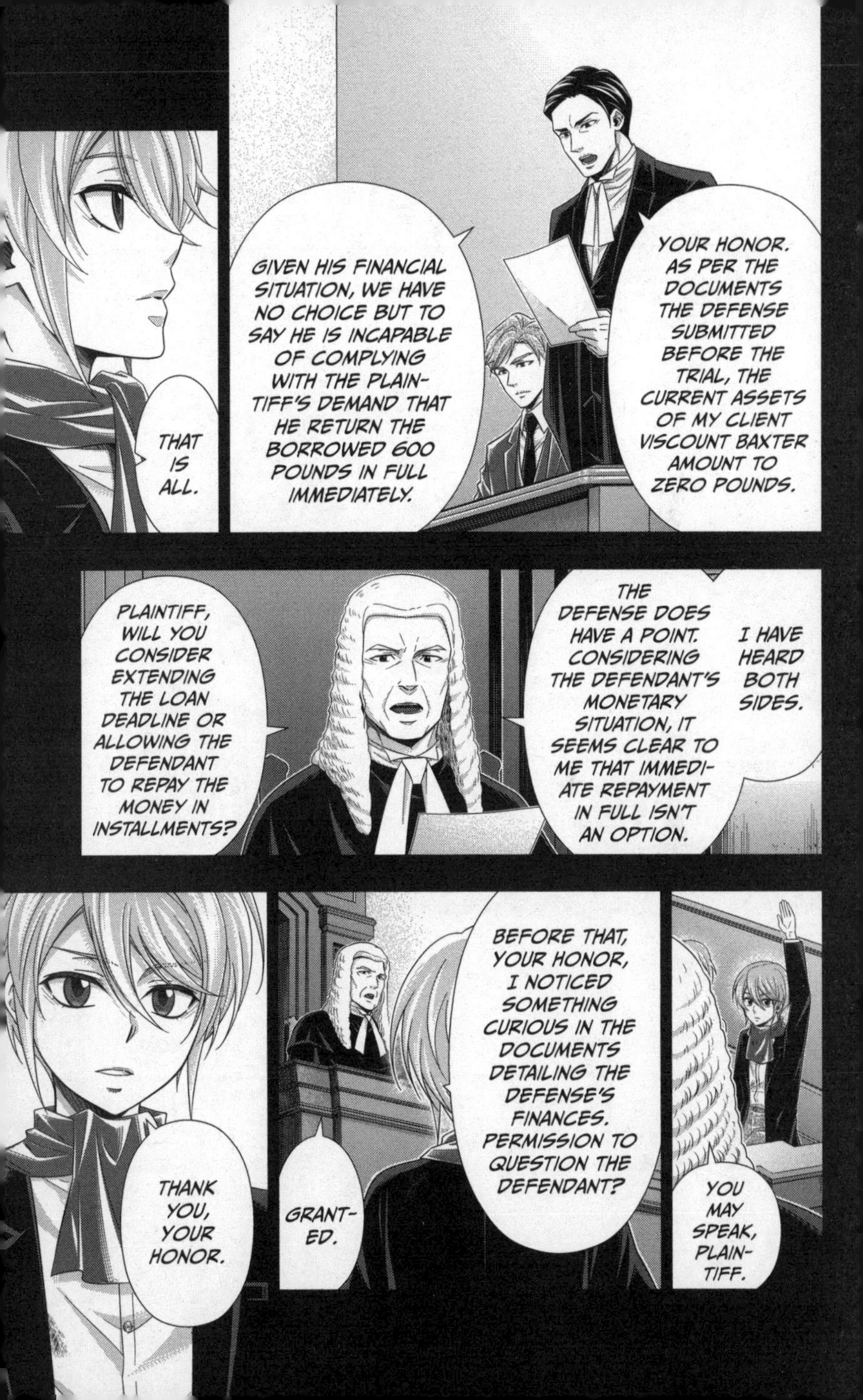
YOUR HONOR. AS PER THE DOCUMENTS THE DEFENSE SUBMITTED BEFORE THE TRIAL, THE CURRENT ASSETS OF MY CLIENT VISCOUNT BAXTER AMOUNT TO ZERO POUNDS.
GIVEN HIS FINANCIAL SITUATION, WE HAVE NO CHOICE BUT TO SAY HE IS INCAPABLE OF COMPLYING WITH THE PLAIN-TIFF'S DEMAND THAT HE RETURN THE BORROWED 600 POUNDS IN FULL IMMEDIATELY.
THAT IS ALL.
I HAVE HEARD BOTH SIDES.
THE DEFENSE DOES HAVE A POINT. CONSIDERING THE DEFENDANT'S MONETARY SITUATION, IT SEEMS CLEAR TO ME THAT IMMEDI-ATE REPAYMENT IN FULL ISN'T AN OPTION.
PLAINTIFF, WILL YOU CONSIDER EXTENDING THE LOAN DEADLINE OR ALLOWING THE DEFENDANT TO REPAY THE MONEY IN INSTALLMENTS?
YOU MAY SPEAK, PLAIN-TIFF.
BEFORE THAT, YOUR HONOR, I NOTICED SOMETHING CURIOUS IN THE DOCUMENTS DETAILING THE DEFENSE'S FINANCES. PERMISSION TO QUESTION THE DEFENDANT?
GRANT-ED.
THANK YOU, YOUR HONOR.

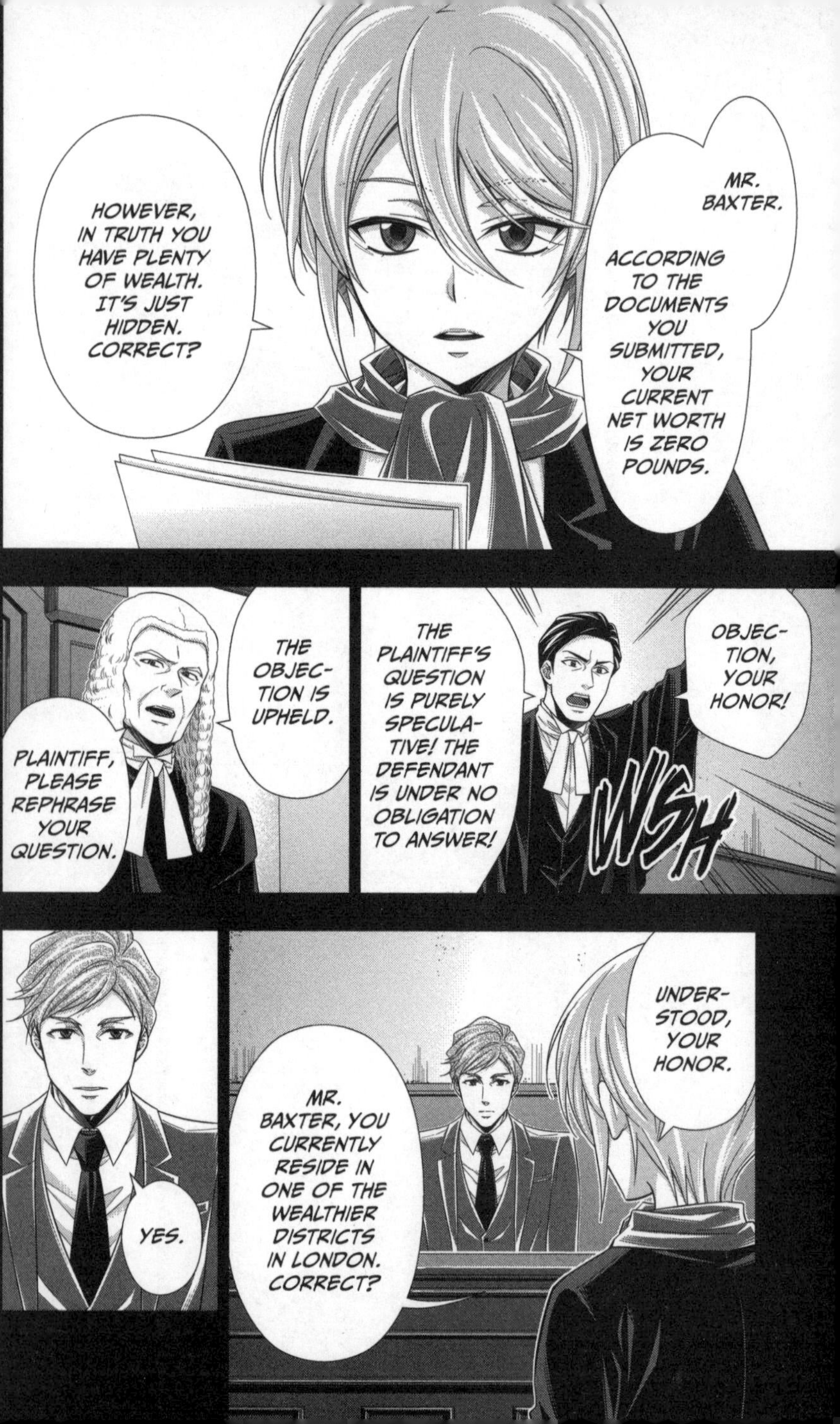
MR. BAXTER.
ACCORDING TO THE DOCUMENTS YOU SUBMITTED, YOUR CURRENT NET WORTH IS ZERO POUNDS.
HOWEVER, IN TRUTH YOU HAVE PLENTY OF WEALTH. IT'S JUST HIDDEN. CORRECT?
OBJECTION, YOUR HONOR!
WSH
THE PLAINTIFF'S QUESTION IS PURELY SPECULATIVE! THE DEFENDANT IS UNDER NO OBLIGATION TO ANSWER!
THE OBJECTION IS UPHELD.
PLAINTIFF, PLEASE REPHRASE YOUR QUESTION.
UNDERSTOOD, YOUR HONOR.
MR. BAXTER, YOU CURRENTLY RESIDE IN ONE OF THE WEALTHIER DISTRICTS IN LONDON. CORRECT?
YES.

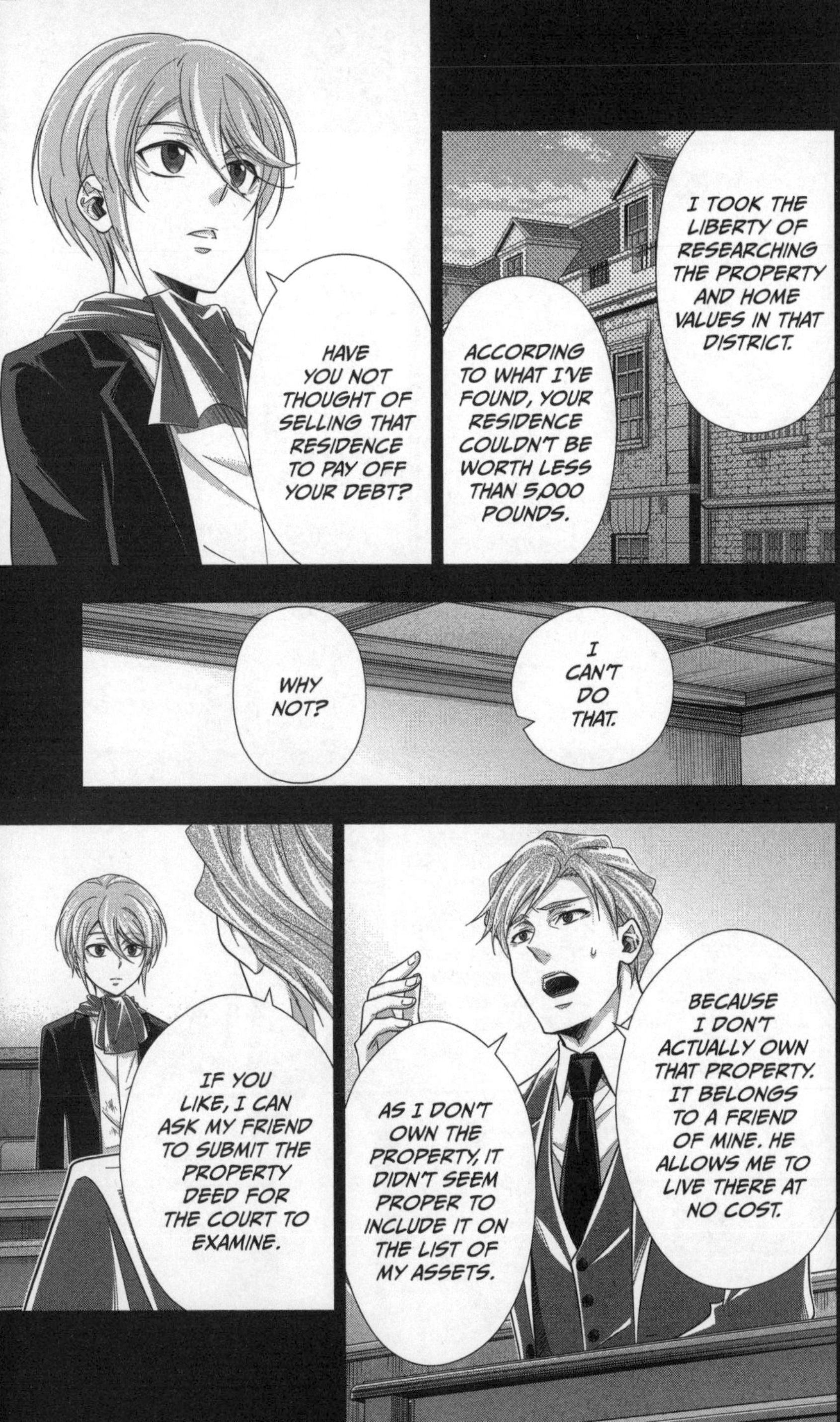
I TOOK THE LIBERTY OF RESEARCHING THE PROPERTY AND HOME VALUES IN THAT DISTRICT.
ACCORDING TO WHAT I'VE FOUND, YOUR RESIDENCE COULDN'T BE WORTH LESS THAN 5,000 POUNDS.
HAVE YOU NOT THOUGHT OF SELLING THAT RESIDENCE TO PAY OFF YOUR DEBT?
I CAN'T DO THAT.
WHY NOT?
BECAUSE I DON'T ACTUALLY OWN THAT PROPERTY. IT BELONGS TO A FRIEND OF MINE. HE ALLOWS ME TO LIVE THERE AT NO COST.
AS I DON'T OWN THE PROPERTY, IT DIDN'T SEEM PROPER TO INCLUDE IT ON THE LIST OF MY ASSETS.
IF YOU LIKE, I CAN ASK MY FRIEND TO SUBMIT THE PROPERTY DEED FOR THE COURT TO EXAMINE.

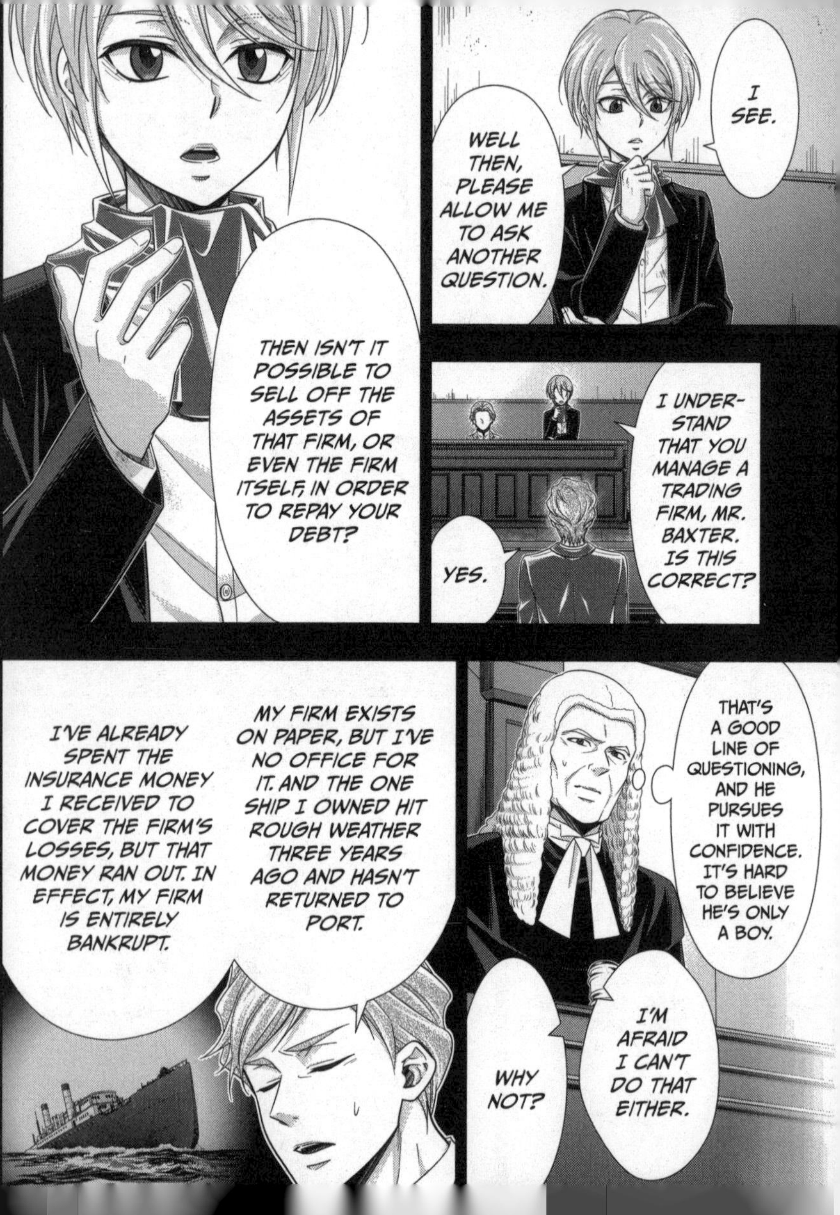
I SEE.
WELL THEN, PLEASE ALLOW ME TO ASK ANOTHER QUESTION.
I UNDER-STAND THAT YOU MANAGE A TRADING FIRM, MR. BAXTER. IS THIS CORRECT?
YES.
THEN ISN'T IT POSSIBLE TO SELL OFF THE ASSETS OF THAT FIRM, OR EVEN THE FIRM ITSELF, IN ORDER TO REPAY YOUR DEBT?
THAT'S A GOOD LINE OF QUESTIONING, AND HE PURSUES IT WITH CONFIDENCE. IT'S HARD TO BELIEVE HE'S ONLY A BOY.
I'M AFRAID I CAN'T DO THAT EITHER.
WHY NOT?
MY FIRM EXISTS ON PAPER, BUT I'VE NO OFFICE FOR IT. AND THE ONE SHIP I OWNED HIT ROUGH WEATHER THREE YEARS AGO AND HASN'T RETURNED TO PORT.
I'VE ALREADY SPENT THE INSURANCE MONEY I RECEIVED TO COVER THE FIRM'S LOSSES, BUT THAT MONEY RAN OUT. IN EFFECT, MY FIRM IS ENTIRELY BANKRUPT.

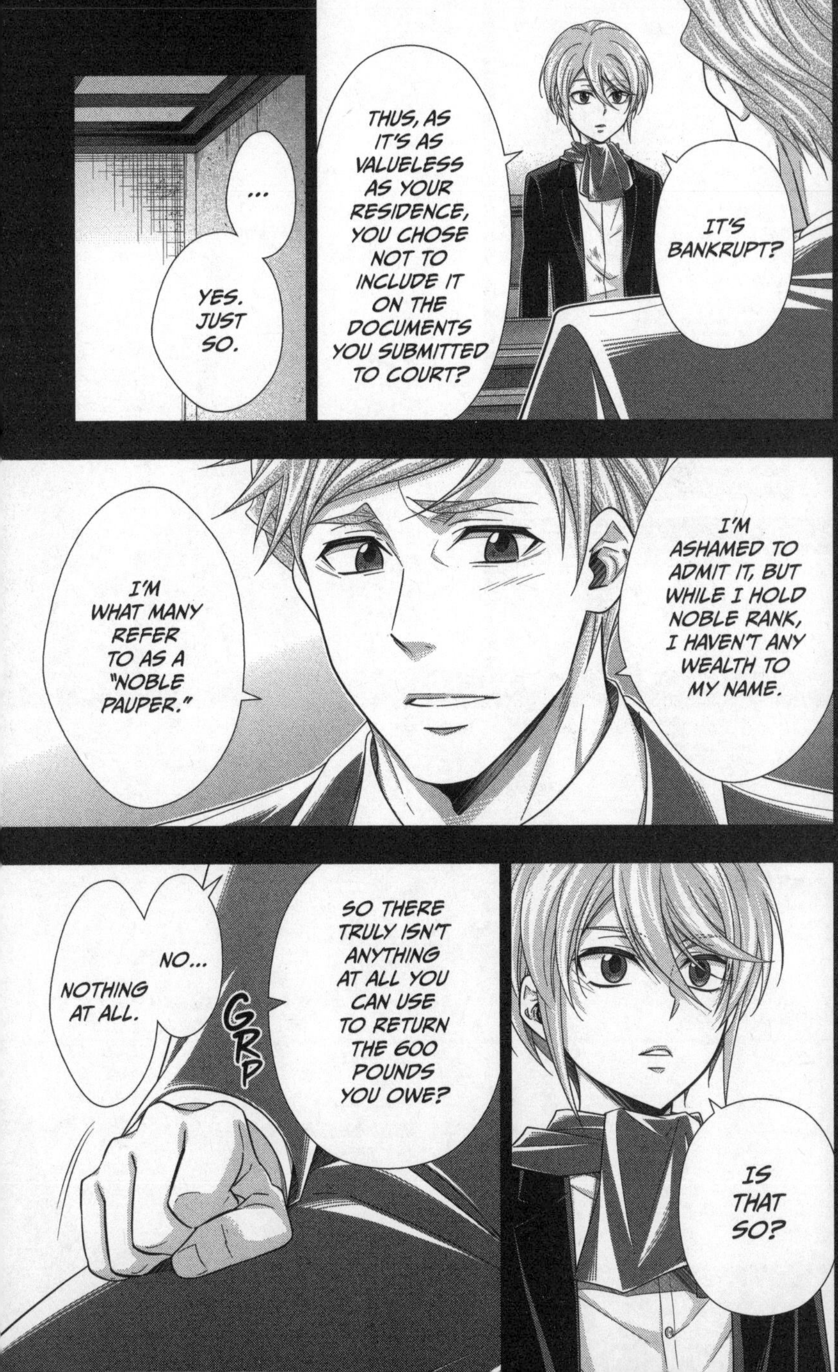
IT'S BANKRUPT?
THUS, AS IT'S AS VALUELESS AS YOUR RESIDENCE, YOU CHOSE NOT TO INCLUDE IT ON THE DOCUMENTS YOU SUBMITTED TO COURT?
...
YES. JUST SO.
I'M ASHAMED TO ADMIT IT, BUT WHILE I HOLD NOBLE RANK, I HAVEN'T ANY WEALTH TO MY NAME.
I'M WHAT MANY REFER TO AS A "NOBLE PAUPER."
IS THAT SO?
SO THERE TRULY ISN'T ANYTHING AT ALL YOU CAN USE TO RETURN THE 600 POUNDS YOU OWE?
GRP
NO...
NOTHING AT ALL.

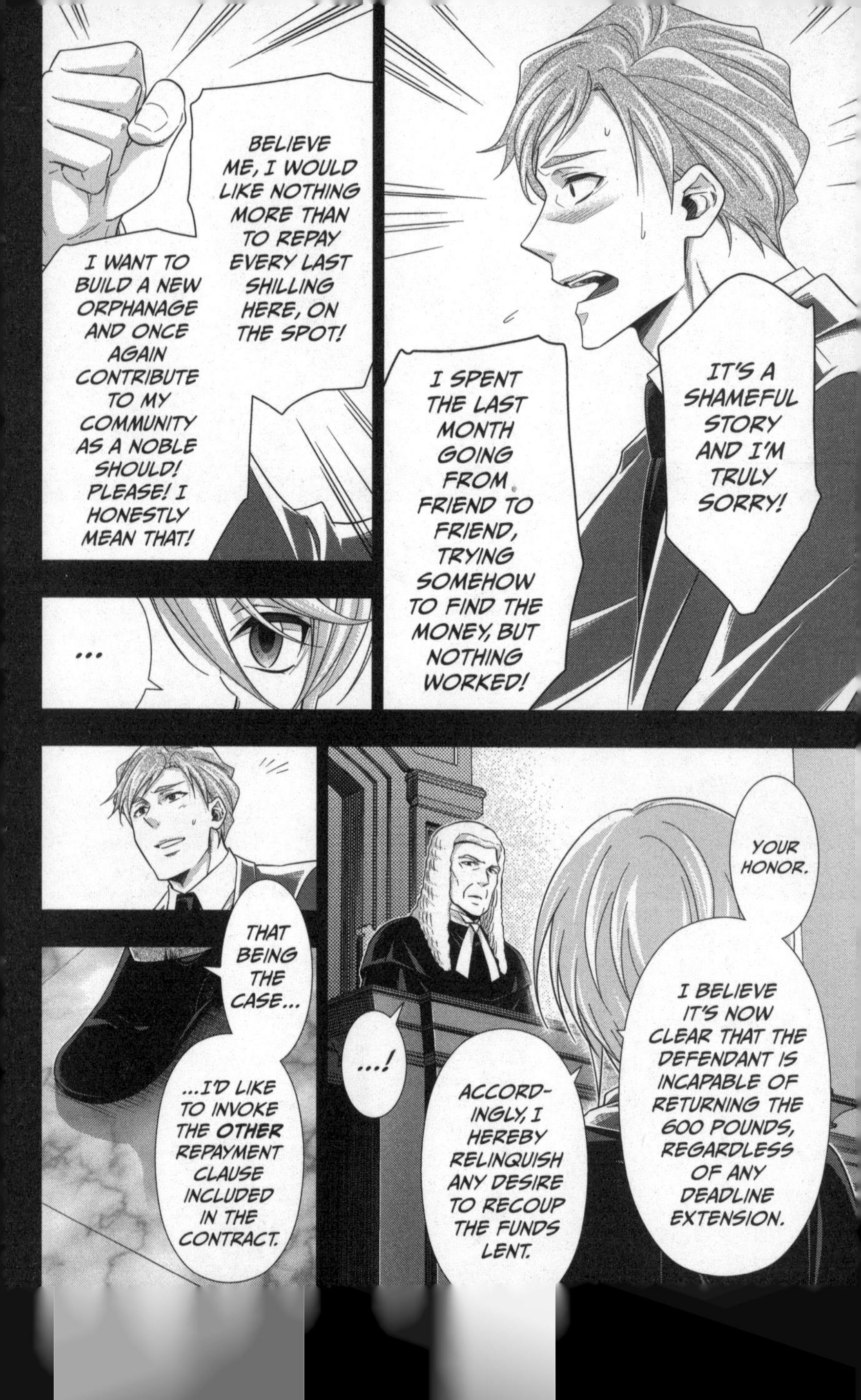
IT'S A SHAMEFUL STORY AND I'M TRULY SORRY!
I SPENT THE LAST MONTH GOING FROM FRIEND TO FRIEND, TRYING SOMEHOW TO FIND THE MONEY, BUT NOTHING WORKED!
BELIEVE ME, I WOULD LIKE NOTHING MORE THAN TO REPAY EVERY LAST SHILLING HERE, ON THE SPOT!
I WANT TO BUILD A NEW ORPHANAGE AND ONCE AGAIN CONTRIBUTE TO MY COMMUNITY AS A NOBLE SHOULD! PLEASE! I HONESTLY MEAN THAT!
...
YOUR HONOR.
I BELIEVE IT'S NOW CLEAR THAT THE DEFENDANT IS INCAPABLE OF RETURNING THE 600 POUNDS, REGARDLESS OF ANY DEADLINE EXTENSION.
ACCORDINGLY, I HEREBY RELINQUISH ANY DESIRE TO RECOUP THE FUNDS LENT.
...!
THAT BEING THE CASE...
...I'D LIKE TO INVOKE THE OTHER REPAYMENT CLAUSE INCLUDED IN THE CONTRACT.

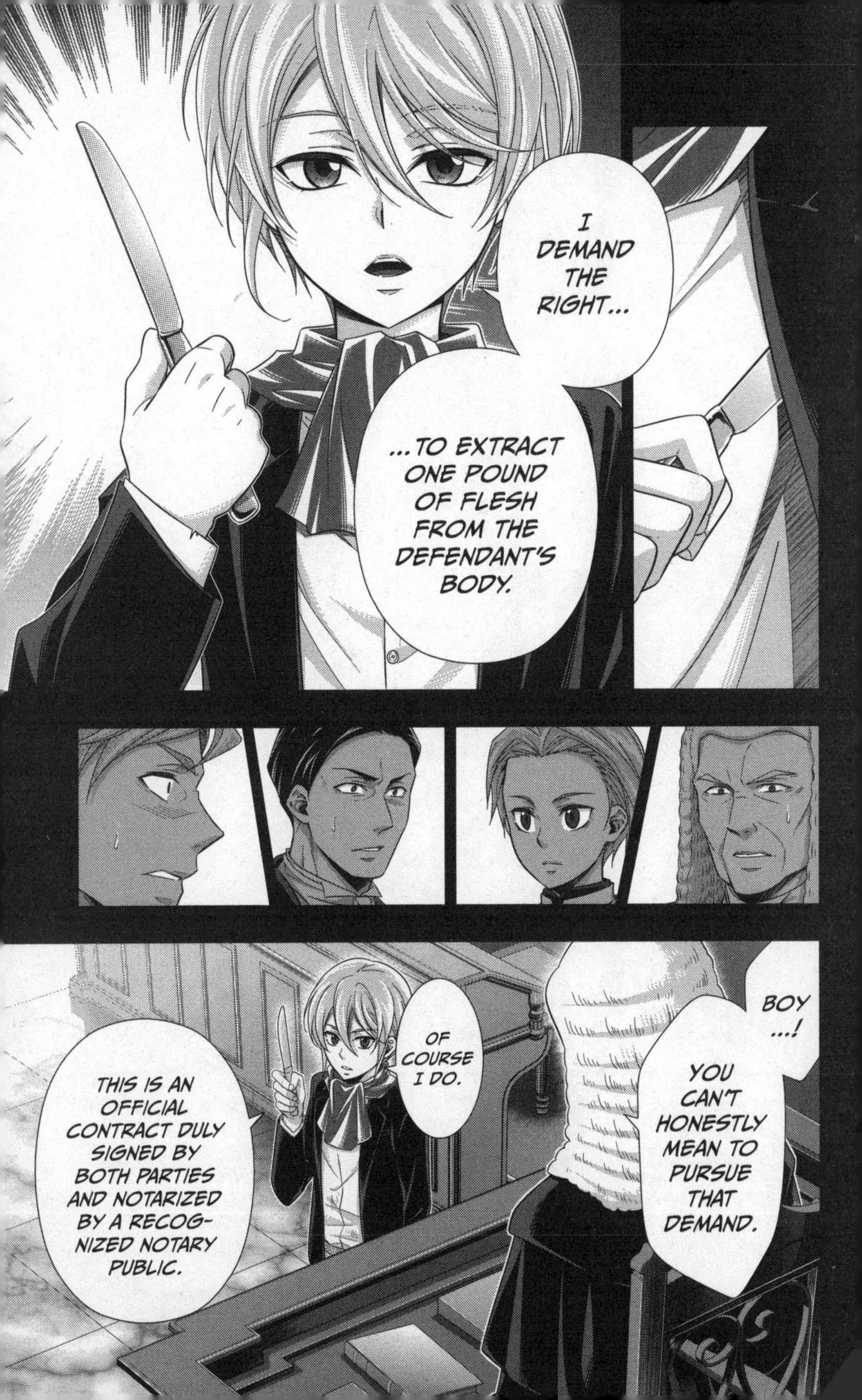
I DEMAND THE RIGHT...
...TO EXTRACT ONE POUND OF FLESH FROM THE DEFENDANT'S BODY.
BOY ...!
YOU CAN'T HONESTLY MEAN TO PURSUE THAT DEMAND.
OF COURSE I DO.
THIS IS AN OFFICIAL CONTRACT DULY SIGNED BY BOTH PARTIES AND NOTARIZED BY A RECOG-NIZED NOTARY PUBLIC.

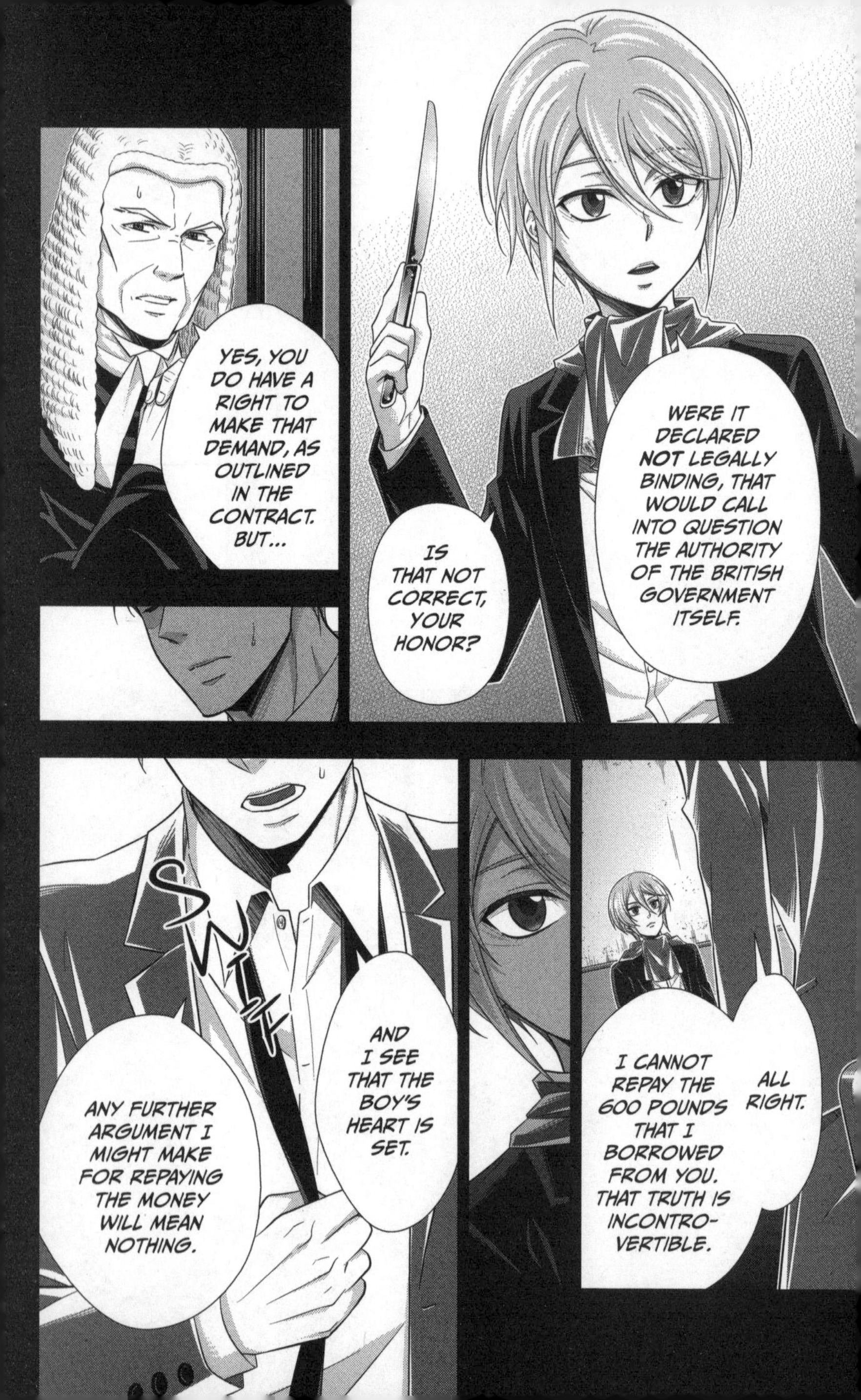
WERE IT DECLARED NOT LEGALLY BINDING, THAT WOULD CALL INTO QUESTION THE AUTHORITY OF THE BRITISH GOVERNMENT ITSELF.
IS THAT NOT CORRECT, YOUR HONOR?
YES, YOU DO HAVE A RIGHT TO MAKE THAT DEMAND, AS OUTLINED IN THE CONTRACT. BUT...
ALL RIGHT.
I CANNOT REPAY THE 600 POUNDS THAT I BORROWED FROM YOU. THAT TRUTH IS INCONTRO-VERTIBLE.
AND I SEE THAT THE BOY'S HEART IS SET.
ANY FURTHER ARGUMENT I MIGHT MAKE FOR REPAYING THE MONEY WILL MEAN NOTHING.

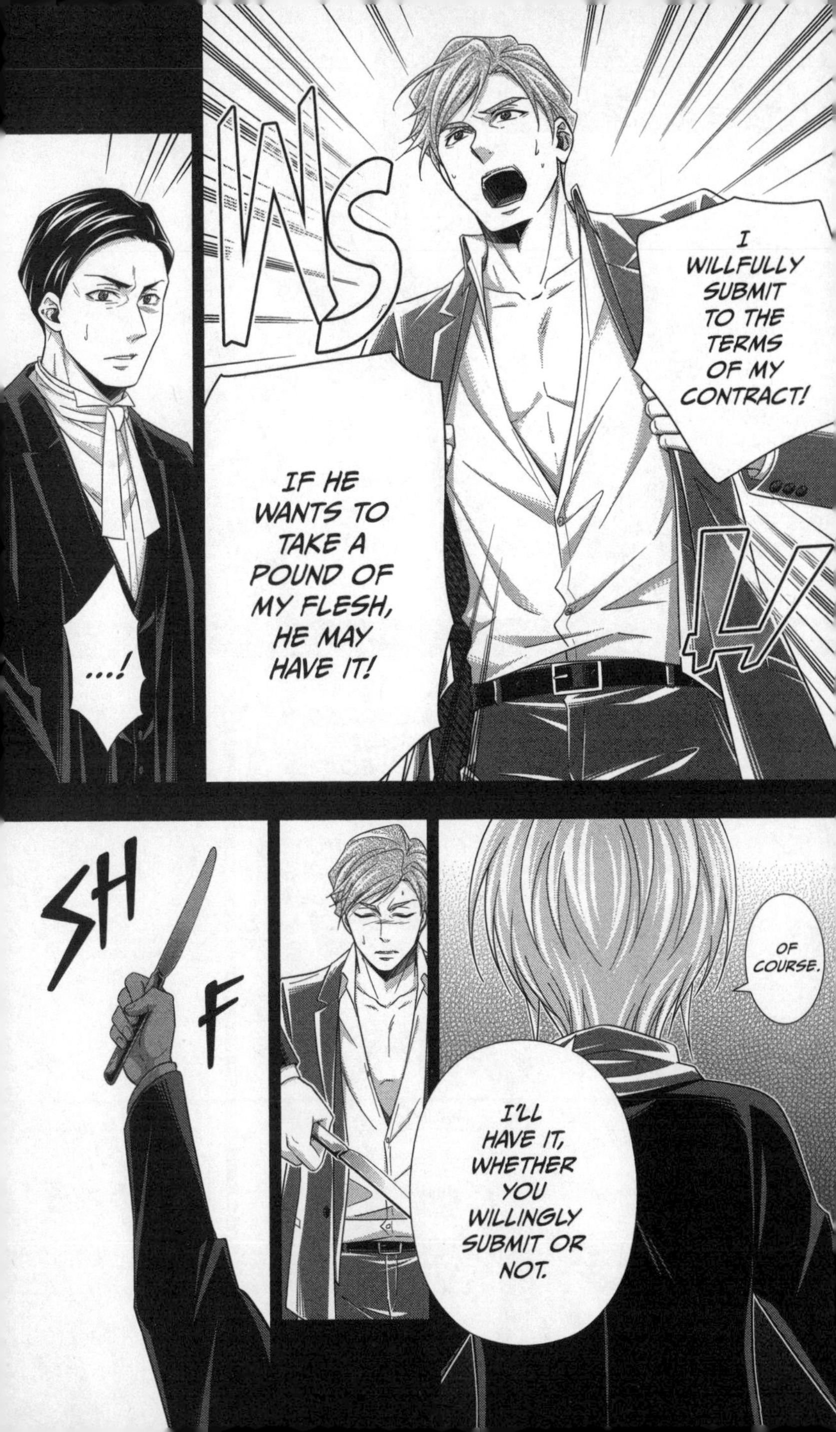
I WILLFULLY SUBMIT TO THE TERMS OF MY CONTRACT!
WS
IF HE WANTS TO TAKE A POUND OF MY FLESH, HE MAY HAVE IT!
...!
OF COURSE.
I'LL HAVE IT, WHETHER YOU WILLINGLY SUBMIT OR NOT.
SH
F

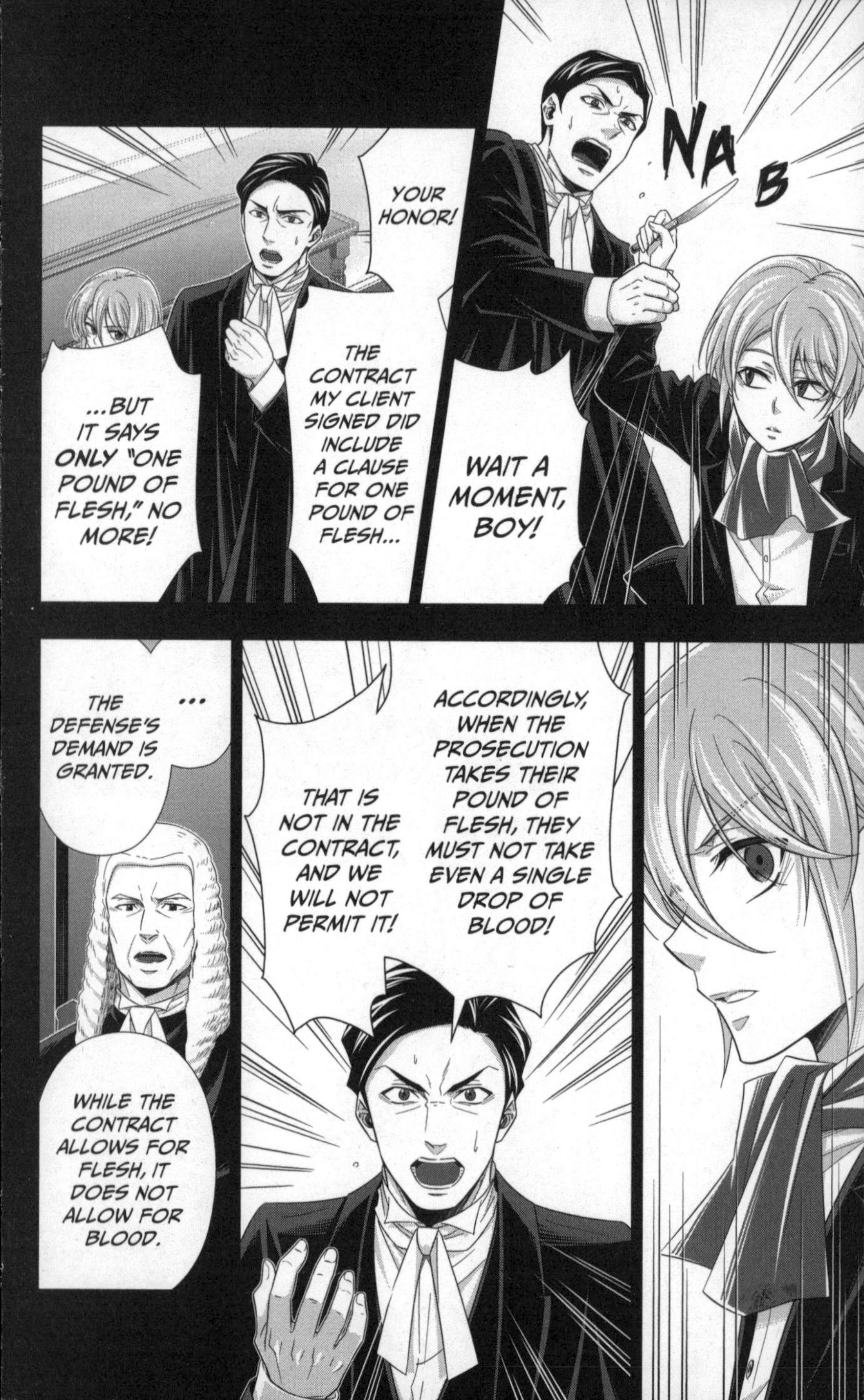
NAB
WAIT A MOMENT, BOY!
YOUR HONOR!
THE CONTRACT MY CLIENT SIGNED DID INCLUDE A CLAUSE FOR ONE POUND OF FLESH...
...BUT IT SAYS ONLY "ONE POUND OF FLESH," NO MORE!
WHILE THE CONTRACT ALLOWS FOR FLESH, IT DOES NOT ALLOW FOR BLOOD.
ACCORDINGLY, WHEN THE PROSECUTION TAKES THEIR POUND OF FLESH, THEY MUST NOT TAKE EVEN A SINGLE DROP OF BLOOD!
THAT IS NOT IN THE CONTRACT, AND WE WILL NOT PERMIT IT!
...
THE DEFENSE'S DEMAND IS GRANTED.

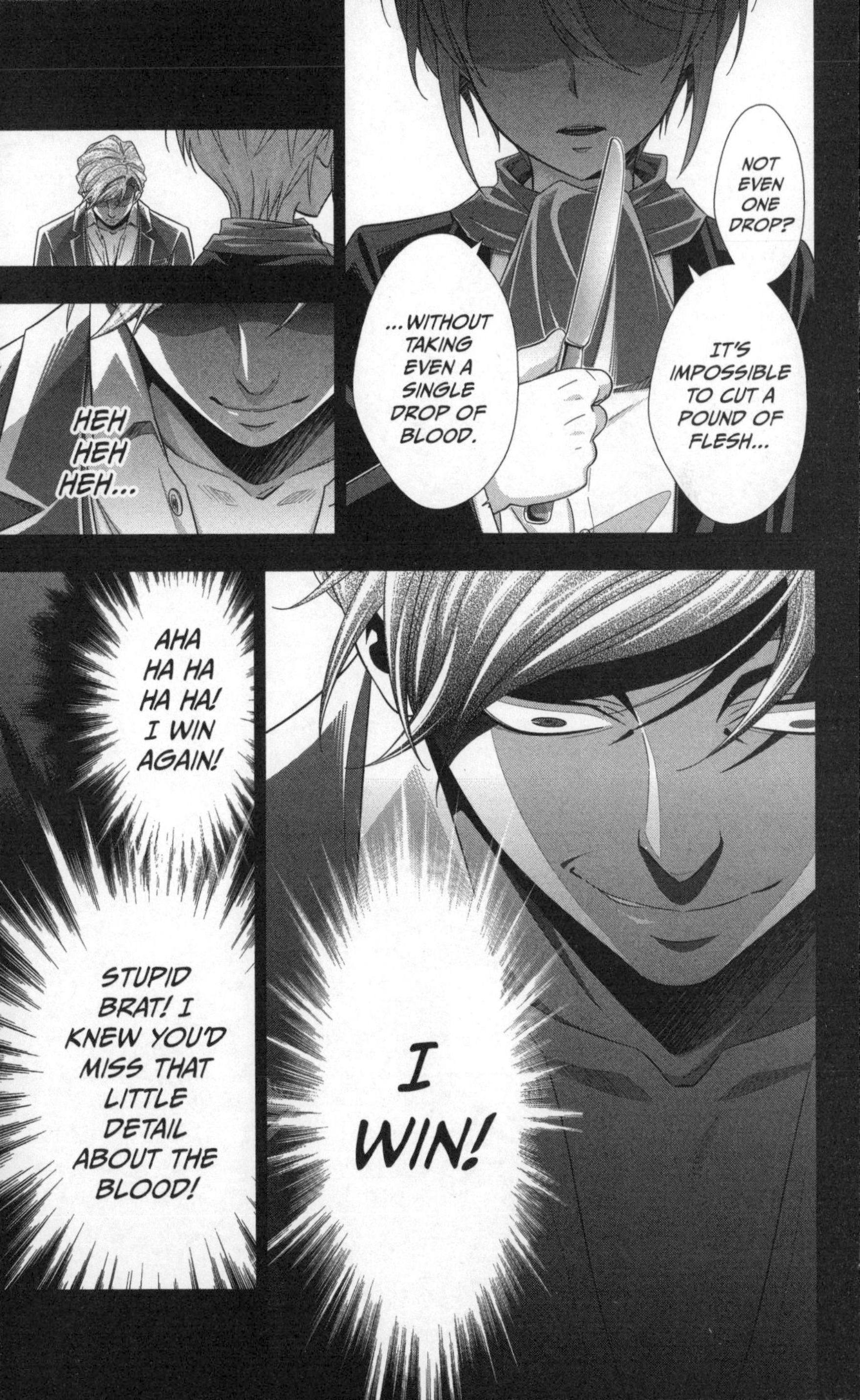
IT'S IMPOSSIBLE TO CUT A POUND OF FLESH...
...WITHOUT TAKING EVEN A SINGLE DROP OF BLOOD.
NOT EVEN ONE DROP?
HEH HEH HEH...
I WIN!
AHA HA HA HA HA! I WIN AGAIN!
STUPID BRAT! I KNEW YOU'D MISS THAT LITTLE DETAIL ABOUT THE BLOOD!

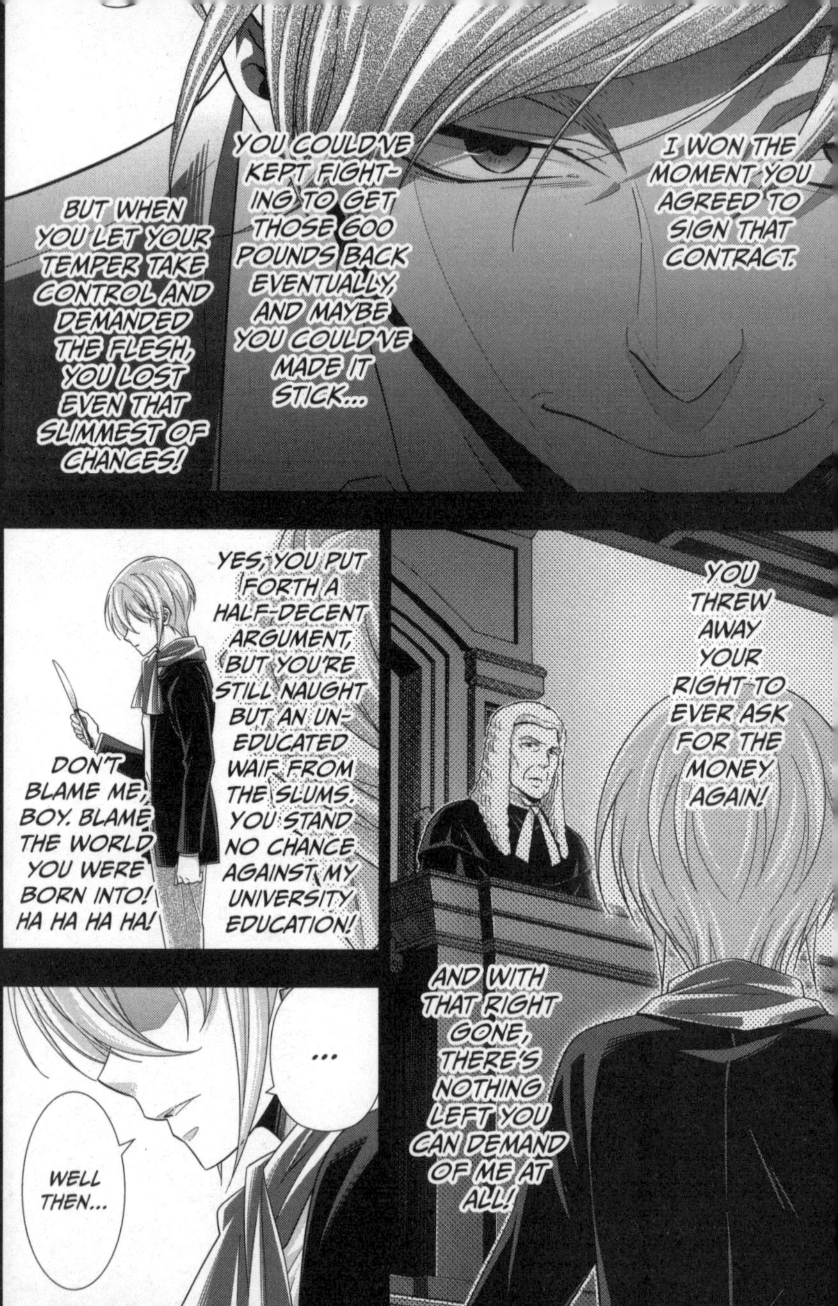
I WON THE MOMENT YOU AGREED TO SIGN THAT CONTRACT.
YOU COULD'VE KEPT FIGHTING TO GET THOSE 600 POUNDS BACK EVENTUALLY, AND MAYBE YOU COULD'VE MADE IT STICK...
BUT WHEN YOU LET YOUR TEMPER TAKE CONTROL AND DEMANDED THE FLESH, YOU LOST EVEN THAT SLIMMEST OF CHANCES!
YOU THREW AWAY YOUR RIGHT TO EVER ASK FOR THE MONEY AGAIN!
AND WITH THAT RIGHT GONE, THERE'S NOTHING LEFT YOU CAN DEMAND OF ME AT ALL!
YES, YOU PUT FORTH A HALF-DECENT ARGUMENT, BUT YOU'RE STILL NAUGHT BUT AN UNEDUCATED WAIF FROM THE SLUMS. YOU STAND NO CHANCE AGAINST MY UNIVERSITY EDUCATION!
DON'T BLAME ME, BOY. BLAME THE WORLD YOU WERE BORN INTO! HA HA HA HA!
...
WELL THEN...

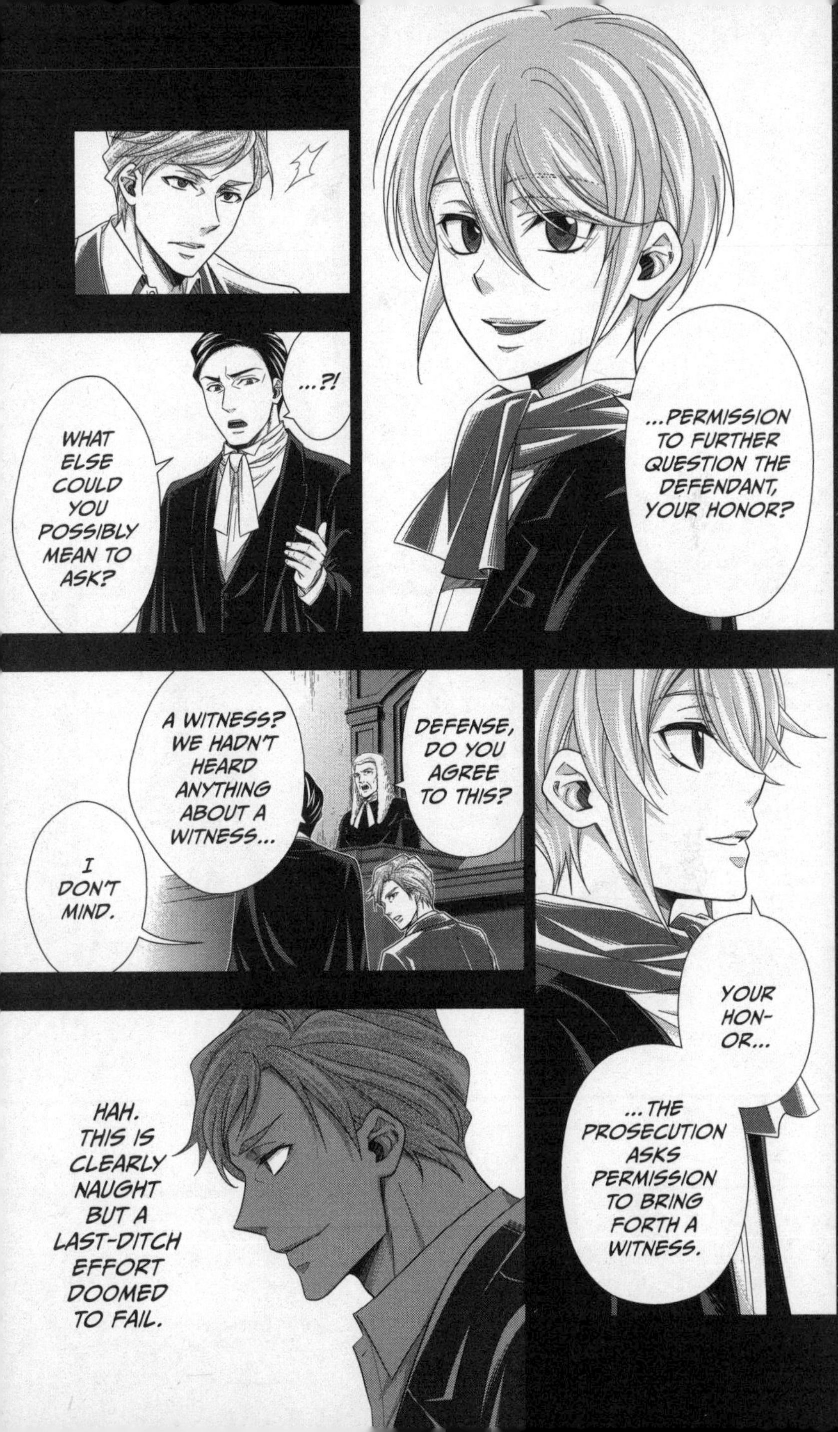
...PERMISSION TO FURTHER QUESTION THE DEFENDANT, YOUR HONOR?
...?!
WHAT ELSE COULD YOU POSSIBLY MEAN TO ASK?
YOUR HON-OR...
...THE PROSECUTION ASKS PERMISSION TO BRING FORTH A WITNESS.
DEFENSE, DO YOU AGREE TO THIS?
A WITNESS? WE HADN'T HEARD ANYTHING ABOUT A WITNESS...
I DON'T MIND.
HAH. THIS IS CLEARLY NAUGHT BUT A LAST-DITCH EFFORT DOOMED TO FAIL.

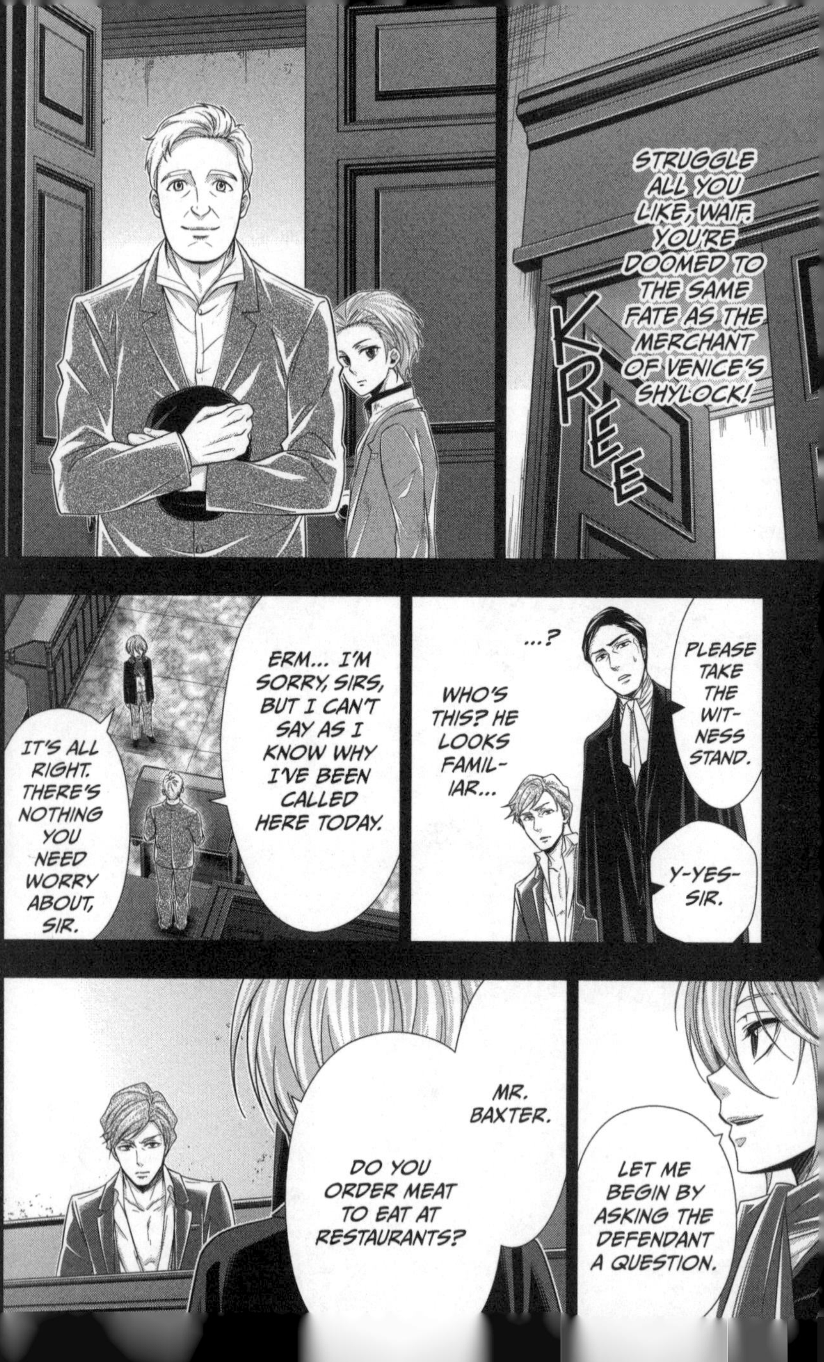
STRUGGLE ALL YOU LIKE, WAIF. YOU'RE DOOMED TO THE SAME FATE AS THE MERCHANT OF VENICE'S SHYLOCK!
KREEE
PLEASE TAKE THE WIT-NESS STAND.
...?
WHO'S THIS? HE LOOKS FAMIL-IAR...
Y-YES-SIR.
ERM... I'M SORRY, SIRS, BUT I CAN'T SAY AS I KNOW WHY I'VE BEEN CALLED HERE TODAY.
IT'S ALL RIGHT. THERE'S NOTHING YOU NEED WORRY ABOUT, SIR.
LET ME BEGIN BY ASKING THE DEFENDANT A QUESTION.
MR. BAXTER.
DO YOU ORDER MEAT TO EAT AT RESTAURANTS?

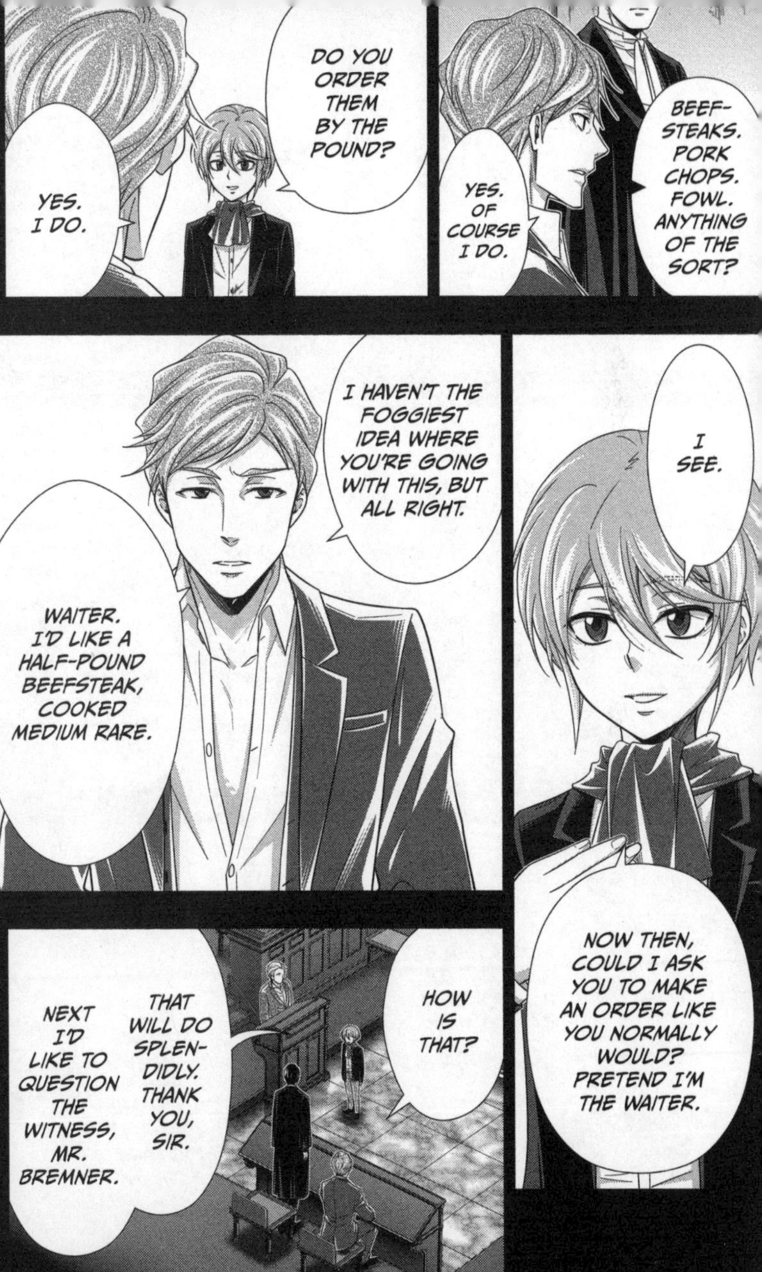
BEEF-STEAKS. PORK CHOPS. FOWL. ANYTHING OF THE SORT?
YES. OF COURSE I DO.
DO YOU ORDER THEM BY THE POUND?
YES. I DO.
I SEE.
NOW THEN, COULD I ASK YOU TO MAKE AN ORDER LIKE YOU NORMALLY WOULD? PRETEND I'M THE WAITER.
I HAVEN'T THE FOGGIEST IDEA WHERE YOU'RE GOING WITH THIS, BUT ALL RIGHT.
WAITER. I'D LIKE A HALF-POUND BEEFSTEAK, COOKED MEDIUM RARE.
HOW IS THAT?
THAT WILL DO SPLENDIDLY. THANK YOU, SIR.
NEXT I'D LIKE TO QUESTION THE WITNESS, MR. BREMNER.

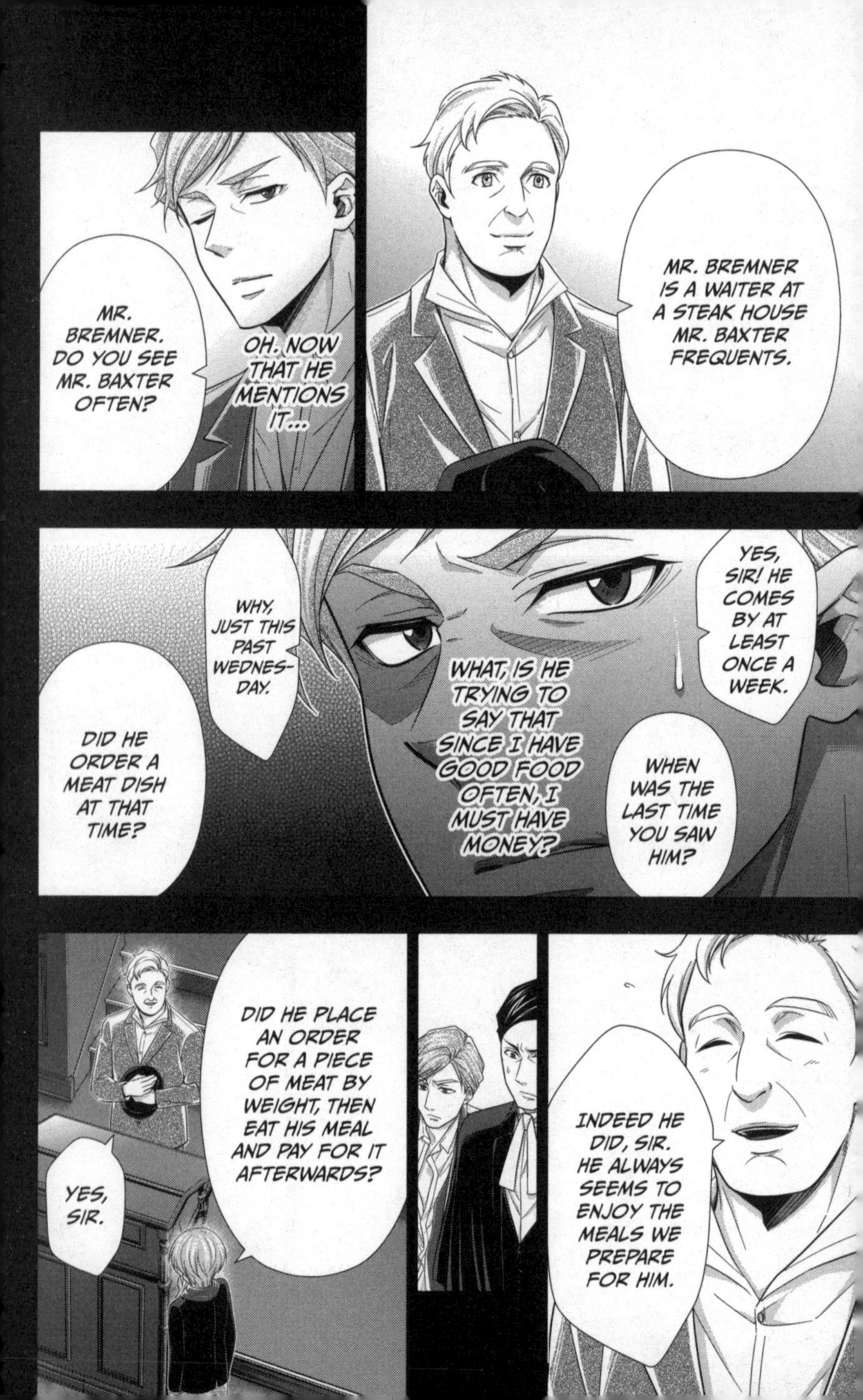
MR. BREMNER IS A WAITER AT A STEAK HOUSE MR. BAXTER FREQUENTS.
MR. BREMNER. DO YOU SEE MR. BAXTER OFTEN?
OH. NOW THAT HE MENTIONS IT...
YES, SIR! HE COMES BY AT LEAST ONCE A WEEK.
WHAT, IS HE TRYING TO SAY THAT SINCE I HAVE GOOD FOOD OFTEN, I MUST HAVE MONEY?
WHEN WAS THE LAST TIME YOU SAW HIM?
WHY, JUST THIS PAST WEDNES-DAY.
DID HE ORDER A MEAT DISH AT THAT TIME?
INDEED HE DID, SIR. HE ALWAYS SEEMS TO ENJOY THE MEALS WE PREPARE FOR HIM.
DID HE PLACE AN ORDER FOR A PIECE OF MEAT BY WEIGHT, THEN EAT HIS MEAL AND PAY FOR IT AFTERWARDS?
YES, SIR.

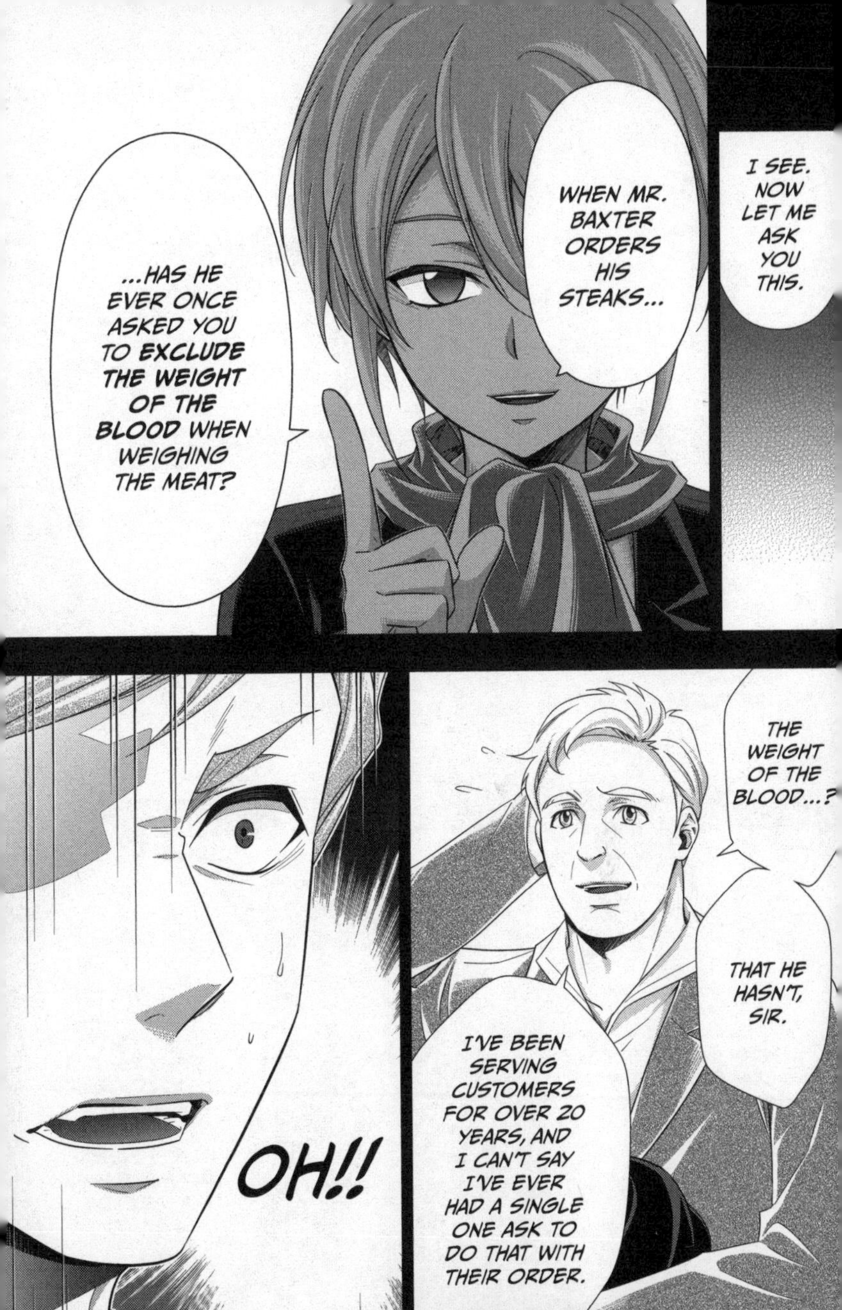
I SEE. NOW LET ME ASK YOU THIS.
WHEN MR. BAXTER ORDERS HIS STEAKS...
...HAS HE EVER ONCE ASKED YOU TO **EXCLUDE THE WEIGHT OF THE BLOOD** WHEN WEIGHING THE MEAT?
THE WEIGHT OF THE BLOOD...?
THAT HE HASN'T, SIR.
I'VE BEEN SERVING CUSTOMERS FOR OVER 20 YEARS, AND I CAN'T SAY I'VE EVER HAD A SINGLE ONE ASK TO DO THAT WITH THEIR ORDER.
OH!!

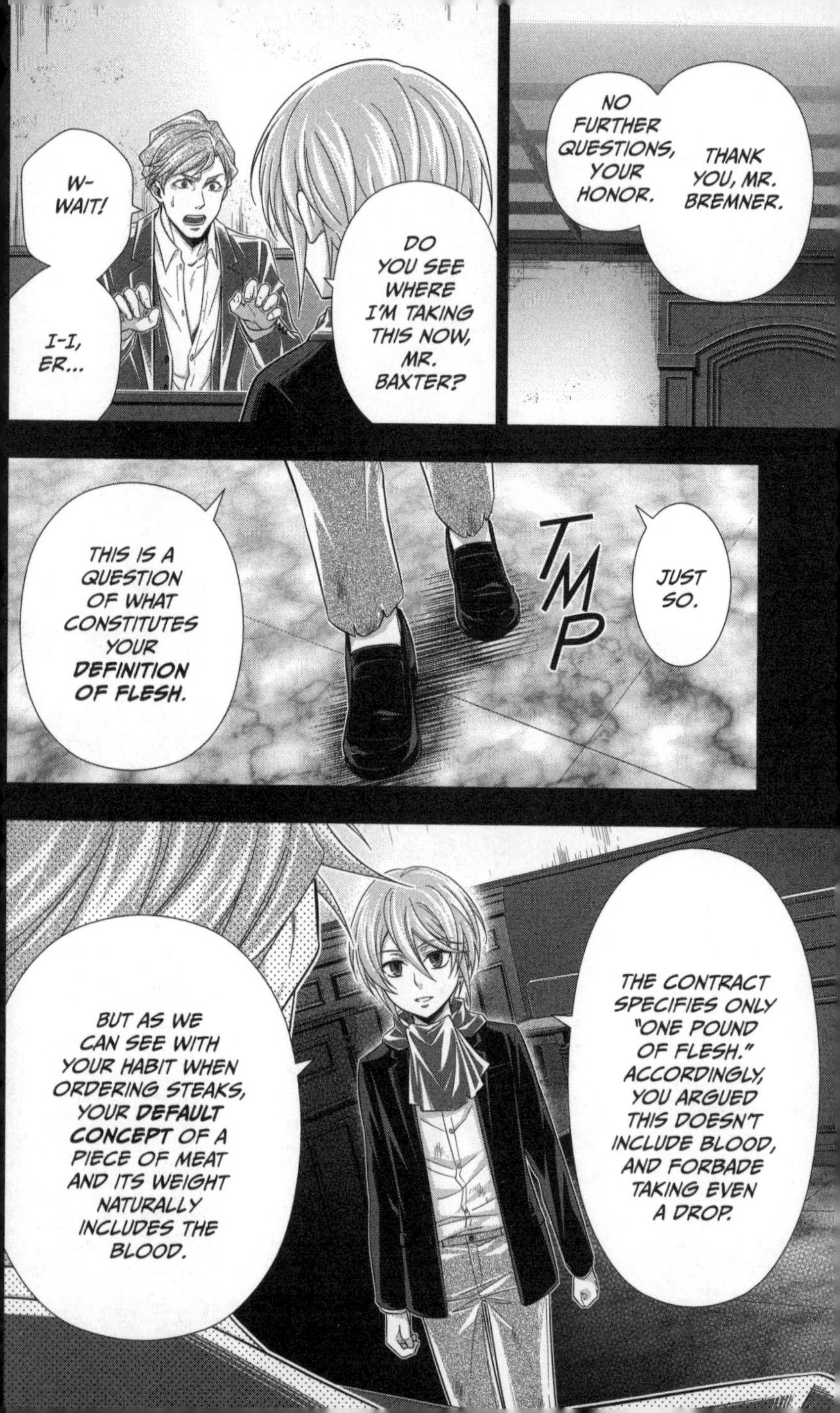
NO FURTHER QUESTIONS, YOUR HONOR.
THANK YOU, MR. BREMNER.
DO YOU SEE WHERE I'M TAKING THIS NOW, MR. BAXTER?
W-WAIT!
I-I, ER...
JUST SO.
TMP
THIS IS A QUESTION OF WHAT CONSTITUTES YOUR **DEFINITION OF FLESH.**
THE CONTRACT SPECIFIES ONLY "ONE POUND OF FLESH." ACCORDINGLY, YOU ARGUED THIS DOESN'T INCLUDE BLOOD, AND FORBADE TAKING EVEN A DROP.
BUT AS WE CAN SEE WITH YOUR HABIT WHEN ORDERING STEAKS, YOUR **DEFAULT CONCEPT** OF A PIECE OF MEAT AND ITS WEIGHT NATURALLY INCLUDES THE BLOOD.

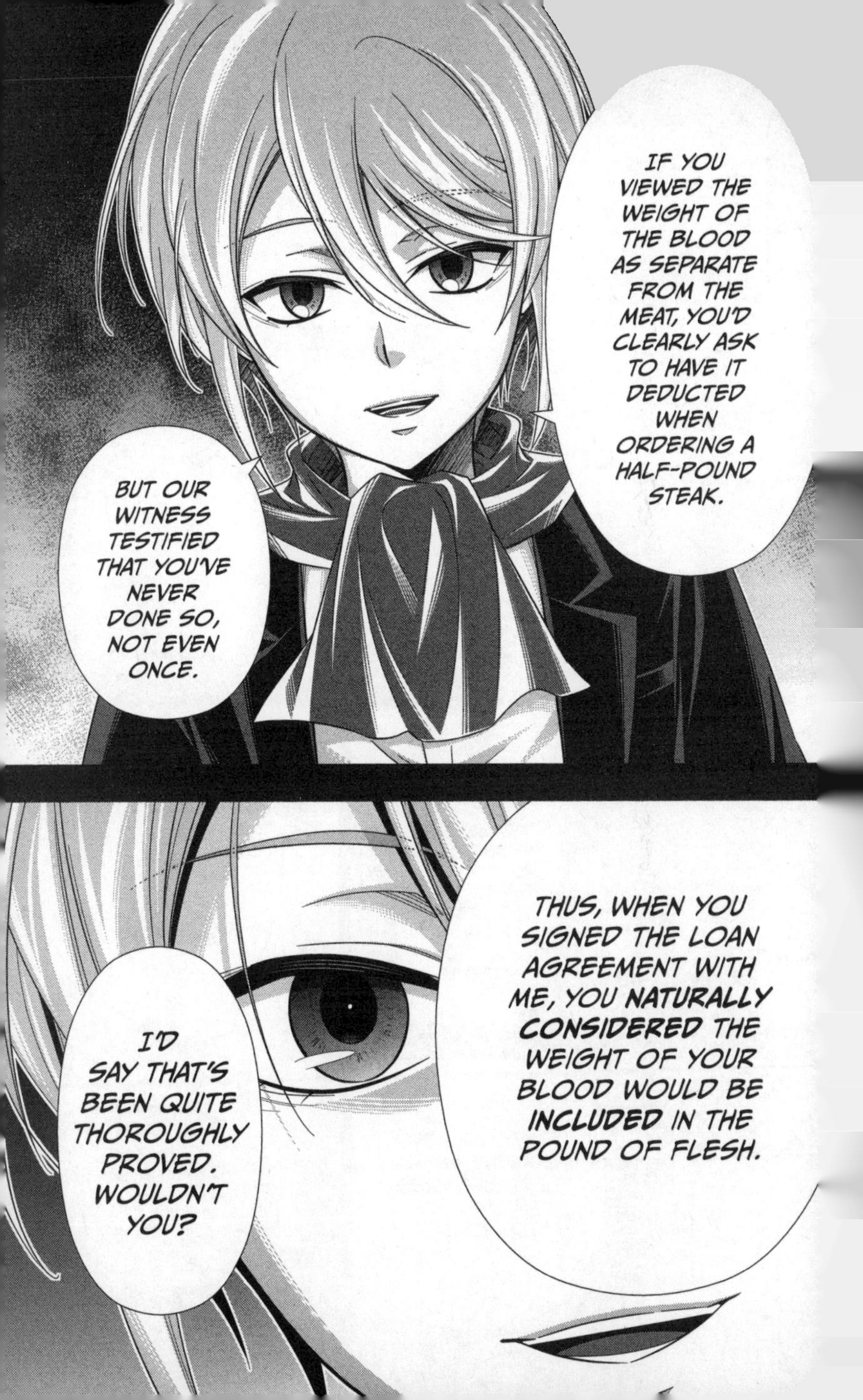
IF YOU VIEWED THE WEIGHT OF THE BLOOD AS SEPARATE FROM THE MEAT, YOU'D CLEARLY ASK TO HAVE IT DEDUCTED WHEN ORDERING A HALF-POUND STEAK.
BUT OUR WITNESS TESTIFIED THAT YOU'VE NEVER DONE SO, NOT EVEN ONCE.
THUS, WHEN YOU SIGNED THE LOAN AGREEMENT WITH ME, YOU NATURALLY CONSIDERED THE WEIGHT OF YOUR BLOOD WOULD BE INCLUDED IN THE POUND OF FLESH.
I'D SAY THAT'S BEEN QUITE THOROUGHLY PROVED. WOULDN'T YOU?

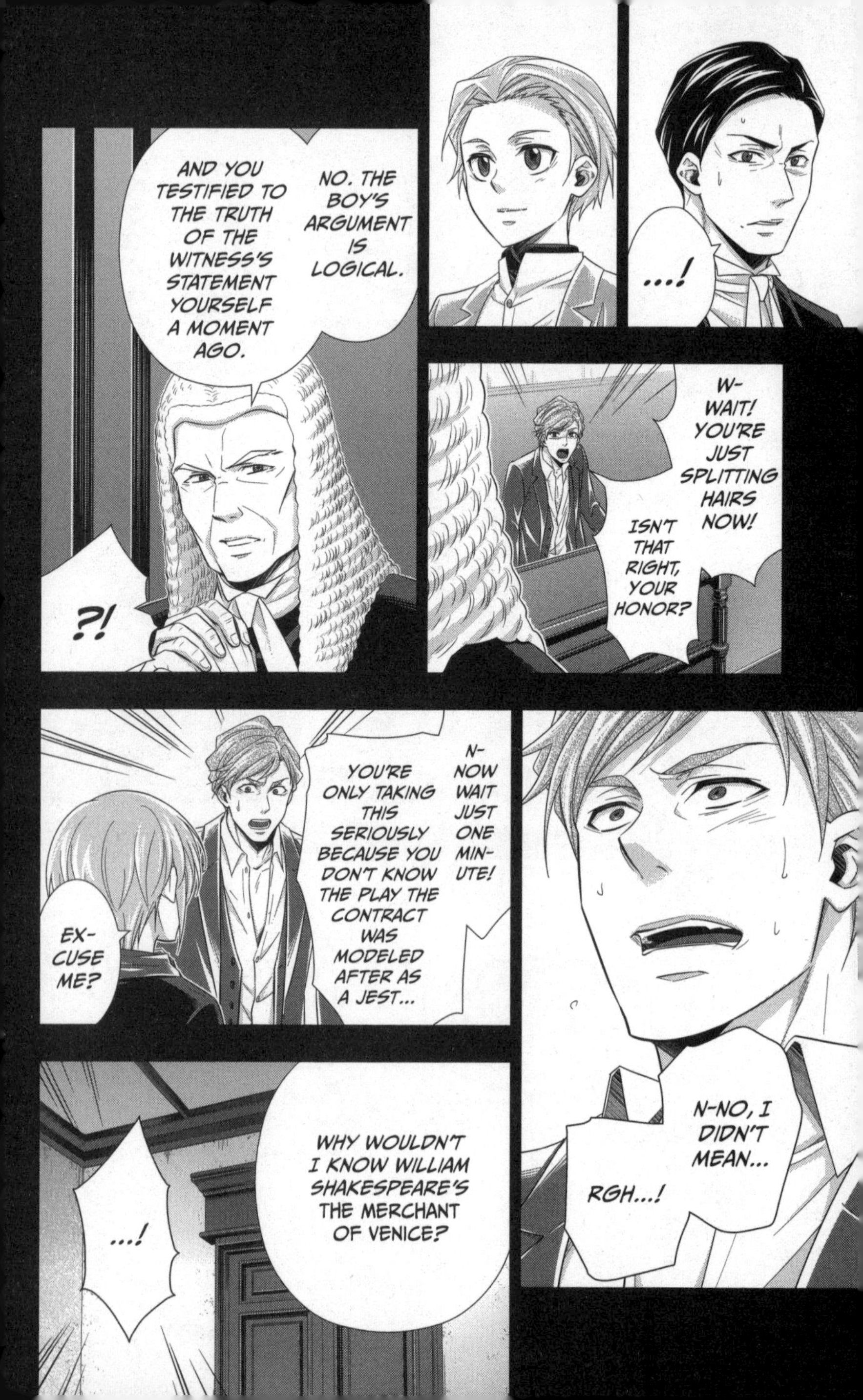
...!
NO. THE BOY'S ARGUMENT IS LOGICAL.
AND YOU TESTIFIED TO THE TRUTH OF THE WITNESS'S STATEMENT YOURSELF A MOMENT AGO.
?!
W-WAIT! YOU'RE JUST SPLITTING HAIRS NOW!
ISN'T THAT RIGHT, YOUR HONOR?
N-NO, I DIDN'T MEAN...
RGH...!
N-NOW WAIT JUST ONE MIN-UTE!
YOU'RE ONLY TAKING THIS SERIOUSLY BECAUSE YOU DON'T KNOW THE PLAY THE CONTRACT WAS MODELED AFTER AS A JEST...
EX-CUSE ME?
WHY WOULDN'T I KNOW WILLIAM SHAKESPEARE'S THE MERCHANT OF VENICE?
...!

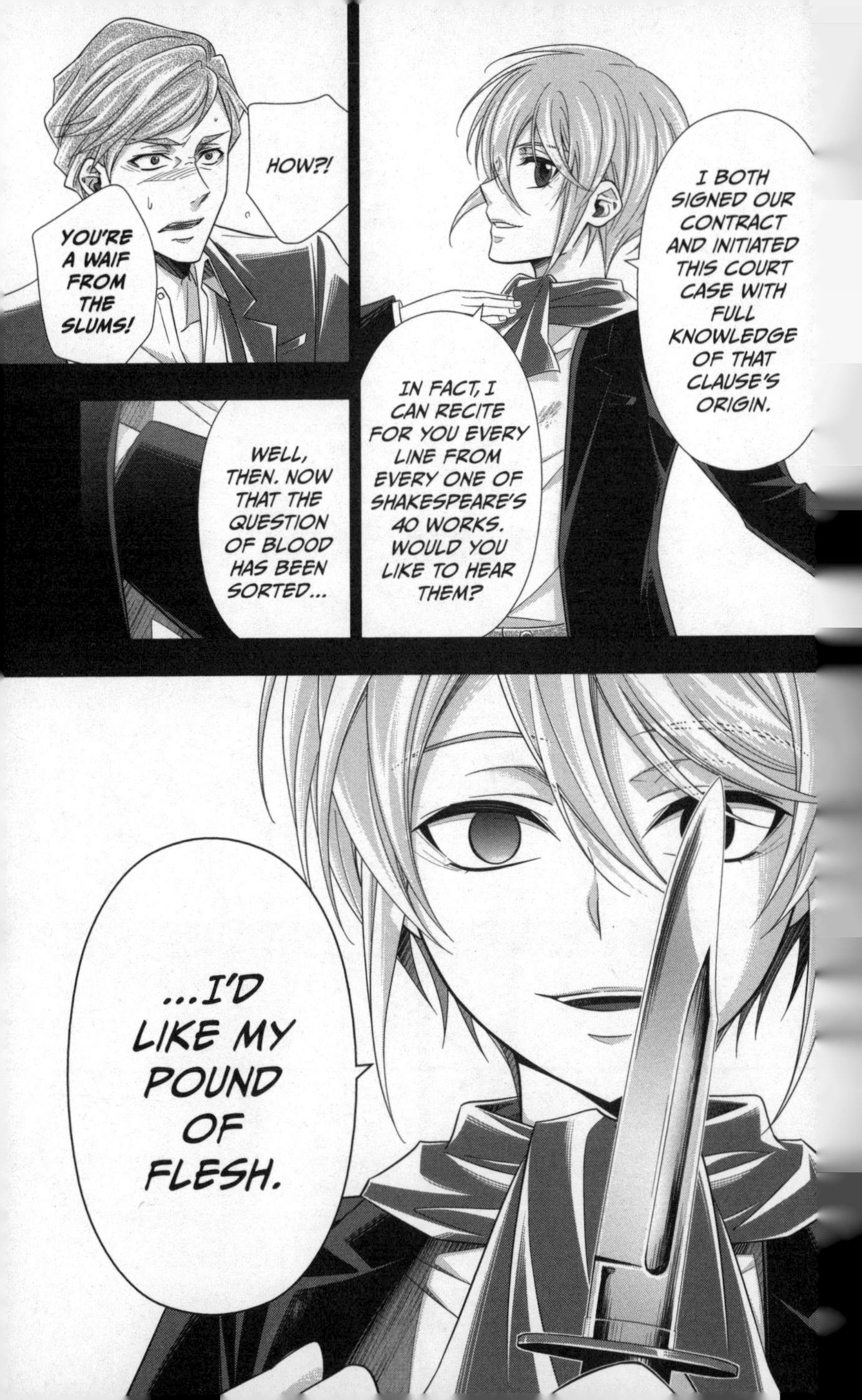
I BOTH SIGNED OUR CONTRACT AND INITIATED THIS COURT CASE WITH FULL KNOWLEDGE OF THAT CLAUSE'S ORIGIN.
IN FACT, I CAN RECITE FOR YOU EVERY LINE FROM EVERY ONE OF SHAKESPEARE'S 40 WORKS. WOULD YOU LIKE TO HEAR THEM?
HOW?!
YOU'RE A WAIF FROM THE SLUMS!
WELL, THEN. NOW THAT THE QUESTION OF BLOOD HAS BEEN SORTED...
...I'D LIKE MY POUND OF FLESH.

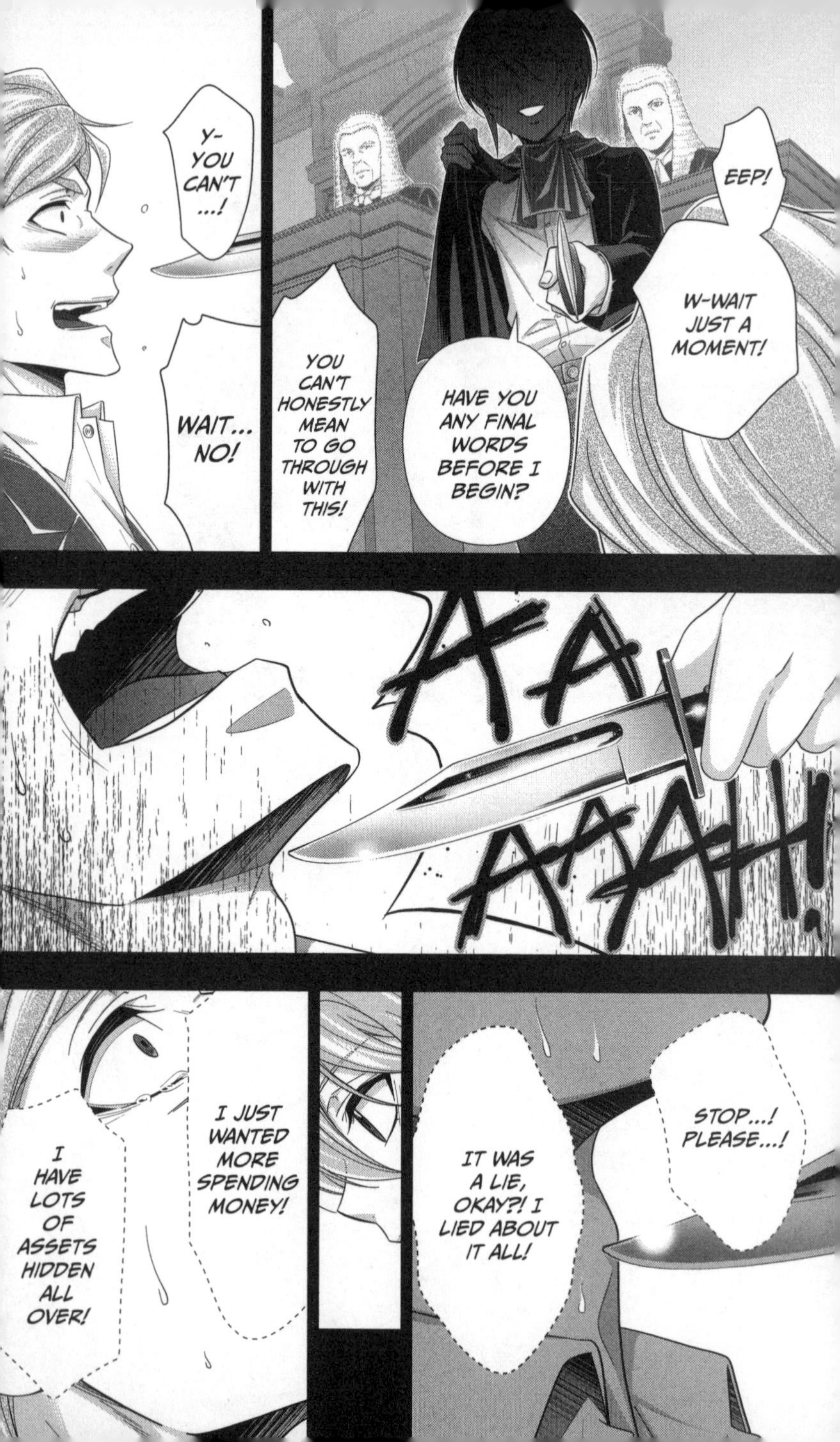
EEP!
W-WAIT JUST A MOMENT!
HAVE YOU ANY FINAL WORDS BEFORE I BEGIN?
YOU CAN'T HONESTLY MEAN TO GO THROUGH WITH THIS!
Y-YOU CAN'T...!
WAIT... NO!
AAAAAH!
STOP...! PLEASE...!
IT WAS A LIE, OKAY?! I LIED ABOUT IT ALL!
I JUST WANTED MORE SPENDING MONEY!
I HAVE LOTS OF ASSETS HIDDEN ALL OVER!

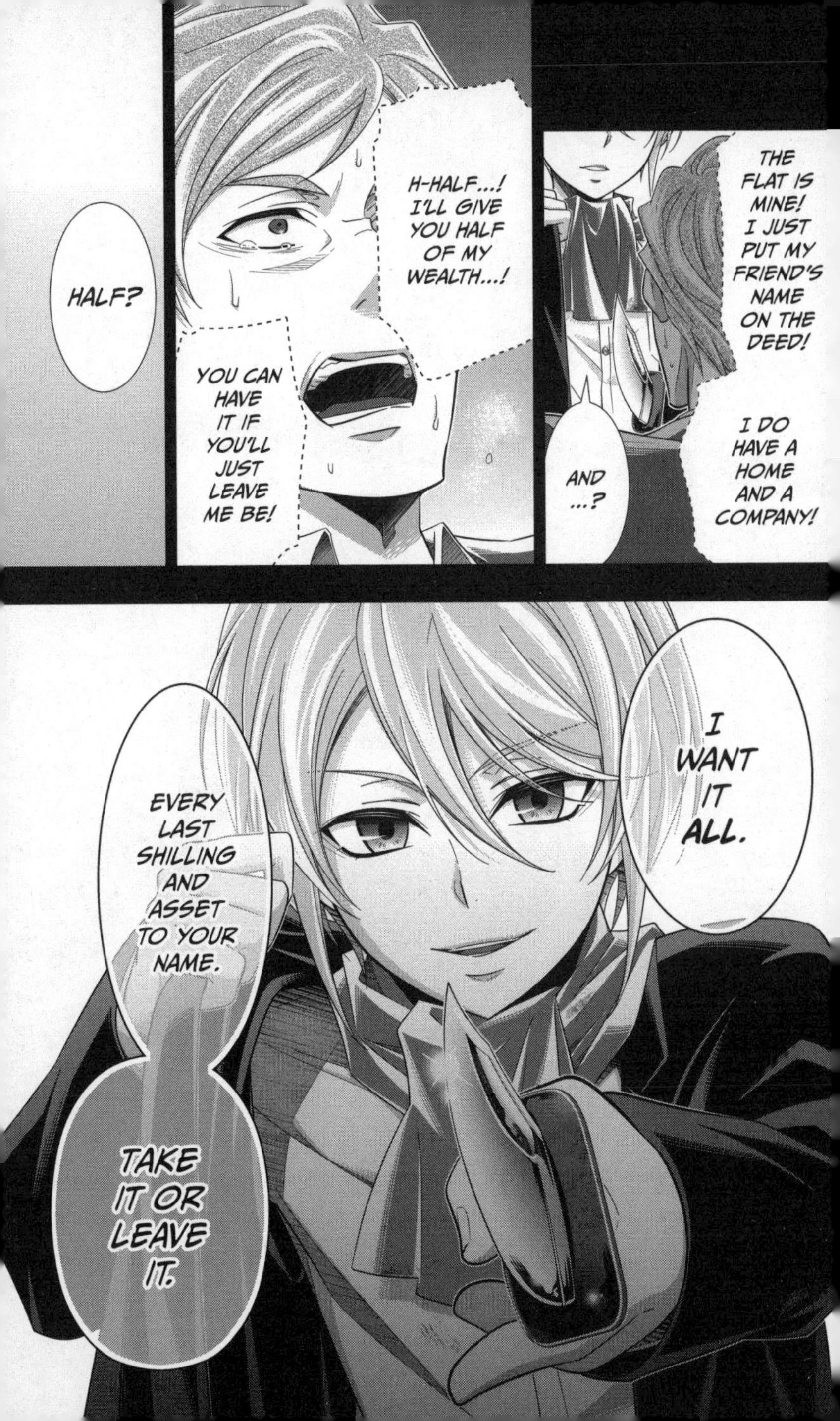
THE FLAT IS MINE! I JUST PUT MY FRIEND'S NAME ON THE DEED!
I DO HAVE A HOME AND A COMPANY!
AND ...?
H-HALF...! I'LL GIVE YOU HALF OF MY WEALTH...!
YOU CAN HAVE IT IF YOU'LL JUST LEAVE ME BE!
HALF?
I WANT IT ALL.
EVERY LAST SHILLING AND ASSET TO YOUR NAME.
TAKE IT OR LEAVE IT.

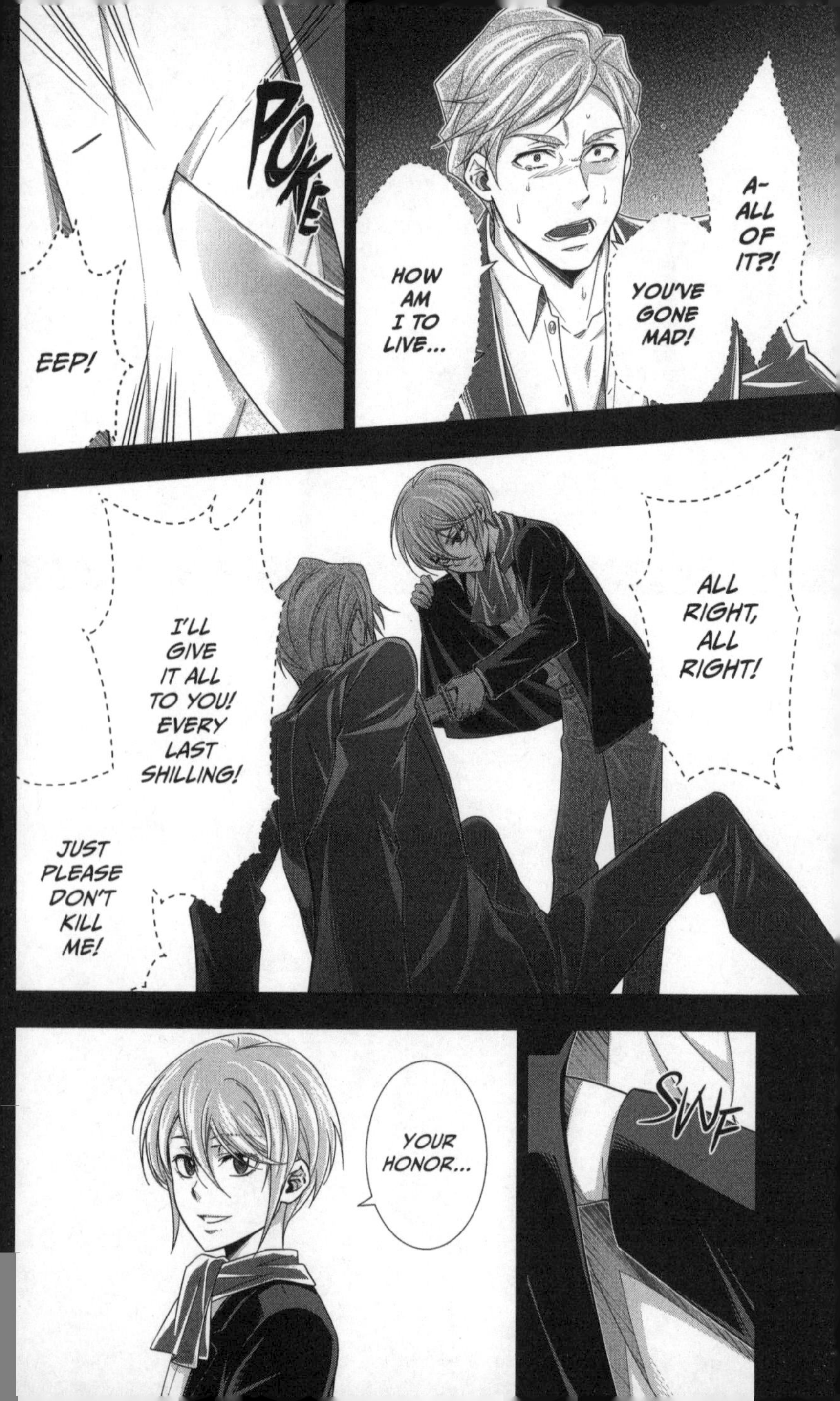
A-ALL OF IT?!
YOU'VE GONE MAD!
HOW AM I TO LIVE...
POKE
EEP!
ALL RIGHT, ALL RIGHT!
I'LL GIVE IT ALL TO YOU! EVERY LAST SHILLING!
JUST PLEASE DON'T KILL ME!
SWF
YOUR HONOR...

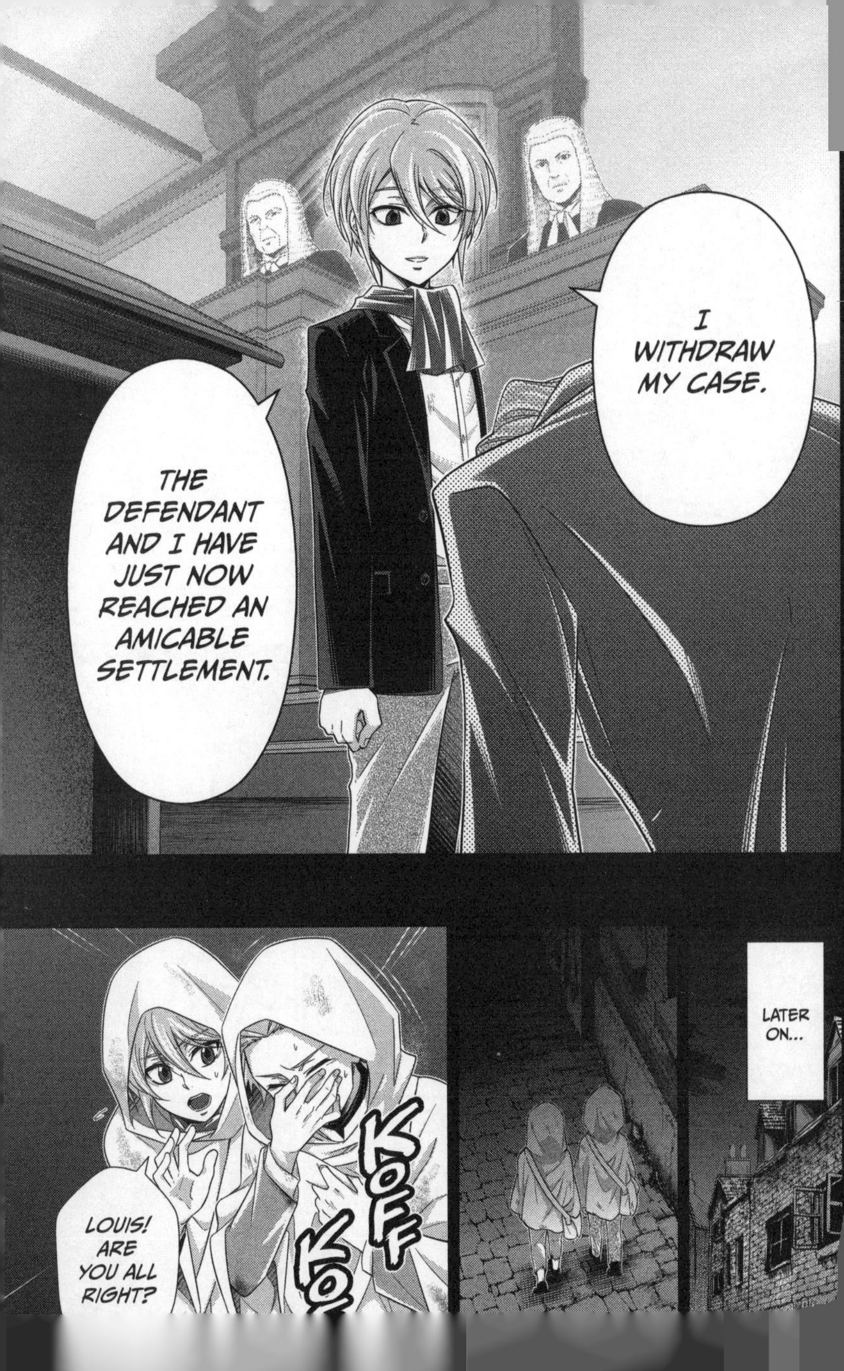
I WITHDRAW MY CASE.
THE DEFENDANT AND I HAVE JUST NOW REACHED AN AMICABLE SETTLEMENT.
LATER ON...
KOFF
KO
LOUIS! ARE YOU ALL RIGHT?

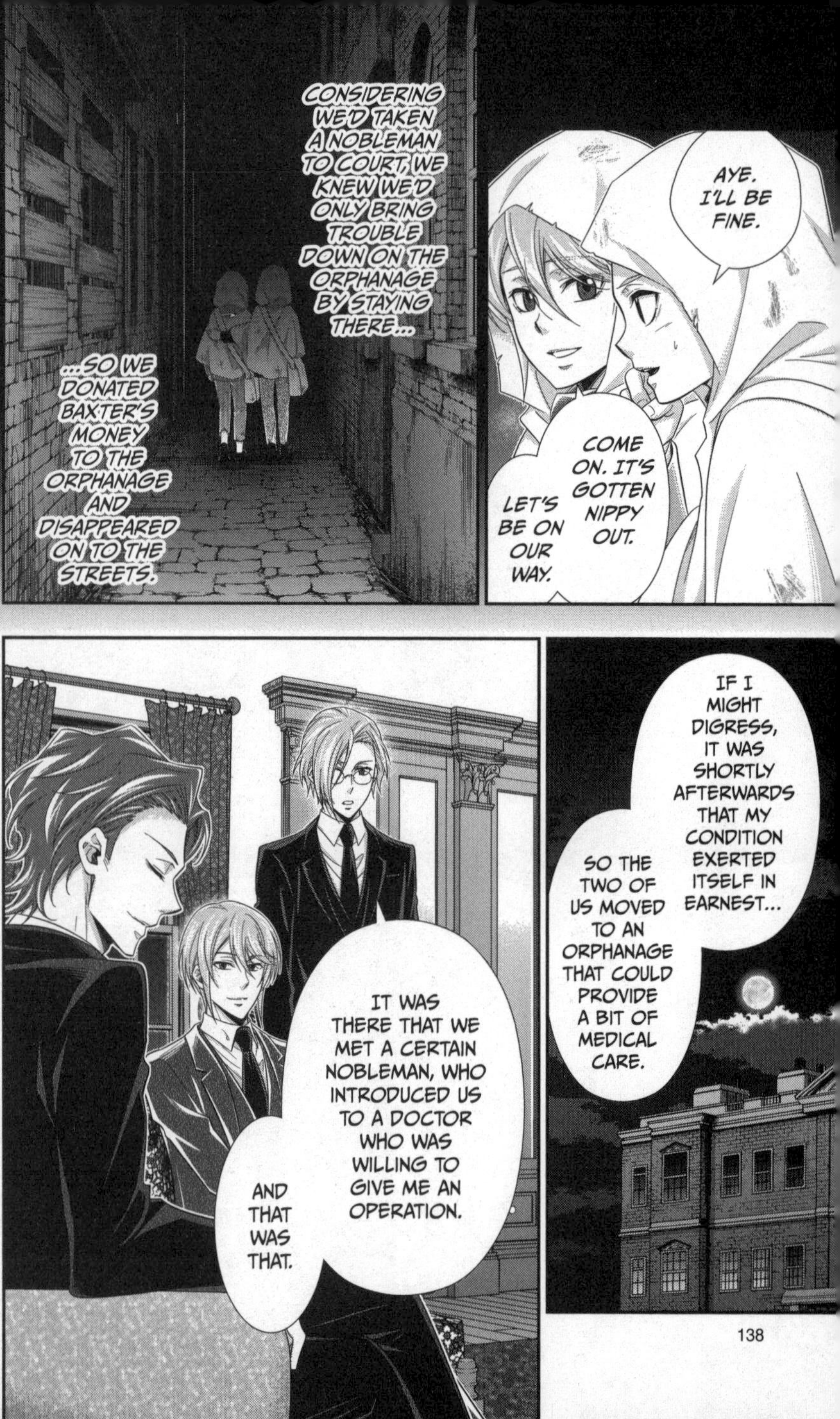
AYE. I'LL BE FINE.
COME ON. IT'S GOTTEN NIPPY OUT.
LET'S BE ON OUR WAY.
CONSIDERING WE'D TAKEN A NOBLEMAN TO COURT, WE KNEW WE'D ONLY BRING TROUBLE DOWN ON THE ORPHANAGE BY STAYING THERE...
...SO WE DONATED BAXTER'S MONEY TO THE ORPHANAGE AND DISAPPEARED ON TO THE STREETS.
IF I MIGHT DIGRESS, IT WAS SHORTLY AFTERWARDS THAT MY CONDITION EXERTED ITSELF IN EARNEST...
SO THE TWO OF US MOVED TO AN ORPHANAGE THAT COULD PROVIDE A BIT OF MEDICAL CARE.
IT WAS THERE THAT WE MET A CERTAIN NOBLEMAN, WHO INTRODUCED US TO A DOCTOR WHO WAS WILLING TO GIVE ME AN OPERATION.
AND THAT WAS THAT.

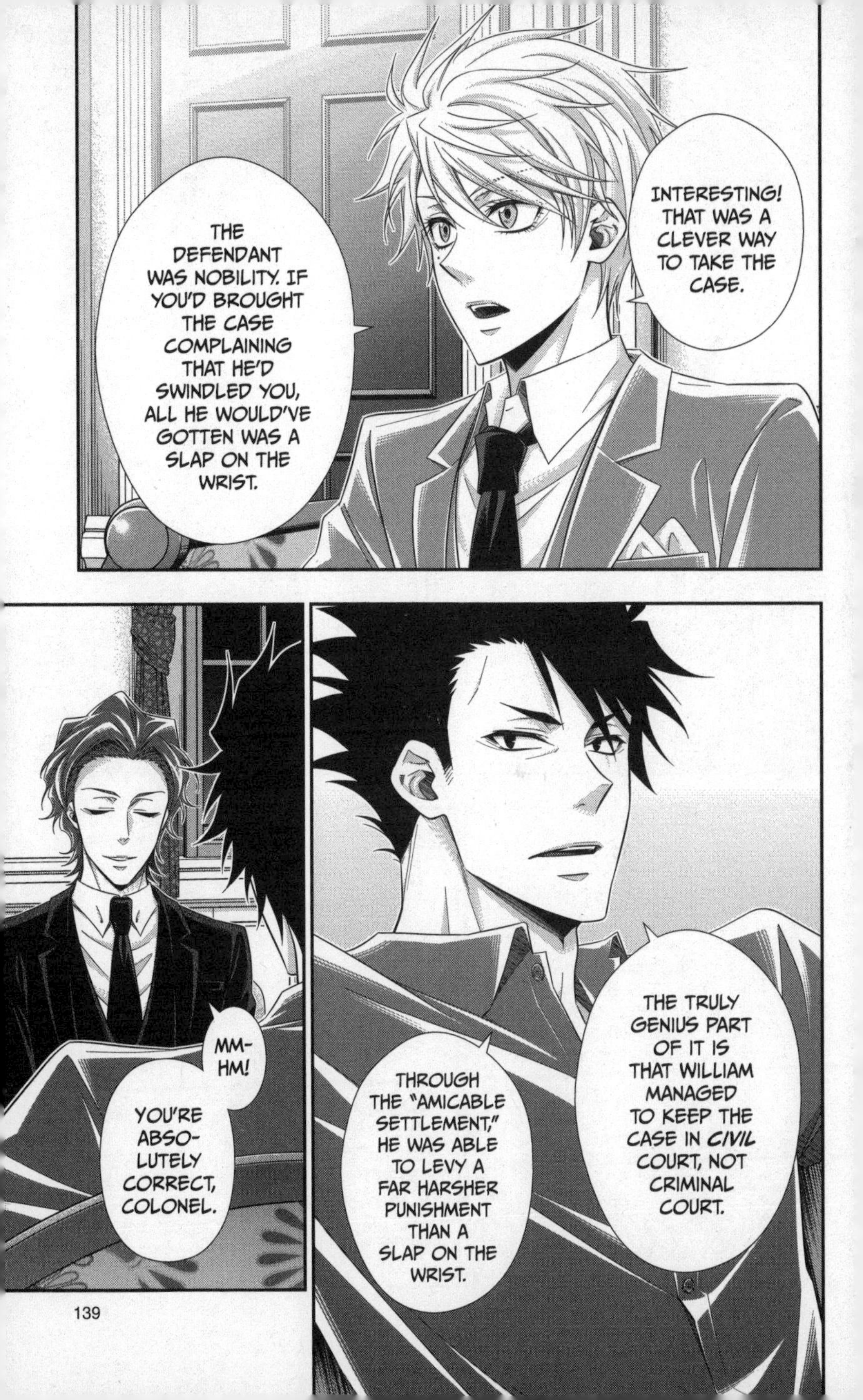
INTERESTING! THAT WAS A CLEVER WAY TO TAKE THE CASE.
THE DEFENDANT WAS NOBILITY. IF YOU'D BROUGHT THE CASE COMPLAINING THAT HE'D SWINDLED YOU, ALL HE WOULD'VE GOTTEN WAS A SLAP ON THE WRIST.
THE TRULY GENIUS PART OF IT IS THAT WILLIAM MANAGED TO KEEP THE CASE IN *CIVIL* COURT, NOT CRIMINAL COURT.
THROUGH THE "AMICABLE SETTLEMENT," HE WAS ABLE TO LEVY A FAR HARSHER PUNISHMENT THAN A SLAP ON THE WRIST.
MM-HM!
YOU'RE ABSO-LUTELY CORRECT, COLONEL.

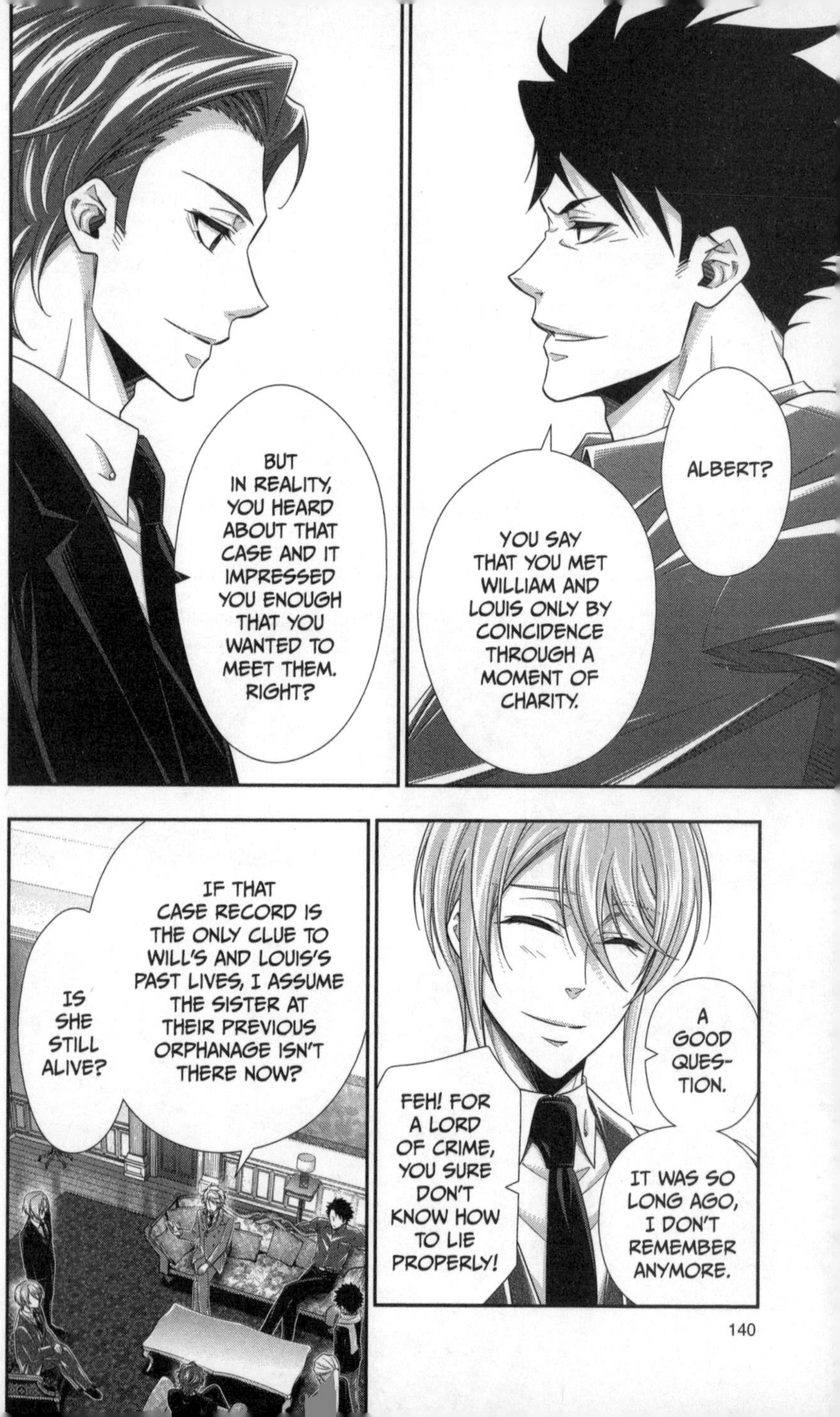
ALBERT?
YOU SAY THAT YOU MET WILLIAM AND LOUIS ONLY BY COINCIDENCE THROUGH A MOMENT OF CHARITY.
BUT IN REALITY, YOU HEARD ABOUT THAT CASE AND IT IMPRESSED YOU ENOUGH THAT YOU WANTED TO MEET THEM. RIGHT?
A GOOD QUES-TION.
IT WAS SO LONG AGO, I DON'T REMEMBER ANYMORE.
FEH! FOR A LORD OF CRIME, YOU SURE DON'T KNOW HOW TO LIE PROPERLY!
IF THAT CASE RECORD IS THE ONLY CLUE TO WILL'S AND LOUIS'S PAST LIVES, I ASSUME THE SISTER AT THEIR PREVIOUS ORPHANAGE ISN'T THERE NOW?
IS SHE STILL ALIVE?

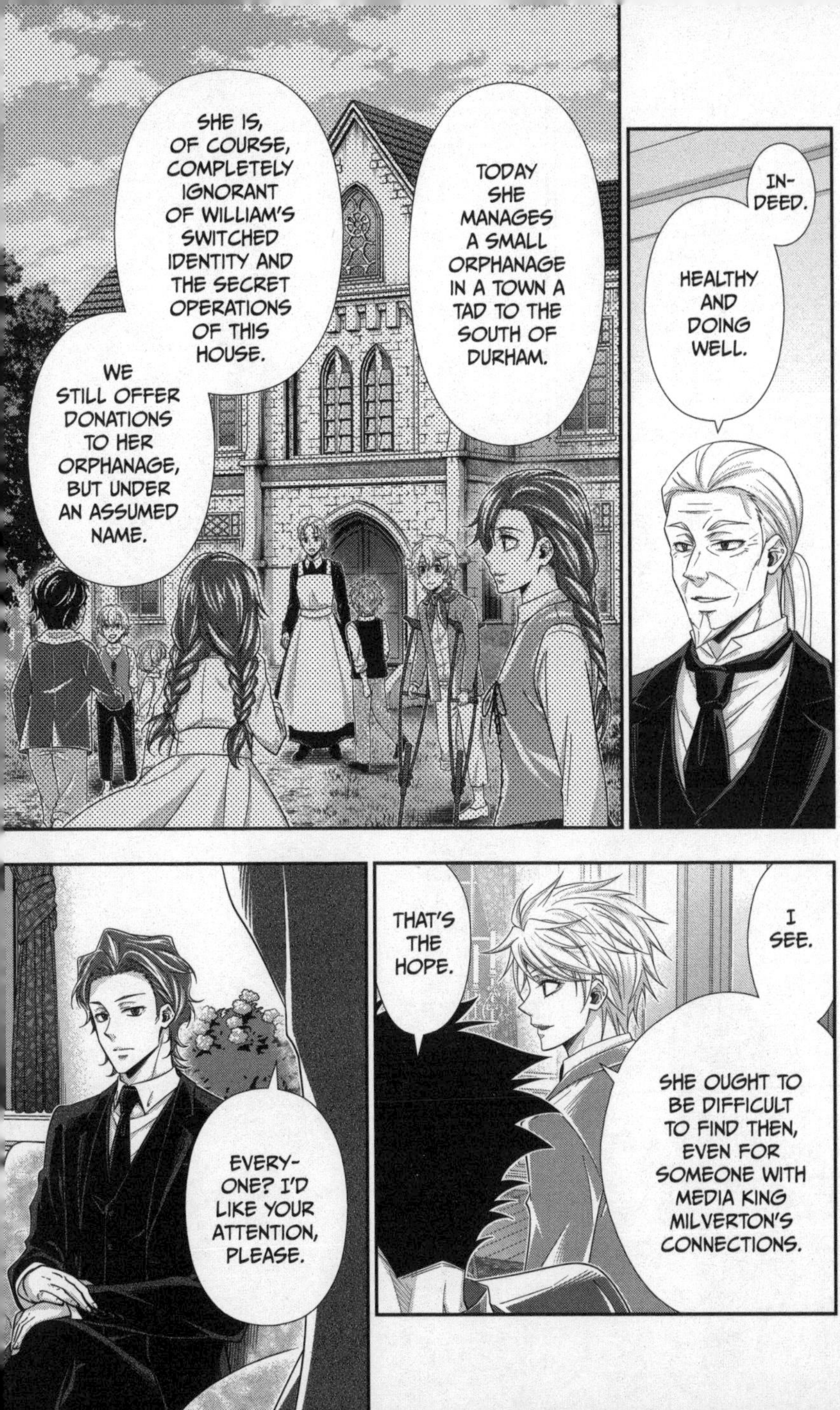
IN-DEED.
HEALTHY AND DOING WELL.
TODAY SHE MANAGES A SMALL ORPHANAGE IN A TOWN A TAD TO THE SOUTH OF DURHAM.
SHE IS, OF COURSE, COMPLETELY IGNORANT OF WILLIAM'S SWITCHED IDENTITY AND THE SECRET OPERATIONS OF THIS HOUSE.
WE STILL OFFER DONATIONS TO HER ORPHANAGE, BUT UNDER AN ASSUMED NAME.
I SEE.
SHE OUGHT TO BE DIFFICULT TO FIND THEN, EVEN FOR SOMEONE WITH MEDIA KING MILVERTON'S CONNECTIONS.
THAT'S THE HOPE.
EVERY-ONE? I'D LIKE YOUR ATTENTION, PLEASE.

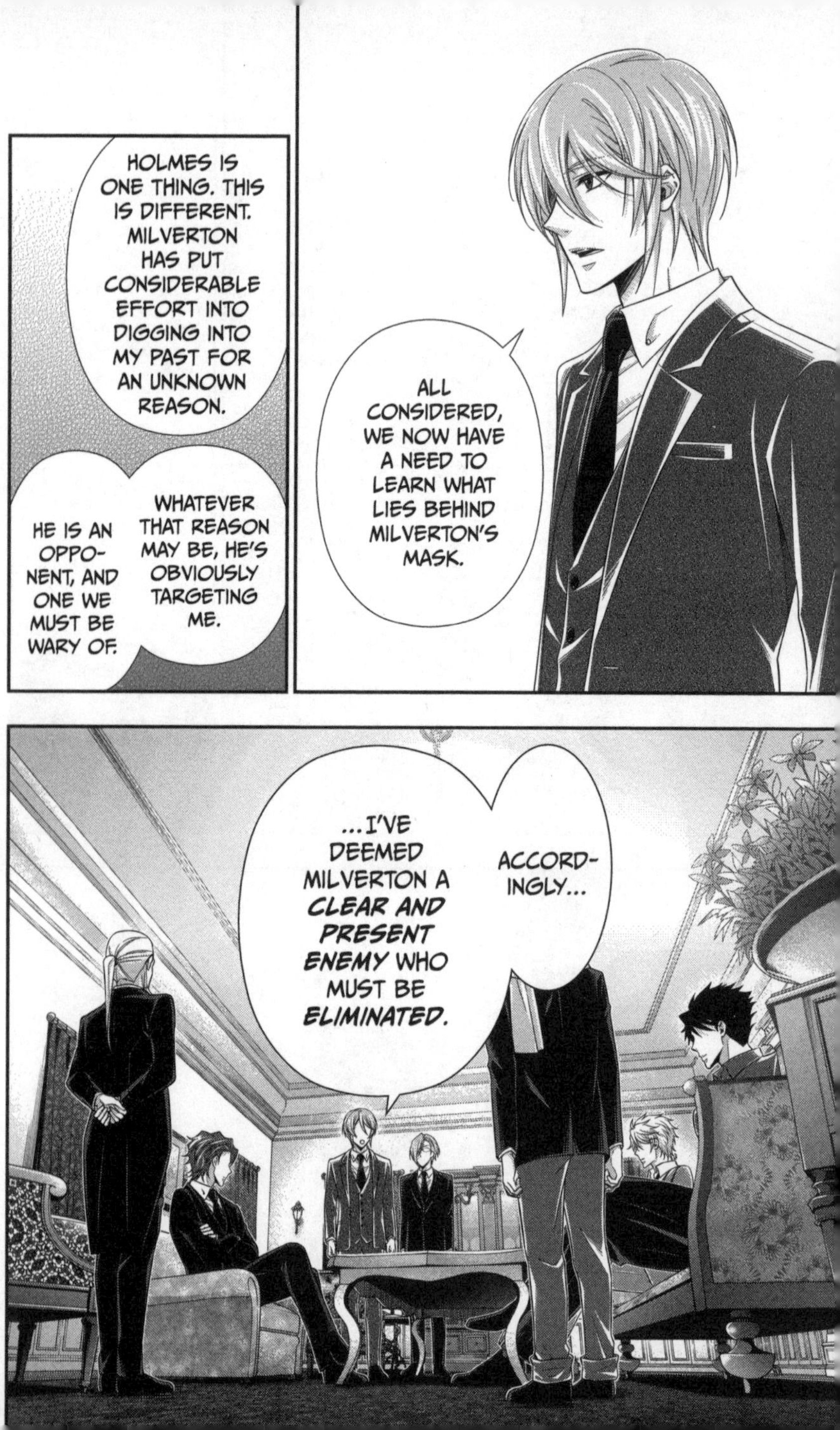
ALL CONSIDERED, WE NOW HAVE A NEED TO LEARN WHAT LIES BEHIND MILVERTON'S MASK.
HOLMES IS ONE THING. THIS IS DIFFERENT. MILVERTON HAS PUT CONSIDERABLE EFFORT INTO DIGGING INTO MY PAST FOR AN UNKNOWN REASON.
WHATEVER THAT REASON MAY BE, HE'S OBVIOUSLY TARGETING ME.
HE IS AN OPPO-NENT, AND ONE WE MUST BE WARY OF.
ACCORD-INGLY...
...I'VE DEEMED MILVERTON A ***CLEAR AND PRESENT ENEMY*** WHO MUST BE ***ELIMINATED.***

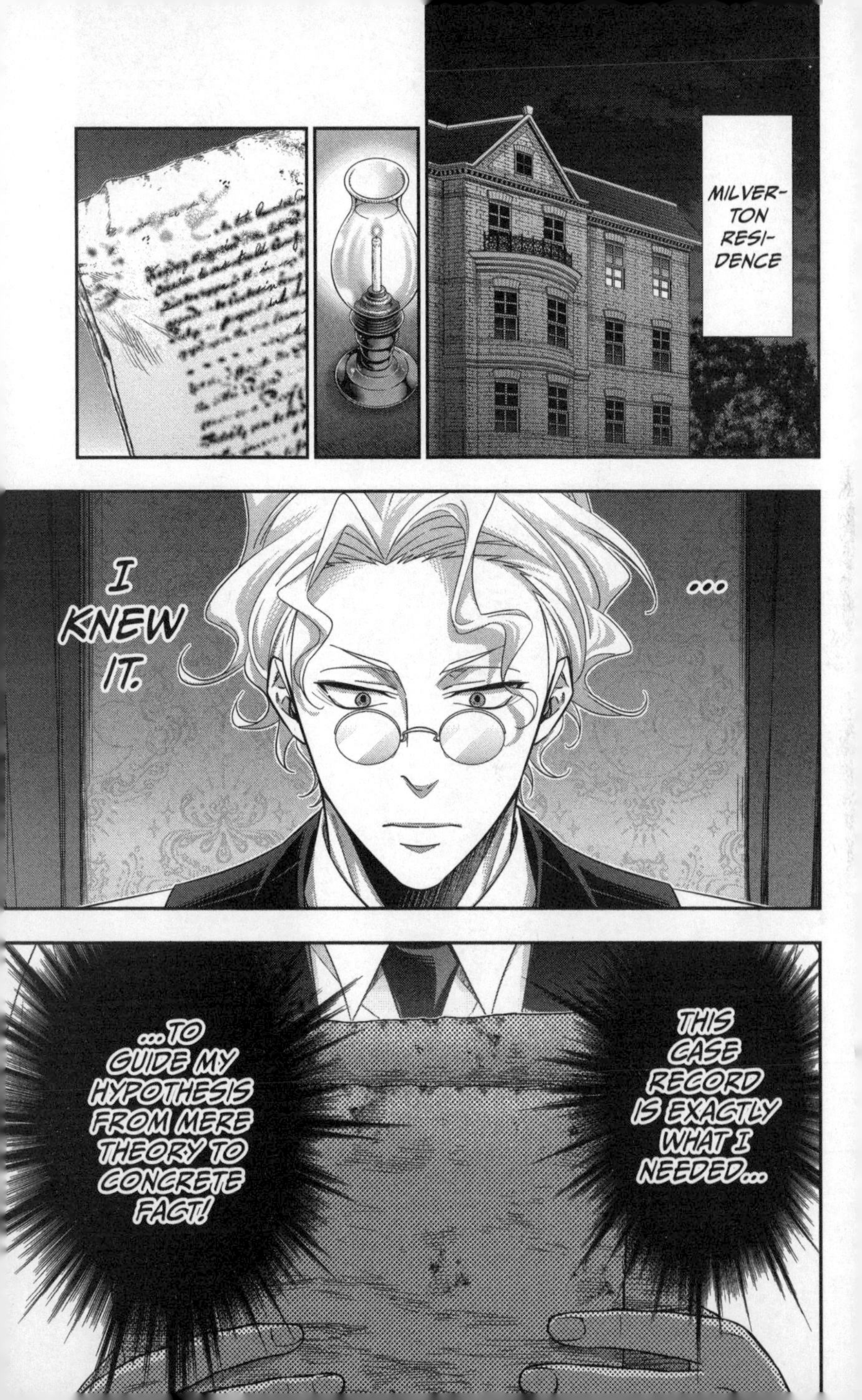
MILVERTON RESIDENCE
...
I KNEW IT.
THIS CASE RECORD IS EXACTLY WHAT I NEEDED...
...TO GUIDE MY HYPOTHESIS FROM MERE THEORY TO CONCRETE FACT!

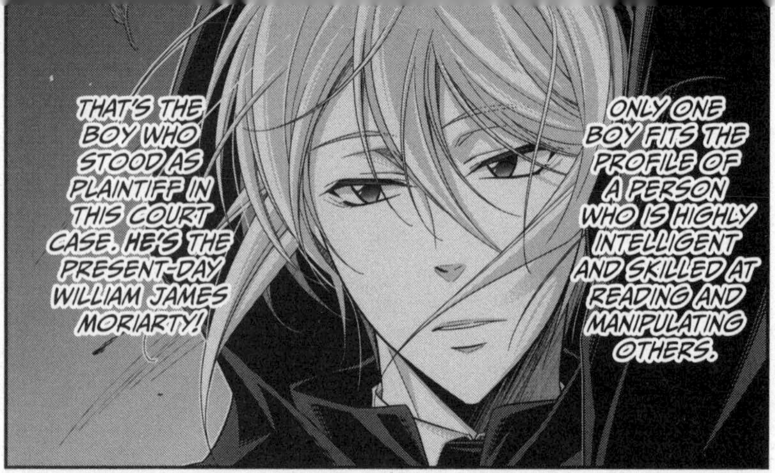
ONLY ONE BOY FITS THE PROFILE OF A PERSON WHO IS HIGHLY INTELLIGENT AND SKILLED AT READING AND MANIPULATING OTHERS.
THAT'S THE BOY WHO STOOD AS PLAINTIFF IN THIS COURT CASE. HE'S THE PRESENT-DAY WILLIAM JAMES MORIARTY!
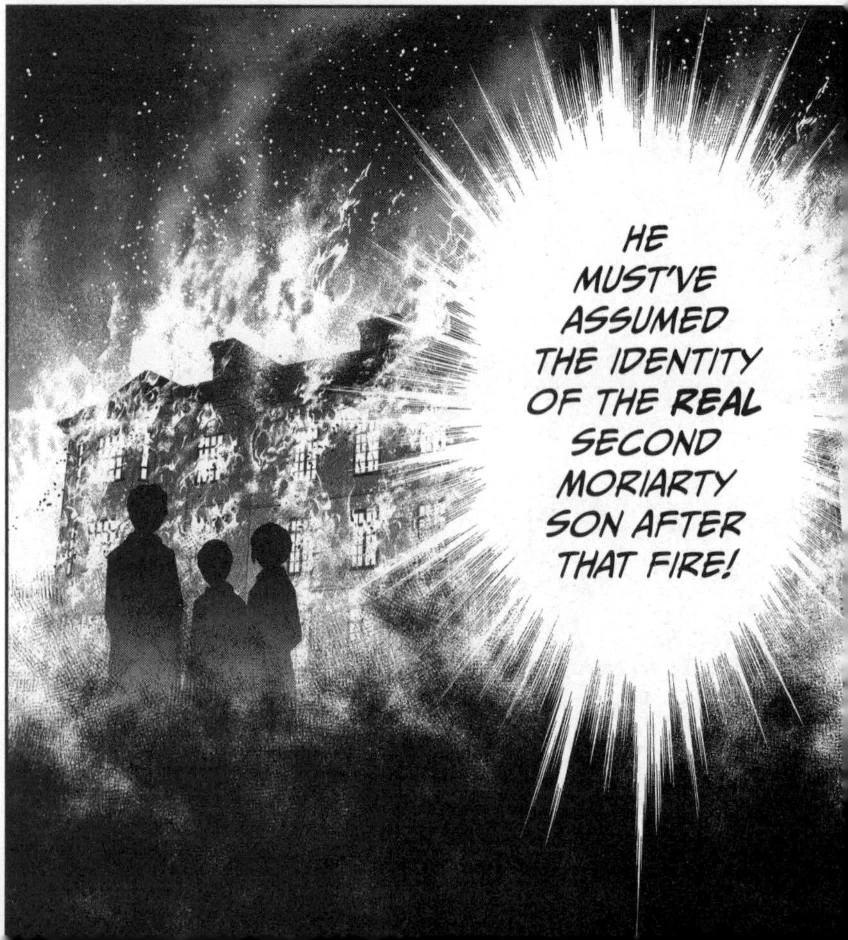
HE MUST'VE ASSUMED THE IDENTITY OF THE **REAL** SECOND MORIARTY SON AFTER THAT FIRE!

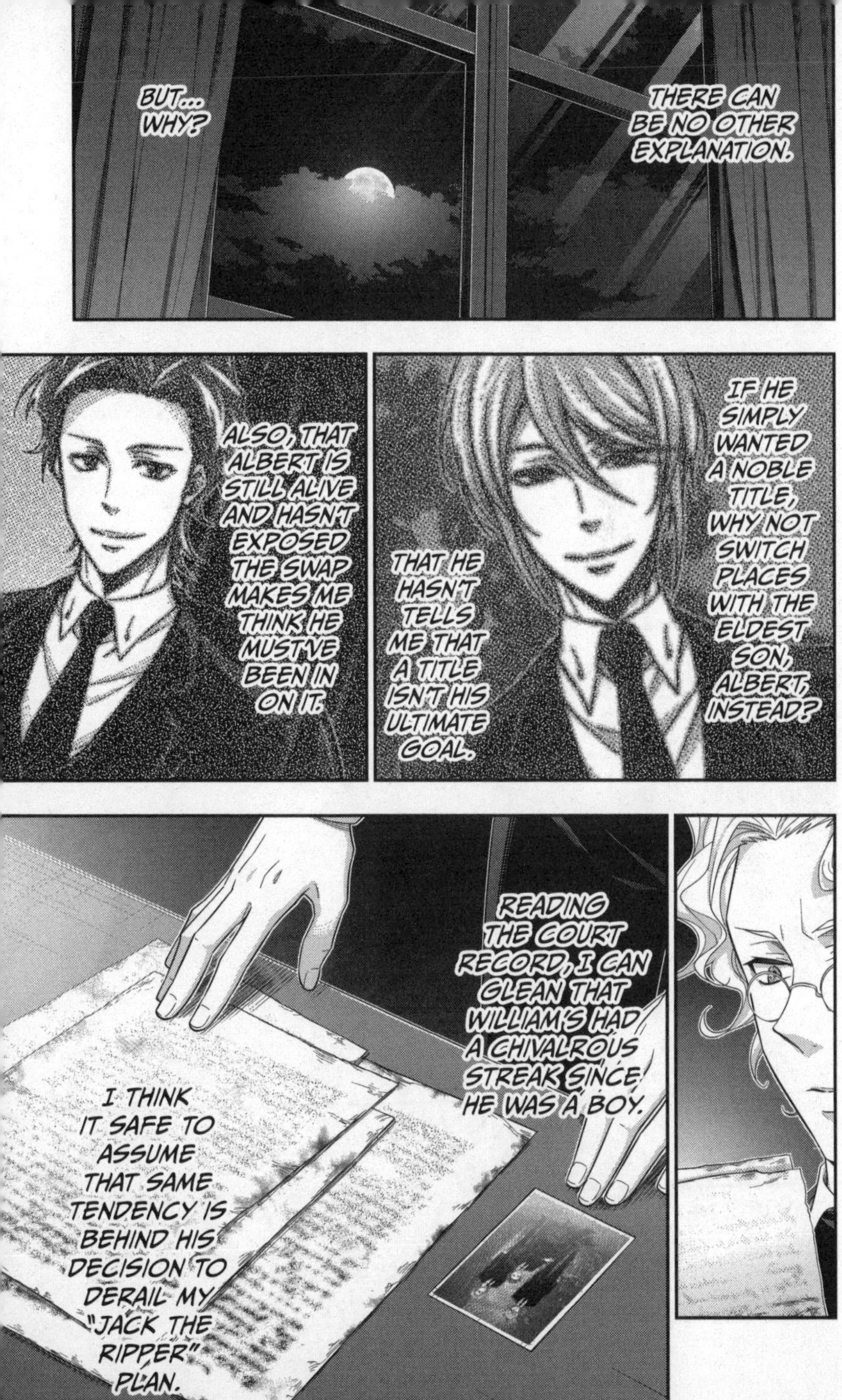
THERE CAN BE NO OTHER EXPLANATION.
BUT... WHY?
IF HE SIMPLY WANTED A NOBLE TITLE, WHY NOT SWITCH PLACES WITH THE ELDEST SON, ALBERT, INSTEAD?
THAT HE HASN'T TELLS ME THAT A TITLE ISN'T HIS ULTIMATE GOAL.
ALSO, THAT ALBERT IS STILL ALIVE AND HASN'T EXPOSED THE SWAP MAKES ME THINK HE MUST'VE BEEN IN ON IT.
READING THE COURT RECORD, I CAN GLEAN THAT WILLIAM'S HAD A CHIVALROUS STREAK SINCE HE WAS A BOY.
I THINK IT SAFE TO ASSUME THAT SAME TENDENCY IS BEHIND HIS DECISION TO DERAIL MY "JACK THE RIPPER" PLAN.

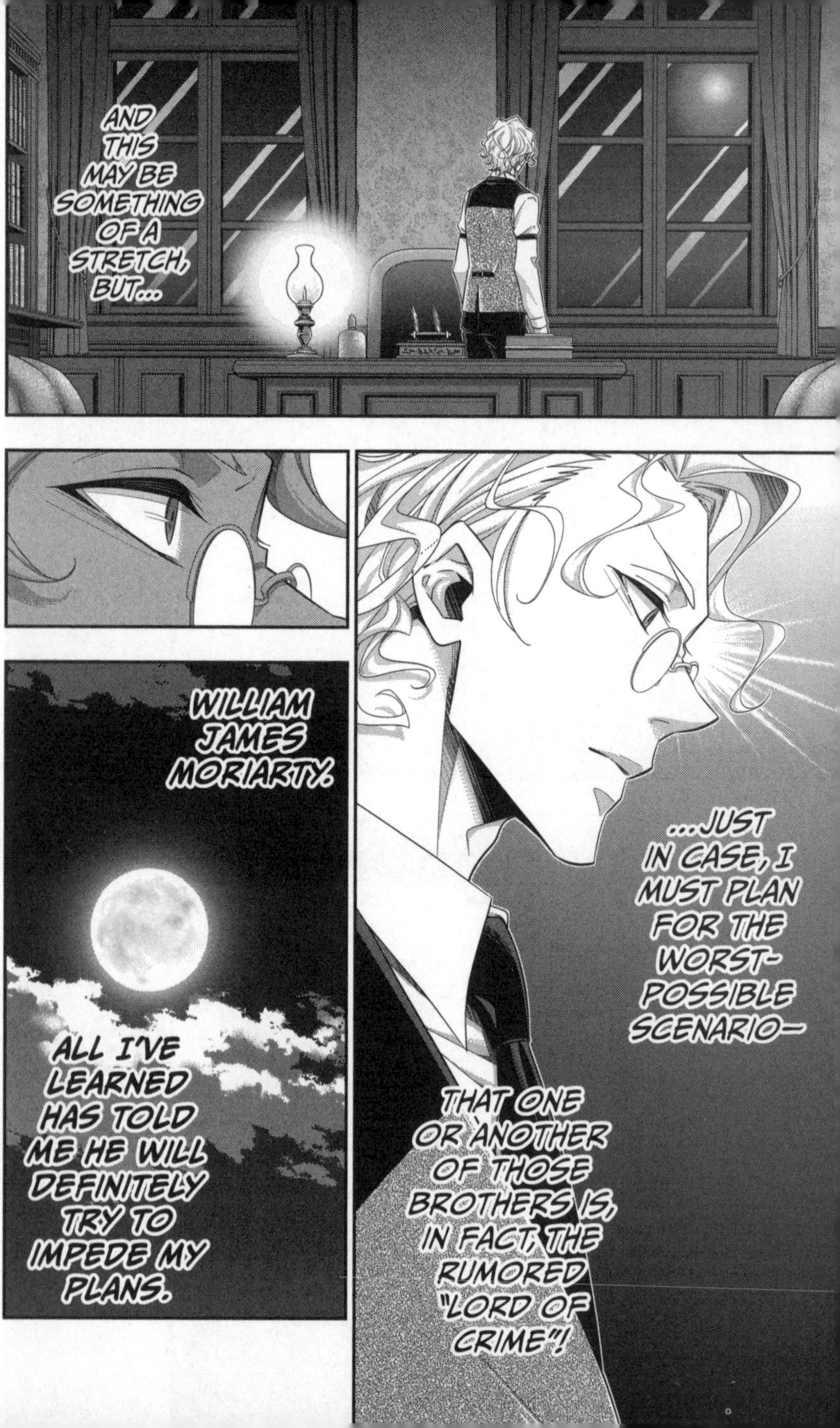
AND THIS MAY BE SOMETHING OF A STRETCH, BUT...
...JUST IN CASE, I MUST PLAN FOR THE WORST-POSSIBLE SCENARIO—
THAT ONE OR ANOTHER OF THOSE BROTHERS IS, IN FACT, THE RUMORED "LORD OF CRIME"!
WILLIAM JAMES MORIARTY.
ALL I'VE LEARNED HAS TOLD ME HE WILL DEFINITELY TRY TO IMPEDE MY PLANS.

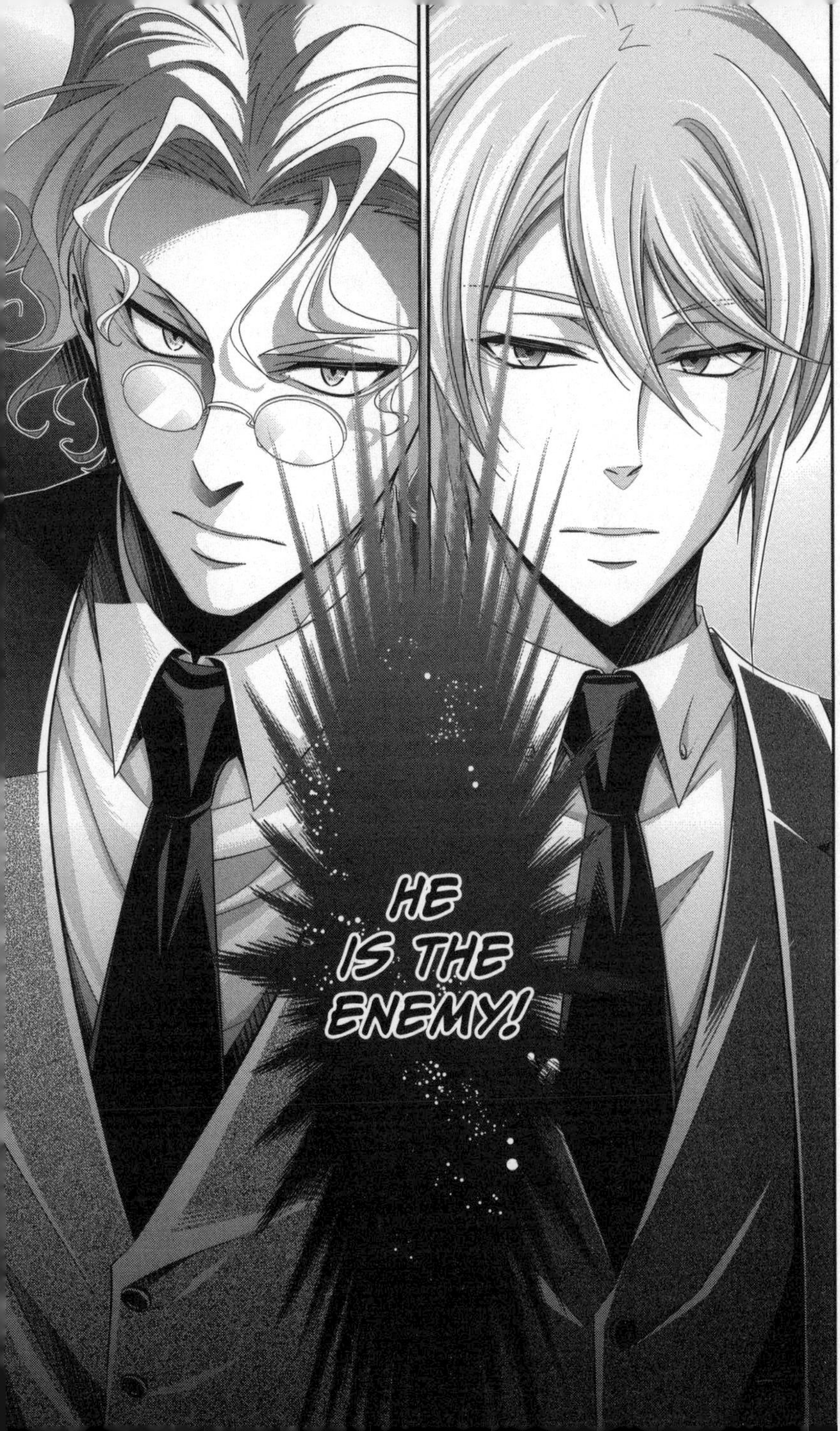
HE IS THE ENEMY!

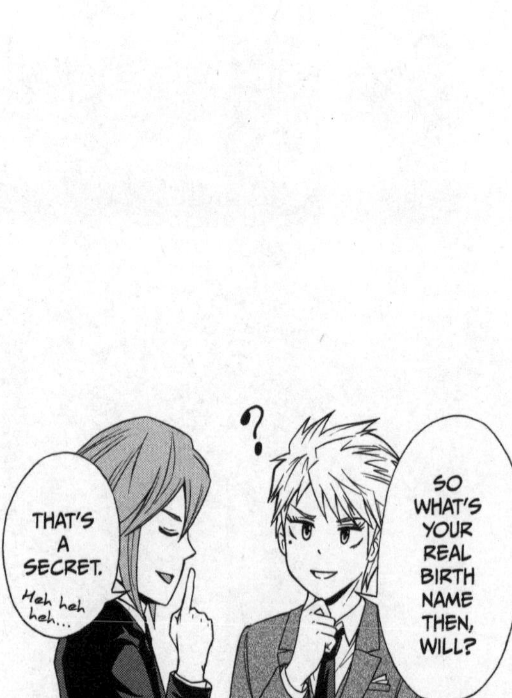
SO WHAT'S YOUR REAL BIRTH NAME THEN, WILL?
THAT'S A SECRET.
Heh heh heh...

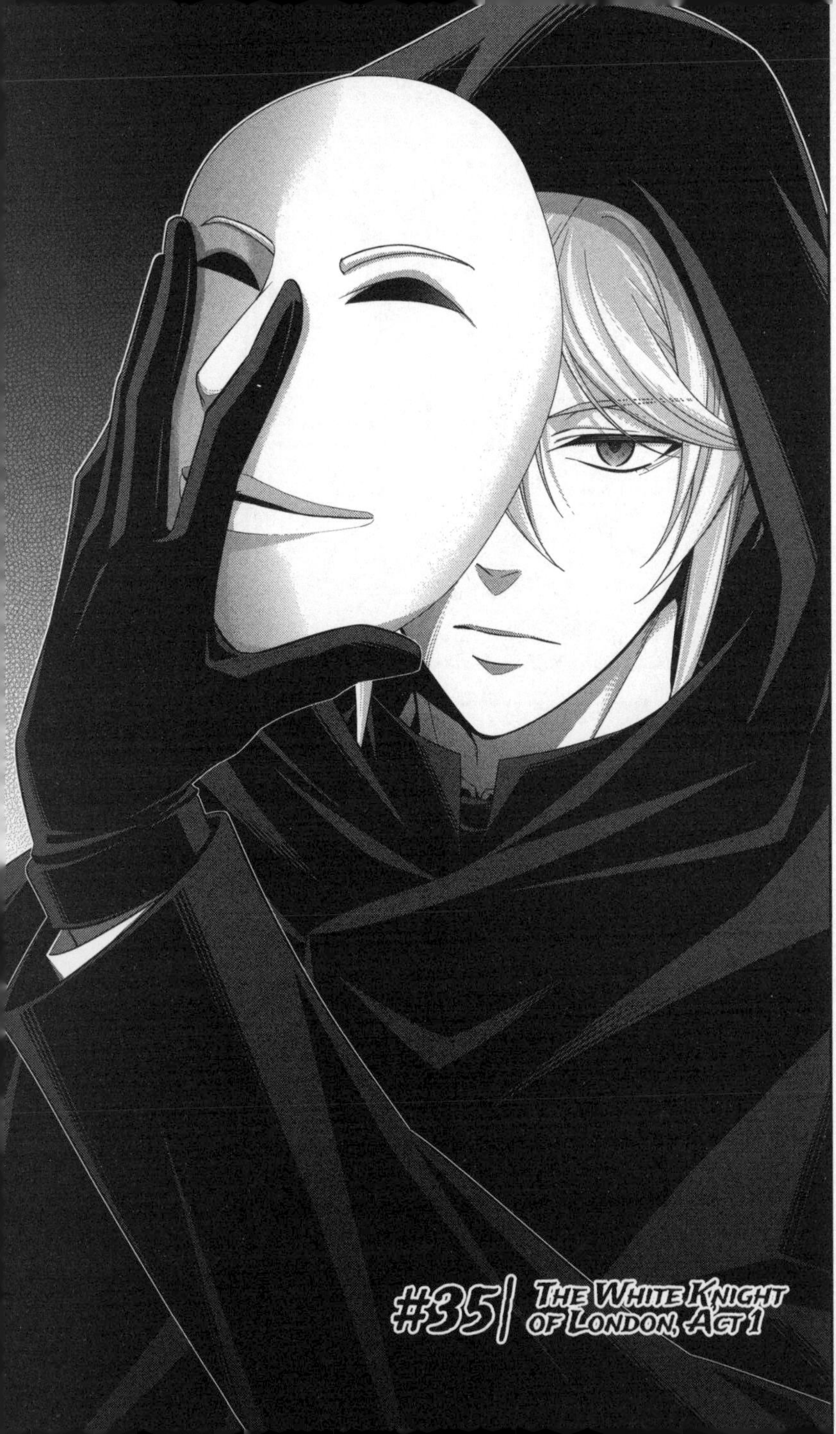
#35 The White Knight of London, Act 1

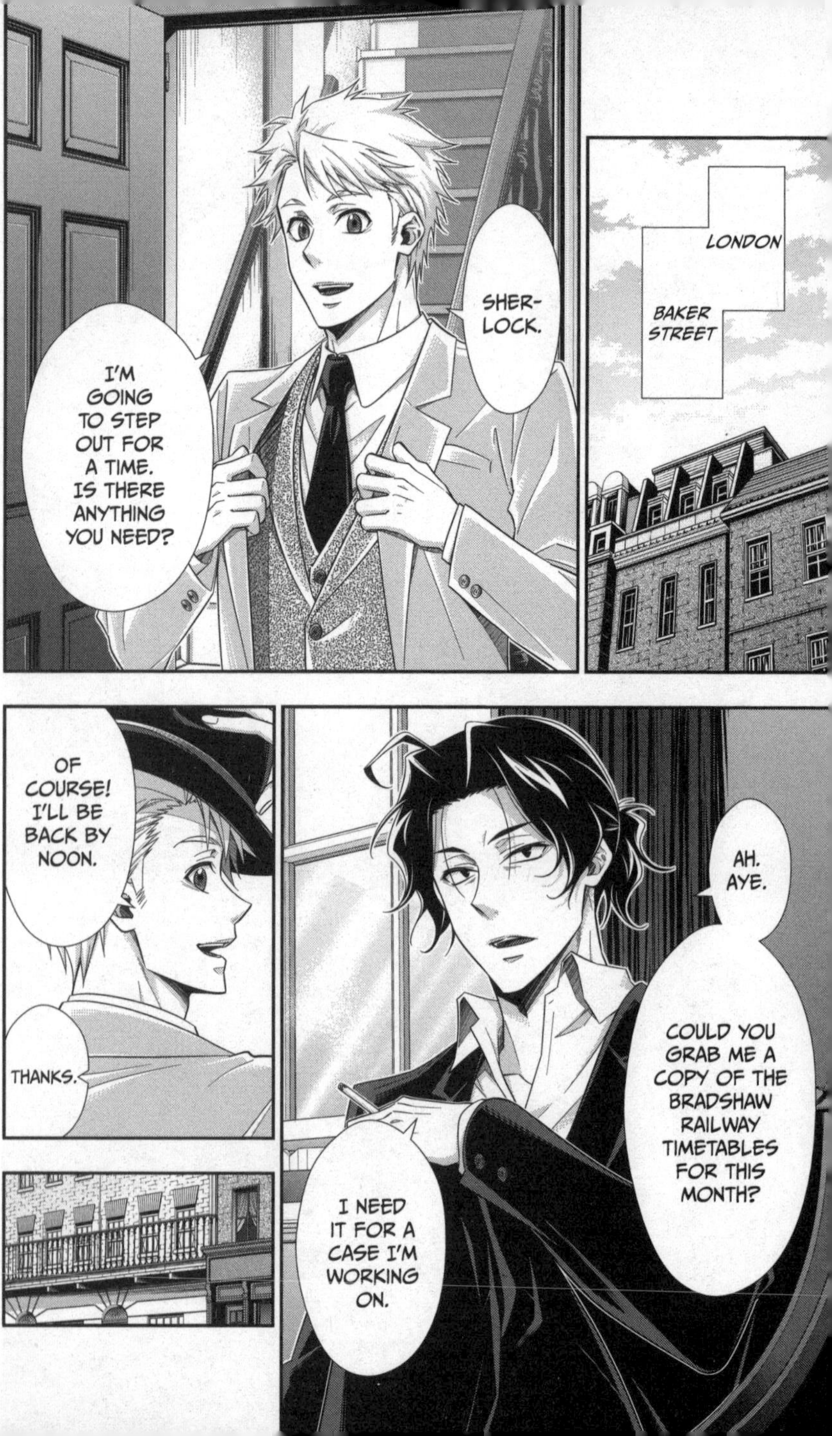
LONDON
BAKER STREET
SHER-LOCK.
I'M GOING TO STEP OUT FOR A TIME. IS THERE ANYTHING YOU NEED?
AH. AYE.
COULD YOU GRAB ME A COPY OF THE BRADSHAW RAILWAY TIMETABLES FOR THIS MONTH?
I NEED IT FOR A CASE I'M WORKING ON.
OF COURSE! I'LL BE BACK BY NOON.
THANKS.

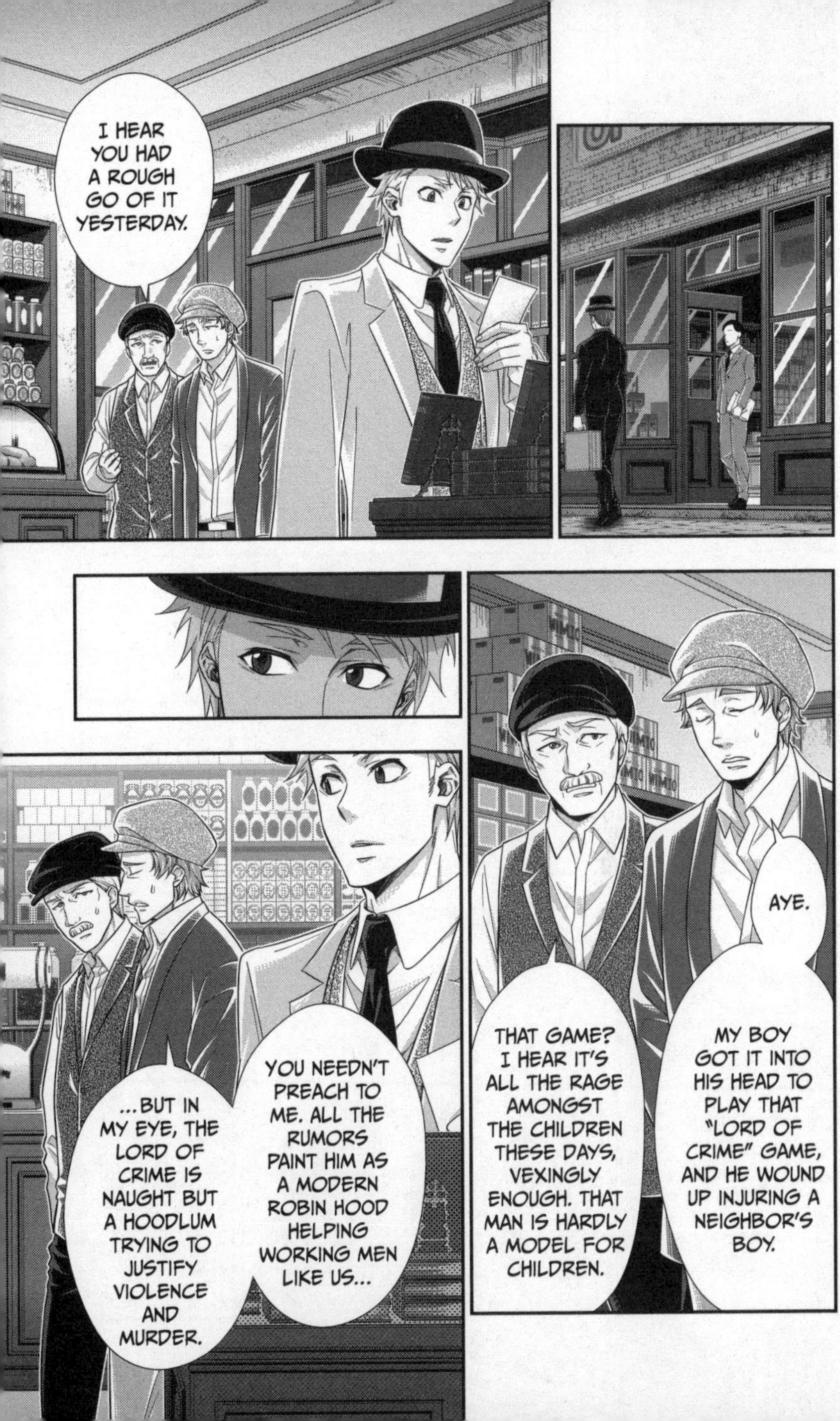
I HEAR YOU HAD A ROUGH GO OF IT YESTERDAY.
AYE.
MY BOY GOT IT INTO HIS HEAD TO PLAY THAT "LORD OF CRIME" GAME, AND HE WOUND UP INJURING A NEIGHBOR'S BOY.
THAT GAME? I HEAR IT'S ALL THE RAGE AMONGST THE CHILDREN THESE DAYS, VEXINGLY ENOUGH. THAT MAN IS HARDLY A MODEL FOR CHILDREN.
YOU NEEDN'T PREACH TO ME. ALL THE RUMORS PAINT HIM AS A MODERN ROBIN HOOD HELPING WORKING MEN LIKE US...
...BUT IN MY EYE, THE LORD OF CRIME IS NAUGHT BUT A HOODLUM TRYING TO JUSTIFY VIOLENCE AND MURDER.

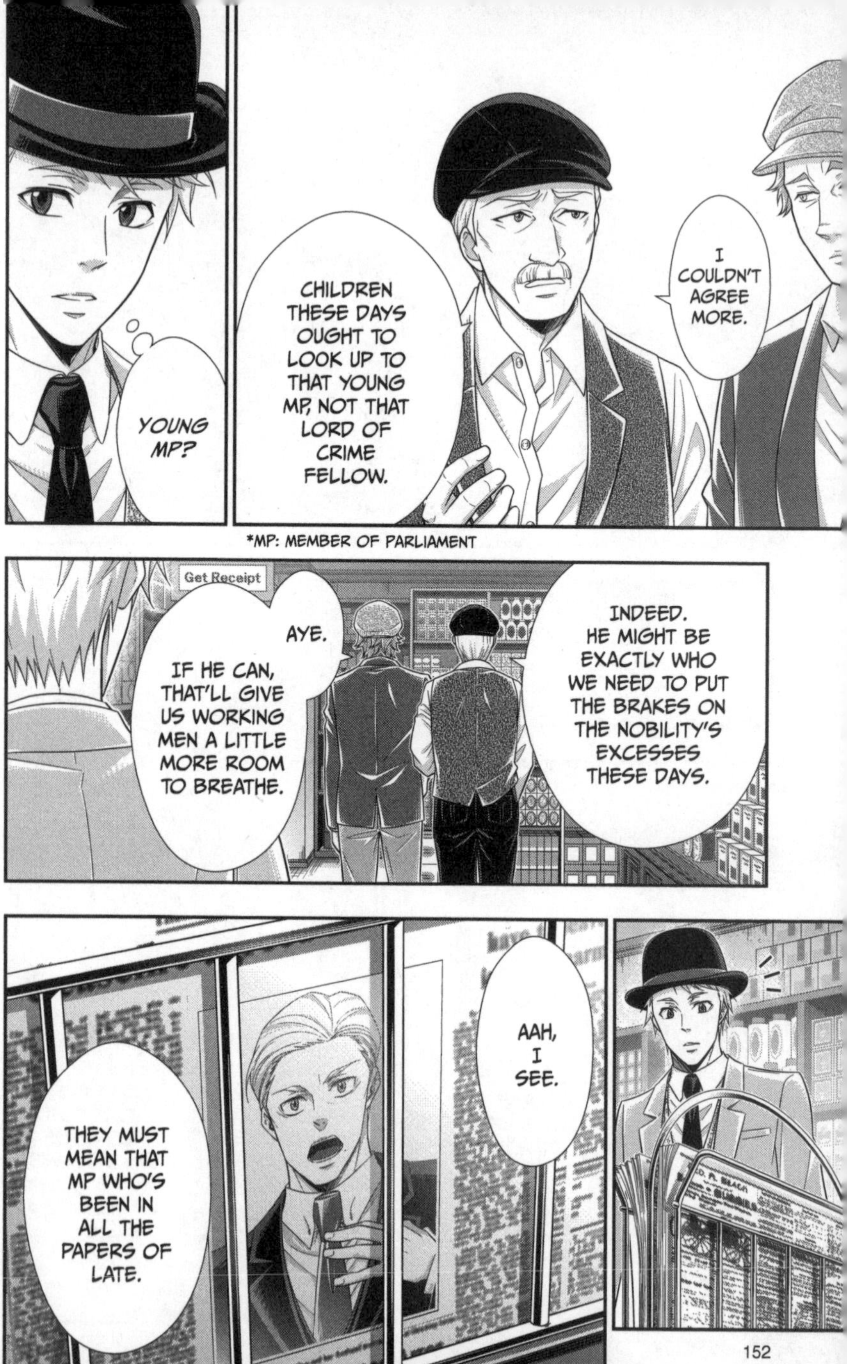
CHILDREN THESE DAYS OUGHT TO LOOK UP TO THAT YOUNG MP, NOT THAT LORD OF CRIME FELLOW.
I COULDN'T AGREE MORE.
YOUNG MP?
*MP: MEMBER OF PARLIAMENT
INDEED. HE MIGHT BE EXACTLY WHO WE NEED TO PUT THE BRAKES ON THE NOBILITY'S EXCESSES THESE DAYS.
AYE.
IF HE CAN, THAT'LL GIVE US WORKING MEN A LITTLE MORE ROOM TO BREATHE.
Get Receipt
AAH, I SEE.
THEY MUST MEAN THAT MP WHO'S BEEN IN ALL THE PAPERS OF LATE.

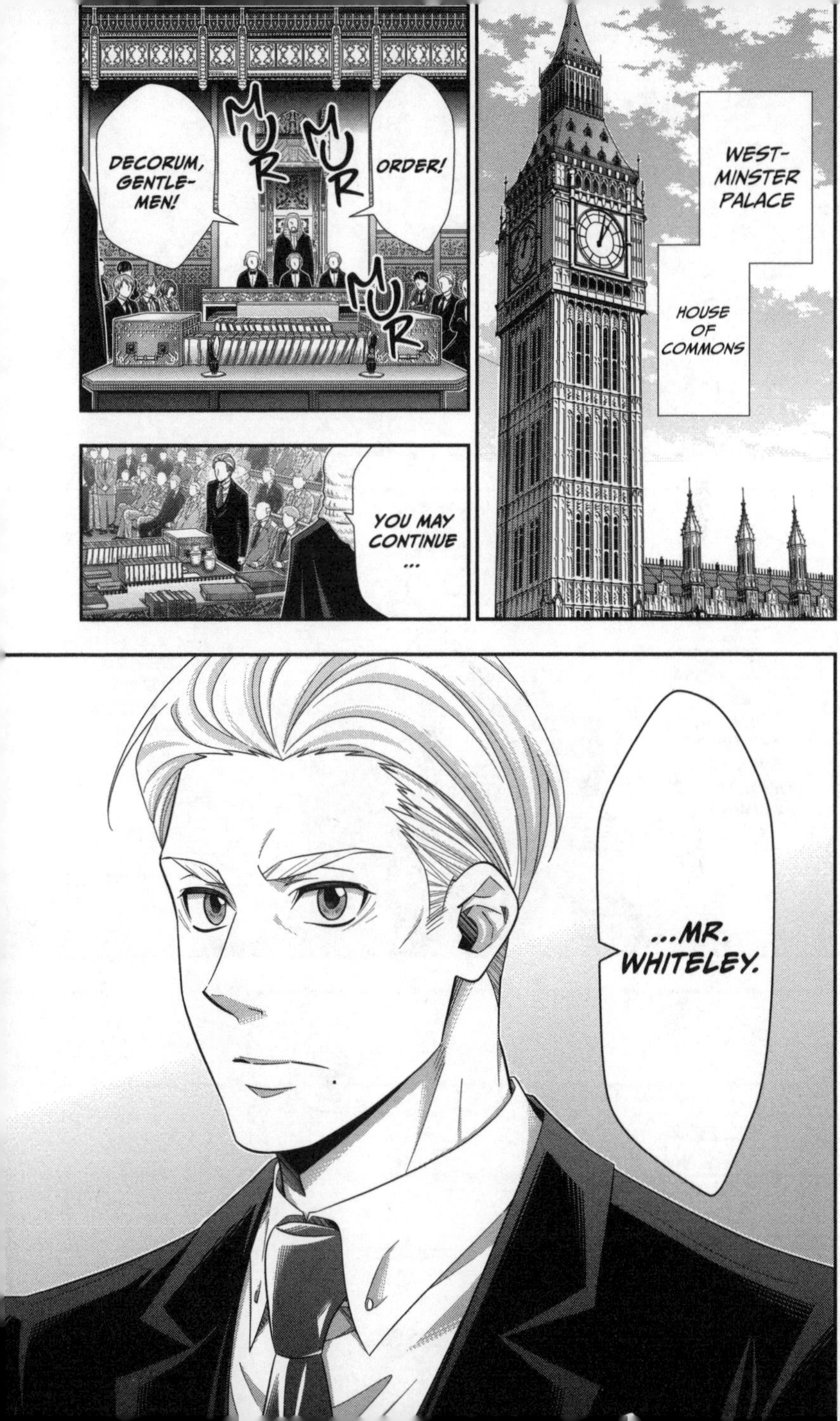
WEST-MINSTER PALACE
HOUSE OF COMMONS
ORDER!
MUR MUR
MUR
DECORUM, GENTLE-MEN!
YOU MAY CONTINUE ...
...MR. WHITELEY.

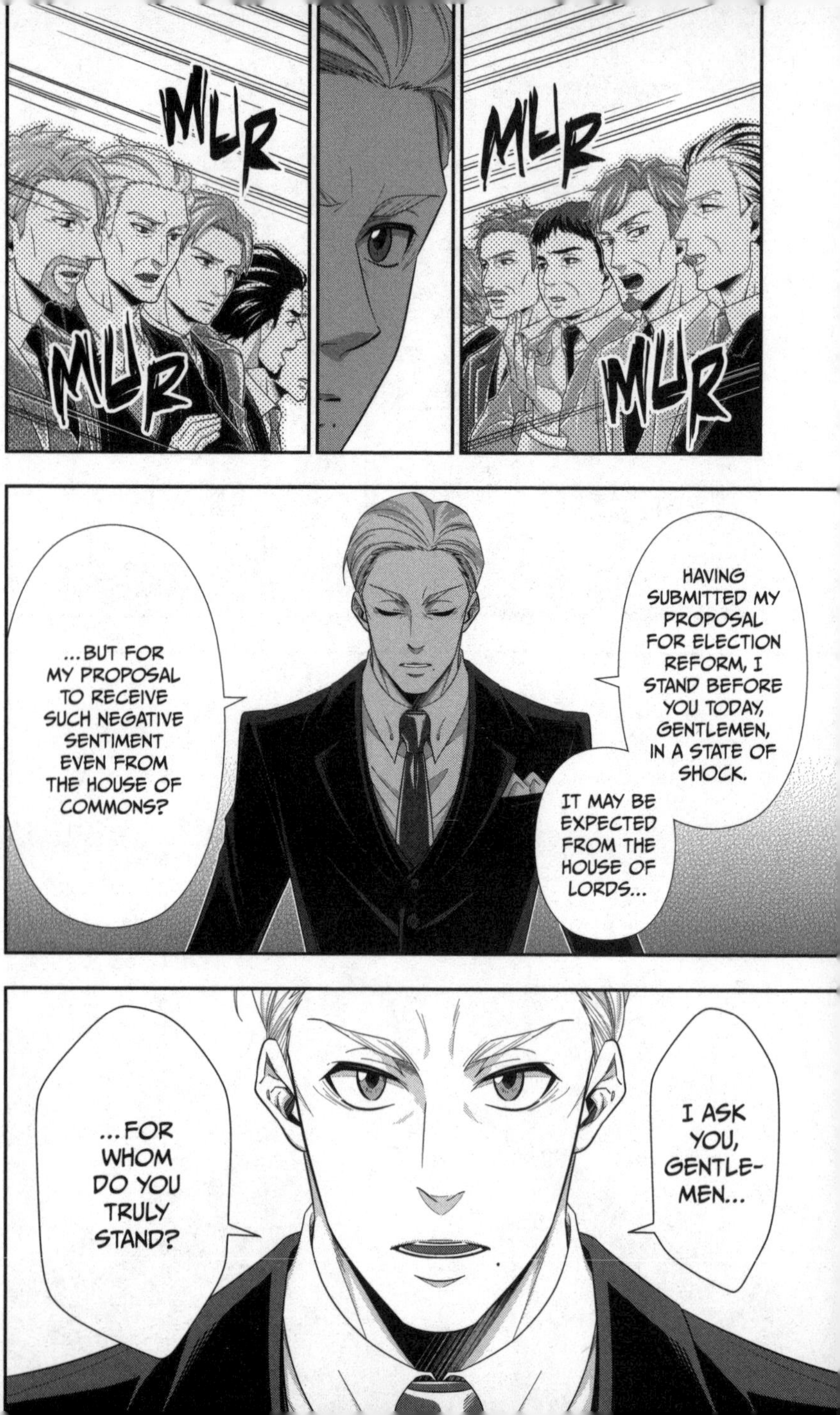
MUR
MUR
MUR
MUR
HAVING SUBMITTED MY PROPOSAL FOR ELECTION REFORM, I STAND BEFORE YOU TODAY, GENTLEMEN, IN A STATE OF SHOCK.
IT MAY BE EXPECTED FROM THE HOUSE OF LORDS...
...BUT FOR MY PROPOSAL TO RECEIVE SUCH NEGATIVE SENTIMENT EVEN FROM THE HOUSE OF COMMONS?
I ASK YOU, GENTLE-MEN...
...FOR WHOM DO YOU TRULY STAND?

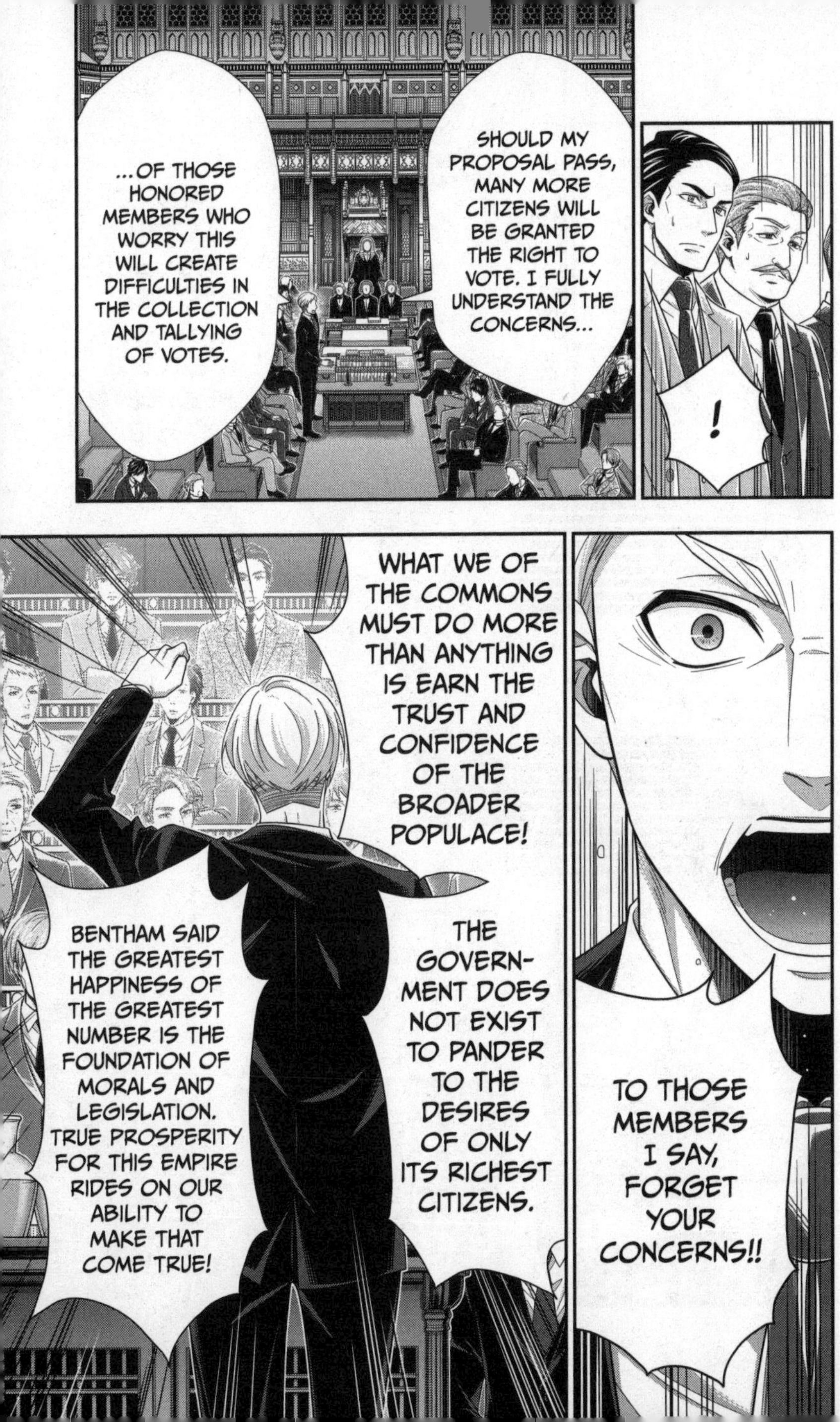
!
SHOULD MY PROPOSAL PASS, MANY MORE CITIZENS WILL BE GRANTED THE RIGHT TO VOTE. I FULLY UNDERSTAND THE CONCERNS...
...OF THOSE HONORED MEMBERS WHO WORRY THIS WILL CREATE DIFFICULTIES IN THE COLLECTION AND TALLYING OF VOTES.
TO THOSE MEMBERS I SAY, FORGET YOUR CONCERNS!!
WHAT WE OF THE COMMONS MUST DO MORE THAN ANYTHING IS EARN THE TRUST AND CONFIDENCE OF THE BROADER POPULACE!
THE GOVERN-MENT DOES NOT EXIST TO PANDER TO THE DESIRES OF ONLY ITS RICHEST CITIZENS.
BENTHAM SAID THE GREATEST HAPPINESS OF THE GREATEST NUMBER IS THE FOUNDATION OF MORALS AND LEGISLATION. TRUE PROSPERITY FOR THIS EMPIRE RIDES ON OUR ABILITY TO MAKE THAT COME TRUE!

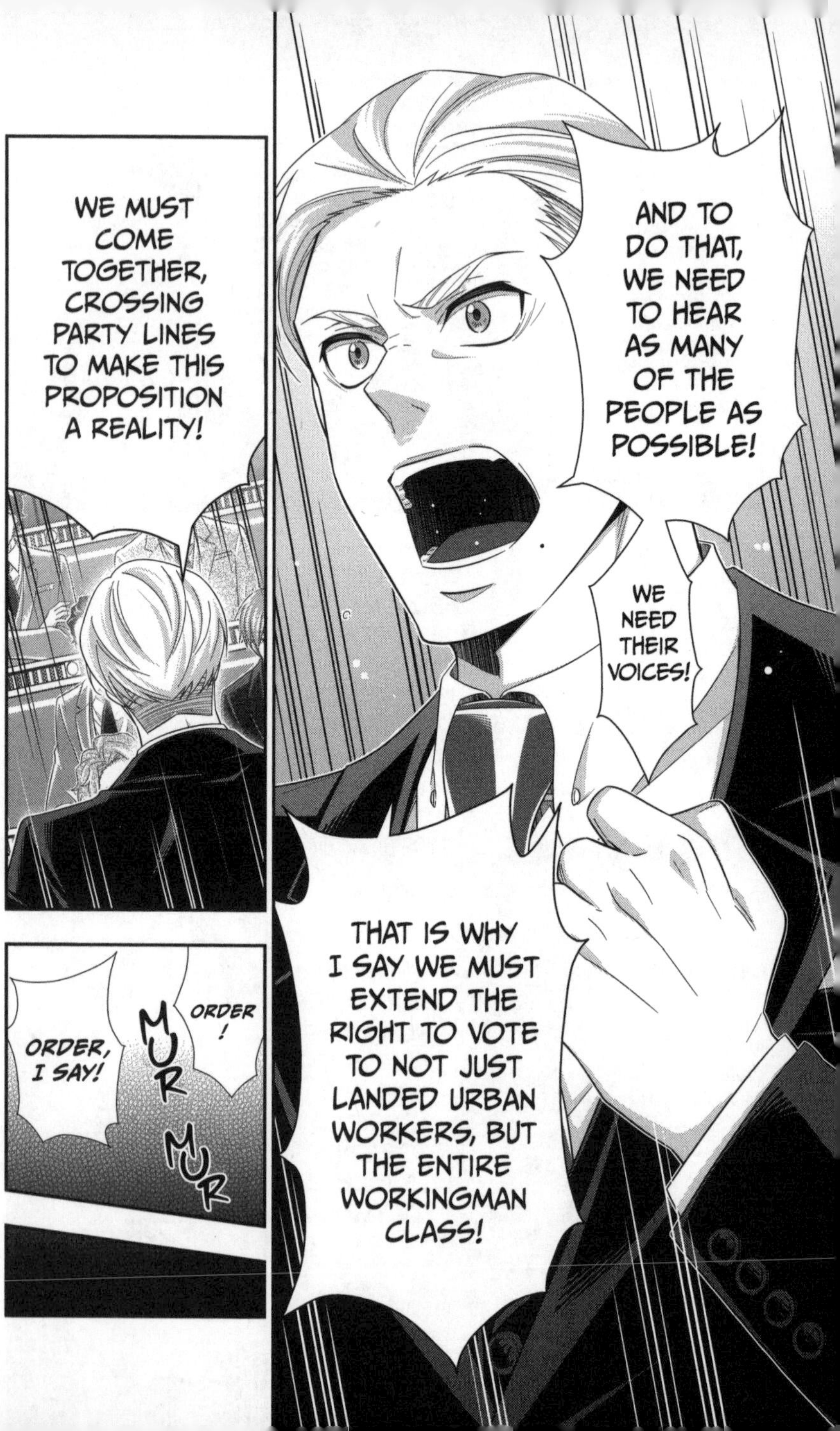
AND TO DO THAT, WE NEED TO HEAR AS MANY OF THE PEOPLE AS POSSIBLE!
WE NEED THEIR VOICES!
THAT IS WHY I SAY WE MUST EXTEND THE RIGHT TO VOTE TO NOT JUST LANDED URBAN WORKERS, BUT THE ENTIRE WORKINGMAN CLASS!
WE MUST COME TOGETHER, CROSSING PARTY LINES TO MAKE THIS PROPOSITION A REALITY!
ORDER!
MUR MUR
ORDER, I SAY!

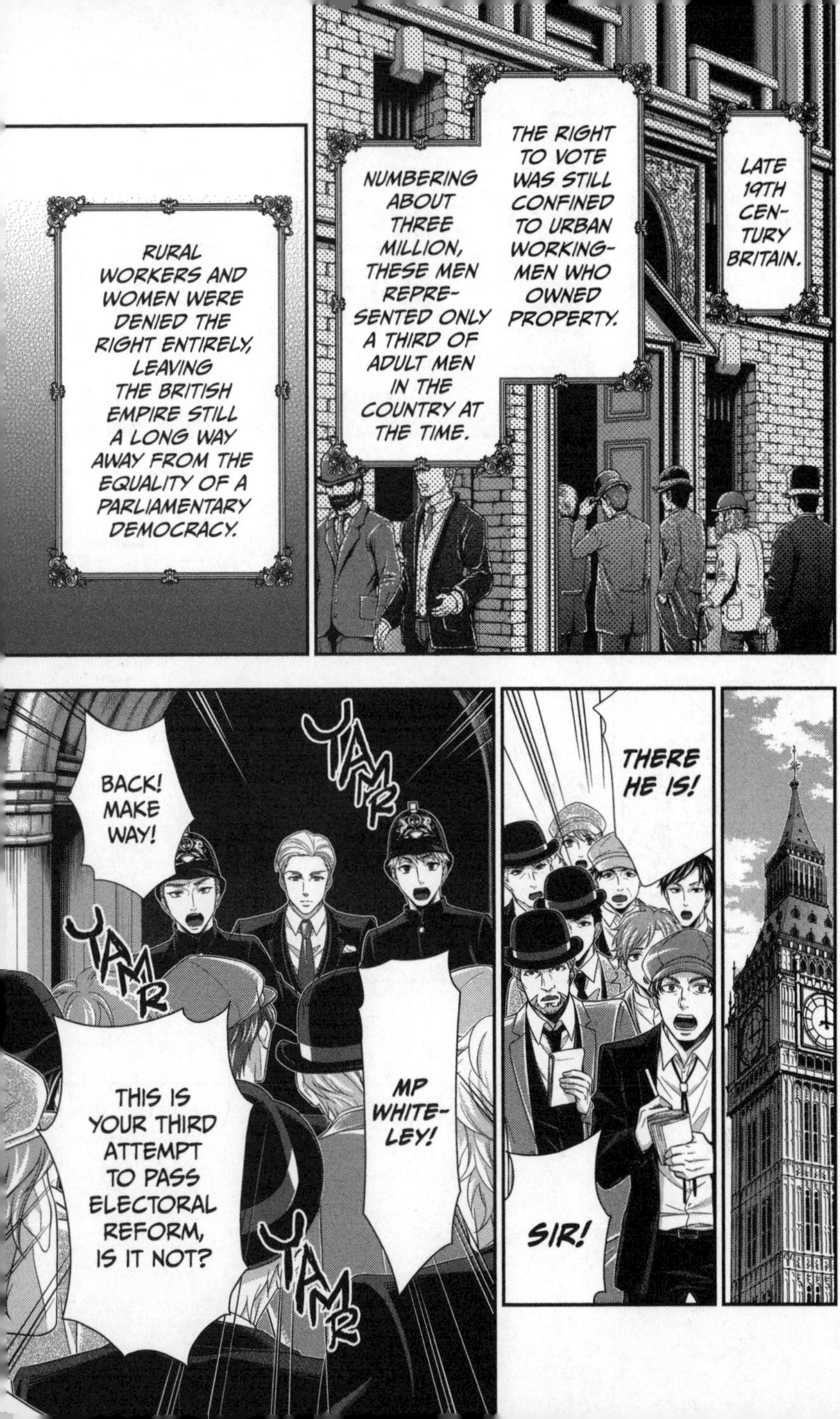
LATE 19TH CENTURY BRITAIN.
THE RIGHT TO VOTE WAS STILL CONFINED TO URBAN WORKINGMEN WHO OWNED PROPERTY.
NUMBERING ABOUT THREE MILLION, THESE MEN REPRESENTED ONLY A THIRD OF ADULT MEN IN THE COUNTRY AT THE TIME.
RURAL WORKERS AND WOMEN WERE DENIED THE RIGHT ENTIRELY, LEAVING THE BRITISH EMPIRE STILL A LONG WAY AWAY FROM THE EQUALITY OF A PARLIAMENTARY DEMOCRACY.
THERE HE IS!
SIR!
YAMR
BACK! MAKE WAY!
YAMR
MP WHITELEY!
THIS IS YOUR THIRD ATTEMPT TO PASS ELECTORAL REFORM, IS IT NOT?
YAMR

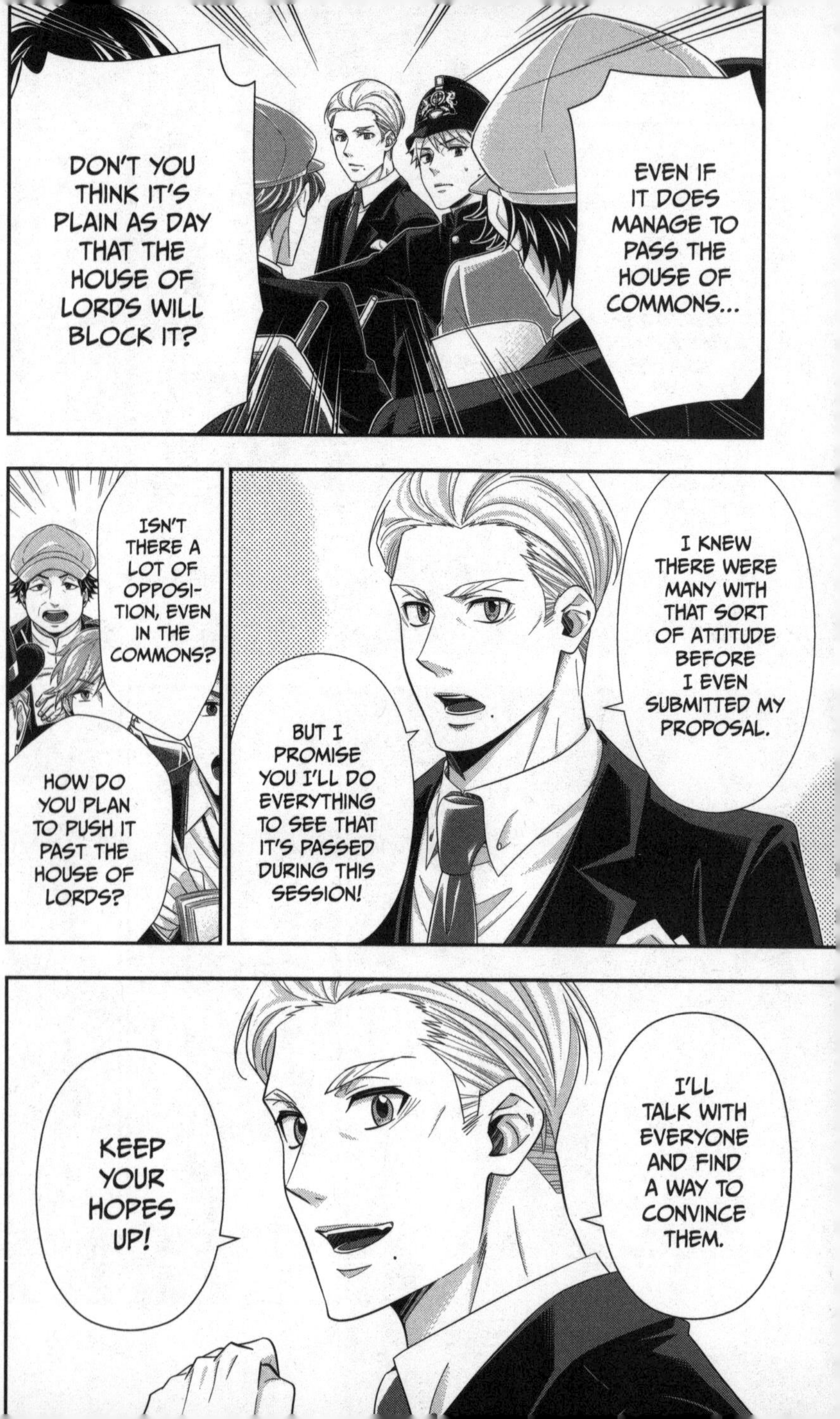
EVEN IF IT DOES MANAGE TO PASS THE HOUSE OF COMMONS...
DON'T YOU THINK IT'S PLAIN AS DAY THAT THE HOUSE OF LORDS WILL BLOCK IT?
I KNEW THERE WERE MANY WITH THAT SORT OF ATTITUDE BEFORE I EVEN SUBMITTED MY PROPOSAL.
BUT I PROMISE YOU I'LL DO EVERYTHING TO SEE THAT IT'S PASSED DURING THIS SESSION!
ISN'T THERE A LOT OF OPPOSI-TION, EVEN IN THE COMMONS?
HOW DO YOU PLAN TO PUSH IT PAST THE HOUSE OF LORDS?
I'LL TALK WITH EVERYONE AND FIND A WAY TO CONVINCE THEM.
KEEP YOUR HOPES UP!

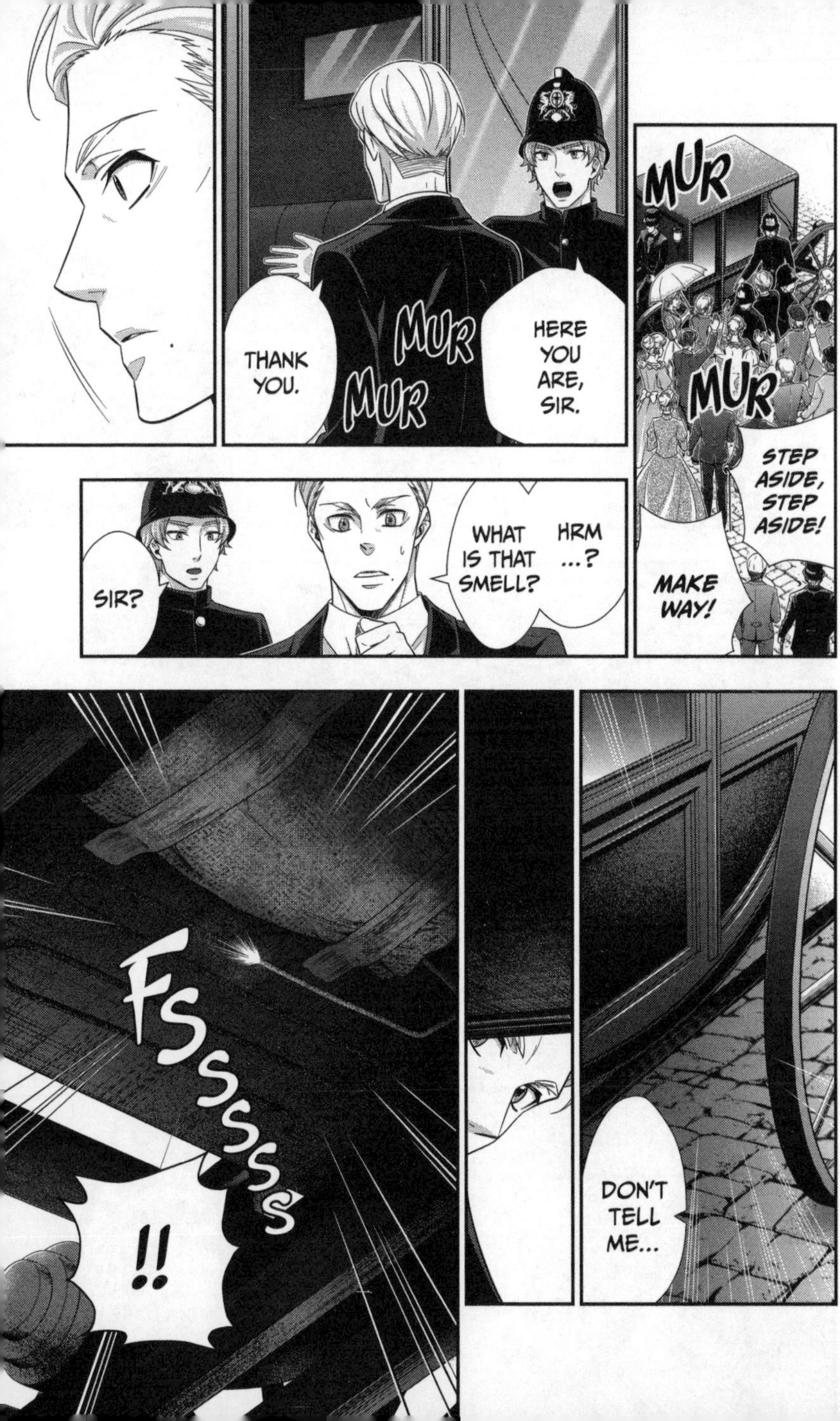
MUR
MUR
STEP ASIDE, STEP ASIDE!
MAKE WAY!
HERE YOU ARE, SIR.
MUR
MUR
THANK YOU.
HRM ...?
WHAT IS THAT SMELL?
SIR?
DON'T TELL ME...
FSSSSSS
!!

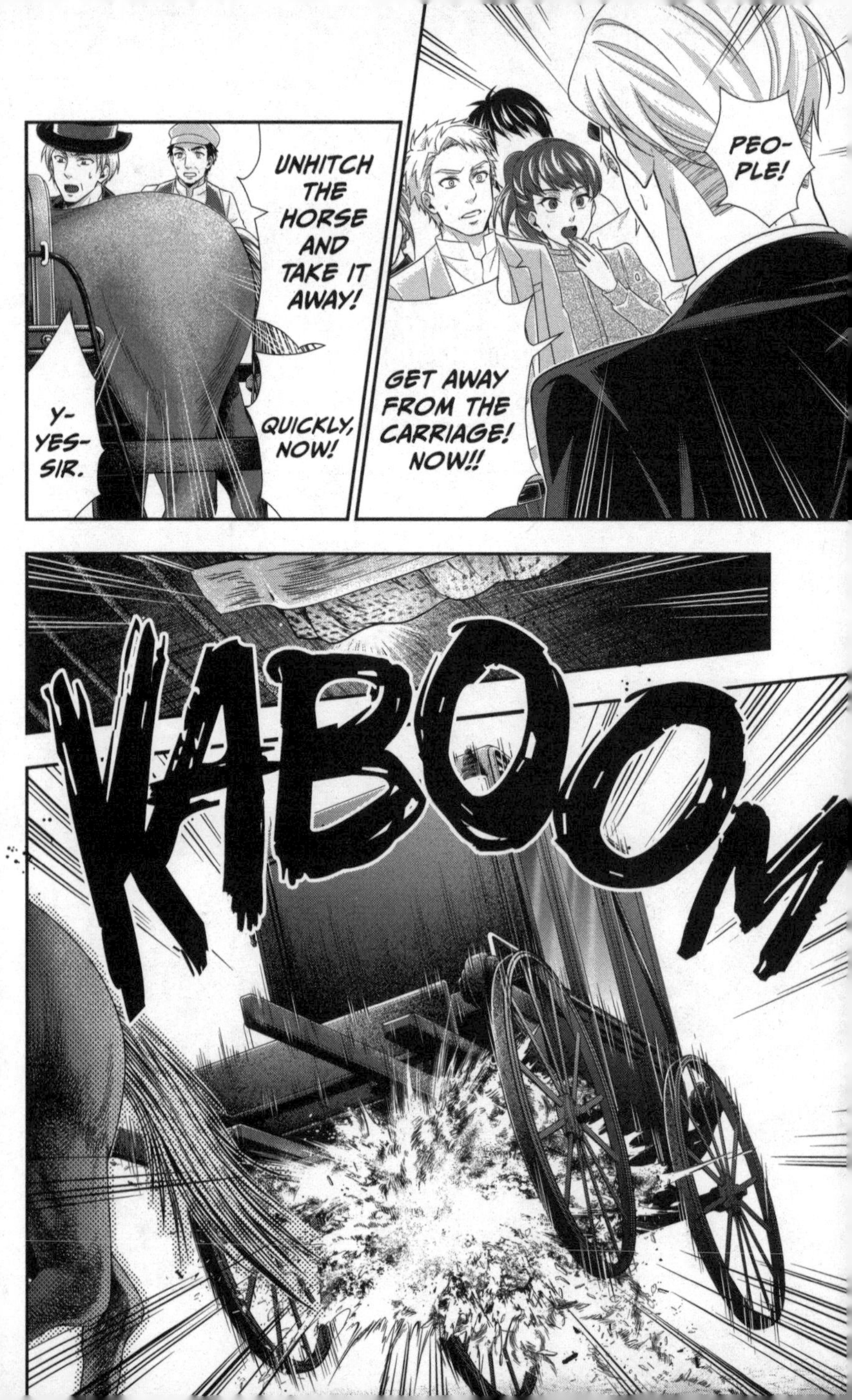
PEO-PLE!
GET AWAY FROM THE CARRIAGE! NOW!!
UNHITCH THE HORSE AND TAKE IT AWAY!
QUICKLY, NOW!
Y-YES-SIR.
KABOOM

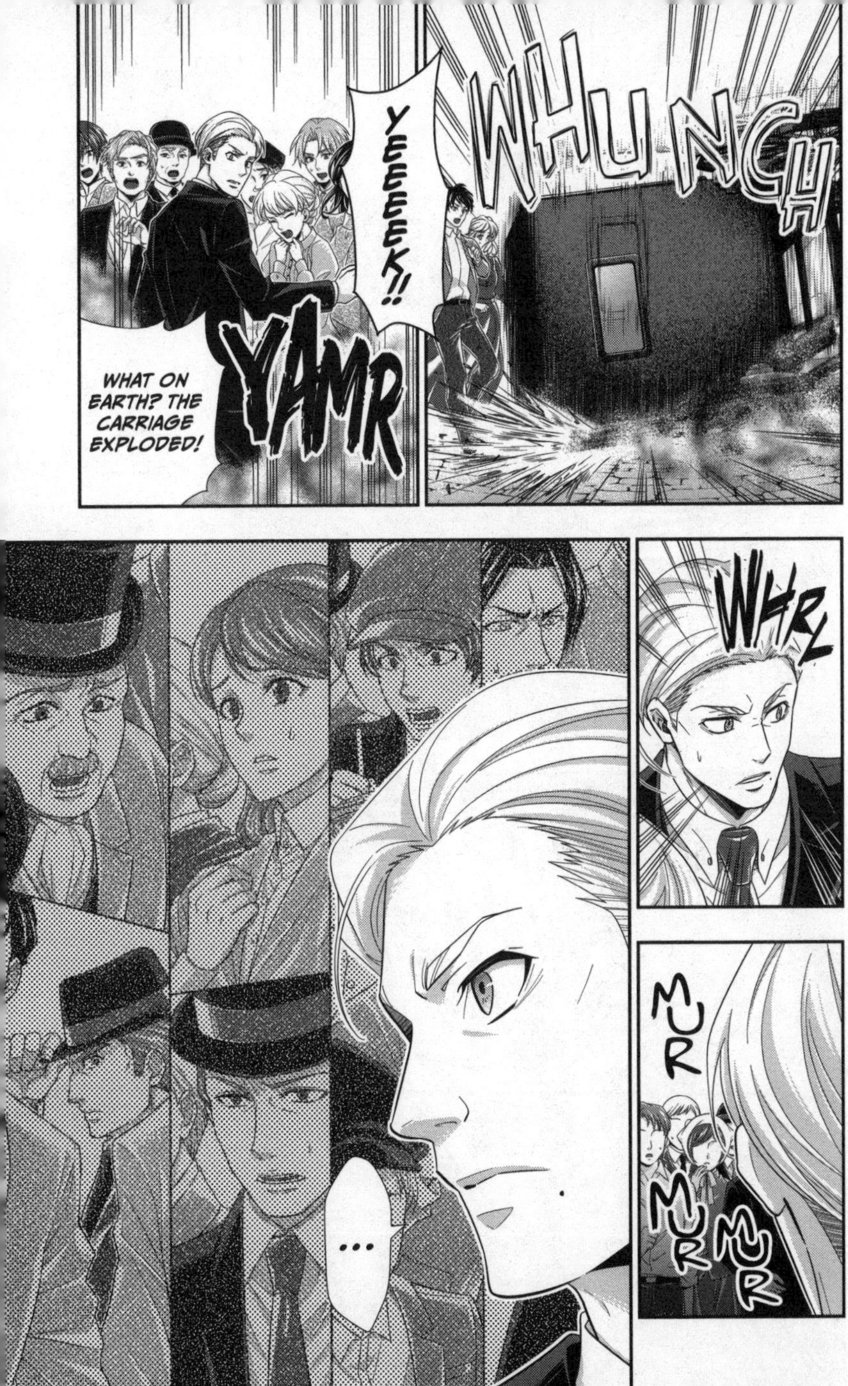
WHUNCH
YEEEEK!!
YAMR
WHAT ON EARTH? THE CARRIAGE EXPLODED!
WHRL
MUR
MUR
MUR
...

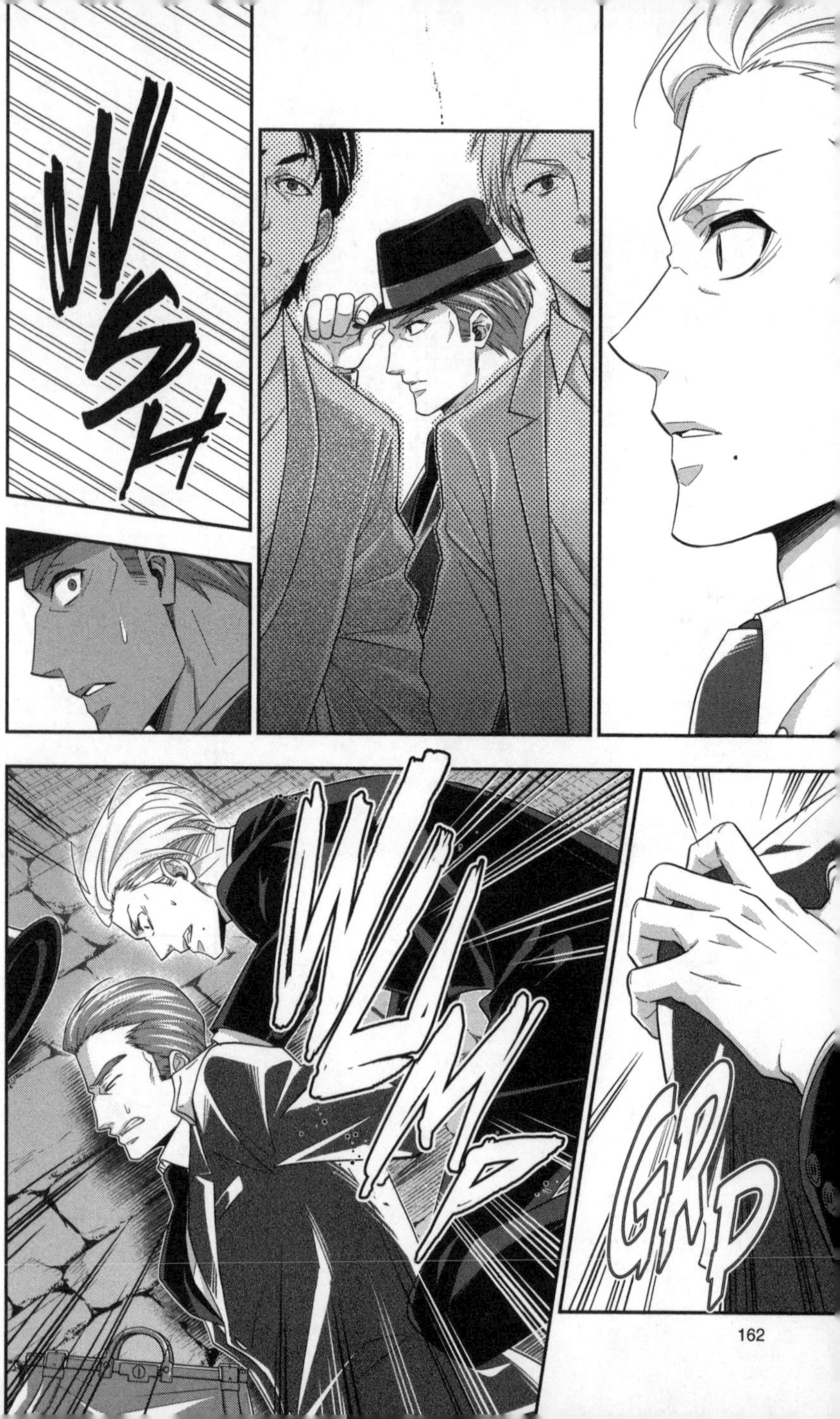
WSH
WUMP
GRP

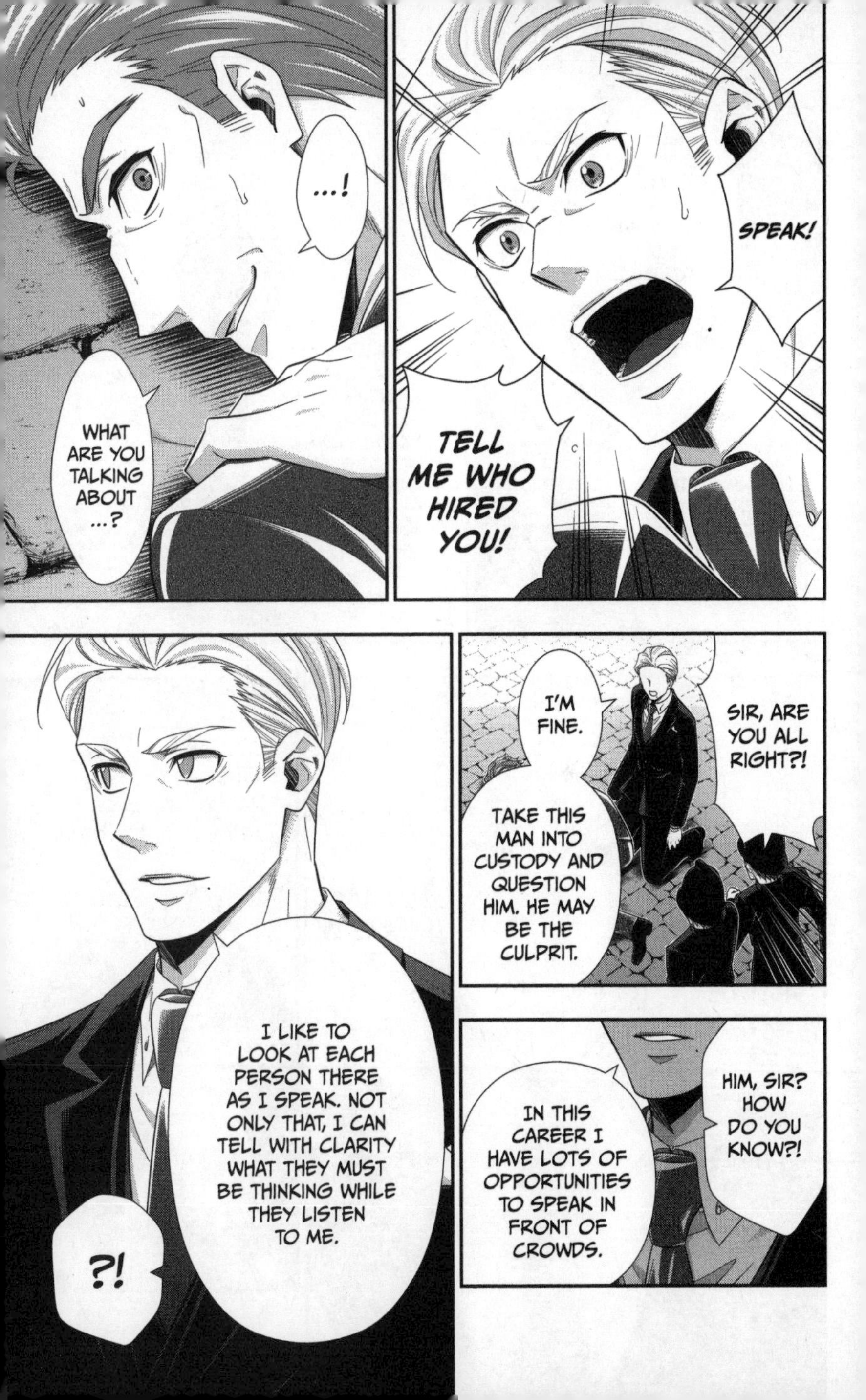
SPEAK!
TELL ME WHO HIRED YOU!
...!
WHAT ARE YOU TALKING ABOUT ...?
SIR, ARE YOU ALL RIGHT?!
I'M FINE.
TAKE THIS MAN INTO CUSTODY AND QUESTION HIM. HE MAY BE THE CULPRIT.
HIM, SIR? HOW DO YOU KNOW?!
IN THIS CAREER I HAVE LOTS OF OPPORTUNITIES TO SPEAK IN FRONT OF CROWDS.
I LIKE TO LOOK AT EACH PERSON THERE AS I SPEAK. NOT ONLY THAT, I CAN TELL WITH CLARITY WHAT THEY MUST BE THINKING WHILE THEY LISTEN TO ME.
?!

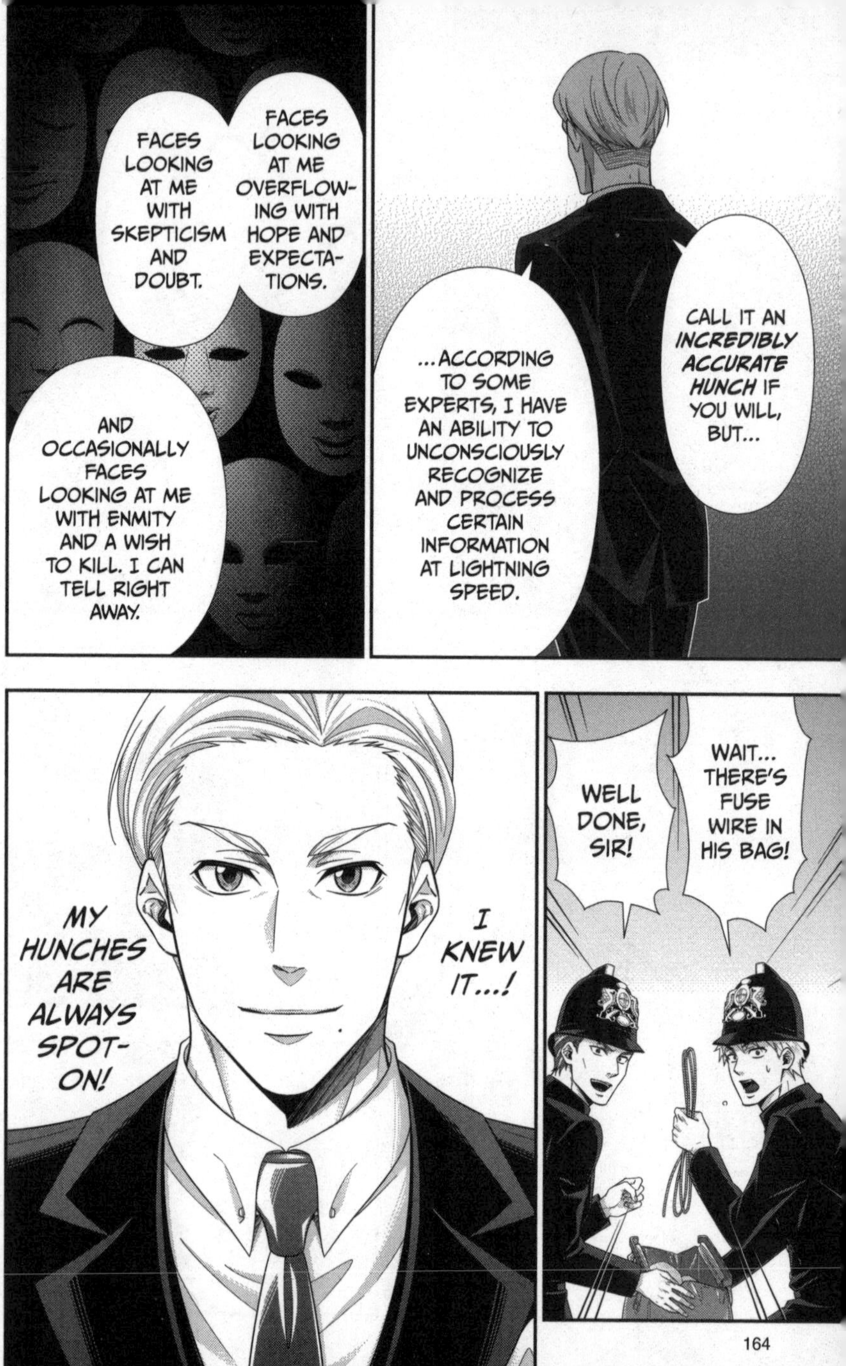
CALL IT AN *INCREDIBLY ACCURATE HUNCH* IF YOU WILL, BUT...
...ACCORDING TO SOME EXPERTS, I HAVE AN ABILITY TO UNCONSCIOUSLY RECOGNIZE AND PROCESS CERTAIN INFORMATION AT LIGHTNING SPEED.
FACES LOOKING AT ME OVERFLOWING WITH HOPE AND EXPECTATIONS.
FACES LOOKING AT ME WITH SKEPTICISM AND DOUBT.
AND OCCASIONALLY FACES LOOKING AT ME WITH ENMITY AND A WISH TO KILL. I CAN TELL RIGHT AWAY.
WAIT... THERE'S FUSE WIRE IN HIS BAG!
WELL DONE, SIR!
I KNEW IT...!
MY HUNCHES ARE ALWAYS SPOT-ON!

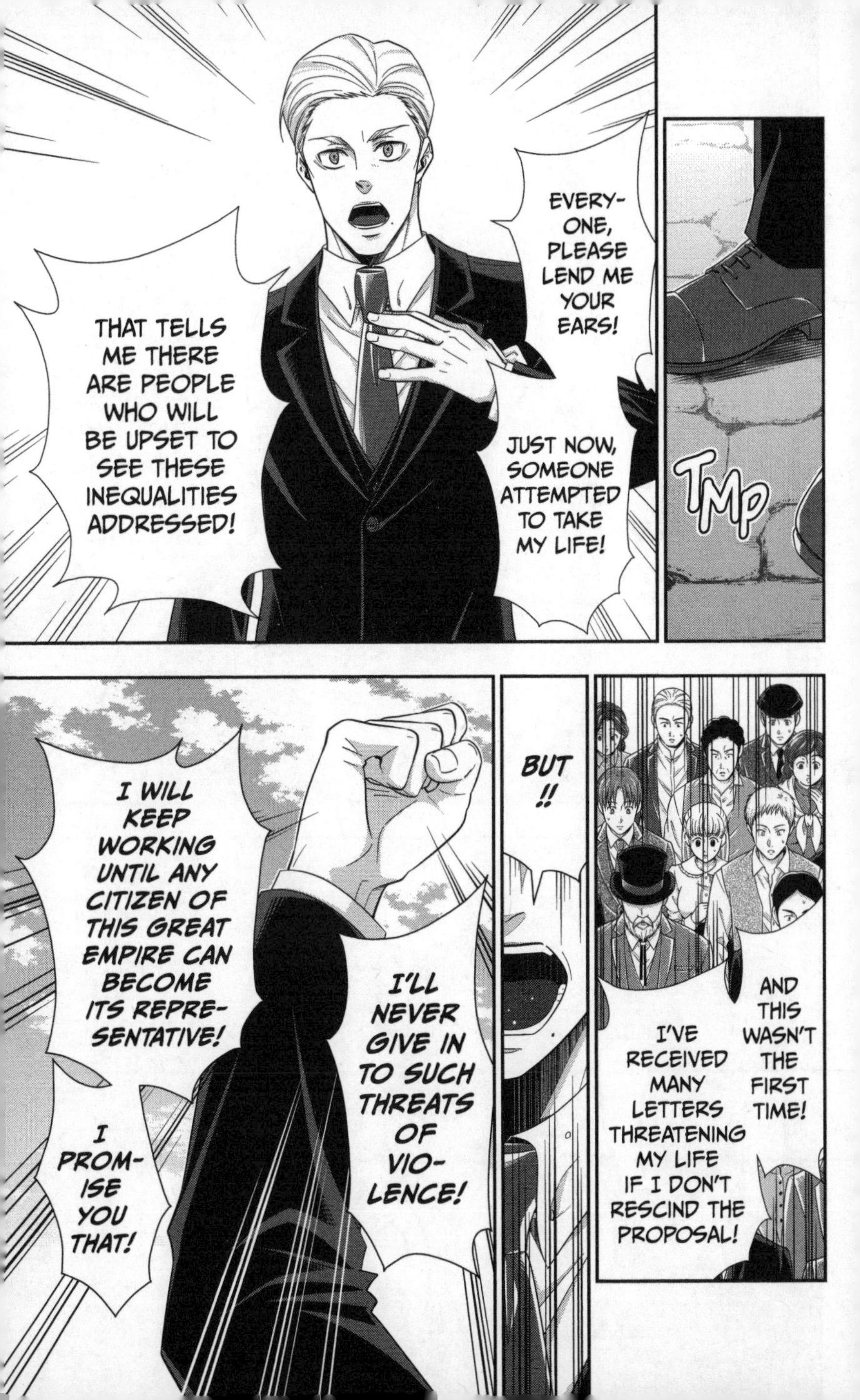
TMP
EVERY-ONE, PLEASE LEND ME YOUR EARS!
JUST NOW, SOMEONE ATTEMPTED TO TAKE MY LIFE!
THAT TELLS ME THERE ARE PEOPLE WHO WILL BE UPSET TO SEE THESE INEQUALITIES ADDRESSED!
AND THIS WASN'T THE FIRST TIME!
I'VE RECEIVED MANY LETTERS THREATENING MY LIFE IF I DON'T RESCIND THE PROPOSAL!
BUT !!
I'LL NEVER GIVE IN TO SUCH THREATS OF VIO-LENCE!
I WILL KEEP WORKING UNTIL ANY CITIZEN OF THIS GREAT EMPIRE CAN BECOME ITS REPRE-SENTATIVE!
I PROMISE YOU THAT!

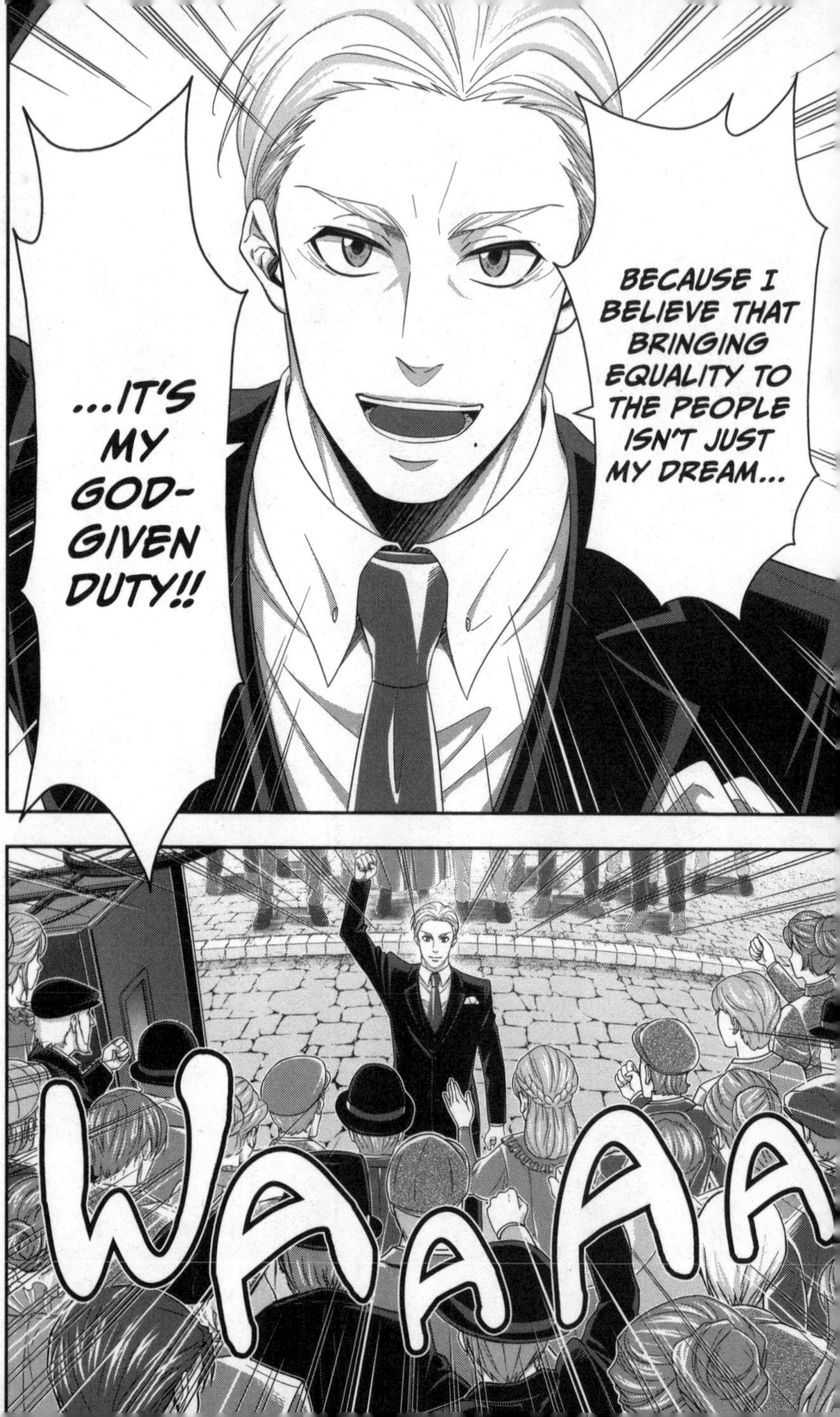
BECAUSE I BELIEVE THAT BRINGING EQUALITY TO THE PEOPLE ISN'T JUST MY DREAM...
...IT'S MY GOD-GIVEN DUTY!!
WAAAA

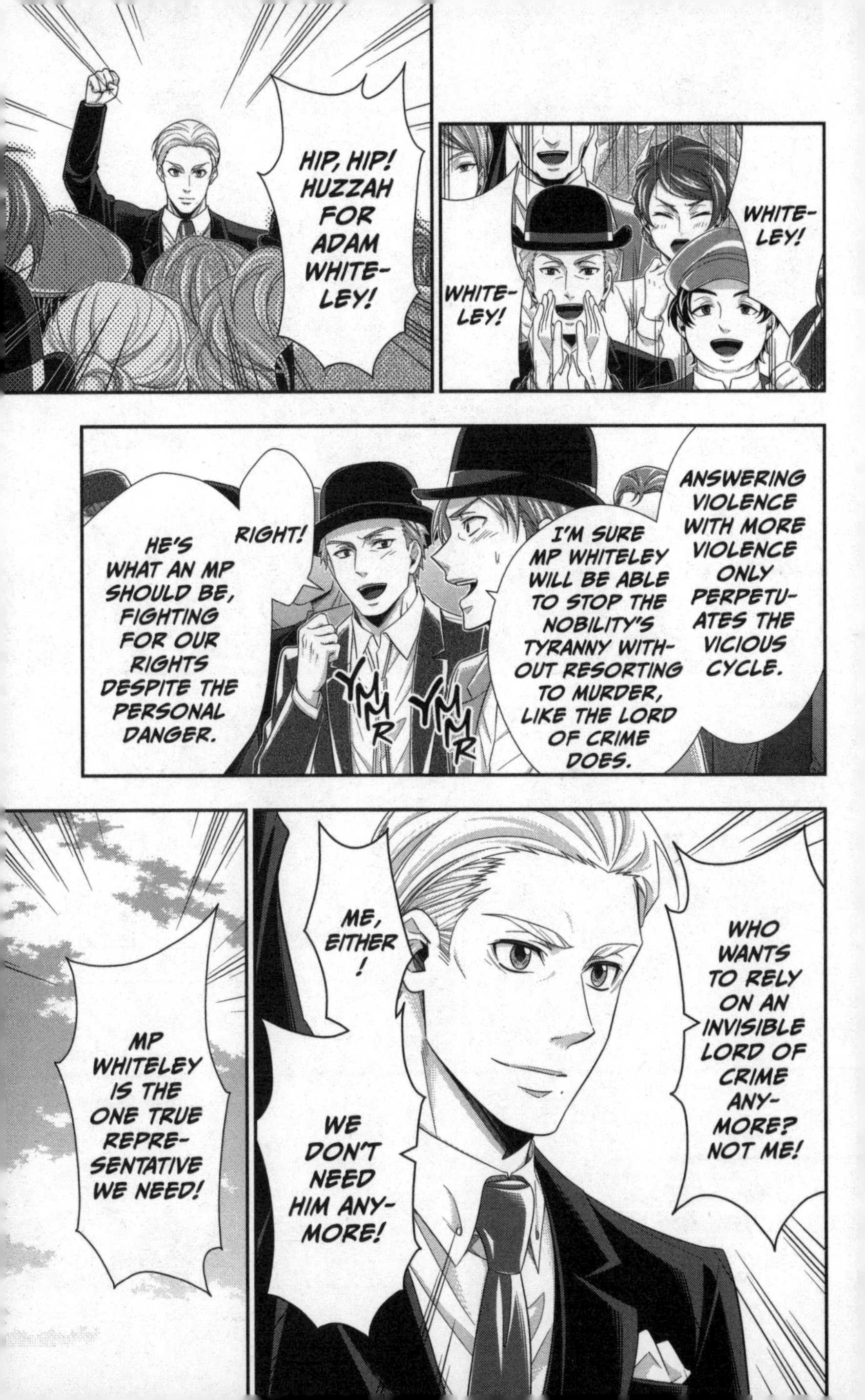
WHITELEY!
WHITELEY!
HIP, HIP! HUZZAH FOR ADAM WHITELEY!
ANSWERING VIOLENCE WITH MORE VIOLENCE ONLY PERPETUATES THE VICIOUS CYCLE.
I'M SURE MP WHITELEY WILL BE ABLE TO STOP THE NOBILITY'S TYRANNY WITHOUT RESORTING TO MURDER, LIKE THE LORD OF CRIME DOES.
RIGHT!
HE'S WHAT AN MP SHOULD BE, FIGHTING FOR OUR RIGHTS DESPITE THE PERSONAL DANGER.
YMMR YMMR
WHO WANTS TO RELY ON AN INVISIBLE LORD OF CRIME ANYMORE? NOT ME!
ME, EITHER!
WE DON'T NEED HIM ANYMORE!
MP WHITELEY IS THE ONE TRUE REPRESENTATIVE WE NEED!

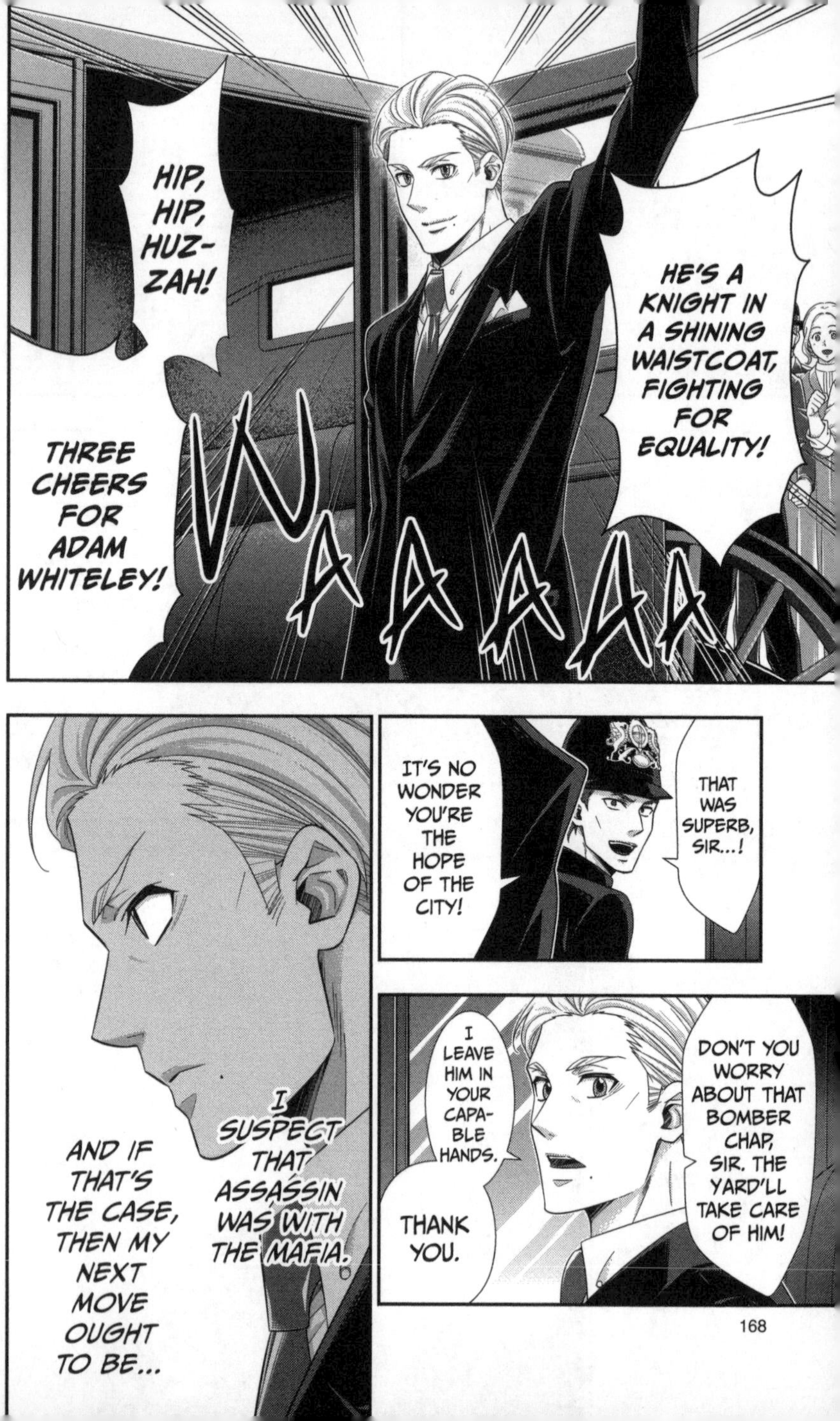

HE'S A KNIGHT IN A SHINING WAISTCOAT, FIGHTING FOR EQUALITY!
HIP, HIP, HUZ-ZAH!
WAAAAA
THREE CHEERS FOR ADAM WHITELEY!
THAT WAS SUPERB, SIR...!
IT'S NO WONDER YOU'RE THE HOPE OF THE CITY!
DON'T YOU WORRY ABOUT THAT BOMBER CHAP, SIR. THE YARD'LL TAKE CARE OF HIM!
I LEAVE HIM IN YOUR CAPA-BLE HANDS.
THANK YOU.
I SUSPECT THAT ASSASSIN WAS WITH THE MAFIA.
AND IF THAT'S THE CASE, THEN MY NEXT MOVE OUGHT TO BE...

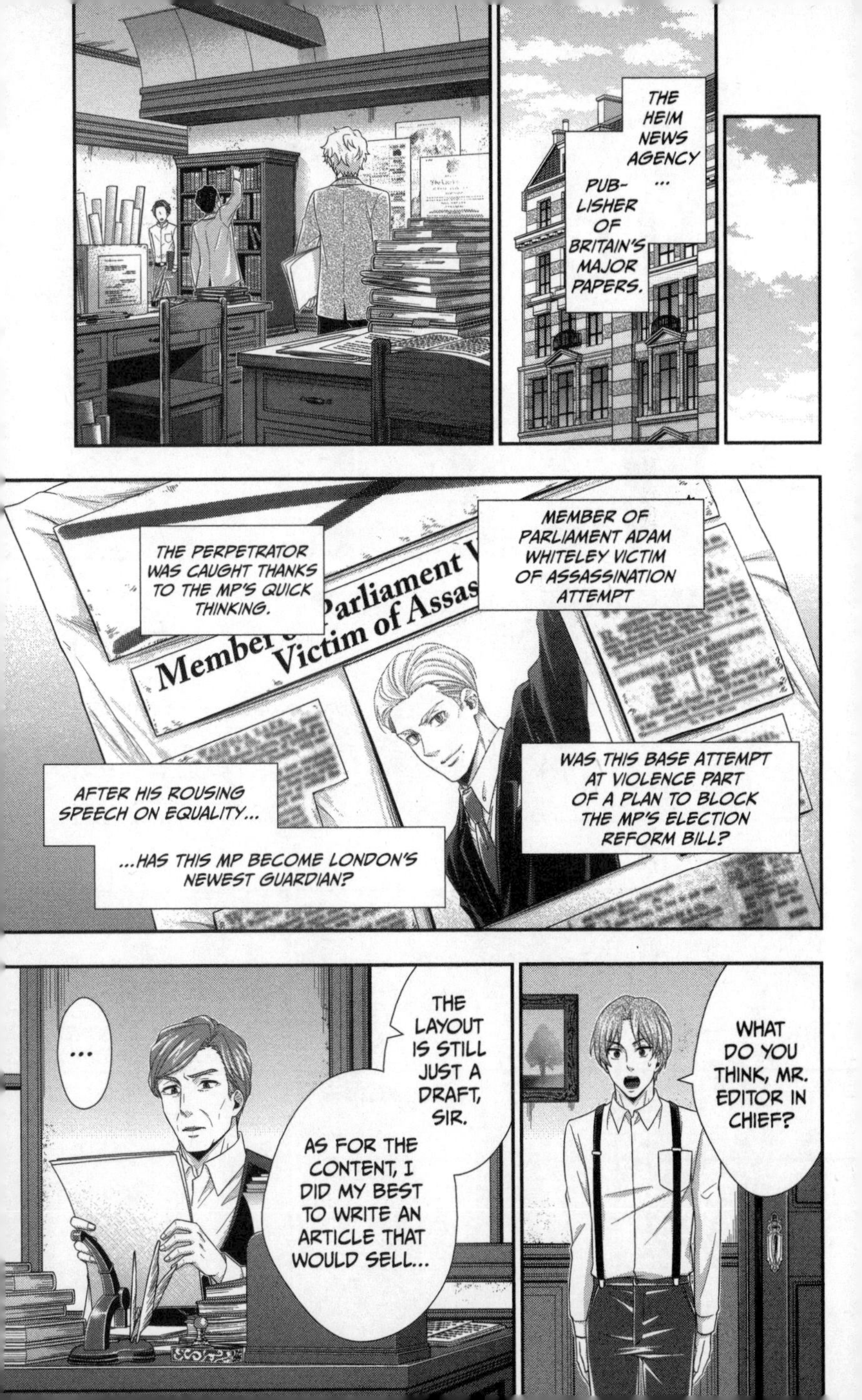

THE HEIM NEWS AGENCY...
PUBLISHER OF BRITAIN'S MAJOR PAPERS.
MEMBER OF PARLIAMENT ADAM WHITELEY VICTIM OF ASSASSINATION ATTEMPT
THE PERPETRATOR WAS CAUGHT THANKS TO THE MP'S QUICK THINKING.
WAS THIS BASE ATTEMPT AT VIOLENCE PART OF A PLAN TO BLOCK THE MP'S ELECTION REFORM BILL?
AFTER HIS ROUSING SPEECH ON EQUALITY...
...HAS THIS MP BECOME LONDON'S NEWEST GUARDIAN?
WHAT DO YOU THINK, MR. EDITOR IN CHIEF?
THE LAYOUT IS STILL JUST A DRAFT, SIR.
AS FOR THE CONTENT, I DID MY BEST TO WRITE AN ARTICLE THAT WOULD SELL...
...

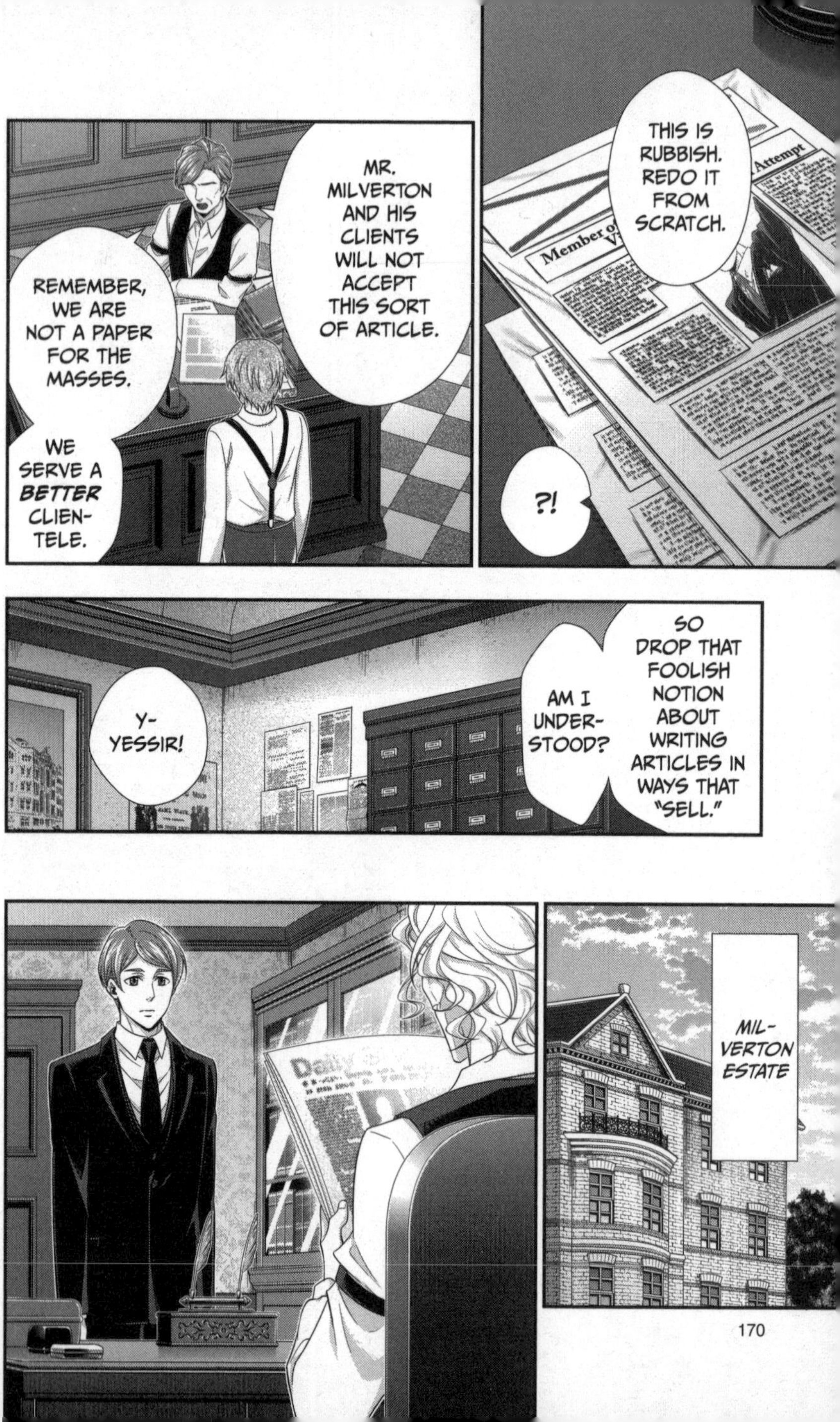
THIS IS RUBBISH. REDO IT FROM SCRATCH.
?!
MR. MILVERTON AND HIS CLIENTS WILL NOT ACCEPT THIS SORT OF ARTICLE.
REMEMBER, WE ARE NOT A PAPER FOR THE MASSES.
WE SERVE A *BETTER* CLIEN-TELE.
SO DROP THAT FOOLISH NOTION ABOUT WRITING ARTICLES IN WAYS THAT "SELL."
AM I UNDER-STOOD?
Y-YESSIR!
MIL-VERTON ESTATE

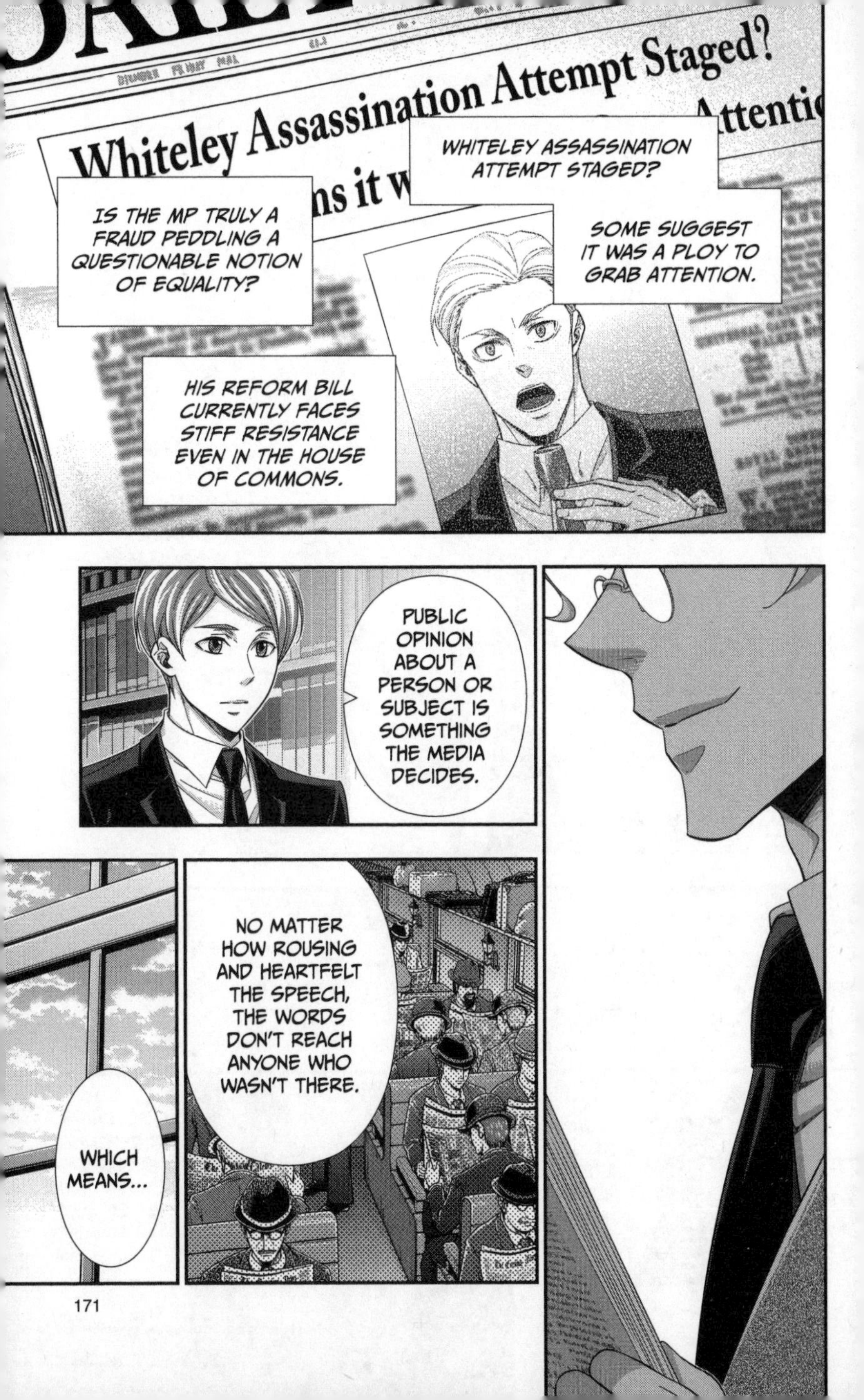
Whiteley Assassination Attempt Staged?
Whiteley Assassination Attempt Staged?
WHITELEY ASSASSINATION ATTEMPT STAGED?
SOME SUGGEST IT WAS A PLOY TO GRAB ATTENTION.
IS THE MP TRULY A FRAUD PEDDLING A QUESTIONABLE NOTION OF EQUALITY?
HIS REFORM BILL CURRENTLY FACES STIFF RESISTANCE EVEN IN THE HOUSE OF COMMONS.
PUBLIC OPINION ABOUT A PERSON OR SUBJECT IS SOMETHING THE MEDIA DECIDES.
NO MATTER HOW ROUSING AND HEARTFELT THE SPEECH, THE WORDS DON'T REACH ANYONE WHO WASN'T THERE.
WHICH MEANS...

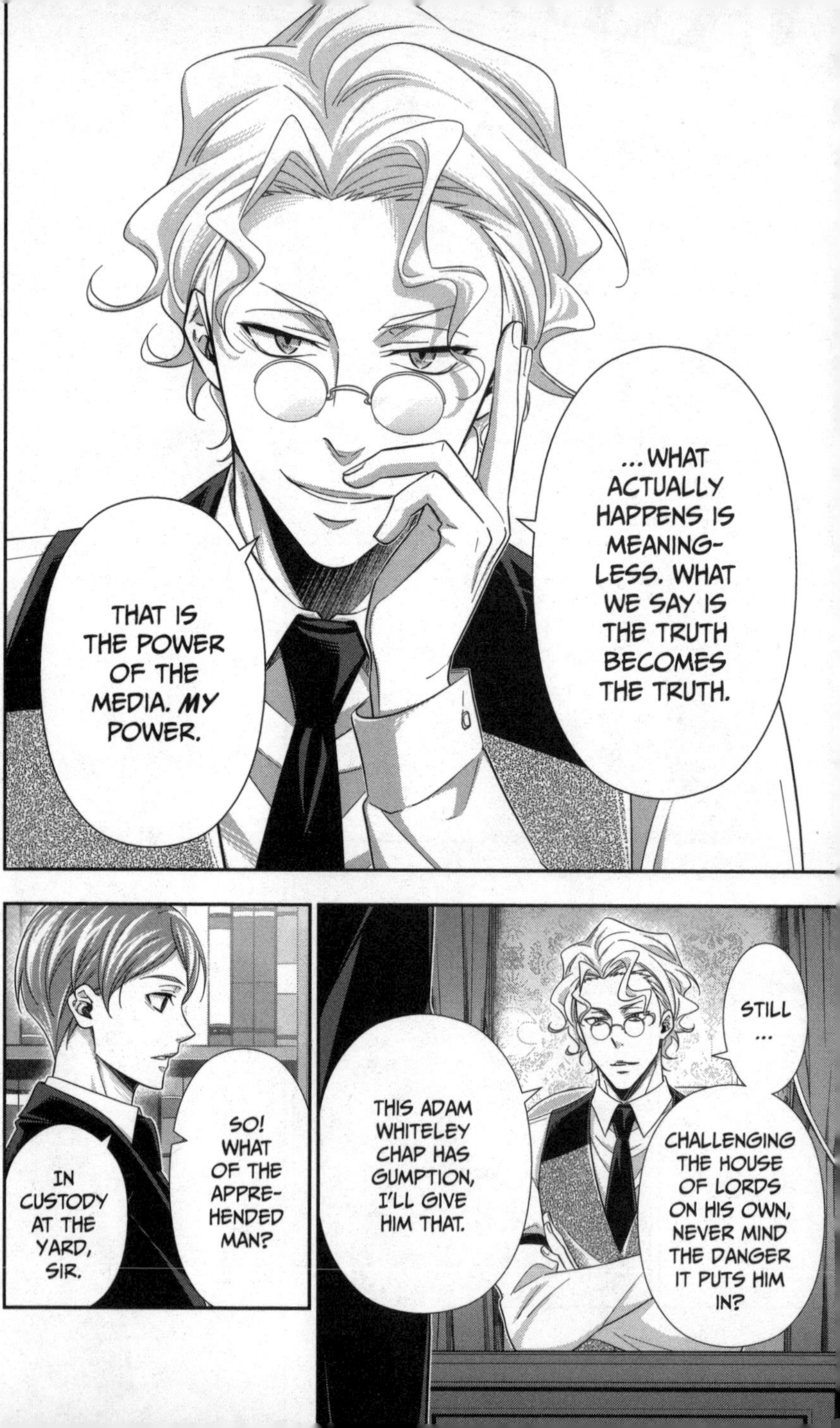
...WHAT ACTUALLY HAPPENS IS MEANING-LESS. WHAT WE SAY IS THE TRUTH BECOMES THE TRUTH.
THAT IS THE POWER OF THE MEDIA. *MY* POWER.
THIS ADAM WHITELEY CHAP HAS GUMPTION, I'LL GIVE HIM THAT.
STILL ...
CHALLENGING THE HOUSE OF LORDS ON HIS OWN, NEVER MIND THE DANGER IT PUTS HIM IN?
SO! WHAT OF THE APPRE-HENDED MAN?
IN CUSTODY AT THE YARD, SIR.

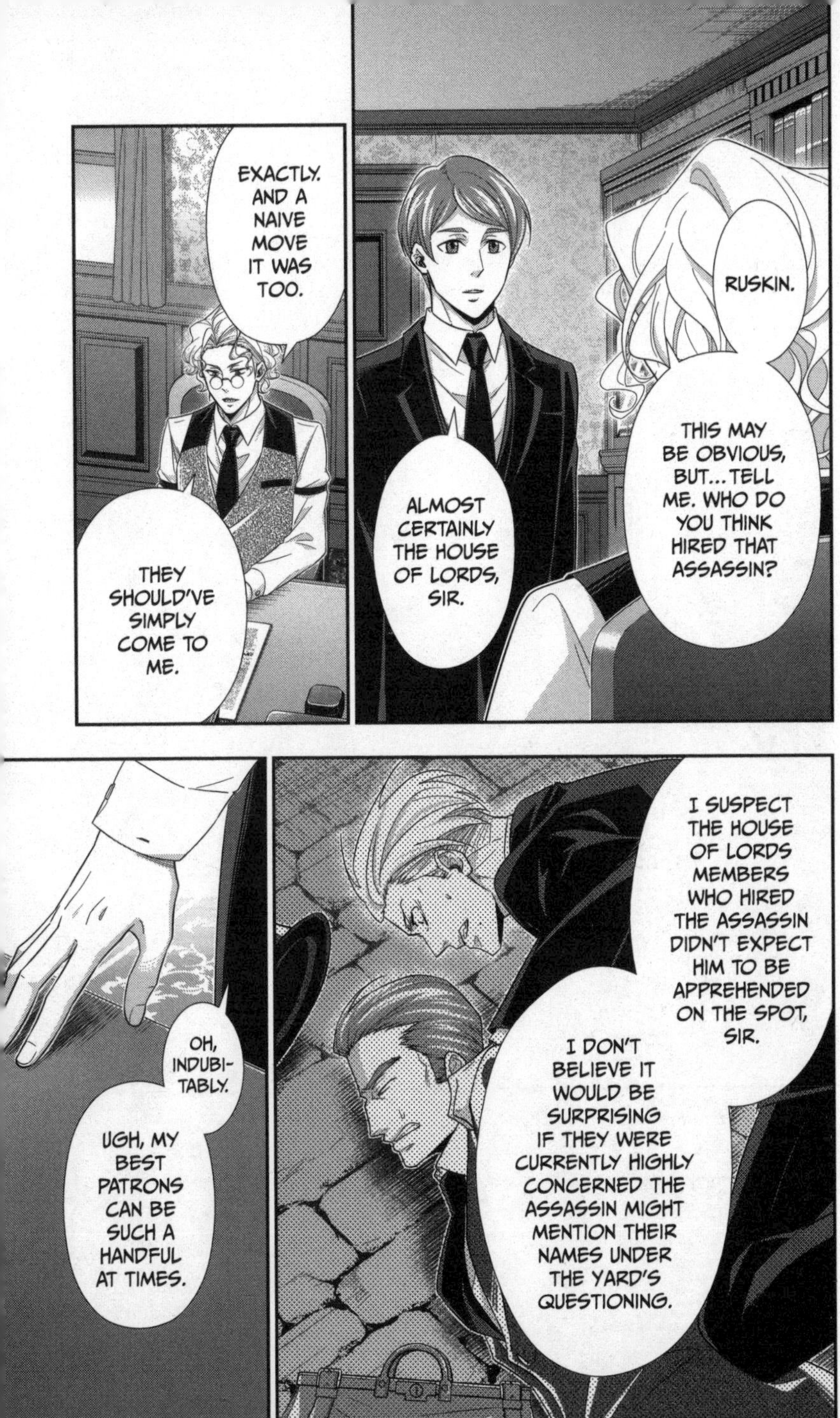
RUSKIN.
THIS MAY BE OBVIOUS, BUT... TELL ME. WHO DO YOU THINK HIRED THAT ASSASSIN?
ALMOST CERTAINLY THE HOUSE OF LORDS, SIR.
EXACTLY. AND A NAIVE MOVE IT WAS TOO.
THEY SHOULD'VE SIMPLY COME TO ME.
I SUSPECT THE HOUSE OF LORDS MEMBERS WHO HIRED THE ASSASSIN DIDN'T EXPECT HIM TO BE APPREHENDED ON THE SPOT, SIR.
I DON'T BELIEVE IT WOULD BE SURPRISING IF THEY WERE CURRENTLY HIGHLY CONCERNED THE ASSASSIN MIGHT MENTION THEIR NAMES UNDER THE YARD'S QUESTIONING.
OH, INDUBITABLY.
UGH, MY BEST PATRONS CAN BE SUCH A HANDFUL AT TIMES.

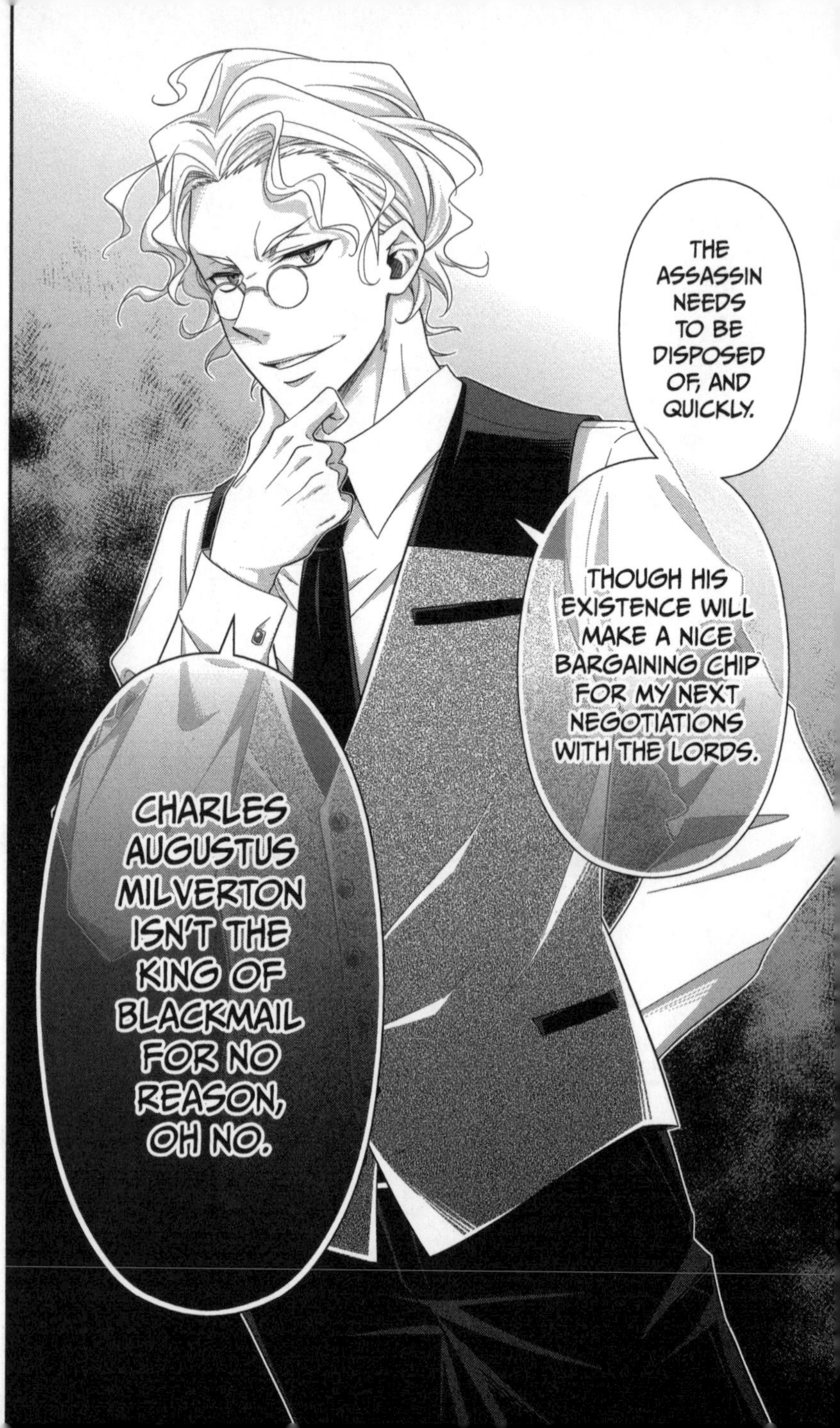
THE ASSASSIN NEEDS TO BE DISPOSED OF, AND QUICKLY.
THOUGH HIS EXISTENCE WILL MAKE A NICE BARGAINING CHIP FOR MY NEXT NEGOTIATIONS WITH THE LORDS.
CHARLES AUGUSTUS MILVERTON ISN'T THE KING OF BLACKMAIL FOR NO REASON, OH NO.

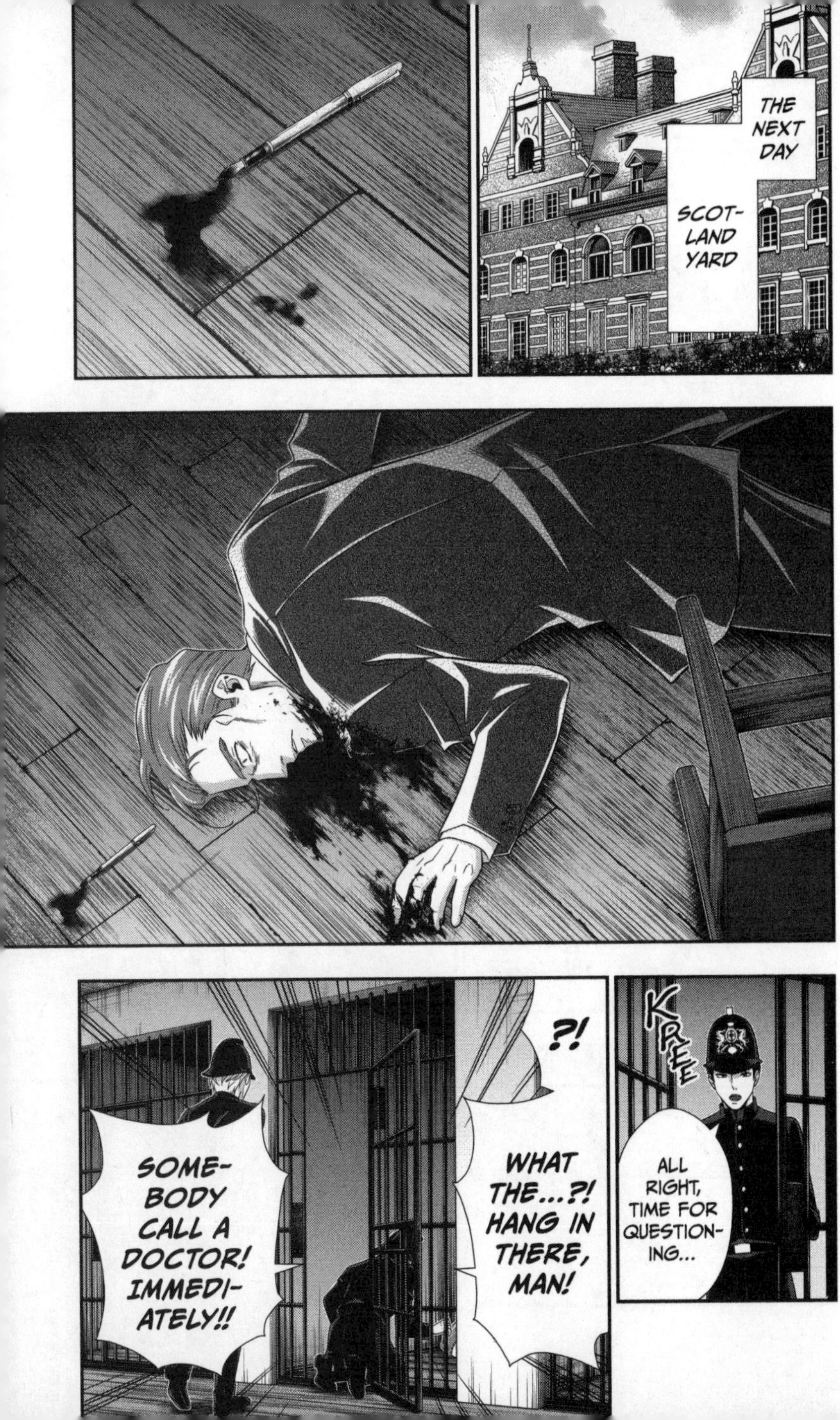
THE NEXT DAY
SCOTLAND YARD
KREE
ALL RIGHT, TIME FOR QUESTIONING...
?!
WHAT THE...?! HANG IN THERE, MAN!
SOMEBODY CALL A DOCTOR! IMMEDIATELY!!

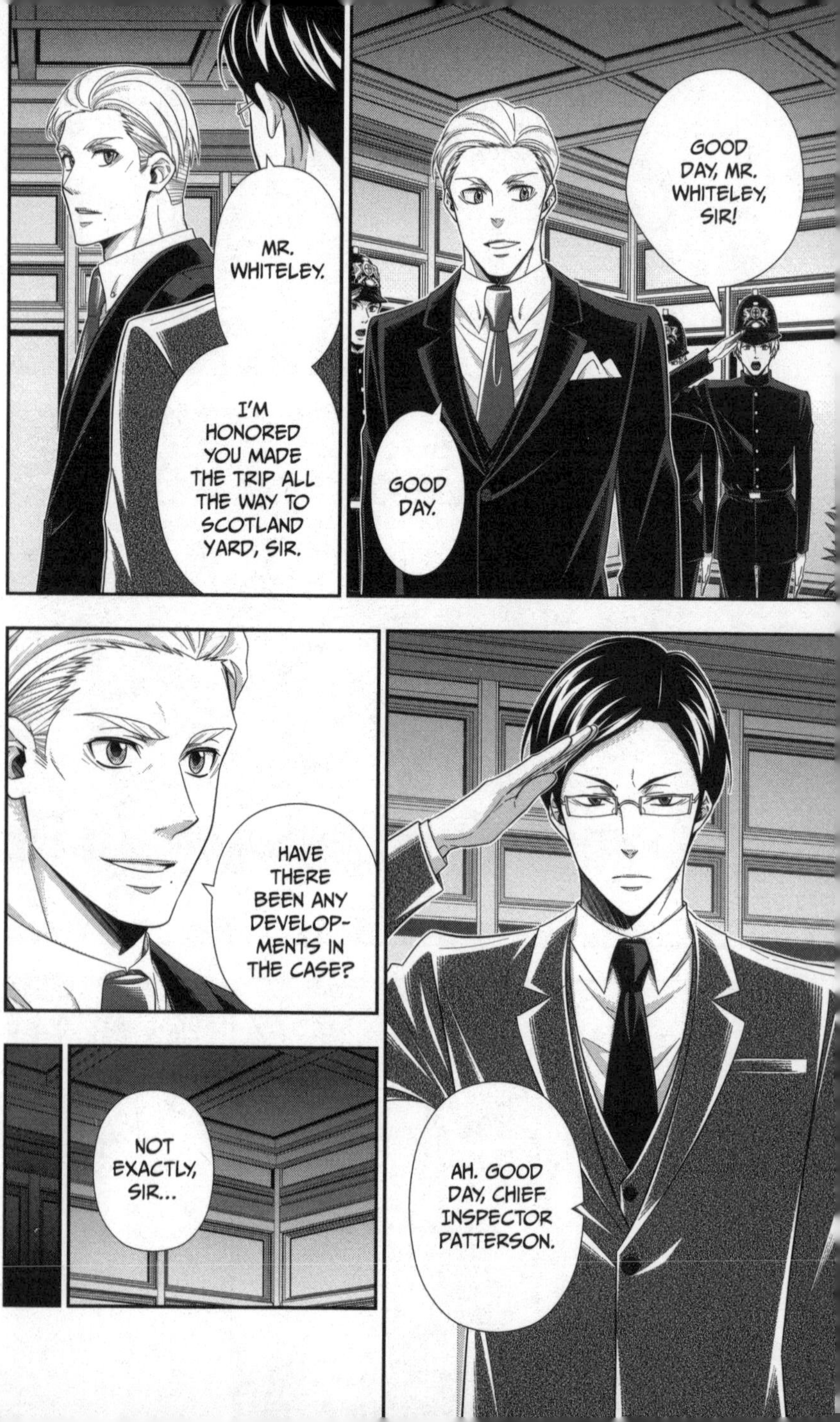
GOOD DAY, MR. WHITELEY, SIR!
GOOD DAY.
MR. WHITELEY.
I'M HONORED YOU MADE THE TRIP ALL THE WAY TO SCOTLAND YARD, SIR.
AH. GOOD DAY, CHIEF INSPECTOR PATTERSON.
HAVE THERE BEEN ANY DEVELOP-MENTS IN THE CASE?
NOT EXACTLY, SIR...

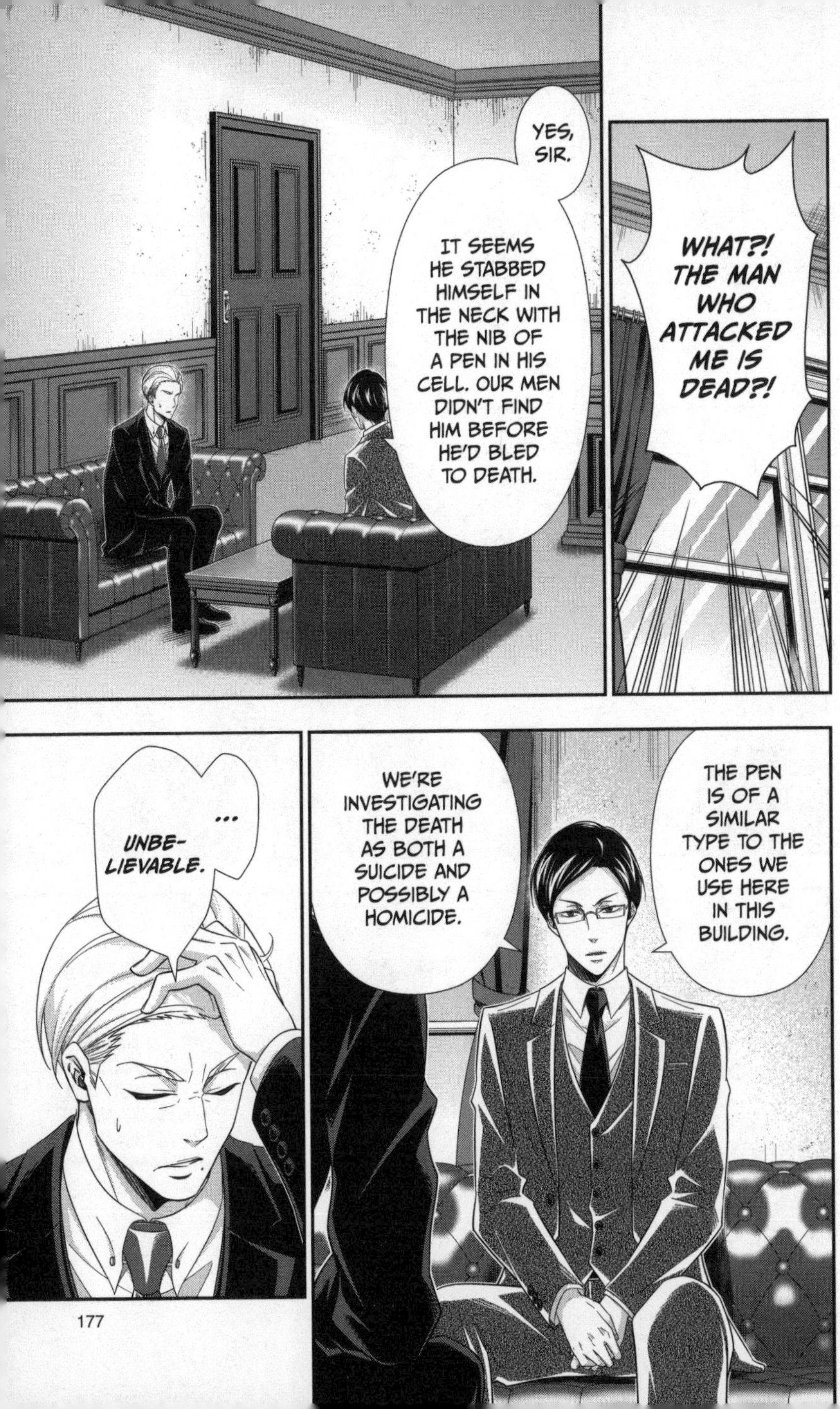
WHAT?! THE MAN WHO ATTACKED ME IS DEAD?!
YES, SIR.
IT SEEMS HE STABBED HIMSELF IN THE NECK WITH THE NIB OF A PEN IN HIS CELL. OUR MEN DIDN'T FIND HIM BEFORE HE'D BLED TO DEATH.
THE PEN IS OF A SIMILAR TYPE TO THE ONES WE USE HERE IN THIS BUILDING.
WE'RE INVESTIGATING THE DEATH AS BOTH A SUICIDE AND POSSIBLY A HOMICIDE.
... UNBE-LIEVABLE.

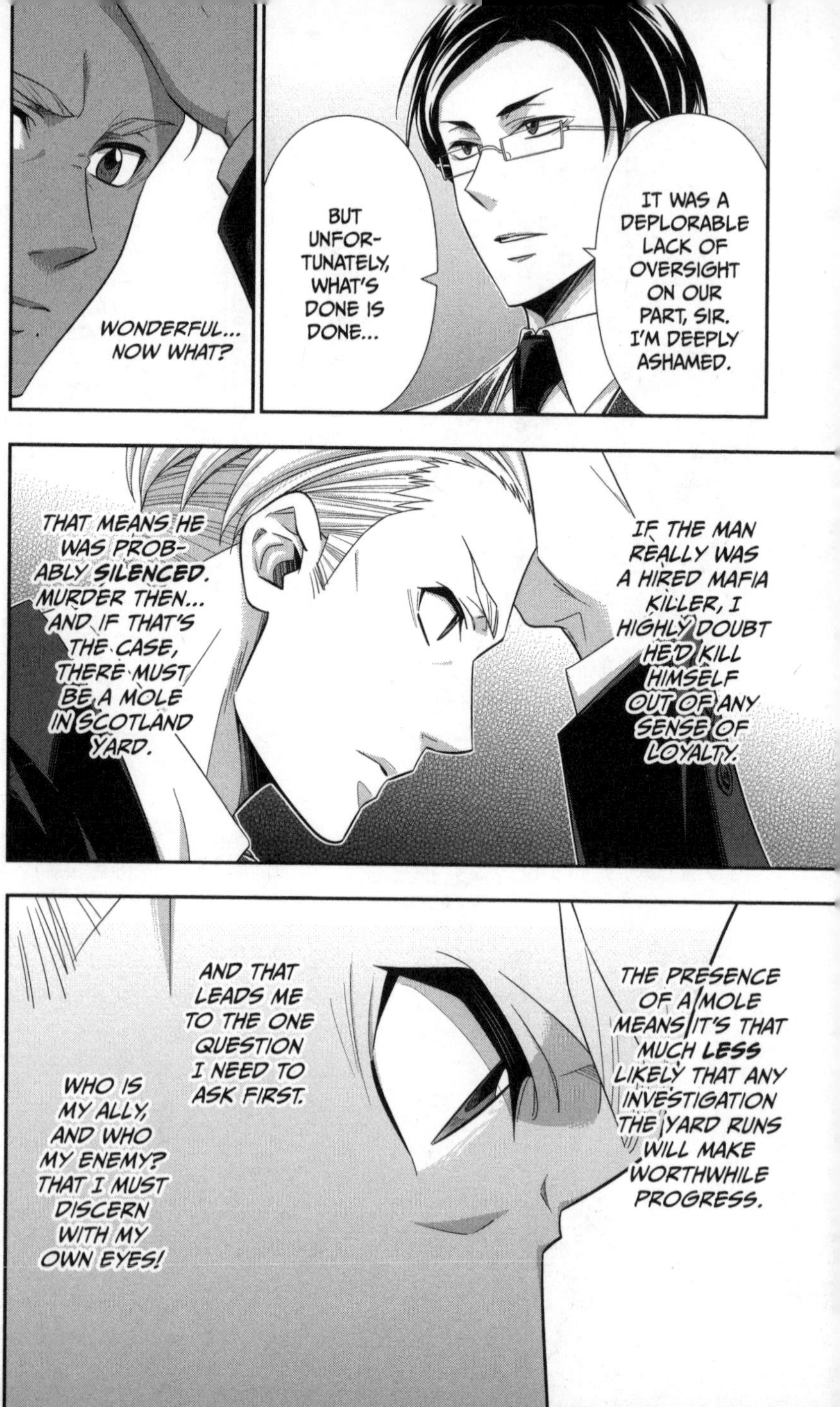
IT WAS A DEPLORABLE LACK OF OVERSIGHT ON OUR PART, SIR. I'M DEEPLY ASHAMED.
BUT UNFOR-TUNATELY, WHAT'S DONE IS DONE...
WONDERFUL... NOW WHAT?
IF THE MAN REALLY WAS A HIRED MAFIA KILLER, I HIGHLY DOUBT HE'D KILL HIMSELF OUT OF ANY SENSE OF LOYALTY.
THAT MEANS HE WAS PROB-ABLY **SILENCED**. MURDER THEN... AND IF THAT'S THE CASE, THERE MUST BE A MOLE IN SCOTLAND YARD.
THE PRESENCE OF A MOLE MEANS IT'S THAT MUCH **LESS** LIKELY THAT ANY INVESTIGATION THE YARD RUNS WILL MAKE WORTHWHILE PROGRESS.
AND THAT LEADS ME TO THE ONE QUESTION I NEED TO ASK FIRST.
WHO IS MY ALLY, AND WHO MY ENEMY? THAT I MUST DISCERN WITH MY OWN EYES!

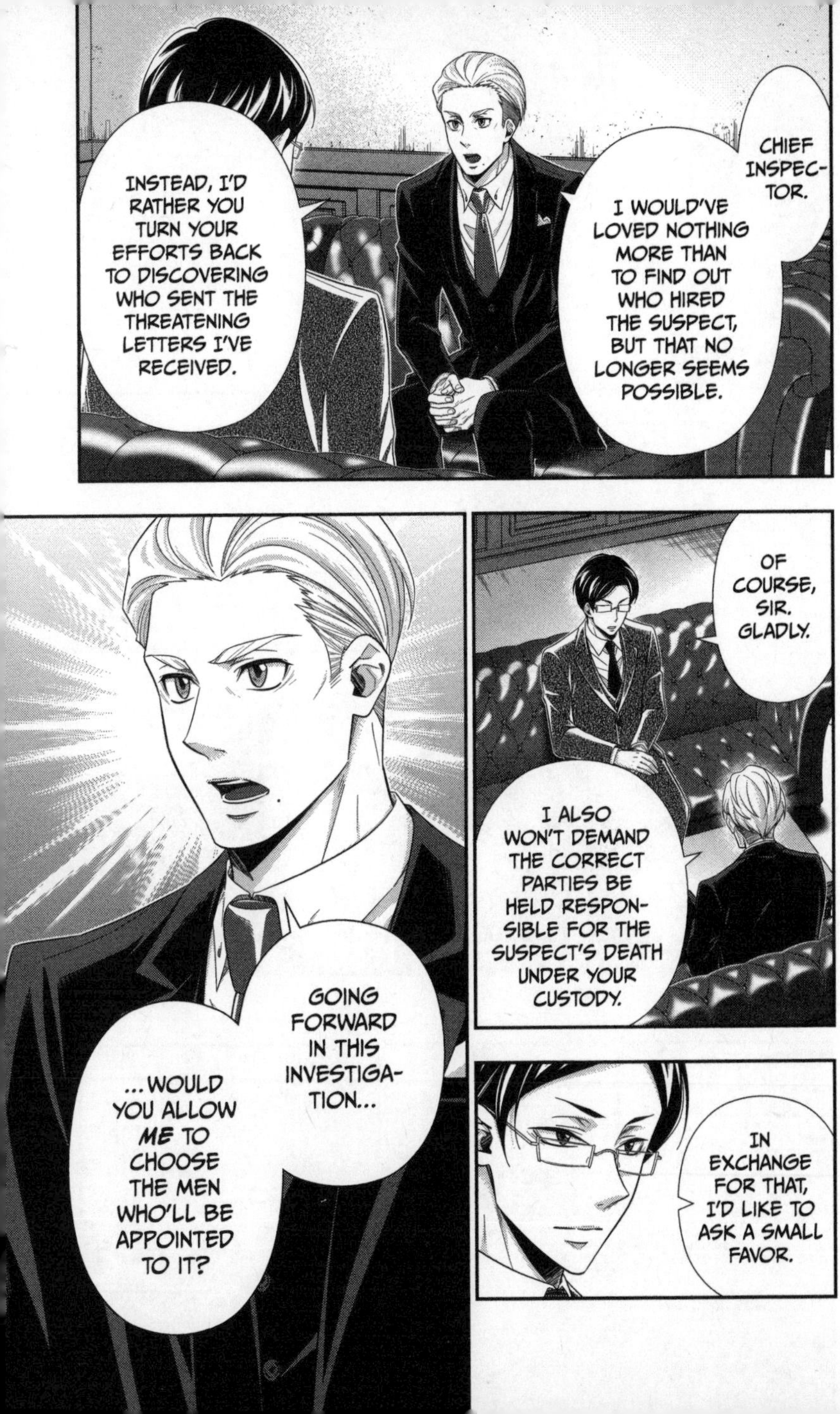
CHIEF INSPECTOR.
I WOULD'VE LOVED NOTHING MORE THAN TO FIND OUT WHO HIRED THE SUSPECT, BUT THAT NO LONGER SEEMS POSSIBLE.
INSTEAD, I'D RATHER YOU TURN YOUR EFFORTS BACK TO DISCOVERING WHO SENT THE THREATENING LETTERS I'VE RECEIVED.
OF COURSE, SIR. GLADLY.
I ALSO WON'T DEMAND THE CORRECT PARTIES BE HELD RESPONSIBLE FOR THE SUSPECT'S DEATH UNDER YOUR CUSTODY.
IN EXCHANGE FOR THAT, I'D LIKE TO ASK A SMALL FAVOR.
GOING FORWARD IN THIS INVESTIGATION...
...WOULD YOU ALLOW *ME* TO CHOOSE THE MEN WHO'LL BE APPOINTED TO IT?

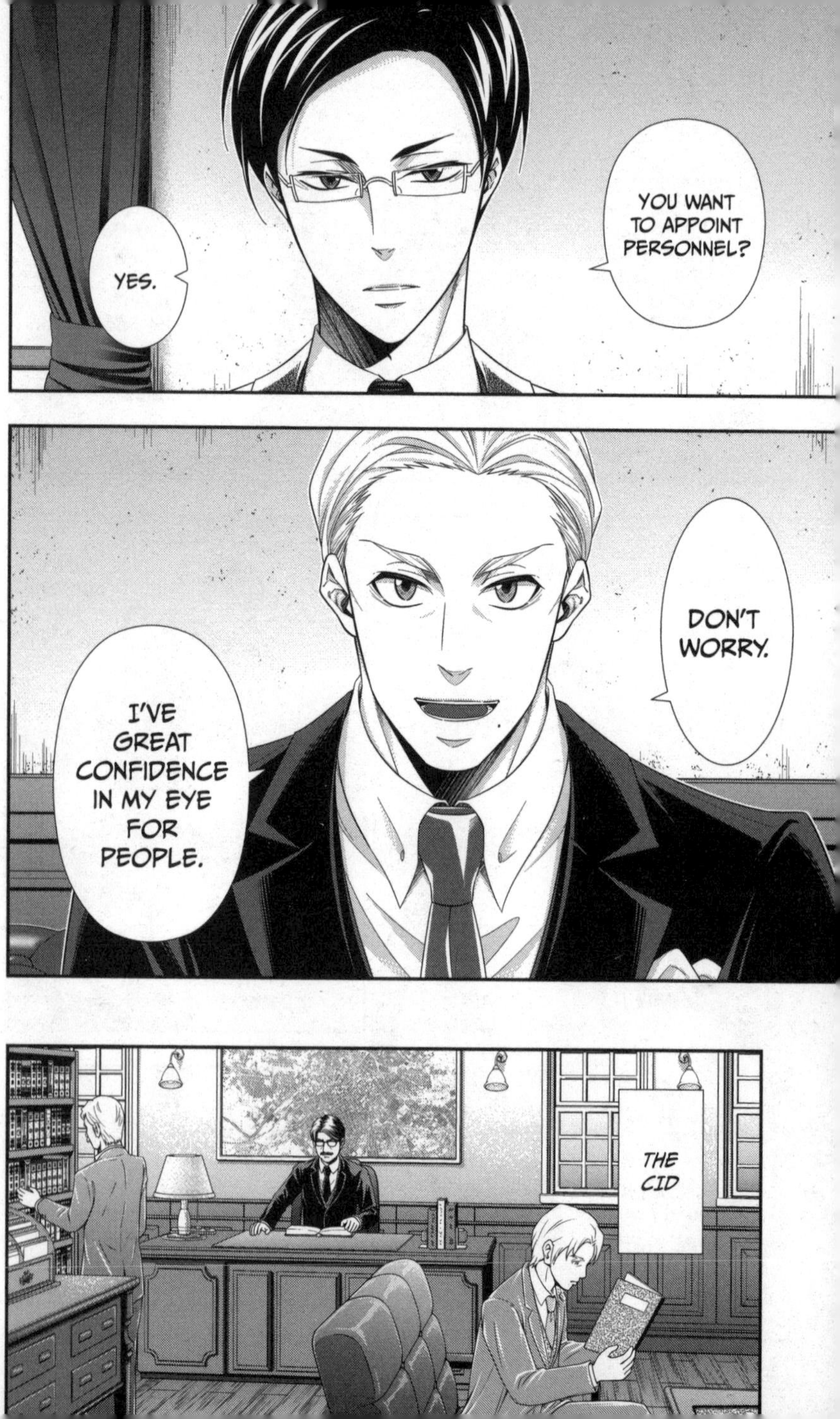
YOU WANT TO APPOINT PERSONNEL?
YES.
DON'T WORRY.
I'VE GREAT CONFIDENCE IN MY EYE FOR PEOPLE.
THE CID

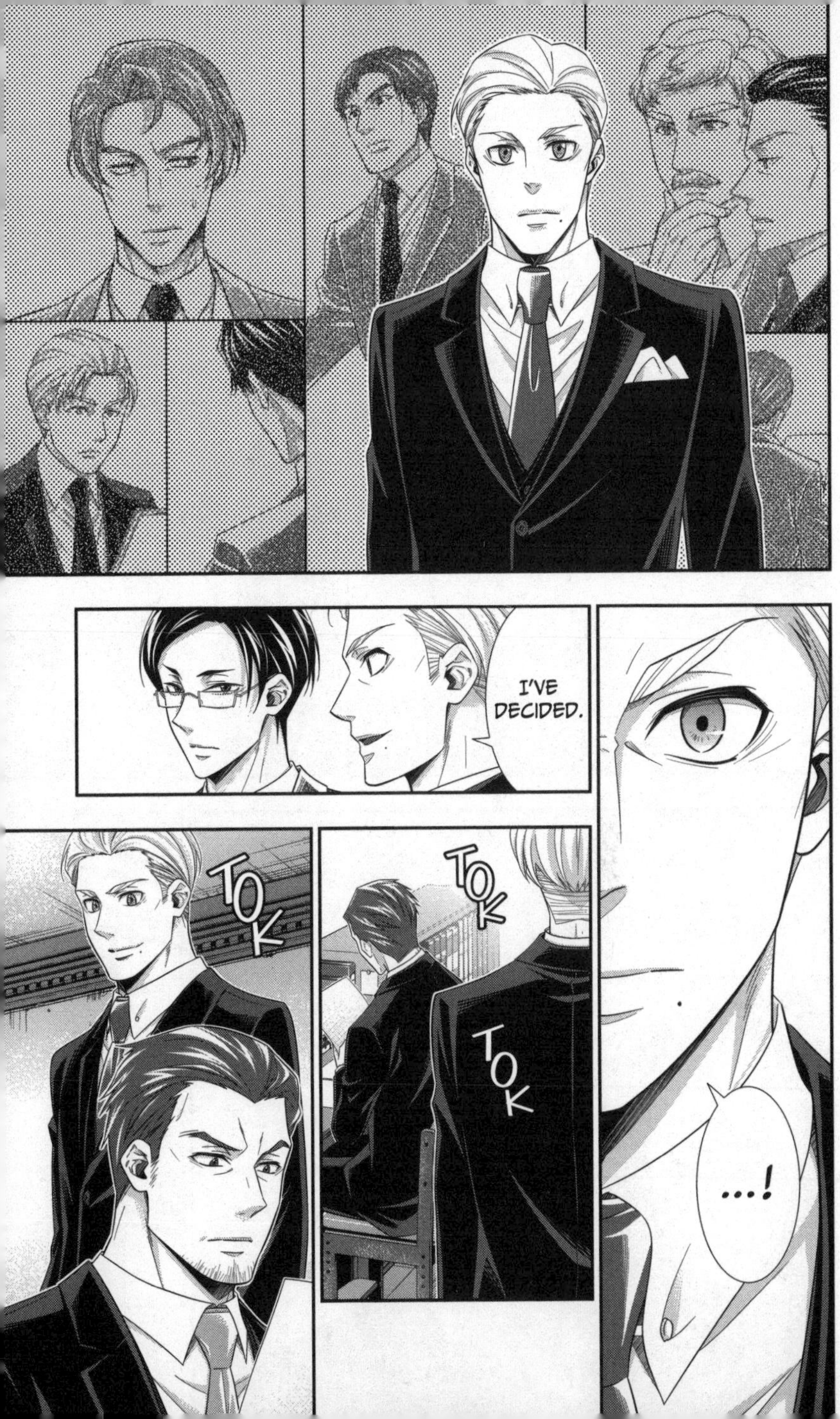
...!
I'VE DECIDED.
TOK
TOK
TOK

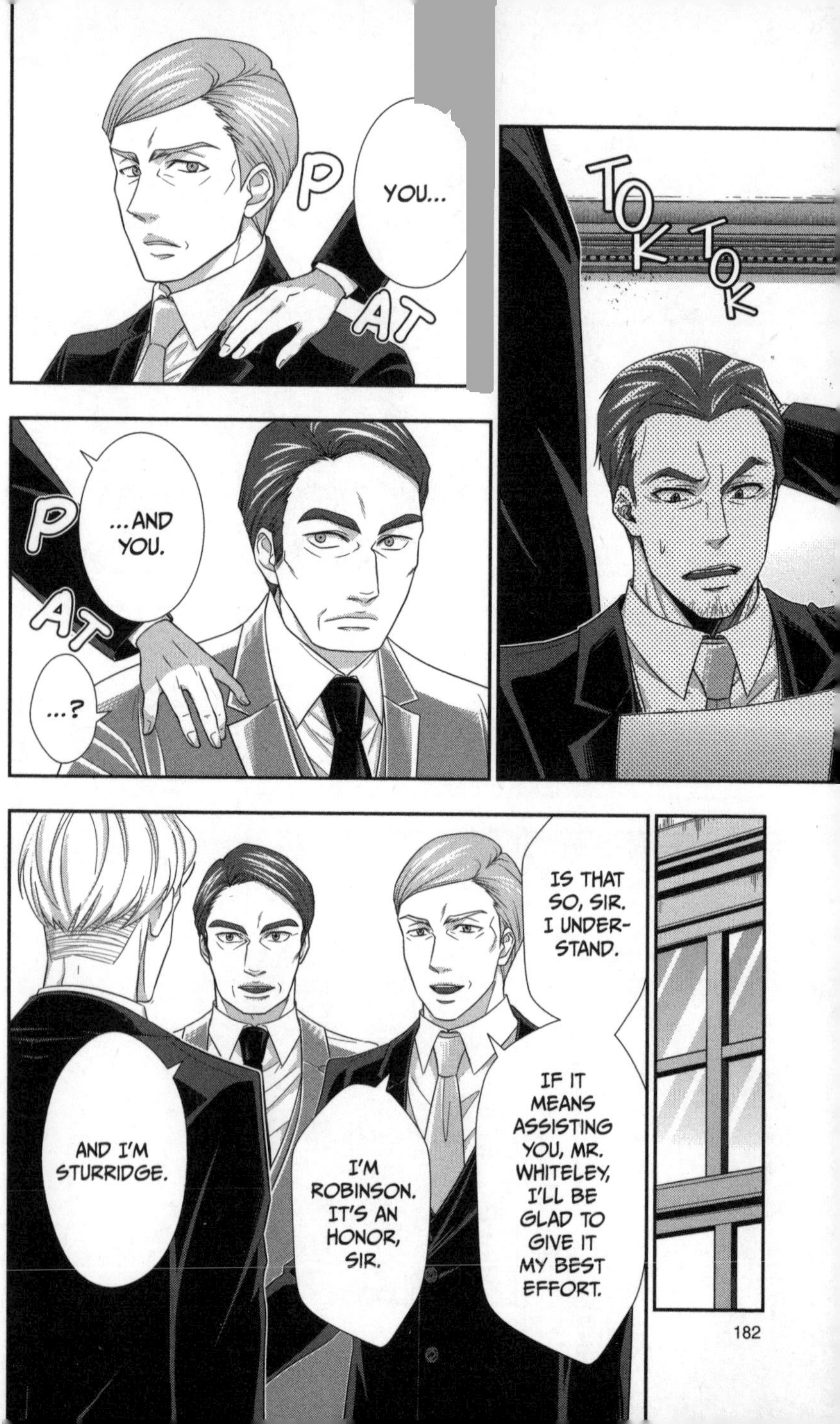
TOK TOK
YOU...
PAT
...AND YOU.
PAT
...?
IS THAT SO, SIR. I UNDER-STAND.
IF IT MEANS ASSISTING YOU, MR. WHITELEY, I'LL BE GLAD TO GIVE IT MY BEST EFFORT.
I'M ROBINSON. IT'S AN HONOR, SIR.
AND I'M STURRIDGE.

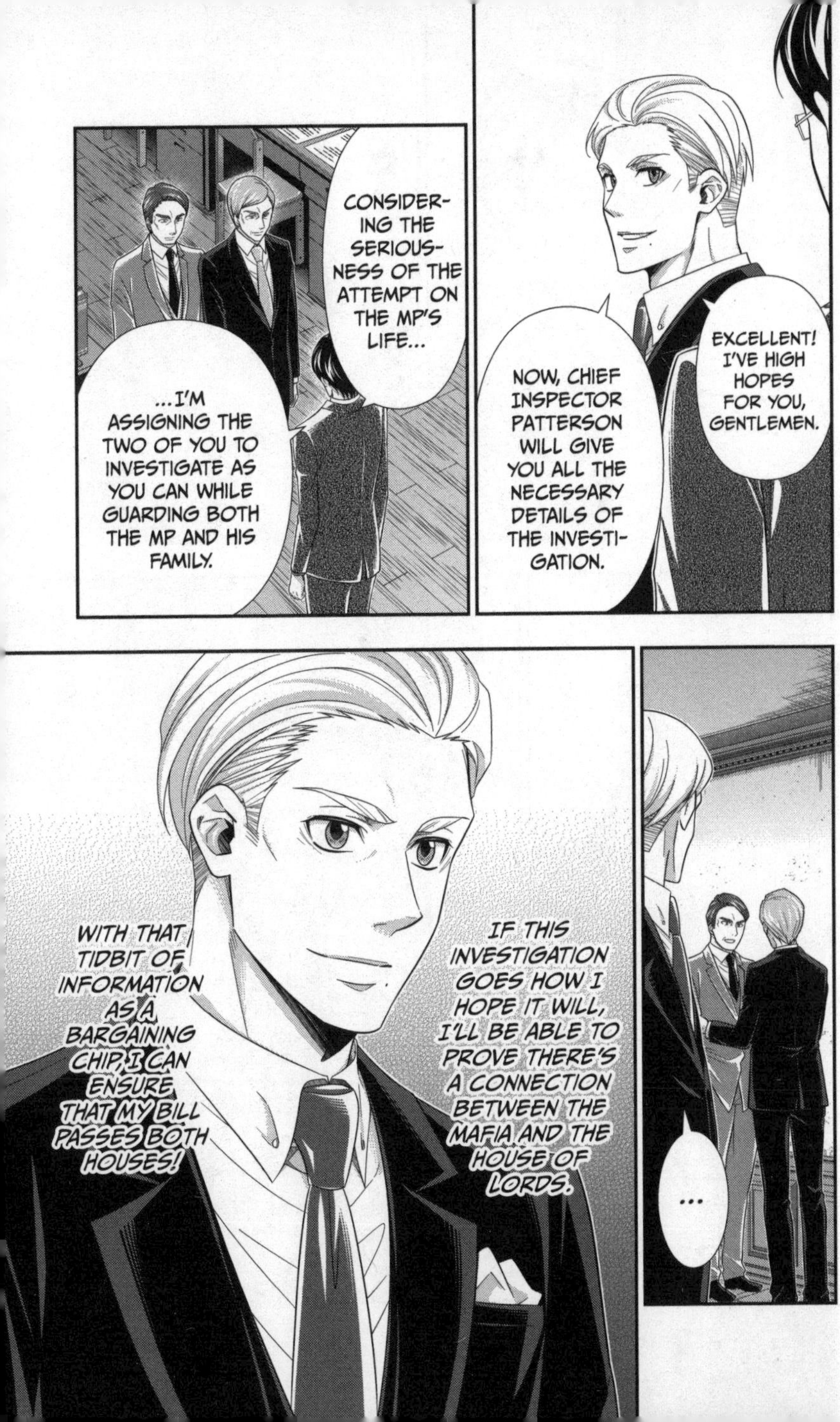
EXCELLENT! I'VE HIGH HOPES FOR YOU, GENTLEMEN.
NOW, CHIEF INSPECTOR PATTERSON WILL GIVE YOU ALL THE NECESSARY DETAILS OF THE INVESTIGATION.
CONSIDERING THE SERIOUSNESS OF THE ATTEMPT ON THE MP'S LIFE...
...I'M ASSIGNING THE TWO OF YOU TO INVESTIGATE AS YOU CAN WHILE GUARDING BOTH THE MP AND HIS FAMILY.
...
IF THIS INVESTIGATION GOES HOW I HOPE IT WILL, I'LL BE ABLE TO PROVE THERE'S A CONNECTION BETWEEN THE MAFIA AND THE HOUSE OF LORDS.
WITH THAT TIDBIT OF INFORMATION AS A BARGAINING CHIP, I CAN ENSURE THAT MY BILL PASSES BOTH HOUSES!

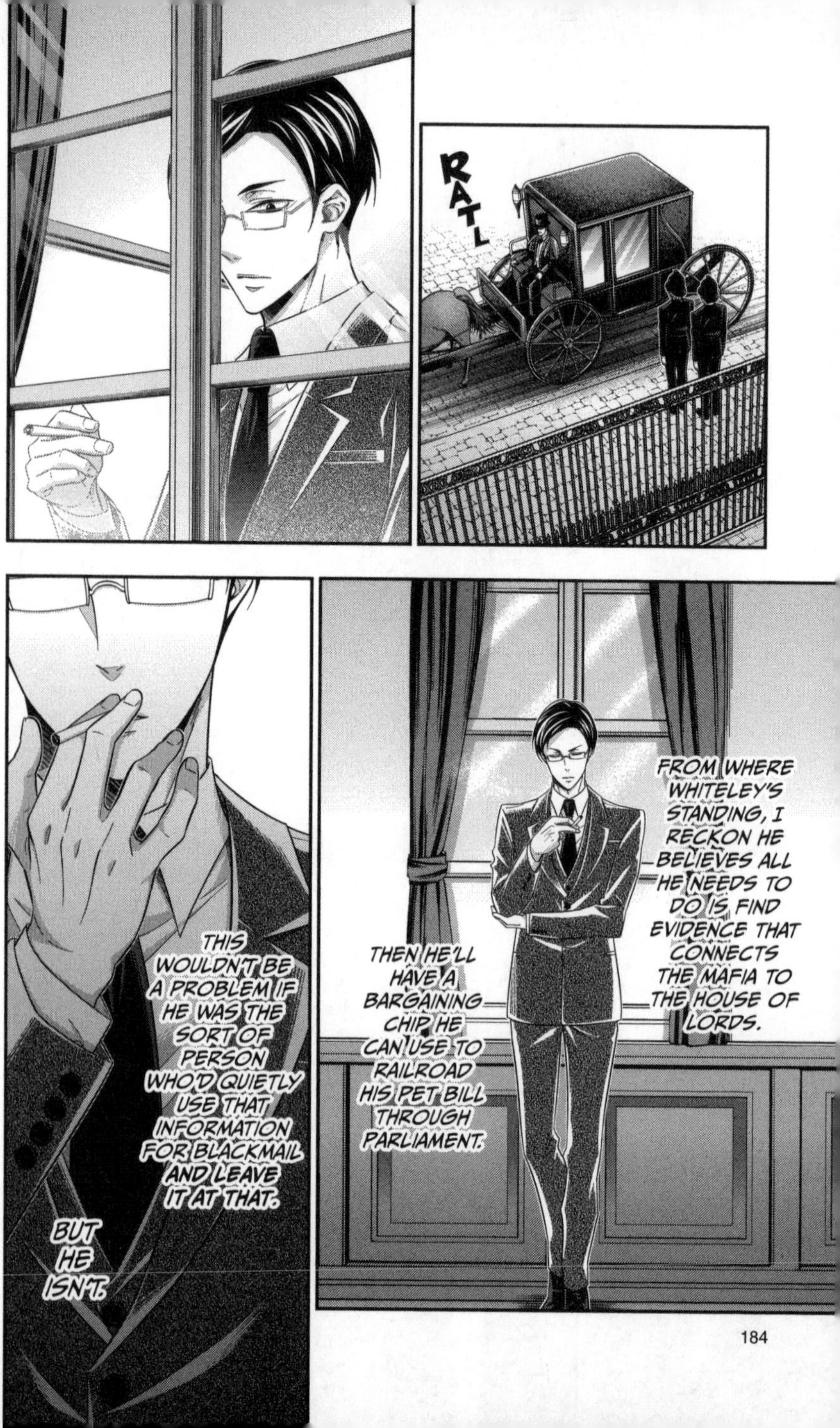
RATL
FROM WHERE WHITELEY'S STANDING, I RECKON HE BELIEVES ALL HE NEEDS TO DO IS FIND EVIDENCE THAT CONNECTS THE MAFIA TO THE HOUSE OF LORDS.
THEN HE'LL HAVE A BARGAINING CHIP HE CAN USE TO RAILROAD HIS PET BILL THROUGH PARLIAMENT.
THIS WOULDN'T BE A PROBLEM IF HE WAS THE SORT OF PERSON WHO'D QUIETLY USE THAT INFORMATION FOR BLACKMAIL AND LEAVE IT AT THAT.
BUT HE ISN'T.

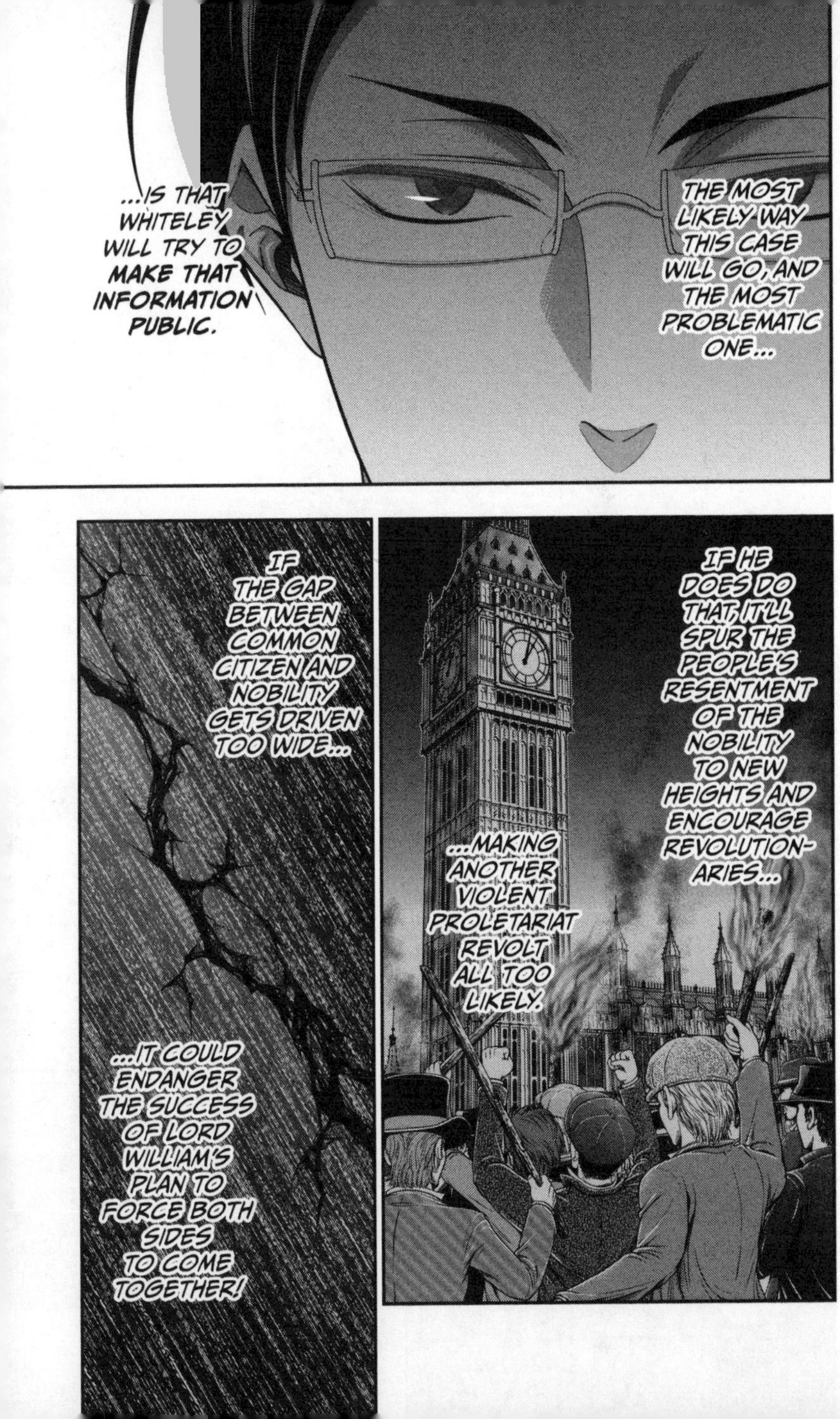
THE MOST LIKELY WAY THIS CASE WILL GO, AND THE MOST PROBLEMATIC ONE...
...IS THAT WHITELEY WILL TRY TO MAKE THAT INFORMATION PUBLIC.
IF HE DOES DO THAT, IT'LL SPUR THE PEOPLE'S RESENTMENT OF THE NOBILITY TO NEW HEIGHTS AND ENCOURAGE REVOLUTION-ARIES...
...MAKING ANOTHER VIOLENT PROLETARIAT REVOLT ALL TOO LIKELY.
IF THE GAP BETWEEN COMMON CITIZEN AND NOBILITY GETS DRIVEN TOO WIDE...
...IT COULD ENDANGER THE SUCCESS OF LORD WILLIAM'S PLAN TO FORCE BOTH SIDES TO COME TOGETHER!

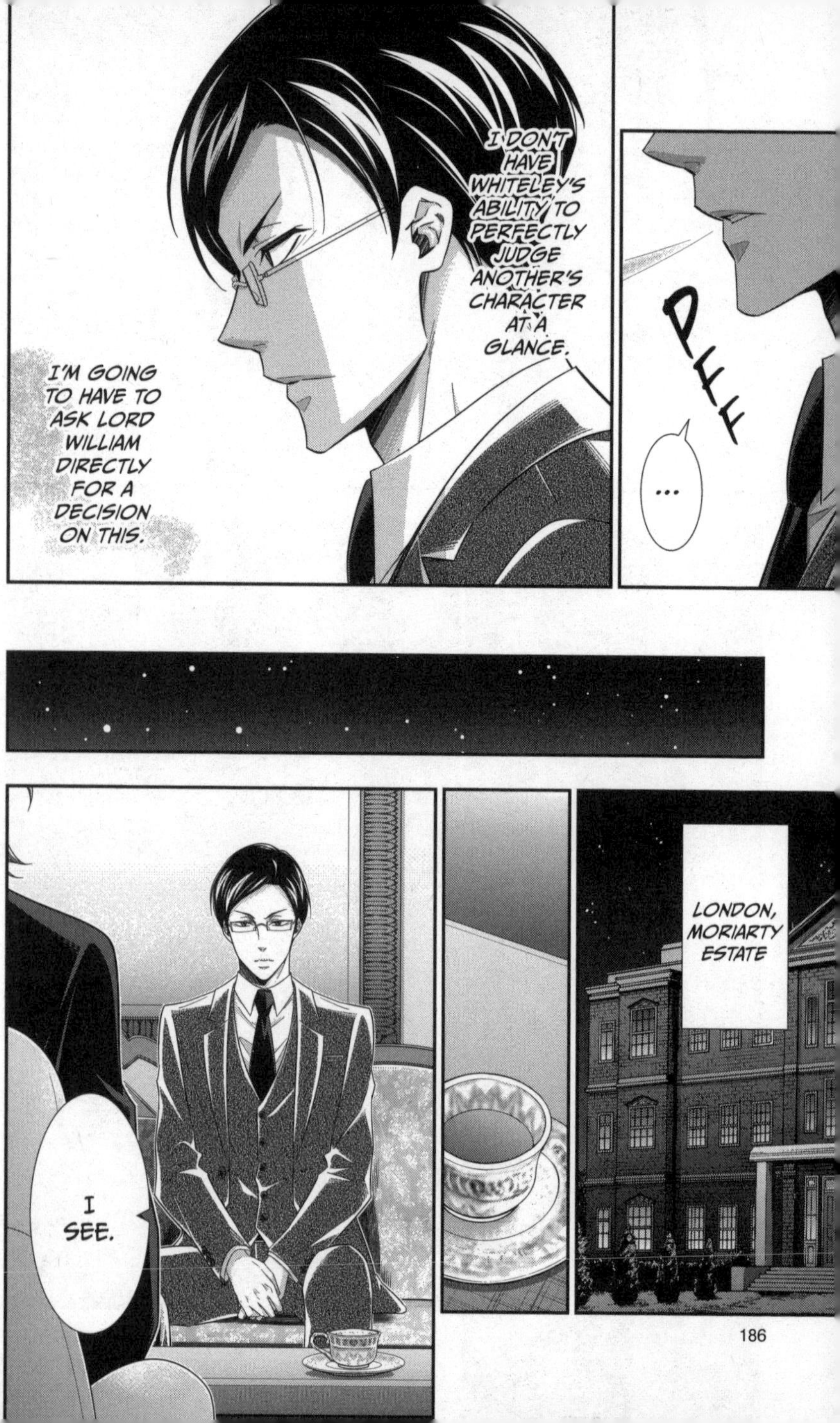
PFFF
...
I DON'T HAVE WHITELEY'S ABILITY TO PERFECTLY JUDGE ANOTHER'S CHARACTER AT A GLANCE.
I'M GOING TO HAVE TO ASK LORD WILLIAM DIRECTLY FOR A DECISION ON THIS.
LONDON, MORIARTY ESTATE
I SEE.

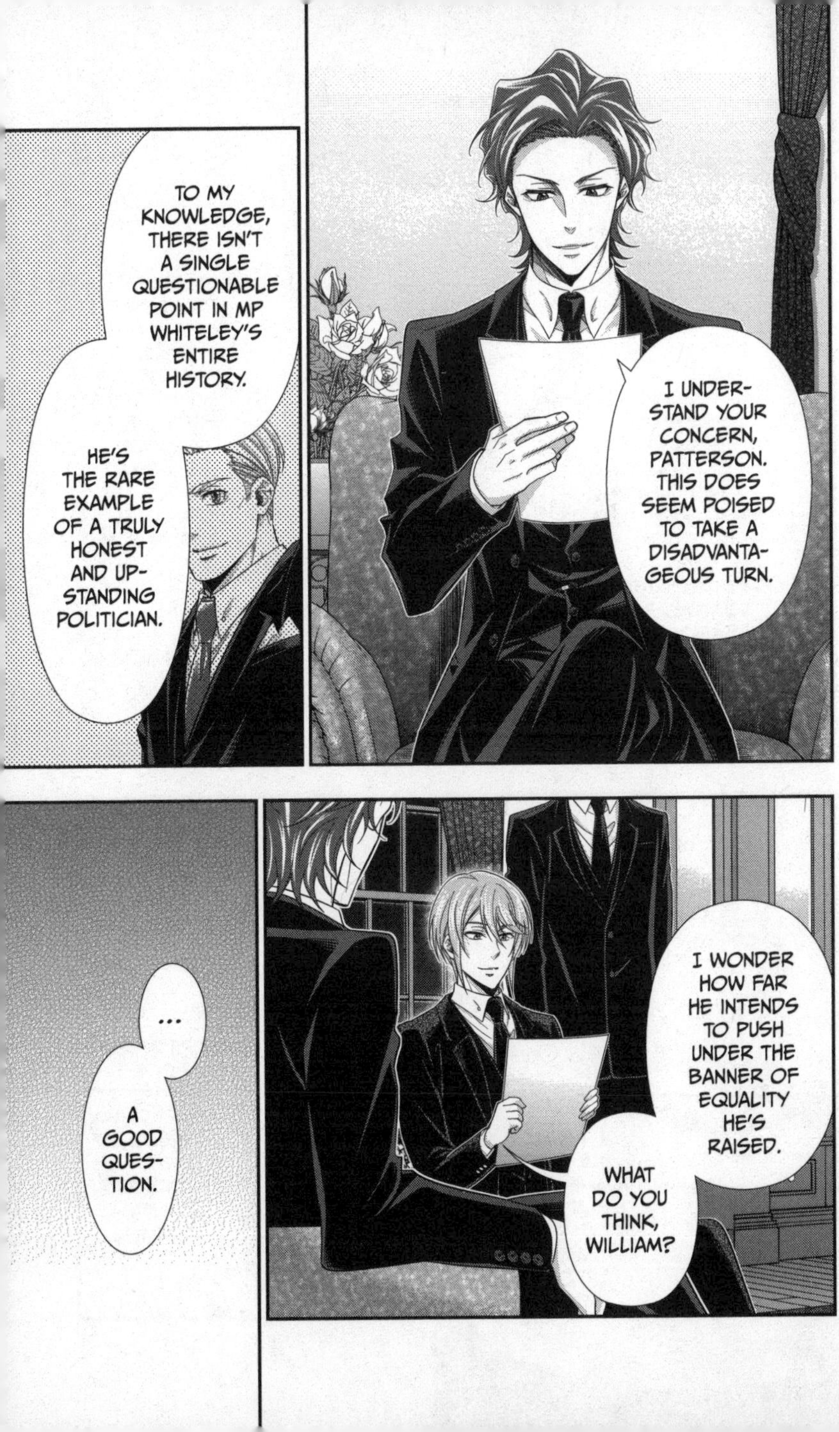
I UNDER-STAND YOUR CONCERN, PATTERSON. THIS DOES SEEM POISED TO TAKE A DISADVANTA-GEOUS TURN.
TO MY KNOWLEDGE, THERE ISN'T A SINGLE QUESTIONABLE POINT IN MP WHITELEY'S ENTIRE HISTORY.
HE'S THE RARE EXAMPLE OF A TRULY HONEST AND UP-STANDING POLITICIAN.
I WONDER HOW FAR HE INTENDS TO PUSH UNDER THE BANNER OF EQUALITY HE'S RAISED.
WHAT DO YOU THINK, WILLIAM?
...
A GOOD QUES-TION.

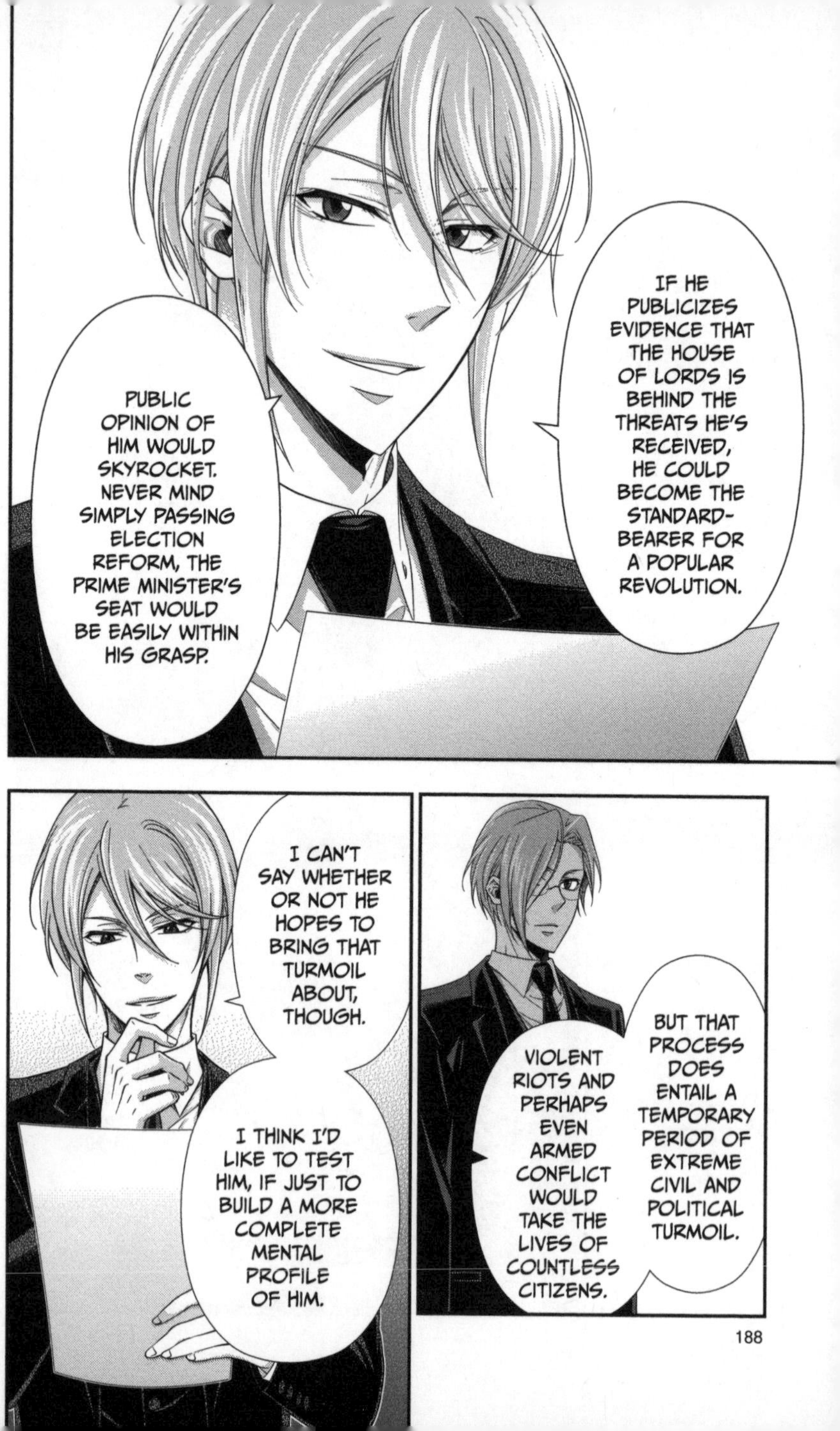
IF HE PUBLICIZES EVIDENCE THAT THE HOUSE OF LORDS IS BEHIND THE THREATS HE'S RECEIVED, HE COULD BECOME THE STANDARD-BEARER FOR A POPULAR REVOLUTION.
PUBLIC OPINION OF HIM WOULD SKYROCKET. NEVER MIND SIMPLY PASSING ELECTION REFORM, THE PRIME MINISTER'S SEAT WOULD BE EASILY WITHIN HIS GRASP.
BUT THAT PROCESS DOES ENTAIL A TEMPORARY PERIOD OF EXTREME CIVIL AND POLITICAL TURMOIL.
VIOLENT RIOTS AND PERHAPS EVEN ARMED CONFLICT WOULD TAKE THE LIVES OF COUNTLESS CITIZENS.
I CAN'T SAY WHETHER OR NOT HE HOPES TO BRING THAT TURMOIL ABOUT, THOUGH.
I THINK I'D LIKE TO TEST HIM, IF JUST TO BUILD A MORE COMPLETE MENTAL PROFILE OF HIM.

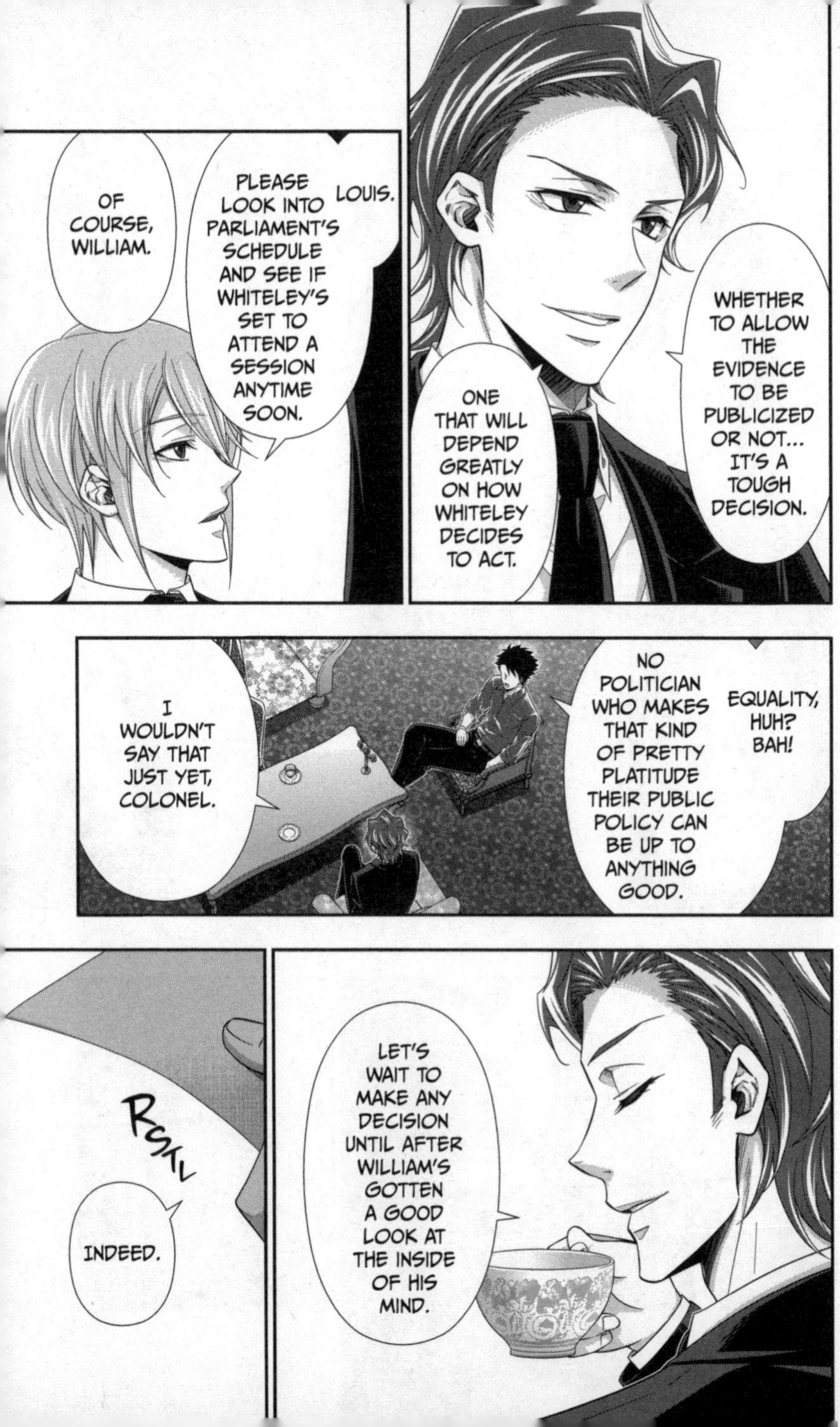
WHETHER TO ALLOW THE EVIDENCE TO BE PUBLICIZED OR NOT... IT'S A TOUGH DECISION.
ONE THAT WILL DEPEND GREATLY ON HOW WHITELEY DECIDES TO ACT.
LOUIS.
PLEASE LOOK INTO PARLIAMENT'S SCHEDULE AND SEE IF WHITELEY'S SET TO ATTEND A SESSION ANYTIME SOON.
OF COURSE, WILLIAM.
EQUALITY, HUH? BAH!
NO POLITICIAN WHO MAKES THAT KIND OF PRETTY PLATITUDE THEIR PUBLIC POLICY CAN BE UP TO ANYTHING GOOD.
I WOULDN'T SAY THAT JUST YET, COLONEL.
LET'S WAIT TO MAKE ANY DECISION UNTIL AFTER WILLIAM'S GOTTEN A GOOD LOOK AT THE INSIDE OF HIS MIND.
RSTL
INDEED.

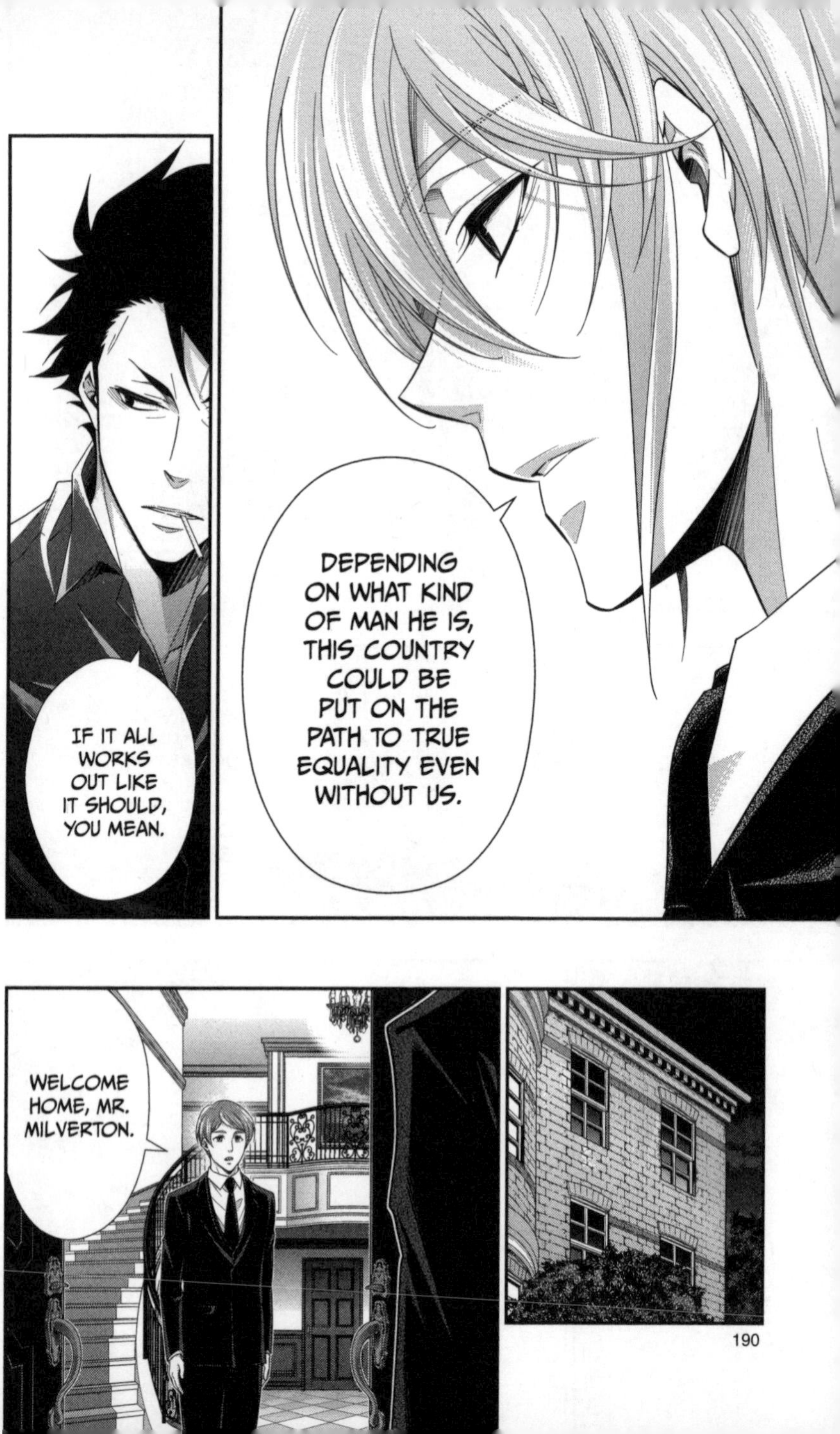
DEPENDING ON WHAT KIND OF MAN HE IS, THIS COUNTRY COULD BE PUT ON THE PATH TO TRUE EQUALITY EVEN WITHOUT US.
IF IT ALL WORKS OUT LIKE IT SHOULD, YOU MEAN.
WELCOME HOME, MR. MILVERTON.

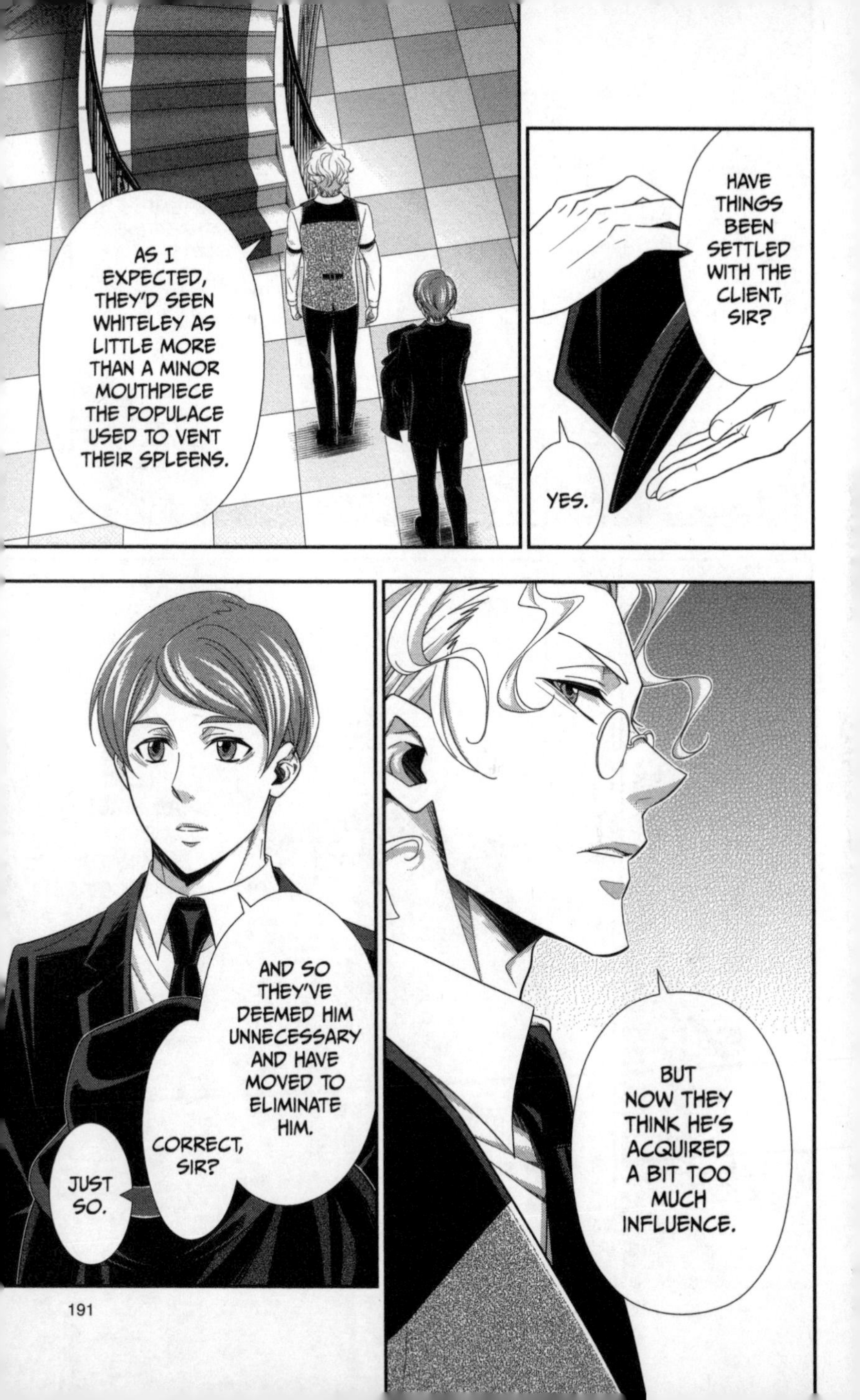
HAVE THINGS BEEN SETTLED WITH THE CLIENT, SIR?
YES.
AS I EXPECTED, THEY'D SEEN WHITELEY AS LITTLE MORE THAN A MINOR MOUTHPIECE THE POPULACE USED TO VENT THEIR SPLEENS.
BUT NOW THEY THINK HE'S ACQUIRED A BIT TOO MUCH INFLUENCE.
AND SO THEY'VE DEEMED HIM UNNECESSARY AND HAVE MOVED TO ELIMINATE HIM.
CORRECT, SIR?
JUST SO.

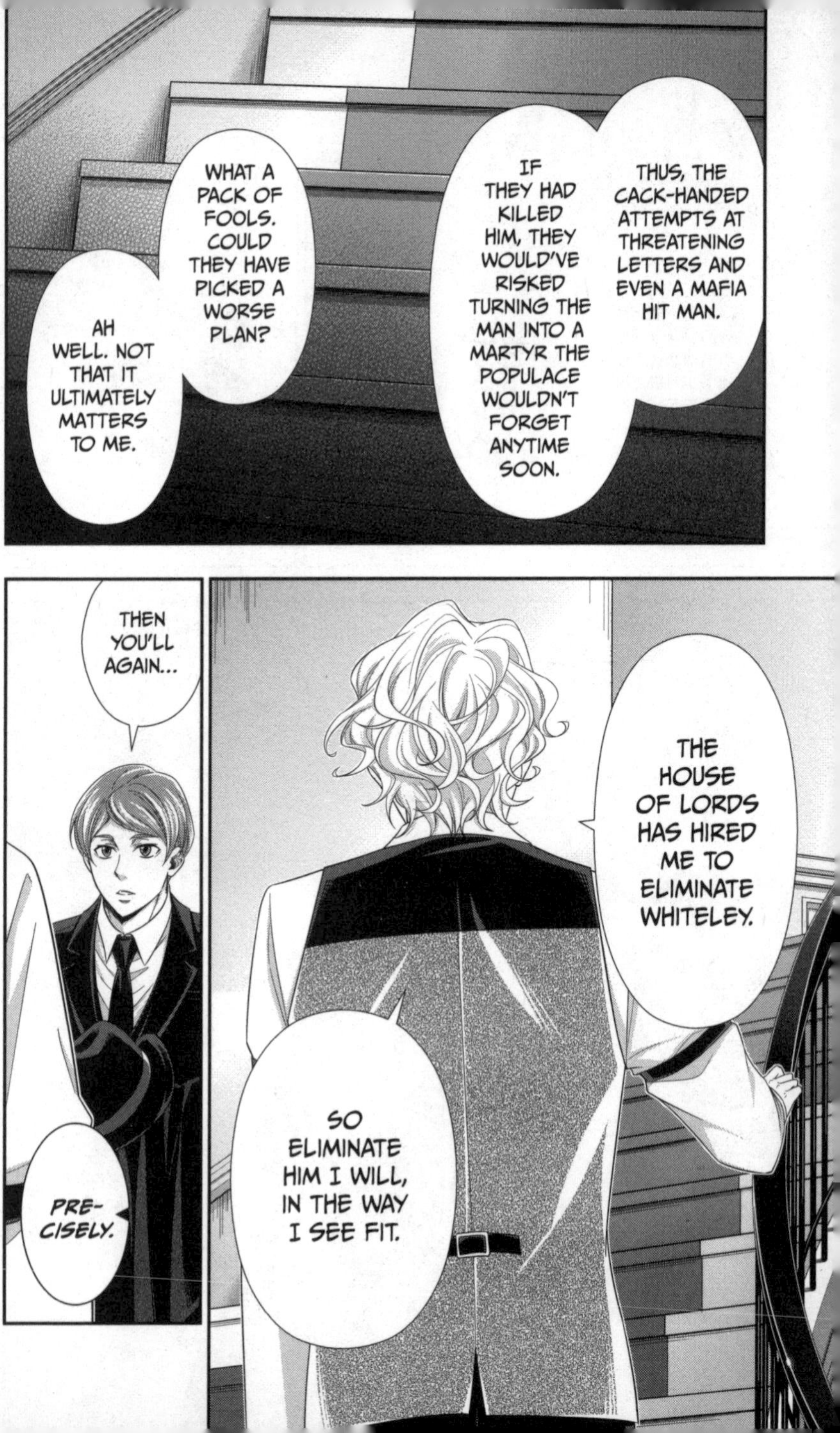
THUS, THE CACK-HANDED ATTEMPTS AT THREATENING LETTERS AND EVEN A MAFIA HIT MAN.
IF THEY HAD KILLED HIM, THEY WOULD'VE RISKED TURNING THE MAN INTO A MARTYR THE POPULACE WOULDN'T FORGET ANYTIME SOON.
WHAT A PACK OF FOOLS. COULD THEY HAVE PICKED A WORSE PLAN?
AH WELL. NOT THAT IT ULTIMATELY MATTERS TO ME.
THE HOUSE OF LORDS HAS HIRED ME TO ELIMINATE WHITELEY.
SO ELIMINATE HIM I WILL, IN THE WAY I SEE FIT.
THEN YOU'LL AGAIN...
PRE-CISELY.

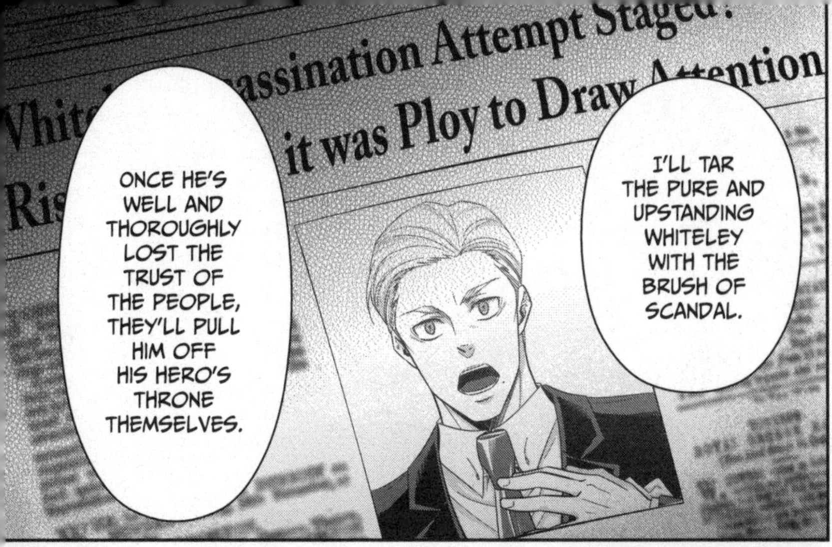
it was Ploy to Draw
I'LL TAR THE PURE AND UPSTANDING WHITELEY WITH THE BRUSH OF SCANDAL.
ONCE HE'S WELL AND THOROUGHLY LOST THE TRUST OF THE PEOPLE, THEY'LL PULL HIM OFF HIS HERO'S THRONE THEMSELVES.

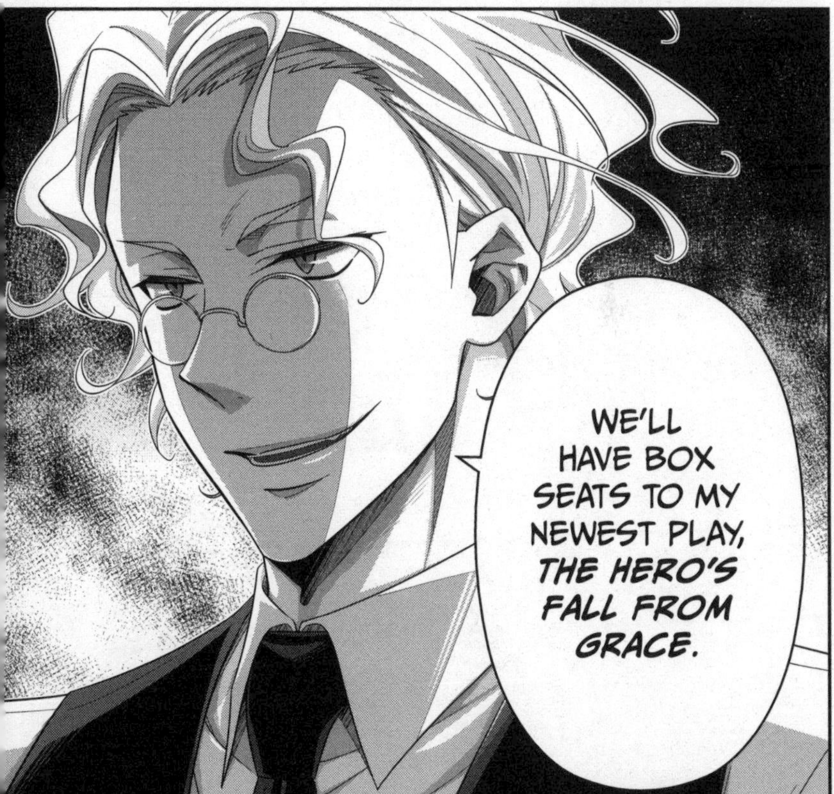
WE'LL HAVE BOX SEATS TO MY NEWEST PLAY, *THE HERO'S FALL FROM GRACE.*

MORIARTY THE PATRIOT VOL. 9: END

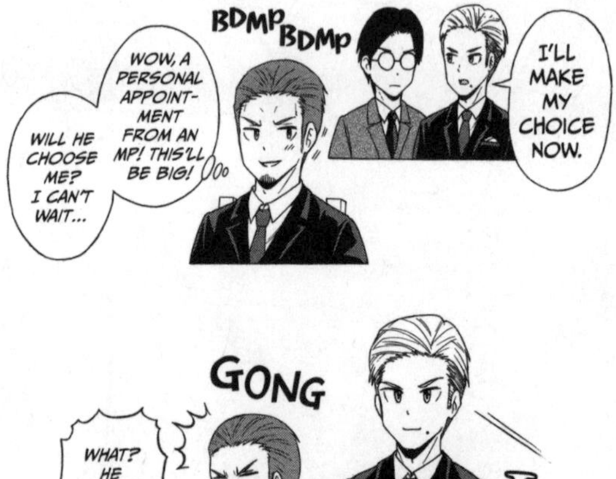
I'LL MAKE MY CHOICE NOW.
BDMP BDMP
WOW, A PERSONAL APPOINT-MENT FROM AN MP! THIS'LL BE BIG!
WILL HE CHOOSE ME? I CAN'T WAIT...
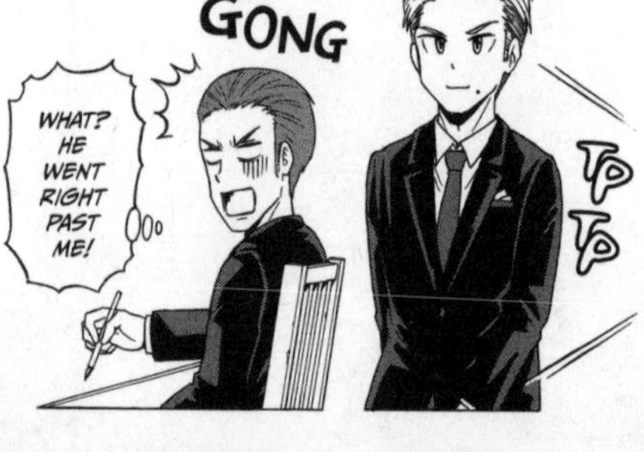
GONG
TP TP
WHAT? HE WENT RIGHT PAST ME!

MORIARTY
THE PATRIOT

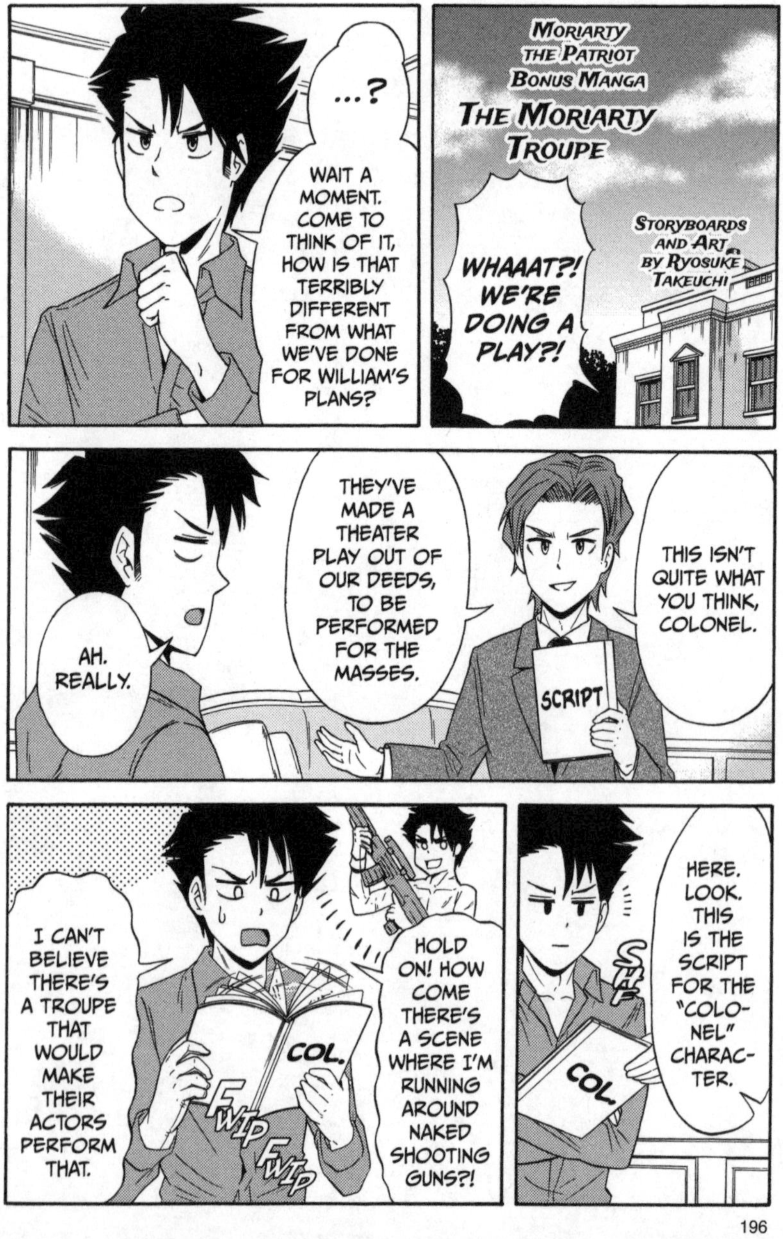
Moriarty the Patriot Bonus Manga
The Moriarty Troupe
Storyboards and Art by Ryosuke Takeuchi
WHAAAT?! WE'RE DOING A PLAY?!
...?
WAIT A MOMENT. COME TO THINK OF IT, HOW IS THAT TERRIBLY DIFFERENT FROM WHAT WE'VE DONE FOR WILLIAM'S PLANS?
THIS ISN'T QUITE WHAT YOU THINK, COLONEL.
SCRIPT
THEY'VE MADE A THEATER PLAY OUT OF OUR DEEDS, TO BE PERFORMED FOR THE MASSES.
AH. REALLY.
HERE. LOOK. THIS IS THE SCRIPT FOR THE "COLONEL" CHARACTER.
SHUF
COL.
HOLD ON! HOW COME THERE'S A SCENE WHERE I'M RUNNING AROUND NAKED SHOOTING GUNS?!
COL.
FWIP FWIP
I CAN'T BELIEVE THERE'S A TROUPE THAT WOULD MAKE THEIR ACTORS PERFORM THAT.

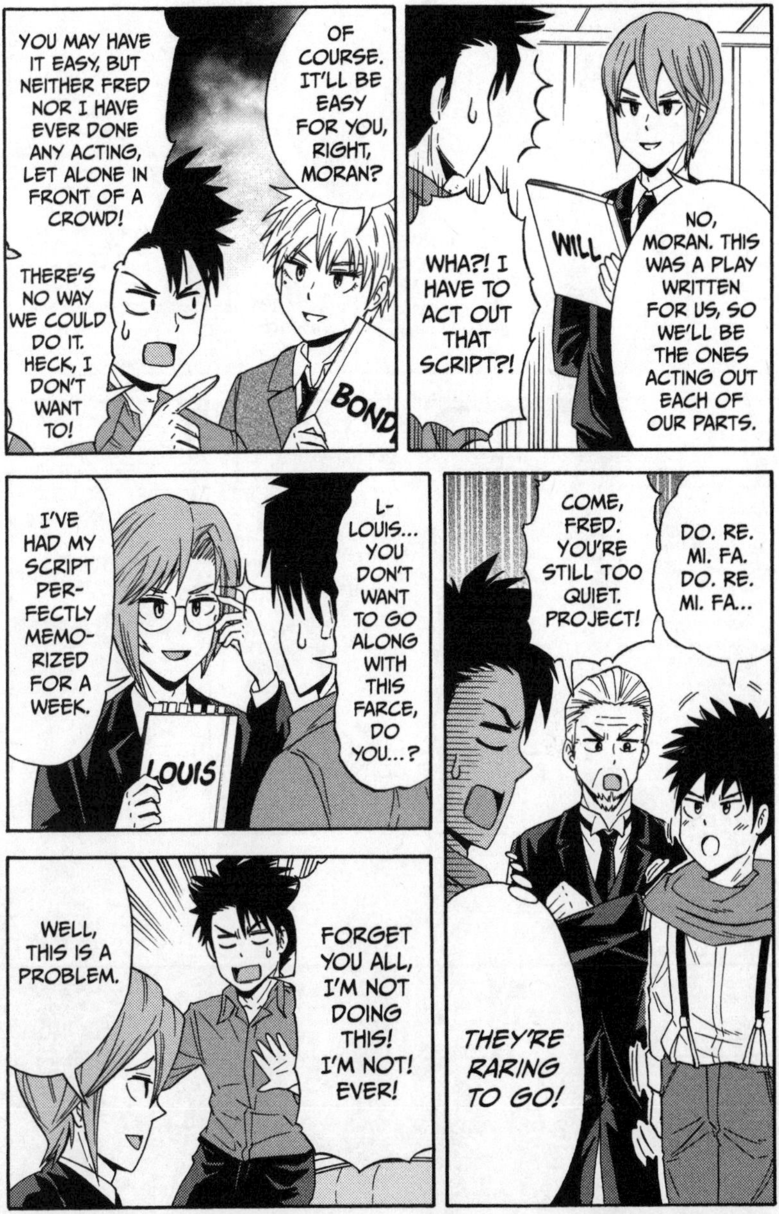
WHA?! I HAVE TO ACT OUT THAT SCRIPT?!
WILL
NO, MORAN. THIS WAS A PLAY WRITTEN FOR US, SO WE'LL BE THE ONES ACTING OUT EACH OF OUR PARTS.
OF COURSE. IT'LL BE EASY FOR YOU, RIGHT, MORAN?
YOU MAY HAVE IT EASY, BUT NEITHER FRED NOR I HAVE EVER DONE ANY ACTING, LET ALONE IN FRONT OF A CROWD!
THERE'S NO WAY WE COULD DO IT. HECK, I DON'T WANT TO!
BOND
DO. RE. MI. FA. DO. RE. MI. FA...
COME, FRED. YOU'RE STILL TOO QUIET. PROJECT!
THEY'RE RARING TO GO!
L-LOUIS... YOU DON'T WANT TO GO ALONG WITH THIS FARCE, DO YOU...?
I'VE HAD MY SCRIPT PERFECTLY MEMORIZED FOR A WEEK.
LOUIS
FORGET YOU ALL, I'M NOT DOING THIS! I'M NOT! EVER!
WELL, THIS IS A PROBLEM.

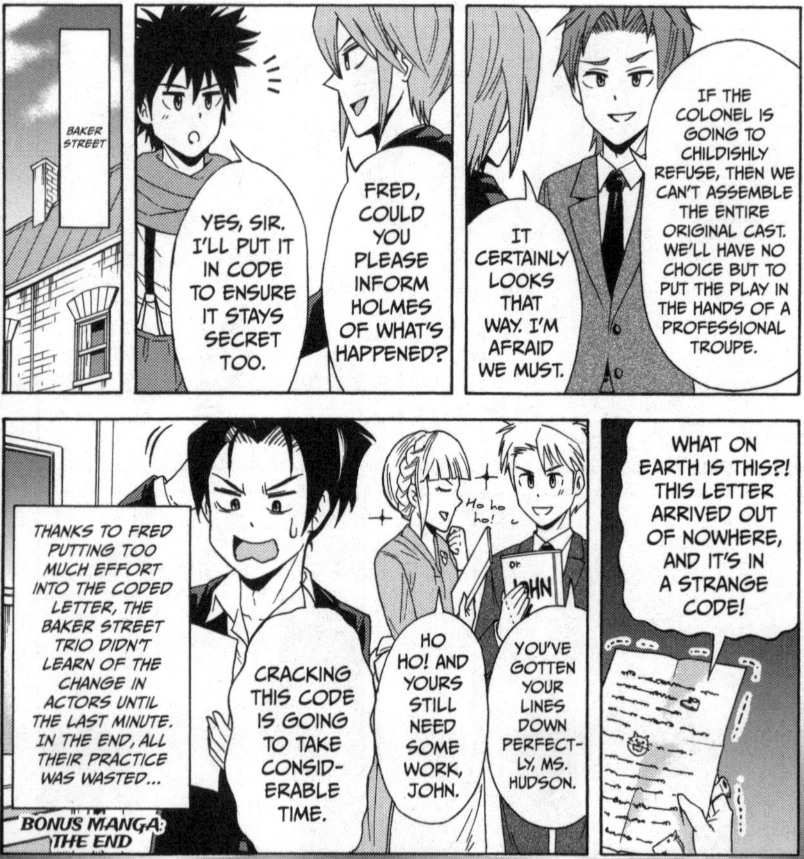
IF THE COLONEL IS GOING TO CHILDISHLY REFUSE, THEN WE CAN'T ASSEMBLE THE ENTIRE ORIGINAL CAST. WE'LL HAVE NO CHOICE BUT TO PUT THE PLAY IN THE HANDS OF A PROFESSIONAL TROUPE.
IT CERTAINLY LOOKS THAT WAY. I'M AFRAID WE MUST.
FRED, COULD YOU PLEASE INFORM HOLMES OF WHAT'S HAPPENED?
YES, SIR. I'LL PUT IT IN CODE TO ENSURE IT STAYS SECRET TOO.
BAKER STREET
WHAT ON EARTH IS THIS?! THIS LETTER ARRIVED OUT OF NOWHERE, AND IT'S IN A STRANGE CODE!
Ho ho ho!
YOU'VE GOTTEN YOUR LINES DOWN PERFECT-LY, MS. HUDSON.
HO HO! AND YOURS STILL NEED SOME WORK, JOHN.
CRACKING THIS CODE IS GOING TO TAKE CONSID-ERABLE TIME.
THANKS TO FRED PUTTING TOO MUCH EFFORT INTO THE CODED LETTER, THE BAKER STREET TRIO DIDN'T LEARN OF THE CHANGE IN ACTORS UNTIL THE LAST MINUTE. IN THE END, ALL THEIR PRACTICE WAS WASTED...
BONUS MANGA: THE END

MORIARTY THE PATRIOT

RYOSUKE TAKEUCHI

I recently moved for the first time in seven years. I originally thought I'd go with the first moving company I got an estimate from, but everyone told me to get another quote. So I went around and asked several other companies for estimates. Eventually I found one that made an offer that was less than half of the first company's estimate. Needless to say, I went with them. It was a really busy time for me to be moving too, but this was a good reminder of how important it is to get multiple estimates.

HIKARU MIYOSHI

The other day, several *Jump SQ* creators and I went for a thorough medical exam together. My results weren't that bad, which is a relief considering the stressful life of a manga creator. The doctor took one look at my fasting blood sugar levels and said, "You eat sweets in the middle of the night a lot, don't you?" He was, embarrassingly enough, dead-on. I...I'll start exercising...

RYOSUKE TAKEUCHI was born November 20, 1980, in Hyogo, Japan, and is a manga artist and writer. He got his big break in 2011 with *ST&RS*, his first serialized *Weekly Shonen Jump* series. He later did the storyboards for *All You Need Is Kill*.

HIKARU MIYOSHI is a manga artist whose previous work includes *Inspector Akane Tsunemori*, which was based on the popular anime *Psycho-Pass*.

Takeuchi and Miyoshi began collaborating on *Moriarty the Patriot* in 2016.

MORIARTY
❖ THE PATRIOT ❖

9

SHONEN JUMP Edition

BASED ON THE WORKS OF Sir Arthur Conan Doyle
STORYBOARDS BY Ryosuke Takeuchi
ART BY Hikaru Miyoshi

TRANSLATION Adrienne Beck
TOUCH-UP ART & LETTERING Annaliese "Ace" Christman
DESIGN Shawn Carrico
EDITOR Rae First

YUKOKU NO MORIARTY © 2016 by Ryosuke Takeuchi, Hikaru Miyoshi
All rights reserved.
First published in Japan in 2016 by SHUEISHA Inc., Tokyo.
English translation rights arranged by SHUEISHA Inc.

Printed in the U.S.A.

Published by VIZ Media, LLC
P.O. Box 77010
San Francisco, CA 94107

10 9 8 7 6 5 4 3 2 1
First printing, October 2022

viz.com